Navigating Virtual Worlds and the Metaverse for Enhanced E-Learning

Nadia Chafiq
Faculty of Sciences Ben M'Sick, Hassan II University, Casablanca, Morocco

Patricia W. Cummins
Virginia Commonwealth University, USA

Khalil Shehadeh Al-Qatawneh
Tafila Technical University, Jordan

Imane El Imadi
Faculty of Sciences Ben M'sick, Hassan II University, Casablanca, Morocco

A volume in the Advances in Educational Technologies and Instructional Design (AETID) Book Series

IGI Global
PUBLISHER of TIMELY KNOWLEDGE

Published in the United States of America by
IGI Global
Information Science Reference (an imprint of IGI Global)
701 E. Chocolate Avenue
Hershey PA, USA 17033
Tel: 717-533-8845
Fax: 717-533-8661
E-mail: cust@igi-global.com
Web site: http://www.igi-global.com

Library of Congress Cataloging-in-Publication Data

Names: Chafiq, Nadia, 1980- editor.
Title: Navigating virtual worlds and the metaverse for enhanced E-learning / edited by Nadia Chafiq, Patricia Cummins, Khalil Shehadeh Al-Qatawneh, Imane El Imadi.
Description: Hershey, PA : Information Science Reference, 2024. | Includes bibliographical references and index. | Summary: "This book aims to provide relevant theoretical frameworks as well as the most recent empirical research findings in the field of digital learning"-- Provided by publisher.
Identifiers: LCCN 2023041796 (print) | LCCN 2023041797 (ebook) | ISBN 9798369310342 (hardcover) | ISBN 9798369310359 (ebook)
Subjects: LCSH: Internet in education. | Web-based instruction. | Virtual reality in education. | Metaverse.
Classification: LCC LB1044.87 .N39 2023 (print) | LCC LB1044.87 (ebook) | DDC 371.33/44678--dc23/eng/20231012
LC record available at https://lccn.loc.gov/2023041796
LC ebook record available at https://lccn.loc.gov/2023041797

This book is published in the IGI Global book series Advances in Educational Technologies and Instructional Design (AE-TID) (ISSN: 2326-8905; eISSN: 2326-8913)

British Cataloguing in Publication Data
A Cataloguing in Publication record for this book is available from the British Library.

Advances in Educational Technologies and Instructional Design (AETID) Book Series

Lawrence A. Tomei
Robert Morris University, USA

ISSN:2326-8905
EISSN:2326-8913

Mission

Education has undergone, and continues to undergo, immense changes in the way it is enacted and distributed to both child and adult learners. In modern education, the traditional classroom learning experience has evolved to include technological resources and to provide online classroom opportunities to students of all ages regardless of their geographical locations. From distance education, Massive-Open-Online-Courses (MOOCs), and electronic tablets in the classroom, technology is now an integral part of learning and is also affecting the way educators communicate information to students.

The **Advances in Educational Technologies & Instructional Design (AETID) Book Series** explores new research and theories for facilitating learning and improving educational performance utilizing technological processes and resources. The series examines technologies that can be integrated into K-12 classrooms to improve skills and learning abilities in all subjects including STEM education and language learning. Additionally, it studies the emergence of fully online classrooms for young and adult learners alike, and the communication and accountability challenges that can arise. Trending topics that are covered include adaptive learning, game-based learning, virtual school environments, and social media effects. School administrators, educators, academicians, researchers, and students will find this series to be an excellent resource for the effective design and implementation of learning technologies in their classes.

Coverage

- Bring-Your-Own-Device
- Instructional Design Models
- Web 2.0 and Education
- E-Learning
- Collaboration Tools
- Higher Education Technologies
- Hybrid Learning
- Adaptive Learning
- Instructional Design
- Virtual School Environments

IGI Global is currently accepting manuscripts for publication within this series. To submit a proposal for a volume in this series, please contact our Acquisition Editors at Acquisitions@igi-global.com or visit: http://www.igi-global.com/publish/.

The Advances in Educational Technologies and Instructional Design (AETID) Book Series (ISSN 2326-8905) is published by IGI Global, 701 E. Chocolate Avenue, Hershey, PA 17033-1240, USA, www.igi-global.com. This series is composed of titles available for purchase individually; each title is edited to be contextually exclusive from any other title within the series. For pricing and ordering information please visit http://www.igi-global.com/book-series/advances-educational-technologies-instructional-design/73678. Postmaster: Send all address changes to above address.

Titles in this Series

For a list of additional titles in this series, please visit:
www.igi-global.com/book-series/advances-educational-technologies-instructional-design/73678

Innovative Instructional Design Methods and Tools for Improved Teaching
Mohamed Khaldi (Abdelmalek Essaadi University, Moocco)
Information Science Reference • © 2024 • 441pp • H/C (ISBN: 9798369331286) • US $300.00

Technological Tools for Innovative Teaching
Mohamed Khaldi (Abdelmalek Essaadi University, Moocco)
Information Science Reference • © 2024 • 433pp • H/C (ISBN: 9798369331323) • US $300.00

The Role of Generative AI in the Communication Classroom
Sanae Elmoudden (St. John's University, USA) and Jason S. Wrench (SUNY New Paltz, USA)
Information Science Reference • © 2024 • 391pp • H/C (ISBN: 9798369308318) • US $230.00

AI in Language Teaching, Learning, and Assessment
Fang Pan (London School of Economics and Political Science, UK)
Information Science Reference • © 2024 • 384pp • H/C (ISBN: 9798369308721) • US $230.00

Restructuring General Education and Core Curricula Requirements
Julie Christina Tatlock (Mount Mary University, USA)
Information Science Reference • © 2024 • 243pp • H/C (ISBN: 9798369303856) • US $230.00

Inclusive Education in Bilingual and Plurilingual Programs
Lidia Mañoso-Pacheco (Autonomous University of Madrid, Spain) José Luis Estrada Chichón (University of Cádiz, Spain) and Roberto Sánchez-Cabrero (Autonomous University of Madrid, Spain)
Information Science Reference • © 2024 • 331pp • H/C (ISBN: 9798369305638) • US $230.00

Transforming Education With Generative AI Prompt Engineering and Synthetic Content Creation
Ramesh C. Sharma (Ambedkar University, Delhi, India) and Aras Bozkurt (Anadolu University, Turkey)
Engineering Science Reference • © 2024 • 550pp • H/C (ISBN: 9798369313510) • US $240.00

Providing Writing Feedback in Online Teaching and Learning The PAUSE Framework
Jennifer L. Robinson (University of Arizona Global Campus, USA)
Information Science Reference • © 2024 • 202pp • H/C (ISBN: 9781668477076) • US $230.00

IGI Global
PUBLISHER of TIMELY KNOWLEDGE

701 East Chocolate Avenue, Hershey, PA 17033, USA
Tel: 717-533-8845 x100 • Fax: 717-533-8661
E-Mail: cust@igi-global.com • www.igi-global.com

Table of Contents

Detailed Table of Contents

Learner's access to an immersive, platform-like digital universe would be seen as an invitation to exist in a different way through a process of routine communication with a mentor (tutor) who enables him or her to break out of anonymity and express himself or herself using tools built into the hosting platform. The characteristics and purposes for using a MOODLE-like platform are obviously different from those of 3D virtual worlds. By fostering relational dynamics that encourage students to revalue their personal and academic identities by reviving their digital identities, the authors show how far the hybrid course can counteract the negative effects of massification. Defining the conceptual and theoretical frameworks, as well as a postulate and a problematic, will be done first in order to provide an account of this recent experience. Before presenting and discussing the findings, they first go over the methodology used to gather and analyze the information from students, both in-person (via the placement test) and virtually (via activity reports and satisfaction surveys).

The chapter evaluates the integration of learning analytics (LA) into Morocco's education system, a task marked by its inherent complexities. A detailed exploration of a case study involving the Provincial Directorate of Education in the Hay Hassani region aids this endeavor. LA's implementation and implications were critically examined, drawing upon the collected data, survey results, and interviews with key stakeholders. A key finding, the Mehnaty project, emerged as a remarkable LA application in the Moroccan context. The analysis indicates that this model, despite logistical and financial constraints, successfully captured age-and-location-based learning requirements, thus informing the design of a more contextually compatible curriculum. This endeavor confirms that implementing LA in the Moroccan educational landscape is viable, albeit with some challenges. The outcome underscores the importance of context in the utilization of LA, advocating for a tailored approach that takes local realities into account to ensure effective learning outcomes.

This research aims to reflect on the integration of digital technologies in teaching French within non-linguistic disciplines. The goal is to think about the academic integration of French in light of various contexts and practices, such as hybrid teaching (both in-person and online via learning platforms dedicated to Edmodo, Moodle, or even MOOCs), combining theory and practice while considering constraints like motivation, organization, and materials. The authors start from the idea that students' poor performance at the university is due to the extensive use of the French language in courses spread over three months, with three hours of class per week. Therefore, various approaches were tested, with a gradual implementation of a hybrid approach known as light in-person classes. Since the fall of 2014, the team of professors has tested three approaches, ranging from enriched in-person classes to 100% online MOOCs. The latter was conducted in the spring of 2016 through a partnership between the Faculty of Sciences at the University Mohammed V in Rabat and the French Institute of Rabat.

Integration of information and communication technologies in education has become a significant phenomenon that provides educators with the resources they need to improve teaching and learning processes. When used on a regular basis, ICTE promotes program objectives and increases student engagement in learning. This can lead to learning experiences that are rapid, interactive, and impactful. Furthermore, the usage of ICTE increases student motivation and simplifies the teaching process. In recent years, there has been considerable growth in the use of tools designed to promote quick learning in many different kinds of countries. These innovative methods aim to simplify the teaching and learning process by speeding up acquisition and decreasing time spent on traditional explanations. Teachers are invited to use these tools to improve the effectiveness of their instruction.

COVID-19 spread through the entire world and has automatically changed student and teacher perceptions of the entire educational system. This serious pandemic has totally affected students and teachers in their diverse pedagogical tasks. It was therefore important to cope with the far-reaching implications of the virus at the educational level. Obviously, those tremendous implications and changes have given us a glimpse at how the whole system of education could actually change for the better or worse. Most governments around the world have taken swift decisions in order to mitigate the impact of this dangerous and full blown pandemic. Like the rest of the world, the Moroccan government opted for the online education as an alternative to secure a good education for thousands and thousands of students in urban and rural areas. Distance education has completely revolutionized the Moroccan society. Surely, after the pandemic, the students are free to opt for the kind of learning that suits their own interests.

Preface

The range of digital instruments that "Digital Learning" provides for professionals to learn is what gives it its rejuvenating power. Because of this, educational players have a great deal of potential to take use of deep learning, serious games, blockchain, collaborative platforms, and learning analytics. learning analytics, fast learning, MOOCs, mobile learning, and online courses and video conferences.

Teaching is now investing in educational Metaverse as a result of the digital transformation of education being accelerated by these digital tools. This technical innovation has made it possible for students to immerse themselves in suitable situations, which improves their learning processes.

According to Basdevant, François, and Ronfard (2022), we frequently speak to "a concept encompassing several immersive technologies such as augmented reality and virtual reality" when discussing Metaverse in today's world. An internet platform that offers shared, permanent, real-time simulations of three-dimensional locations for the sharing of immersive experiences is called a metaverse. Indeed, according to a number of experts, Metaverse has the potential to completely transform remote learning, "where the primary cause of attrition is a sense of loneliness."

We want to facilitate more cooperation and sharing through these virtual environments. Because of this, the metaverse aims to present itself as one of the solutions that may help students by providing them with learning opportunities that are not possible in a traditional classroom. Thus, the book provides a thorough examination of metaverse and virtual world navigation. The metaverse involves virtual worlds in connection to online education. It examines the rising trend of using digital media to connect and learn, raising issues about the repercussions of this change. This book presents a nuanced view of traversing virtual worlds for improved online learning, emphasizing the advantages and disadvantages of this development.

The purpose of this book, which is grounded in field issues, is to offer stimulating reading about training and research endeavors alike. This book's goal is to address some of the queries that come up in the context of digital Learning from the perspectives of the instructor and the student: Which digital remedies which digital tools can be used to improve education? Which certain metaverse improve the experience for users? In a virtual learning environment, how can we gauge student success and engagement? What digital competencies should educators acquire to effectively traverse virtual environments and the metaverse? How may the metaverse's educational opportunities be improved by the moral application of artificial intelligence? What creative uses of the immersive avatar are there to encourage interaction and participation during online courses? These and a lot of other questions are addressed throughout the book's chapters. The majority of educators and learners are aware of the significance of the metaverse and its implications for instruction and training, according to the writers of these chapters. They are in favor of utilizing virtual environments. setting, but necessitates the use of suitable technology tools, efficient training for training in metaverse environments, and digital learning in general. The effectiveness of metaverse can be directly impacted by the key problem of teacher preparation. Thus, it is imperative that educators receive training in order to use this new tool and promote the adoption of new, professional stances.

ORGANIZATION OF THE BOOK

Section 1: Digital Learning

Chapter 1: Digital Textbook and Educational Outcomes – Design to Performance

This research delves at the application of educational technology, with a focus on digital textbooks, as a way to improve the teaching-learning process and tackle issues in the educational system. 362 students participated in the study, which was carried out at two secondary schools at the Casablanca Regional Academy in Morocco. Using digital textbooks in an active pedagogy to enhance student learning and academic results was the main goal. The technique describes the scripting, design, and student implementation steps involved in creating the digital textbook. The findings showed that using a design and scripting paradigm made it easier to create a digital textbook that worked well and improved student learning results. One effective tactic for improving students' academic performance and learning environment is the usage of digital textbooks.

Chapter 2: Expanding Learning Horizons – Investigating the Potential of Serious Games for Student Engagement and Skill Development in Higher Education at Hassan II University

The purpose of this study is to investigate how University Hassan II students' learning results are affected by serious games. The chosen participants, who represented a range of academic fields, took part in an extensive assessment of how well serious games may improve university students' general engagement, skill improvement, and learning of new knowledge.

Using a mixed-methods approach, the study included quantitative and qualitative data gathering techniques. The pool of participants was split into two groups: one that learned through serious games, and another that learned using conventional teaching techniques. Pre- and post-tests were used to measure the amount of information acquired, and questionnaires were used to find out how engaged the students were and how they felt about the learning process.

The results of the study indicate that serious games have a great deal of potential as useful teaching aids. Serious games have been shown to boost student engagement, encourage active learning, and provide a more immersive and dynamic learning environment when they are included into the curriculum. These results support the inclusion of serious games into modern learning techniques and add to the increasing body of data that shows them to have a favorable influence on educational outcomes.

Chapter 3: Getting Started With Augmented Reality (AR) in Inclusive Online Teaching and Learning in Higher Education – An Extended Environmental Scan for Pedagogical Design Leads

This research explores the world of online education, concentrating on programs that require students to take on creative and innovative projects. The study finds a variety of passive, universal cues that support ideational creativity and invention in online learning socio-technical settings, while acknowledging the existence of domain-specific educational techniques. These questions fall into four main categories: (1) course rules and implementation; (2) instructional leadership and guidance; (3) the online learning ecosystem (which includes LMSs and other places); and (4) integrated social media.

Incorporating these strategies promotes inclusive learner engagement while also stimulating creativity and innovation. Through the recognition of the creative capacity present in every person, this research aims to provide a framework that crosses domain boundaries and advances a common strategy for promoting innovation in online education.

This study is based on an extensive review of scholarly research literature, practical experience with online course instructional design, and the use of abductive logic. This multifaceted approach guarantees a thorough comprehension of the material and enhances the formulation of tactics to foster innovation and creativity in the context of online learning.

Essentially, this research adds to the body of knowledge on online learning while also offering useful advice gleaned from actual instructional design projects. The research endeavors to establish a connection between theoretical concepts and practical applications through the utilization of abductive logic, so cultivating an atmosphere that promotes creativity and innovation in the diverse realm of online education.

Section 2: Metaverse and Virtual Environment

Chapter 4: Enhancing E-Orientation Platform Usage via the Metaverse – An Extended TAM Approach for Moroccan University Students

The goal of this chapter is to help Moroccan students adapt and interact with an e-orientation platform in the context of the Metaverse's changing environment. With a particular focus on the Faculty of Sciences Ben M'Sick, the study methodology applies meta-analytic techniques and uses a quantitative approach via a survey administered to students.

The study found important elements impacting the intention to utilize an e-orientation platform in the Metaverse by using Python for data analysis. Perceived quality, trust, perceived utility, and simplicity of use are among the important factors. An expanded version of the Technology Acceptance Model (TAM), specifically designed for e-orientation platforms in the Metaverse, has been created as a result of these findings. The goal is to match the model to the needs and expectations of parents, students.

This study highlights the Metaverse's transformational potential in easing the difficulties related to e-orientation systems. It emphasizes how important user perception is in determining how well e-orientation systems are designed and accepted. The study's conclusions have practical ramifications for improving the usability and uptake of e-orientation platforms inside the dynamic Metaverse, in addition to adding to the body of knowledge about technological acceptability.

Chapter 5: Exploring the Emerging Potential of the Metaverse in Education – Gamification, Advantages, and Limitations

Exploring the dynamic integration of virtual worlds is the focus of this chapter, which also highlights the Metaverse's potential to revolutionize education. It explores the continuous development of instructional techniques that use interactive and immersive learning environments to meet the needs of students who are digital natives today. In these virtual spaces, teachers have a blank canvas on which to create dynamic, customized courses, while students have the freedom to actively direct their own learning.

This chapter's main focus is on the need of digital literacy for teachers and students, with a particular emphasis on the necessity for skillful virtual world navigation. The story emphasizes how important these settings are for encouraging involvement and engagement.

The chapter openly discusses these issues while acknowledging the Metaverse's clear educational advantages. Infrastructure, privacy, security, and ethical issues are carefully examined, taking into account the intricacies present in this environment of digitally mediated education.

In summary, this chapter offers a thorough examination of the changing Metaverse educational environment. In addition to highlighting the transformational potential, it critically analyzes the difficulties and provides a fair analysis of:: the complex relationship between virtual worlds and education.

Chapter 6: Teachers and Schools Navigating Virtual Worlds and the Metaverse for Enhanced E-Learning – Evaluating an E-Capacity Model Approach

This s chapter describes a research that employs an e-capacity model method to assess how well teachers and schools can incorporate technology into a new curriculum. This chapter discusses several important topics related to traversing virtual worlds and the metaverse for improved e-learning. These include legal and ethical issues pertaining to intellectual property laws, societal concerns like social inequality and the digital divide, the investigation of successful tactics and policies for digital integration in education and training, and the hybridization of training approaches (e.g., hybrid, Hy Flex, co-modal approaches). The discussion touches on a variety of subjects, including simulations, the use of artificial intelligence (AI) in training, the metaverse of education, and the larger effects of ICTs (information and communication technologies) on how education is changing. This thorough investigation aims to shed light on the many opportunities and problems related to the use of technology in education. It covers a wide range of topics, from emerging technologies' potential to change education to ethical considerations.

Chapter 7: The Power of AI for the Sake of the Metaverse in Education

Due to its potential to provide students with immersive, customized, and interactive learning experiences, the integration of metaverse technology into education has attracted a lot of attention. With the integration of augmented reality, AI, blockchain, and machine learning technologies, the metaverse, a virtual reality environment, enables user communication. Metaverse technology is distinguished from more conventional e-learning approaches by its higher degrees of personalization and creativity. This novel method mimics the emotional and cognitive processes of in-person learning events, improving user-environment interaction. Metaverse technology provides new potential for enhancing traditional learning activities by offering approaches that are not possible with traditional techniques. Its application in the classroom has the potential to have a revolutionary effect by giving students access to an immersive, customized, and interactive environment that might completely change the way that learning is done.

Chapter 8: University Pedagogy Evaluated by Massification and the Metaverse – The Case of LANSAD Students at the Mohammedia Faculty of Science and Technology

Regular connection with a mentor or teacher facilitates the learner's access to an immersive, platform-like digital environment, which is envisioned as an invitation to exist in a changed manner. This mentor acts as a guide, giving students the tools they need to express themselves and overcome their anonymity through the hosting platform. 3D virtual worlds are very different from platforms such as MOODLE in terms of their goals and features. By rejuvenating their digital personas, this hybrid course seeks to create relationship dynamics that inspire students to reevaluate their academic and personal identities. The goal is to show how the detrimental impacts of educational massification may be offset by this hybrid method. The chapter initially explores the definition of the conceptual and theoretical frameworks, providing a postulate and a dilemma in order to offer a thorough grasp of this current event. The process used to gather and examine data from students is then described; it includes both online and in-person evaluations using activity reports and satisfaction questionnaires in addition to placement exams. This methodical technique prepares the audience for presenting and debating the hybrid course's conclusions.

Section 3: Digital Pedagogy

Chapter 9: Exploring the Evolution and Impact of Learning Analytics in Moroccan Context – A Case Study

This chapter recognizes the inherent complications connected with this undertaking and offers a thorough review of the integration of learning analytics (LA) inside Morocco's educational system. A thorough case study including the Provincial Directorate of Education in the Hay Hassani district supports the investigation. The chapter uses information gathered from surveys, key stakeholder interviews, and collected statistics to critically analyze the use and ramifications of LA.

The Mehnaty project, which has been recognized as a notable LA application in the Moroccan setting, is one of the study's key findings. In spite of budgetary and logistical challenges, this paradigm has shown to be successful in capturing location- and age-based learning requirements. The research shows how the Mehnaty initiative influenced the creation of a curriculum that is more contextually appropriate.

The chapter openly admits the difficulties experienced in adopting LA in the Moroccan educational system, even as it affirms its feasibility. The Mehnaty project is evidence of how crucial it is to take the local context into account while utilizing LA. The chapter promotes a customized strategy that ensures the efficacy of learning outcomes by recognizing and taking into account local characteristics.

This chapter offers insightful information about the possibilities and challenges of incorporating learning analytics into the Moroccan educational system. It highlights the significance of context-sensitive tactics for the effective use of LA, providing a balanced viewpoint that takes into account the advantages and disadvantages of this revolutionary undertaking.

Chapter 10: Hybridization of Approaches and Gradual Investment in ICTs – Toward Innovative University Pedagogy

This study conducts a critical analysis of the use of digital technology in non-linguistic fields for French language instruction. The main goal is to think about how French language education may be included in the classroom while taking different situations and methods into account. These settings include blended learning, which combines traditional classroom instruction with online learning via specialized platforms like Edmodo, Moodle, and MOOCs. The goal of the research is to provide learning materials that are suited for the classroom while taking organizational concerns, student motivation, and other important limitations into account.

This study was motivated by the finding that three months of intensive French instruction, consisting of three hours of class each week, may be detrimental to university students' academic performance. As a result, the study team tried out a number of different teaching strategies before settling on a hybrid model they called "light in-person classes." Since the introduction of this technique in 2014, the professorial team has explored three distinct methodologies: completely online Massive Open Online Courses (MOOCs) to enhanced in-person classes. The latter was carried out in the spring of 2016 as a consequence of cooperation between the French Institute of Rabat and the Faculty of Sciences at University Mohammed V in Rabat.

The research attempts to provide light on the efficacy of digital technology in improving French language training across non-linguistic fields by investigating these various techniques. The experiences and information gathered throughout the course of this multi-year investigation give insightful information on the possibilities of online and hybrid teaching approaches, with implications for future instructional tactics in comparable educational settings.

Chapter 11: Rapid Learning in the Teaching of Physical Education and Sport

A notable and revolutionary development in education is the integration of information and communication technologies (ICTE), which provides teachers with tools to improve the processes of teaching and learning. Frequent use of ICTE promotes quick, engaging, and powerful learning experiences for students while also being in line with program objectives. In addition to being efficient, ICTE in the classroom increases student motivation and simplifies the teaching process. The use of tools intended to speed up learning across national boundaries has increased significantly in recent years. By speeding up the acquisition of knowledge and cutting down on the amount of time that is often spent on explanations, these cutting-edge techniques seek to streamline the teaching and learning process. It is recommended that educators use these resources to increase the efficiency of their teaching, which represents a paradigm shift.

Chapter 12: Student and Teacher Assessments of Digital Education During the COVID-19 Pandemic and After: – The Case of Cadi Ayad and Sultan Moulay Slimane Universities

Within weeks or months, the rapid and pervasive effects of COVID-19 caused a paradigm change in how instructors and students alike saw the whole educational system. This epidemic has caused major disruptions to a variety of educational responsibilities and calls for quick solutions to address its far-reaching effects. Morocco's government, like all other governments, was forced to move quickly to lessen the pandemic's negative effects on schooling. The Moroccan government, like many others, used online learning as a substitute to meet these issues and guarantee that students in both urban and rural locations would always have access to high-quality education. Moroccan society has undergone a dramatic transformation as a result of the acceptance of distant education.

Nadia Chafiq
Faculty of Sciences Ben M'Sick, Hassan II University, Casablanca, Morocco

Patricia W. Cummins
Virginia Commonwealth University, USA

Khalil Shehadeh Al-Qatawneh
Tafila Technical University, Jordan

Imane El Imadi
Faculty of Sciences Ben M'sick, Hassan II University, Casablanca, Morocco

REFERENCES

Basdevant, A., François, C., & Ronfard, R. (2022). Mission exploratoire sur les métavers. Ministère de la Culture; Ministère de l'Économie, des Finances et de la Souveraineté industrielle et numérique.

Acknowledgment

This revolutionary adventure in the educational metaverse has not been completed without teamwork, and we are very appreciative of everyone who has made a substantial contribution to this cause.

Above all, we would want to express our sincere gratitude to Patricia W. Cummins, Nadia Chafiq, Imane ELimadi, and Khalil Shehadeh Al-Qatawneh. Your commitment, wisdom, and resolute assistance have been indispensable to the production of this book. Your varied viewpoints and combined experience have enhanced the text, guaranteeing a thorough examination of the topic.

To Nadia Chafiq, the depth and caliber of this book are forever changed by your painstaking attention to detail and dedication to academic rigor. Your input has been crucial in forming the story and improving the content's overall cohesion.

Imane ELimadi, this project has a dynamic energy because of your unique approach and original thoughts. Your knowledge of cutting-edge technologies and how they may be used in the classroom has been crucial in bringing attention to the metaverse's revolutionary potential.

Patricia W. Cummins, our investigation of educational technology has gained depth and usefulness from your scholarly contributions and abundance of experience. Your knowledge has been crucial in converting abstract ideas into practical tactics that teachers and students can use.

Thank you, Khalil Shehadeh Al-Qatawneh, for enriching the conversation on responsible digital education with your tireless efforts to advance educational innovation and your unwavering commitment to the ethical implications of technology in learning. Your inputs have given our investigation a crucial new angle.

Introduction

The rapid growth of technology in education has changed not just how we teach and learn, but also the fundamental nature of knowledge itself. Having wise counsel becomes crucial as we approach the edge of the educational metaverse. I introduce with great enthusiasm the seminal work *Navigating Virtual Worlds and the Metaverse for Enhanced E-Learning*. This book serves as a guide for academics, educators, and anyone else interested in the direction of education—it is more than just a compilation of observations. The breadth of subjects addressed, which ranges from wellbeing in the classroom to artificial intelligence, is indicative of the complexity and diversity of the digital technologies that are changing the face of education. The educational metaverse is a real, revolutionary force that is changing the way we think about teaching and learning. It is not just a futuristic idea.

The writers have expertly traversed this dynamic terrain, furnishing a guide for those aiming to leverage the possibilities of virtual environments and cutting-edge technology for improved e-learning. The book's examination of the ethical issues that must follow this technological transformation, in addition to the benefits provided by the digital toolbox, is one of its strongest points. We must be guardians of inclusive and responsible education while providing learners with never-before-seen information access and immersive experiences. I invite you to approach each chapter in "Navigating Virtual Worlds and the Metaverse for Enhanced E-Learning" with an open mind and an eagerness to discover the transforming possibilities that each one has to offer. This book is your road map for negotiating the fascinating and confusing terrain of the educational metaverse as the future of education plays out in front of us.

The quickening speed of technology development has changed our perceptions of learning and knowledge in the ever-changing field of education. In this dynamic environment, *Navigating Virtual Worlds and the Metaverse for Enhanced E-Learning* becomes an indispensable guide, providing insights into the many aspects of educational technology.

This book is more than just a compilation of observations; it's a useful guide for academics, educators, and anybody who cares about education in the long run. Covering everything from AI to student well-being in the classroom, it reflects the intricacy of the digital instruments reshaping our educational environment.

Instead of being shown as a far-off dream, the educational metaverse is shown as a real, transforming force influencing the here and now. The writers expertly negotiate this changing terrain, offering advice to those looking to take use of virtual environments and cutting-edge technology for improved e-learning.

This book's examination of the potential and moral dilemmas raised by the digital toolset is one of its strongest points. This handbook highlights the significance of using a responsible and inclusive strategy in order to empower learners with unparalleled access to knowledge and immersive experiences.

Chapter 1
Digital Textbook and Educational Outcomes:
Design to Performance

Kamal Moundy
Hassan II University, Morocco

Nadia Chafiq
Hassan II University, Morocco

Mohammed Talbi
Hassan II University, Morocco

Oussama Bouiri
Hassan II University, Morocco

ABSTRACT

Educational technology has great potential to confront the challenges encountered in the educational system and place itself at the core of the teaching-learning process. The aim of this study is to use the digital textbook to enhance student learning within an active pedagogy and to strengthen the development of students' academic results. The experiments were carried out in two secondary schools belonging to the Casablanca regional academy in the Kingdom of Morocco. The research samples consisted of 362 students. A methodology describes the process of developing a digital textbook, from scripting to design and use with students. The results showed that developing the digital textbook according to a design and scripting model enabled the authors to design a textbook that could be used by students, with remarkable results. The use of digital textbooks enabled students to improve their educational outcome.

DOI: 10.4018/979-8-3693-1034-2.ch001

1. INTRODUCTION

In the era of technology and the internet, digital transformation has put information and communication technologies (ICT) at the core of modernization and accelerated expansion to meet the challenges facing the education system of nations. As a result, it is inadmissible to anticipate the development of the teaching-learning process without having recourse to the integration of ICT to strengthen the teaching-learning process to fulfil its role of producing knowledge and developing students' skills and competencies (Bank, 2017; Hussain et al., 2011; Grabe & Grabe, 2007). To carry out its role properly, the education system requires teaching stakeholders to introduce educational technologies to foster learner engagement and motivation, encourage collaborative work, govern innovative and creative learning, and reinforce knowledge acquisition and skills development.

Furthermore, Gómez-Galán (2020) points out that the introduction of ICT has led to the digitization of the fundamentals of the didactic means of the teaching-learning process, such as digital didactic tools (interactive whiteboard, video projector, computer, tablet ...) and digital teaching resources (interactive courses, self-correcting exercises, animated videos, simulation and demonstration software, serious games ...). In addition, Information and Communication Technologies (ICT) for teaching have enabled students to change their role from passive consumer of knowledge to active co-producer of knowledge, and ICT has a positive effect on learner motivation, engagement and learning outcomes (Ben Youssef et al., 2022).

One of the main didactic means in the teaching-learning process is "textbook", a fundamental and central tool in the teaching-learning process (Memaï & Rouag, 2017) and is generally edited and printed on paper. The textbook has shown itself to be outdated, while digital transformation has swept through several didactic means since the introduction of ICTE (Dutrieux, 2016). As a result, the paper textbook remains an irreplaceable didactic tool that can be used in different contexts and situations, a complement to the teacher's work and a knowledge support for students. Therefore, it will be very difficult to move beyond the use of the textbook in the digital age, but to renovate the design of the textbook to benefit from the potential of digital technology and regain its central place in a digitized educational environment.

Similarly, the advent of Information and Communication Technology (ICT) has led to the emergence of new teaching methods while bolstering existing ones. Lebrun's research in 2011 highlights that integrating ICT can enhance the teaching-learning process, necessitating educators to embrace active pedagogical approaches to fully harness the benefits of educational technologies. One such active pedagogical method that integrates ICT is the flipped classroom, which has evolved alongside advancements in ICT. Moreover, research indicates that both flipped classroom instruction and ICT integration have a favorable impact on student-centered and active learning, elevating student engagement and ultimately enhancing learning outcomes (Aidoo et al., 2022; Romero et al., 2017).

In this respect, on the one hand, modernization is needed during textbook design, addressing restrictions on textbook use, and including the potential of information and communication technologies (ICT). On the other hand, good practice in the integration of ICT requires teachers to adopt an active, student-centered pedagogical method, to benefit more from the latter, and to make students actors in their learning, so that they reach a higher level of cognitive capacity.

The main aim of this study is to use the digital textbook to enhance student learning within an active pedagogy and to strengthen the development of students' academic results.

2. CONCEPTUAL FRAMEWORK

2.1. Definitions

Textbook, academic textbook, exercise book... these are all terminologies we hear today. First, the term textbook is polysemous, changing definition according to its use and function (Choppin, 1992). Textbooks are a fundamental and central teaching resource in the education system, especially in rural, peri-urban and disadvantaged areas. It is a tool for improving the efficiency of the learning process (Gérard & Rogiers, 2009), an essential vehicle for learning (UNESCO, 2005), an essential vehicle for instruction and socialization, a bearer of knowledge and standards and values (Memaï & Rouag, 2017).

The use of the textbook as a vector for learning objects has a central and operative role in the teaching and learning process, helping to enhance the quality of teaching (Memaï & Rouag, 2017), enhances the knowledge to be acquired or the skills targeted (Séré & Bassy, 2010), transmits models of social behavior, norms and values (UNESCO, 2008), and is an essential vector for academic success (Séguin, 1989).

Nowadays, many products are based on ICT, such as the digital textbook, or "e-book", "interactive textbook", "enriched digital textbook", "digitized textbook" or Altman's "I-m@nuel" (2000), which is a type of paper textbook accompanied by a website for the teacher and learner. Lebert (2009) considers that the e-book is a book digitized for dissemination as an electronic file the physical textbook. A new creation and development of the e-book is called the "smartbook", considered to be an evolving, highly interactive, customizable, adaptable, and intelligent e-book, equipped with a rich set of services to support collaborative creation, and reading (Koychev et al., 2009). Other authors name the digital textbook by "connected Textbook", "augmented Textbook" or "hybrid Textbook" which means that the paper version allows you to flash QR codes printed on the textbook to glimpse digital content on nomadic devices (Abensour & Gomariz, 2018).

There is no agreed definition of a digital textbook (Bruillard, 2020). The digital textbook is a complement to the paper textbook with digital resources. It includes not only text and illustrations, but also diversified digital teaching resources such as video capsules, tutorials, educational applications, self-correcting exercises, gamification, 3D images through augmented reality and learning platforms ("spaces for teacher-student interaction"), etc. These resources can be accessed via mobile and nomadic devices (computers, smartphones, tablets, etc.) through short hyperlinks or QR codes.

A digital textbook can be considered as a didactic tool published and distributed online, including content, objectives, methods, teaching resources and assessments (Université du Québec, 2013). Or a dematerialized textbook that can be projected in the classroom or used in paper format, and features sound documents, animations, or videos (SDTICE, 2009). Or a printed work that integrates audiovisual documents, software or tutorials, self-assessment tools, illustrations and other pedagogical resources that present all the major elements of the curriculum (Legendre, 2005).

There are different types of digital textbook depending on the potential for integrating digital teaching resources (Moundy et al., 2021; Cherif & Gekiere, 2017; Bruillard, 2015; Université du Québec, 2013; SDTICE, 2009) (Figure 1):

Figure 1. Types of digital textbooks

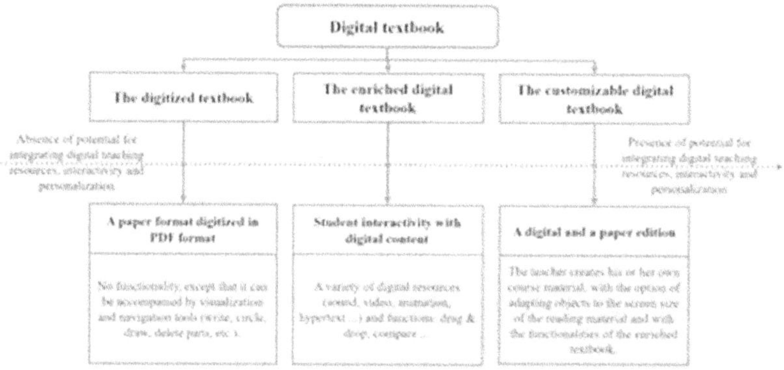

The digitized textbook is an identical format to the paper version, digitized as a PDF document without any functionality, but with options such as writing, circling, drawing, deleting parts using certain tools on a computer, tablet, or interactive whiteboard... Most digital textbooks are of the "enriched" type, i.e., they are enhanced by a set of digital teaching resources (video, sound, application, etc.) enabling interactivity between the student and the digital content, as well as the viewing and navigation functions offered by the type of digitized paper format. Other textbooks of the personalized textbook type are designed with the option of adding features to the textbook by the teacher for example documents or digital content or a workspace (Cherif & Gekiere, 2017).

2.2. From Scripting to Designing a Digital Textbook

The design of a digital textbook begins with a scripting phase. Pedagogical scripting is based on a model (figure 2) that enables the teacher to mobilize his or her professional skills ("to plan, to animate, to evaluate and to regulate") and to consider the characteristics of the students (age, perceptions, learning style, etc.), so as to enable them to be actors in their own learning, to engage in higher-level cognitive pedagogical activities and to develop their abilities and skills (Moundy et al., 2022b).

The necessity of referring to learning theories is essential, providing a frame of reference that guides designers' thinking in proposing content that is conducive to students' needs. In summary, the figure shows a reflection between the principles of pedagogy and the position of learning theories in the teaching-learning process to encourage the acquisition of knowledge and the development of capacities and skills.

At this point, the model of pedagogical scripting intersects with the model of textbook design, to provide script pedagogical sequences and mediatize the content of the digital textbook.

The design of a textbook is not just a linear interaction between an author and a student, but implies a set of scientific, didactic, and technological actors who all take on different roles in the design of the textbook: editors, readers, designers, evaluators, users, publishers, etc. (Gérard & Roegiers, 2009).

Moving on to the design phase (Figure 3), there are three main organizational and methodological steps to follow when designing a digital textbook (Gérard & Roegiers, 2009; Moundy & al., 2021):

Figure 2. The pedagogical scenario model for a digital textbook

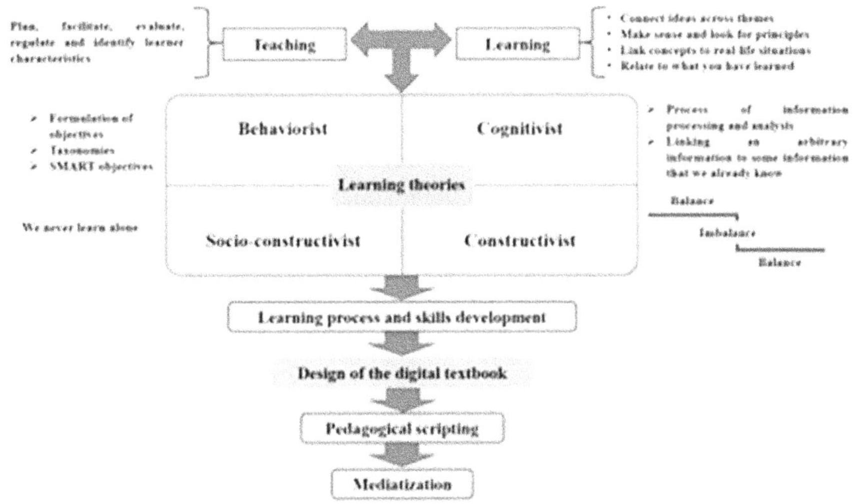

Figure 3. The digital textbook design model

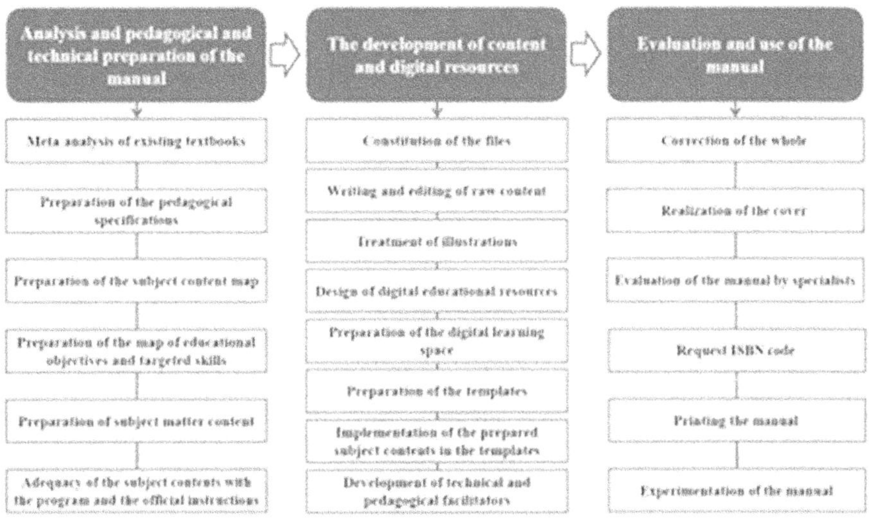

The first phase consists of carrying out a meta-analysis of existing manuals and drawing on their advantages and limitations, preparing pedagogical specifications (manual requirements, pedagogical alignment, type of manual, target audience, etc.) and technical specifications (format, typographic characteristics, colors, timetable, etc.), prepare a subject content map (hard skills and soft skills) for each learning sequence, and a map containing the content program, competencies targeted and pedagogical objectives, prepare subject content (the course) and check that it conforms to the program and official instructions (curriculum).

The second phase consists of creating folders to organize each type of content, writing and correcting the content using word processing software or professional content production software, editing the illustrations using image processing software and ensuring the quality of the illustrations, and designing the various digital resources (videos, podcasts, interactive content, self-correcting exercises, etc.), prepare a digital workspace where the teacher exchanges resources or discusses with students, prepare templates (similar models for all pages), implement the content prepared in the templates, and develop and add technical and pedagogical facilitators to the manual (table of contents, how to use the manual, glossary, index, etc.).

The final phase consists of proofreading the entire manual, producing the manual cover, evaluating the manual by pedagogical specialists (teachers in the manual's specialty) and technical specialists (IT specialists, designers, etc.), requesting the ISBN code for the manual, printing the manual, and testing the manual with a group of students.

For the effective integration of digital teaching resources into the teaching-learning process, the TPACK model (Technological Pedagogical Content Knowledge) is used to present a conceptual framework for matching the technology-pedagogical-content trio (the technological dimension, the pedagogical dimension, and the disciplinary content).

2.3. In the Era of Digital Textbooks

In the digital age, today's generation, or Generation Z, can adapt to technological changes and innovations, as well as adopting new techniques by becoming familiar with them over time. An experiment conducted by Weisberg (2011) to assess students' choice between using e-textbook, tablets, or paper textbooks, found that 87% of students chose the electronic textbook. Similarly, Dennis (2011) noted that up to 84% of learners opted to use a digital textbook.

The Association of American Publisher states that publishing companies have shown that there was a 43% increase in sales of digital books between 2011 and 2013, as well as their use by young people has increased considerably since 2011 (Pew Research Center, 2014). Also, with the growth of ICT in the education system, textbook editors have invested a lot of resources in the development and promotion of digital textbooks (Young, 2013). And Séguin (1989) who experimented that improved textbook provision showed a positive effect on student academic performance.

Students have identified the main factors for adopting a digital textbook to be low cost, portability, and easy search of content (Weisbelg, 2011), similarly, Junco and Clem (2015) showed that using a digital textbook with a class of students also influenced students' learning profiles. Also, Dutrieux (2016) expresses that the graphic disposition and layout of the textbook attract student to use the textbook and learn its content, since today's students don't have the era to learn in classic textbooks, but with other that allows to engage the student's attention.

3.METHODS

3.1. Characteristics of the Sample

The sample is formed by students from two secondary schools located in the prefecture of Casablanca in Morocco. The sample chosen is simple random and composed of students possessing similar characteristics.

The following table (Table 1) shows the characteristics of the study sample by experimental group, grade, gender, number of students and average age. The study opted for a sample of 362 students, including 179 women (49.45%) and 183 men (50.56%). In terms of average age, the sample had an average age of 15.51, which was similar for men and women.

Table 1. Sample characteristics by group, gender, number of students, percentage, and average age

Group	Grade	Gender								
		Man			Woman			Total		
		N	%	Average age	N	%	Average age	N	%	Average age
Experimental group	1st year	26	7,18%	13,48	23	6,35%	14	49	13,54%	13,76
	2nd year	22	6,08%	14,52	25	6,91%	14,55	47	12,98%	14,53
	3rd year	25	6,91%	14,96	25	6,91%	15,44	50	13,81%	15,2
	4th year	32	8,84%	16,4	35	9,67%	16,94	67	18,51%	16,66
	5th year	35	9,67%	17,5	34	9,39%	17,86	69	19,06%	17,68
	Total	140	38,68%	15,37	142	39,23%	15,76	282	77,90%	15,57
Control group	1st year	9	2,49%	14,29	7	1,93%	13,78	16	4,42%	14
	2nd year	9	2,49%	14,5	8	2,21%	14	17	4,70%	14,24
	3rd year	10	2,76%	15,29	7	1,93%	15	17	4,70%	15,12
	4th year	7	1,93%	16,67	9	2,49%	16	16	4,42%	16,38
	5th year	8	2,21%	17,5	6	1,66%	17,5	14	3,87%	17,5
	Total	43	11,88%	15,65	37	10,22%	15,26	80	22,11%	15,45
Overall total		183	50,56%	15,51	179	49,45%	15,51	362	100%	15,51

The sample was composed of secondary school students at 5 grades, divided into two groups (Table 1): an experimental group of 282 students (77.90%), including 142 women and 140 men, and a control group of 80 students (22.11%), including 37 women and 43 men.

3.2. Measuring Instrument

To measure the effect of using and learning from a digital textbook on learners' academic performance, we administered summative assessments (direct questions, problem-solving exercises, group project and student project).

And to achieve the main objective, this sample is divided into two groups: an experimental group will learn using the digital textbook, and a control group will learn in the normal method. The experimentation took place during one teaching semester of a school year.

The data collected were analyzed and processed using SPSS (version 24) statistical analysis software.

4. RESULTS

To achieve the main objective of this study, students passed a series of summative assessments to measure the degree of proficiency of the learning objects. The table below (Table 2) shows the students' average marks after four summative assessments. The table shows that the experimental group had an overall average of 15.96, quite a bit higher than the control group (13.16), and that this difference is noticeable across all four summative assessments and by each grade level.

Table 2. Average score for summative evaluations of students

Group	Grade	Summative Assessments				Overall Average
		Direct Questions	Problem-Solving Exercises	Group Project	Student's Project	
Experimental group	1st year	15,56	15,48	15,36	15,64	15,50
	2nd year	14,80	14,28	14,80	14,88	14,70
	3rd year	15,88	15,24	15,36	15,44	15,48
	4th year	16,04	15,80	16,00	16,20	16,01
	5th year	18,04	18,16	17,84	18,36	18,11
	Total	16,08	15,80	15,88	16,12	15,96
Control group	1st year	12,12	12,76	12,64	12,36	12,47
	2nd year	13,04	11,64	13,28	12,60	12,65
	3rd year	14,00	12,84	13,28	12,00	13,03
	4th year	13,76	14,00	14,64	14,52	14,22
	5th year	12,84	14,28	13,28	13,28	13,43
	Total	13,16	13,12	13,44	12,96	13,16
Total		14,60	14,44	14,64	14,52	14,56

Table 3. Normality test of students' grade averages: Kolmogorov-Smirnov and Shapiro-Wilk

		Kolmogorov-Smirnov			Shapiro-Wilk		
		Statistiques	ddl	p-Value	Statistiques	ddl	p-Value
Direct questions	Experimental group	,200	282	,000	,892	282	,000
	Control Group	,128	80	,002	,944	80	,002
Problem-solving exercises	Experimental group	,170	282	,000	,895	282	,000
	Control Group	,151	80	,000	,935	80	,001
Group project	Experimental group	,200	282	,000	,886	282	,000
	Control Group	,110	80	,018	,947	80	,002
Student's project	Experimental group	,204	282	,000	,882	282	,000
	Control Group	,132	80	,002	,948	80	,003
grade averages	Experimental group	,116	282	,000	,901	282	,000
	Control Group	,094	80	,078	,961	80	,015

The bellow table (Table 3) presents the results of normality tests of student grade averages according to Kolmogorov-Smirnov and Shapiro-Wilk. The results show that the data from both groups follow a normal distribution, since the p-value values are less than 0.5.

The table (Table 4) presents the independent samples test of the summative assessments passed by the experimental and control groups. The results show that there is a highly significant difference between the experimental and control groups, as shown in Table 2. This difference is remarkable on all four summative assessments, with p-values below .001.

Table 4. Test of independent samples of summative evaluations passed by students

Independent Samples Test										
		Levene's Test for Equality of Variances		t-Test for Equality of Means						
		F	Sig.	t	ddl	(Bilateral) Sig.	Average Difference	Standard Error Difference	Confidence Interval of 95% Difference	
									Lower	Upper
Direct questions	Assumption of equal variances	8,407	,004	6,904	360	,000	3,04486	,44103	2,17753	3,91218
	Hypothesis of unequal variances			6,247	112,126	,000	3,04486	,48744	2,07907	4,01065
Problem-solving exercises	Assumption of equal variances	8,232	,004	6,381	360	,000	2,92163	,45788	2,02118	3,82208
	Hypothesis of unequal variances			5,894	114,838	,000	2,92163	,49569	1,93975	3,90351
Group project	Assumption of equal variances	6,888	,009	5,619	360	,000	2,59628	,46204	1,68765	3,50490
	Hypothesis of unequal variances			5,139	113,516	,000	2,59628	,50517	1,59549	3,59706
Student's project	Assumption of equal variances	5,310	,022	7,404	360	,000	3,35869	,45364	2,46658	4,25080
	Hypothesis of unequal variances			6,857	115,196	,000	3,35869	,48981	2,38848	4,32889
grade averages	Assumption of equal variances	7,716	,006	7,845	360	,000	2,98036	,37992	2,23323	3,72750
	Hypothesis of unequal variances			7,108	112,315	,000	2,98036	,41927	2,14966	3,81106

5. DISCUSSION

Mainly, the aim of this study is to use the digital textbook to enhance student learning within an active pedagogy and to strengthen the development of students' academic results.

Using and learning from a digital textbook enabled students to achieve better learning outcomes, which is approved by the results that the experimental group achieved rather higher overall averages than the control group (m1=15.96; m2 =13.16), this difference is similar by grade level and types of assessment. These were also approved by tests that reported p-values below .001.

These findings were confirmed by Junco and Clem (2015) that students who are engaged and learn through a digital textbook could achieve remarkable academic results. Similarly, Daniel and Woody (2013) and Landrum (2012) state that using and learning through a textbook has a significant association with improved academic performance.

In the same sense, learning through the flipped classroom will enable students to benefit more fully from the contributions of a digital textbook, by making available a set of digital teaching resources that can be used both outside and inside the classroom. In this way, the use of the flipped classroom as an active teaching method during the experiment has enabled us to better create a learning environment and help students achieve outstanding academic results.

According to several authors, the use of the flipped classroom enables students to achieve outstanding academic results (Dong et al., 2021; Öza & Abaan, 2021; Birgili et al., 2021; Strelan et al., 2020; Hoang-Oanh, 2020; Murillo-Zamorano et al., 2019; Lin, 2019; Lope & Soares, 2018). Thus, results have shown that the use of the flipped classroom with the exploitation of information and communication technology (ICT) tools enable students to learn better Bhat et al. (2020). And according to Birgili et al (2021), who show that traditional teaching methods should give way to flipped classroom learning based on the use of ICT.

6. CONCLUSION

No one can deny the importance of integrating information and communication technology tools into the teaching-learning process, as a rich environment of pedagogical and digital resources for improving teachers' professional practices and enhancing student learning.

The development of digital textbooks following a design and scripting model has enabled us to design a textbook that can be used by students, with remarkable results. The use of digital textbooks has enabled students to improve their academic results. In this way, learning through the flipped classroom has helped students achieve better academic results.

REFERENCES

Abensour, C., & Gomariz, F. (2018). L'édition d'éducation face aux défis du numérique (1re éd.). Éditions du Cercle de la Librairie.

Aidoo, B., Macdonald, M. A., Vesterinen, V. M., Pétursdóttir, S., & Gísladóttir, B. (2022). Transforming Teaching with ICT Using the Flipped Classroom Approach: Dealing with COVID-19 Pandemic. *Education Sciences*, *12*(6), 421. doi:10.3390/educsci12060421

Altman, P. (2000). I-M@NUEL Une nouvelle génération de Manuels scolaires. *La Revue De l'Epi*, 99.

Bank, A. D. (2017). Innovative Strategies for Accelerated Human Resource Development in South Asia: Information and Communication Technology for Education: Special Focus on Bangladesh, Nepal, and Sri Lanka. Asian Development Bank.

Ben Youssef, A., Dahmani, M., & Ragni, L. (2022). ICT Use, Digital Skills and Students' Academic Performance: Exploring the Digital Divide. *Information (Basel)*, *13*(3), 129. doi:10.3390/info13030129

Bhat, S., Raju, R., Bhat, S., & D'Souza, R. (2020). Redefining Quality in Engineering Educa-tion through the Flipped Classroom Model. *Procedia Computer Science*, *172*, 906–914. doi:10.1016/j.procs.2020.05.131

Birgili, B., Seggie, F. N., & Oğuz, E. (2021). The trends and outcomes of flipped learning re-search between 2012 and 2018: A descriptive content analysis. *Journal of Computers in Education*, *8*(3), 365–394. doi:10.1007/s40692-021-00183-y

Bruillard, É. (2015). Digital textbooks Current trends in secondary education in France. In Digital Textbooks: What's new? Universidade de Santiago de Compostela.

Bruillard, É. (2020, mars). *Les modes d'appropriation des ressources numériques: Caractériser l'offre des ressources numériques éducatives*. Groupes thématiques de la Direction du numérique pour l'Éducation. https://eduscol.education.fr/2115/groupe-thematique-numerique-6-mode-d-appropriation-des-ressources

Cherif, S., & Gekiere, G. (2017). *Enseigner Autrement Avec Le Numérique: La Boîte à Outils Du Professeur*. Dunod.

Choppin, A. (1992). *Les Manuels scolaires: histoire et actualité*. Hachette Éducation Paris.

Daniel, D. B., & Woody, W. D. (2013). E-textbooks at what cost? Performance and use of electronic v. print texts. *Computers & Education*, *62*, 18–23. doi:10.1016/j.compedu.2012.10.016

Dennis, A. (2011). *E-Textbooks at Indiana University: A Summary of Two Years of Research. Indiana University Kelly School of Busness Research Report*. Indiana University.

Dong, Y., Yin, H., Du, S., & Wang, A. (2021). The effects of flipped classroom characterized by situational and collaborative learning in a community nursing course: A quasi-experimental design. *Nurse Education Today*, *105*, 105037. doi:10.1016/j.nedt.2021.105037 PMID:34247009

Dutrieux, L. (2016). *De quelles manières la mise en page et la présentation graphique des manuels scolaires peuvent-elles aider le jeune en apprentissage?* (Olivier Ruol, interview réalisé le 28 avril 2016). https://medium.com/liove/de-quelles-mani%C3%A8res-la-mise-en-page-et-la-pr%C3%A9sentation-graphique-des-manuels-scolaires-peuvent-1afdca651ea2

Gérard, F. M., & Roegiers, X. (2009). *Des manuels scolaires pour apprendre. Concevoir, évaluer, utiliser*. De Boeck Supérieur. doi:10.3917/dbu.gerar.2009.01

Gómez-Galán, J. (2020). Media Education in the ICT Era: Theoretical Structure for Innovative Teaching Styles. *Information (Basel)*, *11*(5), 276. doi:10.3390/info11050276

Grabe, M., & Grabe, C. (2007). *Integrating technology for meaningful learning* (5th ed.). Houghton Mifflin.

Hoang-Oanh, T. T. (2020). The Impact of a Flipped Classroom on Student Learning Achieve-ments in EFL Classrooms. Education. *Language and Sociology Research*, *1*(2), 13. doi:10.22158/elsr.v1n2p13

Hussain, A. J., Morgan, S., & Al-Jumeily, D. (2011, December). How Does ICT Affect Teachings and Learning within School Education. In *Developments in E-systems Engineering (DeSE), 2011* (pp. 250–254). IEEE. doi:10.1109/DeSE.2011.50

Junco, R., & Clem, C. (2015). Predicting course outcomes with digital textbook usage data. *The Internet and Higher Education*, *27*, 54–63. doi:10.1016/j.iheduc.2015.06.001

Junco, R., & Clem, C. (2015). Predicting course outcomes with digital textbook usage data. *The Internet and Higher Education*, *27*, 54–63. doi:10.1016/j.iheduc.2015.06.001

Koychev, I., Nikolov, R., & Dicheva, R. (2009). Smartbook -The future e-book and educatonal hypermedia. *10th IFIP Working Conference on Virtual Enterprises*, Thessaloniki, Greece.

Landrum, R. E., Gurung, R. A. R., & Spann, N. (2012). Assesments of textbook usage and the relarionship to student course performance. *College Teaching*, *60*(1), 17–24. doi:10.1080/87567555.2011.609573

Lebrun, M. (2011). Impacts des TIC sur la qualité des apprentissages des étudiants et le développement professionnel des enseignants: Vers une approche systémique. *Sciences et Technologies de l'Information et de la Communication pour l'Éducation et la Formation*, *18*(1), 287–316. doi:10.3406/stice.2011.1028

Legendre, R. (2005). Dictionnaire actuel de l'éducation (3e éd.). Guérin éditeur Montréal.

Lin, Y. T. (2019). Impacts of a flipped classroom with a smart learning diagnosis system on students' learning performance, perception, and problem-solving ability in a software engineering course. *Computers in Human Behavior*, *95*, 187–196. doi:10.1016/j.chb.2018.11.036

Lopes, A. P., & Soares, F. (2018). Perception and performance in a flipped Financial Mathe-matics classroom. *International Journal of Management Education*, *16*(1), 105–113. doi:10.1016/j.ijme.2018.01.001

Memaï, A., & Rouag, A. (2017). Le manuel scolaire: Au-delà de l'outil pédagogique, l'objet politico-social. *Éducation et socialisation*, 43. doi:10.4000/edso.2014

Moundy, K., Chafiq, N., & Talbi, M. (2021). Comparative Analysis of Student Engagement in Digital Textbook Use during Quarantine. *Education Sciences*, *11*(7), 352. doi:10.3390/educsci11070352

Moundy, K., Chafiq, N., & Talbi, M. (2022b). A Model for Scripting and Designing a Digital Textbook. *International Journal of Emerging Technologies in Learning*, *17*(21), 296–311. doi:10.3991/ijet.v17i21.34603

Murillo-Zamorano, L. R., López Sánchez, J. N., & Godoy-Caballero, A. L. (2019). How the flipped classroom affects knowledge, skills, and engagement in higher education: Effects on students' satisfaction. *Computers & Education*, *141*, 103608. doi:10.1016/j.compedu.2019.103608

Öza, G. Z., & Abaan, S. (2021). Use of a flipped classroom "Leadership in Nursing" course on nursing students' achievement and experiences: A quasi-experimental study. *Journal of Professional Nursing, 37*(3), 562–571. doi:10.1016/j.profnurs.2021.02.001 PMID:34016315

Pew Research Center. (2014). *E-Reading Rises as Device Ownership jumps*. WayBackMachine. https://web.archive.org/web/20140327053903/http://www.pewinternet.org/files/old-media/Files/Reports/2014/PIP_E-reading_011614.pdf

Romero, E., Artal-Sevil, J. S., Casanova, O., & Serrano, R. M. (2017). Flipped learning + ICT: An instructional model in higher education. *INTED Proceedings*. 10.21125/inted.2017.2201

SDTICE. (2009). *Les manuels numériques CG*. CNDP. http://www.cndp.fr/crdp-rouen/images/cddp27/pdf/tuic/les_manuels_numeriques_cg.pdf

Séguin, R. (1989). *L'élaboration des manuels scolaires: Guide méthodologique. Division des sciences de l'éducation contenus et méthodes*. UNESCO.

Séré, A., & Bassy, A.-M. (2010, juillet). *Le manuel scolaire à l'heure du numérique: Une « nouvelle donne » de la politique des ressources pour l'enseignement* (No 087). Ministère de l'éducation nationale ministère de l'enseignement supérieur et de la recherche. https://www.vie-publique.fr/sites/default/files/rapport/pdf/114000048.pdf

Strelan, P., Osborn, A., & Palmer, E. (2020). The flipped classroom: A meta-analysis of ef-fects on student performance across disciplines and education levels. *Educational Research Review, 30*, 100314. doi:10.1016/j.edurev.2020.100314

UNESCO. (2005). Stratégie globale d'élaboration des manuels scolaires et des matériels didactiques. Paris: UNESCO: Organisation des Nations unies pour l'éducation, la science et la culture.

UNESCO. (2008). *Comment promouvoir l'égalité entre les sexes par les manuels scolaires? Guide méthodologique à l'attention des acteurs et actrices de la chaîne du manuel scolaire*. UNESCO.

Université du Québec. (2013). *Guide de conception et d'utilisation du manuel numérique universitaire*. https://www.puq.ca/catalogue/livres/guide-conception-utilisation-manuel-numerique-universitaire-2664.html

Weisberg, M. (2011). Student Attitudes and Behaviors Towards Digital Textbooks. *Publishing Research Quarterly, 27*(2), 188-196. doi:10.1007/s12109-011-9217-4

Young, J. (2013). The object formerly known as the textbook. *The Chronicle of Higher Education*.

Chapter 2

Expanding Learning Horizons:
Investigating the Potential of Serious Games for Student Engagement and Skill Development in Higher Education at Hassan II University

Imane Elimadi
Faculty of Sciences Ben M'Sick, Hassan II University, Casablanca, Morocco

Khalil Shehadeh Al-Qatawneh
Tafila Technical University, Jordan

ABSTRACT

The purpose of this study is to investigate the impact of serious games on student learning outcomes at University Hassan II. To participate in the study, a group of students from various disciplines was chosen. The primary goal was to evaluate the efficacy of serious games in improving knowledge acquisition, skill development, and engagement among university students. The study took a mixed-methods approach, collecting data using both quantitative and qualitative methods. Participants were divided into two groups: one that used serious games as part of their learning experience and one that used traditional instructional methods. Pre- and post-tests were used to assess knowledge gain, and surveys were used to assess student engagement and learning experience perceptions. These findings highlight the potential of serious games as effective educational tools. Incorporating serious games into the curriculum can boost student engagement, promote active learning, and create a more immersive and interactive learning environment.

DOI: 10.4018/979-8-3693-1034-2.ch002

REVIEW OF LITERATURE

The potential of serious games to improve student engagement and skill development in higher education is examined in the essay "Expanding Learning Horizons: Investigating the Potential of Serious Games for Student Engagement and Skill Development in Higher Education". The use of serious games as an inventive instructional tool has received a lot of attention in the field of education, and there has been much discussion of it in scholarly publications.

Serious Games in Education

Serious games are instructional and interactive digital games created with a particular learning objective in mind. They have been identified as a viable method of getting students involved in the learning process. The research demonstrates how they might improve both the effectiveness and enjoyment of learning (Gee, 2003).

Serious games are a dynamic and cutting-edge method of teaching and learning. They are often referred to as instructional or educational games. These interactive online games are painstakingly created with certain learning goals in mind. Because of their capacity to captivate and inspire students, they have attracted a great deal of interest in educational research and practice. Studies have indicated that the successful incorporation of serious games into the curriculum may greatly improve the efficiency and enjoyment of the educational process (Hamari, Koivisto, & Sarsa, 2014).

They provide a special fusion of experiential learning, intrinsic motivation, and interaction, which makes them an invaluable resource for instructors and instructional designers. Studies like "Does Gamification Work? — A Literature Review of Empirical Studies on Gamification" by Hamari, Koivisto, and Sarsa (2014) and "What Video Games Have to Teach Us About Learning and Literacy" by Gee (2003), for example, highlight the implications of gamification and serious games in education by emphasizing how they can enhance motivation, skill development, and knowledge acquisition, ultimately leading to more successful and pleasurable learning experiences.

Active Learning and Engagement

The fundamental component of serious games' educational value is active learning. With the use of technology, these games offer an improved learning experience that actively engages students in making decisions, solving problems, and applying their knowledge. Serious games foster critical thinking abilities in addition to increasing student motivation and knowledge retention by delivering an immersive and interactive learning environment. In order to promote a deeper grasp of difficult subjects and better prepare students for issues they will face in the real world, this technology-enabled approach to active learning makes sure that students are active participants in their educational journey rather than passive users of knowledge. (Wouters, van Nimwegen, van Oostendorp, & van Der Spek, 2013). Because serious games are interactive, they can be customized and adapted to meet the unique learning needs of each player, which increases engagement and improves skill development.

It is impossible to overestimate the importance of serious games and active learning. These games act as a link between more conventional teaching strategies and interactive, tech-enhanced learning. Serious games provide new life to the classroom by actively involving students in problem-solving, decision-making, and experiential learning. They maintain students' engagement and commitment to their academic path by having a significant influence on student motivation. (Annetta, Minogue, Holmes, & Cheng, 2009) Furthermore, serious games' participatory format helps players retain complex information. Pupils who actively engage in their education typically retain and apply the information more successfully. (Steinkuehler & Duncan, 2008) Serious games also help students build higher-order cognitive skills by fostering critical thinking by pushing them to assess results, apply theory to practical circumstances, and analyze consequences.

This ability to think critically goes beyond the game and prepares students for the challenges of both their academic and professional careers. (De Grove, Bourgonjon, & Van Looy, 2012) The degree of customization and flexibility that serious games provide emphasizes how important they are even more. Through individualized learning experiences, each student's specific requirements are met, increasing engagement and skill development. In conclusion, serious games have completely changed the way that education is delivered. They provide students with an engaging, dynamic, and technologically advanced method of active learning that enhances their comprehension, motivation, and critical thinking skills. (Anderson & Dill, 2000)

Research Questions

This article tries to answer the following questions:

What effects can serious games have on student motivation, engagement, and knowledge acquisition in higher education—especially at University Hassan II—when compared to traditional teaching methods? What are the implications for enhancing learning outcomes?

What are the main obstacles to and possibilities for incorporating serious games into the university curriculum, and how can teachers use these games to encourage students in a variety of subjects to learn via experience, critical thinking, and active learning?

A mixed-methods study methodology is suggested to look into how serious games affect University Hassan II students' learning results. This strategy will provide a thorough comprehension of the topic and offer data for analysis that is both quantitative and qualitative. This is a recommended approach:

1. Structure of Research:
   To gather and evaluate data from a bigger sample in an effective manner, use a quantitative research strategy.

2. Selection of Participants:
   Pick 100 university students at random from a variety of academic programs.

3. Division of Groups:
   Split the 100 participants into two groups: the experimental group, which will learn through serious games, and the control group, which will follow conventional teaching techniques.

4. Gathering Data:
   Pre- and post-tests: Give knowledge exams to each participant both before and after the research to gauge their level of understanding.

Surveys:

Utilize surveys to gather information on student motivation, engagement, and opinions on the two groups' educational experiences.

Findings

This table clearly displays the pre-test and post-test scores for both the experimental and control groups, allowing for simple comparison of knowledge gain. Important details about engagement levels are also included by reporting increased engagement using percentages. For more accurate quantification of the group differences, statistical metrics such as mean and standard deviation may be useful.

Table 1. Knowledge acquisition and engagement

Group	Pre-Test Score	Post-Test Score	Percentage Reporting Higher Engagement
Experimental	50	75	85%
Control	48	60	50%

This table gives a clear picture of the proportion of students who have experienced good learning experiences and who are showing better critical thinking. It's clear and simple to comprehend. Incorporating qualitative feedback or remarks from survey participants concerning their experiences may augment the breadth of comprehension.

Table 2. Skill development and learning experience

Group	Percentage Demonstrating Improved Critical Thinking	Percentage with Positive Learning Experience
Experimental	70%	90%
Control	40%	60%

This table effectively conveys the proportion of students who report working together more, having hardware issues, and not being computer literate. It is lucid and educational. You can think about adding extra details to make it more thorough, including the particular difficulties students who reported hardware problems had.

Table 3. Collaboration, communication, and challenges

Group	Percentage Reporting Increased Collaboration	Percentage Facing Hardware Challenges	Percentage Lacking Electronic Literacy
Experimental	80%	20%	N/A
Control	45%	N/A	15%

DISCUSSION

The information displayed in these tables clarifies how serious games affect University Hassan II students' learning objectives. 100 students from various academic programs participated in the mixed-methods study; they were split into two groups: one for the experimental group, which used serious games, and the control group, which used standard teaching techniques.

The experimental group, which used serious games, had a significant gain in information acquisition, according to Table 1's data. This progress is evident in the pre-test and post-test scores, with the post-test average score being considerably higher than the pre-test level. Furthermore, a sizable portion of students in the experimental group reported higher involvement, according to the survey data. This implies that serious games foster greater levels of student involvement, which is essential for efficient learning, in addition to improving information acquisition.

Table 2 shows that a sizable portion of pupils in the experimental group showed better critical thinking abilities as a result of using serious games. This suggests that serious games, through their problem-solving and decision-making elements, might promote the development of critical thinking skills. Serious games have a favorable effect on generating engaging and immersive learning environments, as seen by the high percentage of students in the experimental group who reported positive learning experiences. The control group, on the other hand, showed lower percentages for both pleasant learning experiences and skill growth.

According to Table 3's statistics, a far larger percentage of students in the experimental group reported feeling more collaborative, suggesting that multiplayer-enabled serious games encourage social contact and teamwork. But it's important to recognize that difficulties were also noted. A subset of the experimental group experienced hardware issues, highlighting the significance of guaranteeing that every student has access to appropriate equipment. Furthermore, some of the control group's students did not possess technological literacy, which may have made it difficult for them to interact with technology-based learning resources even if it is not specifically mentioned in the table.

The results of this study point to the benefits that serious games may have for college students' critical thinking, cooperation, engagement, skill development, and acquisition of knowledge. These findings are consistent with the larger body of research on the advantages of learner-centered methods, interactive educational resources, and active learning. To guarantee fair access to these cutting-edge teaching strategies, it is imperative to address issues with digital literacy and technological access. The findings of this study have ramifications for academics, instructional designers, and legislators who aim to improve student learning outcomes in higher education by including serious games.

CONCLUSION

The University Hassan II study on the effects of serious games on learning outcomes for students has shed important light on the possible advantages of these cutting-edge teaching aids. A mixed-means strategy was used in the study, with 100 students from various academic programs being split into two groups: one experimental group that played serious games, and the control group that received instruction using conventional methods.

The study's findings, as shown in the tables, point to a positive correlation between improved learning outcomes and the usage of serious games. Significant gains in information acquisition, skill development, engagement, and pleasant learning experiences were shown by the experimental group. These results are consistent with the larger body of literature that highlights the benefits of student-centered learning, interactive educational resources, and active learning.

Serious games, in particular, have been demonstrated to develop critical thinking abilities, encourage teamwork and communication, and offer immersive and interesting educational opportunities. These findings have important ramifications for improving postsecondary education and designing dynamic, engaging, and productive learning environments.

To guarantee equal access to these cutting-edge teaching strategies, it is imperative to address the issues around digital literacy and technological access. Policymakers and educational institutions need to pay attention to this, particularly in terms of making sure that all students have access to the right gear and digital literacy.

According to the study's findings, serious games have the power to completely transform learning objectives and experiences in the classroom. These cutting-edge resources foster critical thinking and student participation in addition to improving knowledge and skill development. Serious games may be a key component of more accessible and productive learning environments in higher education—that is, if the problems are carefully considered and addressed.

REFERENCES

Annetta, L. A., Minogue, J., Holmes, S. Y., & Cheng, M. T. (2009). Investigating the impact of video games on high school students' engagement and learning about genetics. *Computers & Education*, *53*(1), 74–85. doi:10.1016/j.compedu.2008.12.020

De Grove, F., Bourgonjon, J., & Van Looy, J. (2012). Digital games in the classroom? A contextual approach to teachers' adoption intention of digital games in formal education. *Computers & Education*, *59*(4), 1155–1166.

Gee, J. P. (2003). What Video Games Have to Teach Us About Learning and Literacy. *Computers in Entertainment*, *1*(1), 20–20. doi:10.1145/950566.950595

Hamari, J., Koivisto, J., & Sarsa, H. (2014). Does gamification work? — A literature review of empirical studies on gamification. *2014 47th Hawaii international conference on system sciences*, 3025-3034.

Steinkuehler, C., & Duncan, S. (2008). Scientific habits of mind in virtual worlds. *Journal of Science Education and Technology*, *17*(6), 530–543. doi:10.1007/s10956-008-9120-8

Wouters, P., van Nimwegen, C., van Oostendorp, H., & van Der Spek, E. D. (2013). A meta-analysis of the cognitive and motivational effects of serious games. *Journal of Educational Psychology*, *105*(2), 249–265. doi:10.1037/a0031311

Chapter 3
Getting Started With Augmented Reality (AR) in Inclusive Online Teaching and Learning in Higher Education:
An Extended Environmental Scan for Pedagogical Design Leads

Shalin Hai-Jew
https://orcid.org/0000-0002-8863-0175
Hutchinson Community College, USA

ABSTRACT

With the mass-scale adoption of augmented reality (AR) in the commercial space, and student interest in 3d- and 4d experiential learning, higher education is starting to look towards digital augmentations of real spaces for teaching and learning. University creative shops are exploring whether they can get into the game of producing AR-enhanced experiences: campus tours, interactive gaming, virtual laboratories, exploratory art spaces, simulations, design labs, online / offline / blended teaching and learning modules, and other AR applications. This work offers a basic environmental scan of the AR space for inclusive online teaching and learning, and it includes pedagogical design leads from the current research, technological knowhow, hands-on design / development / deployment of learning objects, and online teaching and learning methods. This work does not take a pedagogical theory approach although several theories are mentioned. Rather, the focus is on applied AR in teaching and learning.

DOI: 10.4018/979-8-3693-1034-2.ch003

INTRODUCTION

Historically, "augmented reality" is said to have been first conceptualized and used by Thomas P. Caudell and David W. Mizell, both engineers and researchers of The Boeing Company (in 1990) (Interactive Design Foundation, 2020, "Augmented reality…" (Vertucci, D'Onofrio, Ricciardi, & De Nino, 2023, p. 41). Specifically, AR was harnessed to superimpose information "on the visual field to make it easier for workers to lay aircraft cables" (Caudell & Mizell, 1992, as cited in Doerner, Broll, Jung, Grimm, Göbel, & Kruse, 2022, p. 25). While AR has been studied since the early 1990s, the rise of smart phones in the 2010s raised interest several decades later. The first conceptualization of augmented reality was in the 1960s, with the first commercial AR tools emerging in the 1980s ((Vertucci, D'Onofrio, Ricciardi, & De Nino, 2023, p. 35). Augmented reality (AR) is famously defined by R.T. Azuma (1997) as a system that "combines real and virtual," is "interactive in real time," and is registered in three dimensions (p. 356), which looks more real-world. Interactivity is considered "the most important characteristic of 3D-LOs" (learning objects) in the VR/AR environment, so people may engage in "touching, moving, exploring, annotating and triggering behaviors" (Mangina, Oct. 2017, p. 5) of the digital objects.

Instead of only going with off-the-shelf products, services, and subscriptions, university creative shops are exploring whether they can get into the game of producing AR-enhanced experiences: campus tours, interactive gaming, virtual laboratories, exploratory art spaces, simulations, design labs, online / offline / blended teaching and learning modules, and other AR applications.

This work offers a basic environmental scan of the AR space for online teaching and learning. From this information and hands-on instructional design work, this chapter explores what a Midwestern university would need to stand-up an initial AR shop: talent for staffing, requisite equipment, requisite software, physical spaces (studios, offices, labs, and production spaces), and others. This is an early and exploratory work that explores the promises and challenges of AR in higher education.

There is an additional brief applied "use case" defined lightly for immigrant learners. Vibrant societies often have strong inflows and outflows of peoples because they engage the world. One byproduct of this involves immigration and emigration (optimally more of the first than the latter, more inflow than outflow). A subset of the immigrants includes immigrant learners, of all ages. In terms of AR spaces, immigrant learners can perhaps relate to the sudden shifts in reality, given the adjustments to different peoples, new locales, novel practices, new cultures, shifts in worldviews, and other practices. They may experience augmentary changes with ease and engagement. More on this use case follows later on.

REVIEW OF THE LITERATURE

Augmented reality is considered "a variation of *Virtual Environments* (VE)" (Azuma, 1997, p. 2) or virtual reality (VR). Both are synthetic environments although AR is considered more annotative, and VR may include a more complete synthetic world surround. Azuma writes:

VE technologies completely immerse a user inside a synthetic environment. While immersed, the user cannot see the real world around him. In contrast, AR allows the user to see the real world, with virtual objects superimposed upon or composited with the real world. Therefore, AR supplements reality, rather than completely replacing it. (Azuma, 1997, p. 2)

AR is thought to harness the strengths of the real world along with the virtual. AR involves the adding of "objects that were not perceptible a priori" (Mohamed & Mohamed, July 2012, p. 1). From early days, it was used to enhance human workplace performance:

Augmented Reality enhances a user's perception of and interaction with the real world. The virtual objects display information that the user cannot direct detect with his own senses. The information conveyed by the virtual objects helps a user perform real-world tasks. AR is a specific example of what Fred Brooks calls Intelligence Amplification...: using the computer as a tool to make a task easier for a human to perform. (Azuma, 1997, p. 3)

The AR visuals are expected to dynamically update. One researcher writes:

It is crucial that this augmentation does not happen statically and at once...but continuously and adapted to the current point of view of the respective viewer. In simplified terms and neglecting individual alternatives, AR can be realized through the following five steps:

1. *Video capturing*
2. *Tracking*
3. *Registration*
4. *Visualization*
5. *Output* (Broll, 2022, p. 292)

Geometric registration has to occur to ensure correct anchoring of the artificial content into the physical reality (Broll, 2022, p. 293).

The core definition of augmented reality has stood the test of time even as the technologies and methods have been updated (Azuma, Baillot, Behringer, Feiner, Julier, & MacIntyre, 2001).

Some definitions hearken to a more idealistic definition and perhaps a sense of full immersion of the human by technology:

In perfect VR, all of the sensory impressions of the user would be generated by the computer, in the same quantity and quality as people are used to in the real world. Human actions in VR would have the same effects and virtual objects would affect people as they do in the real world. Today's VR systems are by no means perfect, but the development of VR technology is aimed at ever more realistic experiences. (Doerner, Broll, Jung, Grimm, Göbel, & Kruse, 2022, p. 16)

Similarly, AR itself would be "immediate" and "seamless" melding of the ambient real and the virtual in real-time, with "the latter resembling reality to the largest extent possible regarding its characteristics, appearance, and behavior, so that (if desired) sensory impressions from reality and virtuality may become indistinguishable (for any senses)" (Doerner, Broll, Jung, Grimm, Göbel, & Kruse, 2022, p. 19). One witty team describes AR as "Click-and-Mortar" (a play on "brick and mortar") (Li, Chen, & Kang, July 2022, p. 49). Photorealistic rendering for AR does enable virtual objects to "appear consistent with their physical environment. Making virtual objects blend seamlessly with the physical environment has many desirable applications. Primarily, the immersive experience is greatly improved. Several works in photorealistic rendering for AR exist, the majority involve sophisticated techniques to make it real-time, render reflective virtual objects, improve illumination, etc." (Del Gallego, Nov. 2020, p. 115). Researchers observe:

Virtual objects must be aligned with the real world properly and dynamically; otherwise, the expected consistency of the virtual and real scene will not be achieved. Failure of geometric consistency will lead to jitter or drift of the virtual objects, which can be perceived by users easily. (Gao, Wang, & Bian, July 2016, p. 928)

The objects need to fuse, the virtual with the real, and vice versa.

Traditional VR is dedicated to fully immersing users in the computer-generated virtual world, which requires accurate modelling of the environment and a huge amount of work…AR to eliminate the modeling for the environment, the core idea is: in the real world fusion computer-generated virtual objects and make the virtual objects and reality of the world as an organic whole, enhances the learner…perception and understanding of the real world. (Liying, Weng, Liyao, Maozheng, & Xiaoping, Dec. 2021, p. 298)

Placing virtual objects in a real scene requires some knowledge of the light in that scene so that the AR objects can be "visually coherent with real objects" (Lee, Jeong, Choi, Kim, & Moon, 2022, p. 109498). Higher-end AR systems can handle this automatically to enable "realistic AR" (Lee, Jeong, Choi, Kim, & Moon, 2022, p. 109508), but others may only enable deterministic lighting.

More recent definitions seem perhaps more informal: Augmented reality is an "overlay" (Lichty, 2020, p. 264); "the draping of virtual reality onto a physical model" (Kundu, Muhammad, & Sattar, Dec. 2017, p. 13). AR serves as "a visualization technology" (Arce-Lopera, Gomez, & Montoya, Nov. 2019, p. 193). Some types of AR are location-based, in-situ, in outside or indoor environments. For example, a game is set up in a room with augmentations, in a so-called "spatial augmented environment" (Oswald, Tost, & Wettach, Nov. 2014, p. 1). While most games have predefined environments, this work describes their instantiation of "a real-time video game level editor that allows users to interact with their own environment to create game content with real everyday objects, making them part of the level design" (Oswald, Tost, & Wettach, Nov. 2014, p. 1). Here, the player is a creator, and they act as "level designers" and the real world is a "video game stage" (Oswald, Tost, & Wettach, Nov. 2014, p. 2, p. 4).

AR affects the person's sense of the world's "light field":

The real world is visualized via numerous light rays, which the human eye captures from different locations and directions by changing its focus. With head motion, human eyes can always focus on the object of interest, even if the object is surrounded by a changing environment. The collection of light rays that people perceive from different locations and directions in their surroundings is the light field. (Yu, 2017, p. 105)

AR is thought to enable both embodied and disembodied cognition. For example, by moving around or into an AR object, people can change their sense of perspective or what the researchers have dubbed "perspective change through movement" (Radu & Antle, Mar. 2017, p. 1). The cognitive load of learners is thought to be displaced into some of the physical objects as well: The researchers write:

When a problem is being solved using physical components, such as when a student is solving a jigsaw puzzle or solving a math problem using physical blocks, part of the student's cognition is being offloaded into the physical world. Distributed cognition theory explores how human cognition occurs both inside the mind and outside in the physical environment. (Radu & Antle, Mar. 2017, p. 1)

In other words, people are engaging in distributed cognition (Figure 1).

Figure 1. Distributed cognition in augmented reality

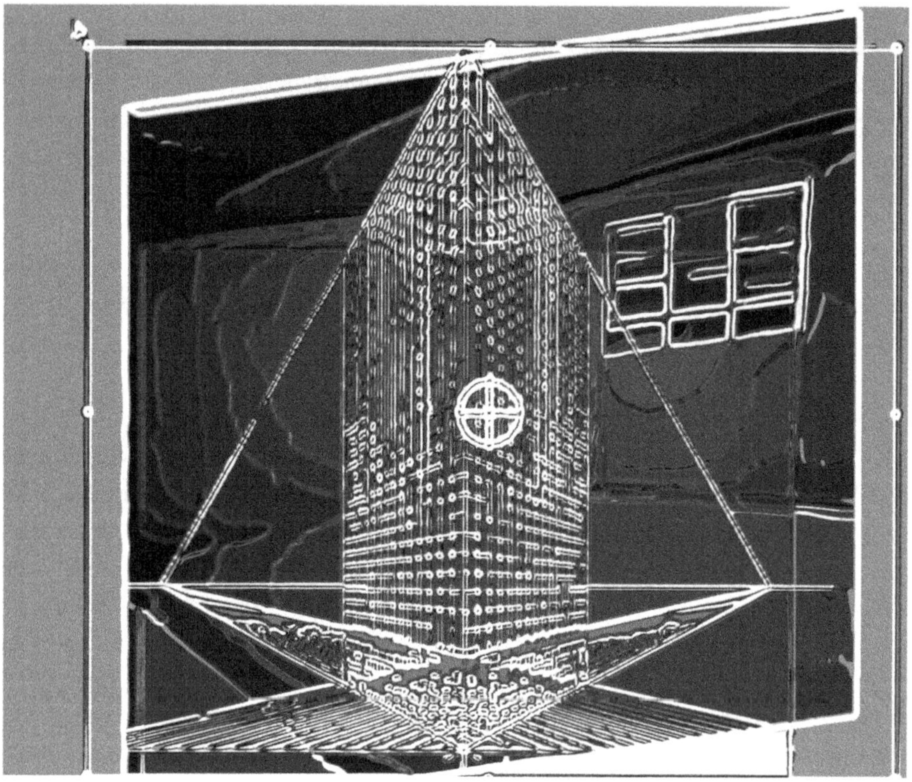

Narrative is considered an ancient form of communication by which people share knowledge and pass down culture and values. Story may help string together related information; bring coherence; improve learning; improve long-term memory of the learning. AR-based storytelling is sometimes built around a particular physical location (Ancient & Teeuw, July 2020) in a "locative" or "in situ" way.

AR enables a multisensory surround, absorption in a story, engagement with a presented challenge (Agrawal & Bech, 2023, p. 321), so there are various ways to engage deeply in AR. AR may be built around story plotlines, created worlds, characters, and there may be game elements for friendly competitions to motivate the learning. Virtual instructors as pedagogical agents have been built into AR (Doswell, 2008, p. 215). Learners themselves may embody digital puppets or avatars in a way that motivates them based on "AR-induced fantasy" and "learner self-similarity" (Zuo, Spek, Hu, & Birk, (Dec. 2021, p. 279). One work explored the uses of AR for social supports, with representations of social support figures as virtual dogs and virtual people. The research participants "significantly preferred, and more positively evaluated, the virtual dog support figure than the other conditions" (albeit not a lessening of physiological stress as indicated by average heart rates) (Norouzi, Kim, Bruder, Bailenson, Wisniewski, & Welch, 2022, p. 1).

Often, the term "immersive" is used in the contexts of both virtual reality / augmented reality (VR/AR). IVR refers to immersive VR, and IAR refers to immersive AR (Bourguet & Romero-Gonzalez, May 2021, p. 3). The "immersion" refers to full-surrounds of visuals and sounds and perhaps even touch, as well as various combinations. It also refers to psychological engagement, how individuals and groups interact with the contents, involve themselves mentally, and invest of themselves in it. One researcher writes:

Immersion is a metaphorical term derived from the physical experience of being submerged in water. We seek the same feeling from a psychologically immersive experience that we do from a plunge in the ocean or swimming pool: the sensation of being surrounded by a completely other reality, as different as water is from air, that takes over all of our attention, our whole perceptual apparatus. (Murray, 2017, p. 99, as cited in Agrawal & Bech, 2023, p. 320)

AR has been harnessed for gaming, marketing, entertainment, customer experiences, art, museum displays, cultural heritage experiences, night shows, citizen participation in civics projects (Saßmannshausen, Radtke, Bohn, Hussein, Randall, & Pipek, June 2021, p. 250), raising awareness of sea level rise and global warming, enhancing a magic show performance (Carreras & Sora, Oct. 2009), and others. Art installations and mobile projects engage the larger publics in conversations about meaning, philosophies, aesthetics, political power, the human condition, and other dimensions (Geroimenko, 2022). Cathedrals are made "intelligent" using augmented reality, virtual reality, and artificial intelligence to create "an intense cultural, historical, and religious visitor experience" (Allal-Chérif, 2022, p. 1). Digital technological overlays are seen as welcome even in sacred spaces and "architectural masterpieces" in the "collective imagination" (Allal-Chérif, 2022, p. 1). Another project involved digitally reviving a historical stone obelisk landmark at a university campus and enabling 3d engagement with it and even the ability to explore details of each stone in the obelisk (and the mine it came from) (Klippel, Wallgrün, Masrur, Zhao, & LaFemina, Mar. 2019, p. 1022).

One sense of the historical sequence for learning goes as follows: distance learning, electronic learning, mobile learning, virtual reality, and augmented reality (with the sub-element of Mobile Augmented Reality or "MAR") (Al-Azawi, Apr. 2018, p. 219). AR is harnessed along with learning management systems, virtual labs, and assessments for game-based learning (Rozinaj, Vančo, Vargic, Minárik, & Polakovič, June 2018, p. 1). AR is integrated into e-learning systems, such as a system about 3d geometry (Patil, Prabhu, Neogi, Joshi, & Katre, Aug. 2016, p. 1). AR is integrated into Massively Multiplayer Online (MMO) worlds and Massively Multiplayer Online Role Playing Games (MMORPGs) (Lang, MacIntyre, & Zugaza, Mar. 2008, p. 67). Researchers see advantages to building AR to persistent platforms:

The major strength we foresee in applying MMOs to AR lies in the immersive, intuitive and collaborative nature of MMO-based AR design; the same can also be said for their potential for VR experience design. The evolving AR experiences are always online, persistent and open to changes. (Lang, MacIntyre, & Zugaza, Mar. 2008, p. 70)

It is used for healthcare diagnostics (Bichlmeier, Wimmer, Heining, & Navab, 2007), therapeutics (Daher, Mar. 2017, p. 417), patient-specific modeling for surgery (De Backer, Simoens, Creemers, Vermijs, Matthys, Bravi,... & Decaestecker, 2022, p. 1), and others. AR 3d holographic models are used to stand in for some anatomy lab hours in medical school and other areas that require anatomy education (Uribe, Harmon, Laguna, & Courtier, 2022, p. 1). An AR app is used to provide therapeutic education for those with diabetes (Calle-Bustos, Juan, Abad, & Mollá, July 2019, p. 337).

AR is used with a range of technologies, including "presentations, a webcam, a file sharing app, and voting systems" (Murodillaevich, Eshpulatovich, & Kuvondik, Nov. 2020, p. 1). It is used for first responder trainings. AR has been used to help television personalities gesture against green screens without accidentally covering over important visuals. AR has long been used for aerospace maintenance training and work. It has been used to interact with data, in social collaboration with others (Gundala, Alamuri, Firdaus, & Kumar, Feb. 2022, p. 1). It is a significant part of Industry 4.0. For example, Tangible Augmented Reality has been used for "creating design representation for usability testing of industrial products" (Jain & Choi, July 2020, p. 43). [Tangible Augmented Reality (TAR) is "where virtual components are registered to physical components and virtual components can be manipulated by interacting with physical components in the real world" (Jain & Choi, July 2020, p. 43).]

AR has been built into apps to assist drivers for improved driving and route learning (Yount, Kass, & Arruda, 2022). It has been used in treadmills to give a sense of walking and running through different locales. It is central to healthcare training and applied work.

AR has been built into assistive devices as well. One work describes an assistive optical see-through AR system for children with autism spectrum disorder to better interpret other's emotions. This tool enables the children to see an emoticon or emoji face where others' faces would be for easier emotion understanding in real time (Sun, Haraldsson, Zhao, & Belongie, Oct. 2019). Another work descries the use of AR and VR to help children with autism spectrum disorder (ASDE) focus during trainings (Lakshmiprabha, Santos, Mladenov, & Beltramello, Sept. 2014, p. 277). Another AR app helps teach "autistic eating skills" (Bouaziz, Alhejaili, Al-Saedi, Mihdhar, & Alsarrani, Dec. 2020, p. 239). There are other apps for those with cognitive disabilities to increase their autonomy in daily life activities, such as setting a table for a meal, collecting garbage and identifying objects for recycling (Garzotto, Torelli, Vona, & Aruanno, Dec. 2018, p. 189). In this app, a virtual assistant provides tips and clear visual examples in multimodal ways (Garzotto, Torelli, Vona, & Aruanno, Dec. 2018, p. 190). A passive haptic AR feedback device re-directs walking for those with visual impairments (Chen, Li, Wang, Steinicke, & Zhao, Oct. 2021).

A mixed reality learning space enabled more accessible learning, for "non-native English speakers, students with hearing disabilities and students with language-based learning disabilities" (Aljowaysir, Ozdemir, & Kim, June 2019, p. 1). AR learning is seen to meet a more diversified range of learning needs in a classroom. Three-dimensional visualizations may enable "support of individualism" (Murodillaevich, Eshpulatovich, & Kuvondik, Nov. 2020, p. 7).

A different AR simulation was created to emulate what the world may be like for those with autism spectrum disorder (ASD), in terms of the sensory-perceptual difficulties. This is a simulation to evoke empathy (what it is like to be in a world where there is near-constant sensory overload) in those stakeholders who know or work with those with ASD. The researchers say that this app is for parents, for special educators, for therapists (professionals), and others (Mikropoulos, Delimitros, Gaintatzis, Iatraki, Stergiouli, Tsiara, & Kalyvioti, June 2020, p. 86).

AR is a "learning medium" (Kurniawan, Purwanto, & Mansur, Nov. 2019, p. 85). AR refers to "a technology that connects the real world with the virtual world" (Saritha, Mankad, Venkataswamy, & Bapu, Dec. 2018, p. 1). AR is seen as a conduit for the delivery of information for learning, as a composite of "text, sound, images, and animation" (Kurniawan, Purwanto, & Mansur, Nov. 2019, p. 85). The respective positionality of the respective elements is important. It affects first impressions. It informs where the learner attention goes, what is foregrounded, what is backgrounded. The layout also informs the sequence of the experienced AR. It affects last impressions.

Some suggest that AR is "a mature technology for creating learning experiences" based on several studies (Iqbal, Mangina, & Campbell, Oct. 2019, p. 12; Santos, Chen, Taketomi, Yamamoto, Miyazaki, & Kato, 2013, p. 38), but seen as "an emerging technology that has yet to be a mature consumer product" (Ghazwani & Smith, Feb. 2020, p. 39) by others. While the technologies have advanced in the commercial market, in education, AR is seen as "emerging" (Iqbal, Mangina, & Campbell, Oct. 2019, p. 12). The AR and VR technologies are "not commonplace today" even as they have improved (Doerner & Horst, 2022, p. 3). There is a high sense of potential, though, for AR in learning (Al-Azawi, Apr. 2018, p. 218).

A major challenge has been how to harness AR for effective educational opportunities (Molnár & Sik, Oct. 2019) and perhaps untested. AR is seen to enhance "student outcomes by engaging them during the learning process" (Murodillaevich, Eshpulatovich, & Kuvondik, Nov. 2020, p. 7). AR "reveals itself as having different modalities as an educational channel. Among these modalities, these are defined by the author as the developmental (teaching AR design), didactic (AR as creative/educational tool), and demonstrative (illustrative, which one will distinguish from the didactic)". The use of each of these has a different communicative quality that assist (sic) in the education of design principles" (Lichty, 2020, p. 265). There is the sense that AR and VR may become "a standard tool in education" and fundamentally change education (Mangina, Oct. 2017, p. 1), either as a complement to more traditional learning technologies or even as a replacement for some traditional approaches.

Education-wise, AR is an "instructional aid" (Erofeeva & Klowait, May 2021, p. 1). An Augmented Reality Learning Environment (ARLE) refers to the learning space that may be acquired from particular AR, both subjectively and objectively. ARLEs have existed since the 1990s "in complex early forms" (Drljević, Wong, & Botički, 2017, p. 419). [Some works refer to "Augmented Reality Learning Experiences" as "ARLEs" as well.]

A meta-analytic study of ARLEs found…

A widely variable effect on student performance from a small negative effect to a large effect, with a mean effect size of 0.56 or moderate effect. To complement this finding, we performed a qualitative analysis on the design aspects for ARLEs: display hardware, software libraries, content authoring solutions, and evaluation techniques. We explain that AR incur(s) three inherent advantages: real world annotation, contextual visualization, and vision-haptic visualization. (Santos, Chen, Taketomi, Yamamoto, Miyazaki, & Kato, 2013, p. 38)

An Augmented Reality Learning Object (ARLO) refers to a base unit of an AR digital learning object, which may be a stand-alone and even portable (ubiquitous) digital piece. A portable piece may be harnessed for "nomadic usage" such as via mobile devices (Broll, 2022, p. 318). [A "digital learning object" is a base unit used for online learning.] Researchers suggest that now it is still early years in terms of designing for the "educational possibilities of AR" (Jang, Ko, Shin, & Han, 2021, p. 6798).

Teachers who have taught using AR/VR have observed "…the high workload involved with the preparation of hands-on experiences, the large amount of course time that needs to be devoted" (Doerner & Horst, 2022, p. 1). Specifically, teachers may not be accepting of VR and AR technologies since adopting AR requires significant effort to deploy. Technology-makers are working hard to make technologies easier to adopt for teachers (Cubillo, Martin, Castro, Diaz, Colmenar, & Botički, Oct. 2014). One study found that the Technological Pedagogical and Content Knowledge (TPACK) model was found to have "a significant influence on perceived usefulness (PU) and perceived ease of use (PEU) while SN (social norms) influenced PU (perceived usefulness" of new technologies (Jang, Ko, Shin, & Han, 2021, p. 6798). Educators "must be creative and innovative to implement technology in the teaching and learning process" (Kiat, Ali, Abd Halim, & Ibrahim, Oct. 2016, p. 23). One study in a developing country found that primary school teachers identified a number of barriers to adoption of AR: "lack of competency, limited instructional design, lack of focused attention, lack of time, and limited environmental resources" (Alalwan, Cheng, Al-Samarraie, Yousef, Alzahrani, & Sarsam, 2020, p. 1). A BYOD (bring your own device) policy is another barrier not only for teachers but learners. One work surrounding a chemistry lab suggests the usefulness of prior learning before entering the lab, such as learning about "experiment manipulation and scientific concepts before they actually enter the real chemistry laboratory" (Hou & Lin, July 2017, p. 1005). This particular AR experience is described as "a game-based learning system integrated with augmented reality, anchored instruction, and virtual laboratory" (Hou & Lin, July 2017, p. 1005).

How AR is harnessed in the developing world is also of interest. One work conceptualizes educating students in remote areas using AR by beaming images of a 3d lecturer to a classroom of learners connectivity (Ghulamani & Zareen, Mar. 2018). It is unclear how practicable that would be given weak cyber connectivity in many places of the world (including in parts of the developed world).

One study about a tourism class in higher education during the pandemic also applied the Technology Acceptance Model (TAM) to learners. They found that "perceived usefulness, hedonic motivation and price value are important predicting factors for Chinese students' adoption and use of these applications" (Shen, Xu, Sotiriadis, & Wang, 2022, p. 1). Part of an instructional design of AR for learning should consider learner openness to using particular technologies as an indicator of behavioral intention.

Some AR installations can be highly complex. One work describes a virtual diorama created at a natural history museum. The AR Perpetual Garden App is "an international collaboration between digital media artists, game developers, and natural history museum scientists and botanists"; it is comprised of "two immersive AR environments that are constructed as data visualizations of plant populations intended to communicate a complex scientific educational narrative about trophic cascades" (Harrington, June 2020, p. 70). The display involves complex bioacoustics. Participants experience a real-world field of view. The information fidelity is high, in terms of "plant facts and concepts…, photorealism…, realistic landscape layouts…, data-based bioacoustics, story…, multimodal signals" and "data visualization and simulation" among others (Harrington, June 2020, p. 74). Museum visitors may engage in a "full-body" sort of exploration of the AR space (Harrington, June 2020, p. 74).

Another project involves the VR reconstruction of the flora and fauna of a national park for learning (Ortiz, Guevara, Espinosa, Santana, Tamayo, & Andaluz, June 2020, p. 1), with a special focus on photorealism in order to ensure the "complete immersion" of learners (p. 5). The higher fidelity of the photorealistic objects require increased effort and computer processing load and so needs to be justified.

In another museum exhibit, the focus is on the depiction of prehistoric wildlife and lives and times that are biologically irrecuperable. This exhibit enabled educational pathways using both structured narration (and also free-roaming options); further, the exhibits were designed with considerations for both adults and children in their mixed reality depiction of the Pleistocene Age (Apostolakis, Margetis, & Stephanidis, Nov. 2020, p. 237).

Researchers have laid the groundwork for contextualizing various types of realities. Specifically, Milgram and Kishino's "Taxonomy of Mixed Reality Visual Displays" from 1994 serves as the basis for Table 1. There is the unmediated and unaugmented world to the left. At the right is the virtual world, unmediated and unaugmented by reality. In the middle is mixed reality, with various types of augmentations and enrichments, diminishments (such as erasing or overlaying or occluding / blocking parts of reality or parts of virtuality), and other additions, subtractions or mixes of both. AR enables some "magical" effects, including "production, vanishing, transformation, restoration, teleportation, prediction, levitation" and other effects that may be partially or in whole supported with augmented reality technologies (Carreras & Sora, Oct. 2009, p. 26). An older work refers to "segmented reality" in which "divided" elements come together to form a coherent experience (De Michelis, De Paoli, Pluchinotta, & Susani, April 2000, p. 82), with the mix of the physical and the virtual, with various forms of loose and tight coupling of the real and the technologically augmented.

Table 1. Mixes of realities and imaginaries from unmediated to fully built-out augmentations, diminishments, and virtualities: Present evolution of the milgram and kishino taxonomy of mixed reality visual displays (from 1994)

Perceptual In-World "Reality"	**Mixed Reality (and Mediated Reality), eXtended Reality**			**Perceptual In-Virtual-World "Imaginary"**
Fully Real Environment (unaugmented, undiminished, or unmediated by the virtual)	**Augmented (or Enriched) Reality, Diminished Reality (+ or -, or mixture of + and -) (multimodal and multimedia)**	**Augmented Reality, Diminished Reality, Augmented Virtuality, Diminished Virtuality, Mixed Modalities**	**Augmented Virtuality, Diminished Virtuality (+ or -, or mixture of + and -) (multimodal and multimedia)**	**Fully Virtual Environment (unaugmented, undiminished, or unmediated from the real)**
Full-surround real world without inputs from digital or computational systems (becoming rarer)	Virtual objects emplaced on real scenes; perceptual inputs from both the real-world surround and digital and computational systems simultaneously • Head-mounted display / device (HMD) • Haptic gloves • Tangibles (wands, objects, cards) • Tabletops • Body suits • Mobile device • Light projectors • Virtual keyboards • And others (including unaided)	Cobbled AR, VR, MR, in a coherent and cohesive experience	Real-informed objects placed in virtual scenes; perceptual inputs from both the virtual world surround and real-world inputs such as data, visualizations, and other often real-time and automated streams	Full-surround virtual world without inputs from the real-world except for human-embodied avatar-based characters

The table includes some mentions of technologies, but the core definitions do not mention requisite technologies per se. While the categories may seem fully mutually exclusive, especially on the two extremes, there is not really absolute purity: no full reality without leavening by imagination, no real without any virtual, no virtual without some intrusion of the real. An older work conceptualizes a "weak" and a "strong" AR; in the weak, the augmentations to the physical space are light but enable people to collaborate at a distance; in the strong, the ICT augmentations to the physical space are extensive and change people's "space perception" (De Michelis, De Paoli, Pluchinotta, & Susani, April 2000, p. 82).

In these early days, it is thought that AR better aligns with topics that have "a spatial component" in a visual sense (Billinghurst & Duenser, 2012, p. 60). What is missing in the physical environment for particular learning? is a particular question that may be asked.

The visuals in augmented reality may be two-dimensional (on a flat plane, especially when one positions to the side of the visual); three-dimensional (including the x-axis or volume or mass); or four-dimensional (including animation or motion as the fourth dimension), that is 2d, 3d, and / or 4d. The visuals may be high-fidelity and photo-realistic for an authentic learning experience. In other cases, the visuals are more representational, low-fidelity, and low-resolution. Regardless, not everything is depicted because such depictions would require too heavy of a development load (on the instructional designers and developers) and technical load on the AR technologies and cognitive load on the learners. Proper design of visuals requires general appearance, proportionality, scale, compositing or layout, color, texture, and other aspects. Textures may be designed in 2d and applied to 3d objects, based on UV mapping and tri-planar mapping, and other methods. They also require proper behaviors in terms of how digital objects interact within the artificial space, interact with other digital objects, and may be used by the human learners. (Depending on the system, the AR may be lit by a global or other singular light, or each object may have to be programmed to reflect light a particular way with select shadow effects. It is important for the visuals to be aligned and non-distractive to be effective for learning. It helps if visuals may be viewed from different angles, instead of being pixel-flat from the side. The idea is that the AR visuals have to maintain some level of illusion to enable the learning. The augmented reality world should main its illusions, too.) The physical location where the display is shown and the technologies required also affect the design. For example, some AR scenes depict through mobile devices on tabletops. Others may require head-mounted displays. Some designs are very smartphone screens (small), and others for mobile laptops and other devices, and still others designed rooms, and still others for ambient outdoor spaces. For proper depth cues to be conveyed in various AR contexts, the proper type and direction and intensity of light (and often sound) are needed to inform spatial perception (Doerner, Broll, Jung, Grimm, Göbel, & Kruse, 2022, p. 29). Still others need no aid to human perception and only display through projectors, speakers, and other devices in real spaces or against buildings. "Mid-air imaging" technologies can show computer graphics (CGs) moving physically in the real world. One approach involves using reflective surfaces and different light sources to show such motion-based objects in real space (Osato & Koizumi, 2020).

Three-dimensional registration technologies that track artificial markers in a scene have also improved for the computational recognizing of objects. Some AR systems can track motion of various objects to enable sensitive "collision" effects between the virtual objects. Collision detection adds to the physical characteristics of virtual objects:

Collision detection is an important aspect of virtual reality systems. High-precision, real-time collision detection technology plays a vital role in enhancing the practicability of 3D simulation. The hierarchical bounding box algorithm was used for microscope simulation. The collider was constructed for the nosepiece, coarse focus knob, fine focus knob and other components such as the slide of the microscope required for interaction. All colliders should match the shape of components of the microscope as much as possible for collision detection to be accurate. (Zhou, Tang, Lin, & Han, 2020, p. 321)

The physics aspects of various AR authoring tools vary and are part of interactive behavior between objects.

In an AR/VR space, sound conveys “information about the spaciousness of a scene including the location of sound sources and the reverberance or size of a virtual environment. In this way, audio can be regarded as a channel to provide semantic information and spatial information and improve the sense of presence and immersion at the same time” (Brinkmann & Weinzierl, 2023, pp. 145-146). There are various methods to assess audio quality, “ranging from classic psychoacoustic methods like alternative forced-choice tests to more recent approaches such as quality taxonomies and plausibility” (Brinkmann & Weinzierl, 2023, p. 145). An idealized standard in a simulation that includes sound is “that is indistinguishable from the physical sound field it is intended to simulate” (Brinkmann & Weinzierl, 2023, p. 149), through ambient sound files and / or mixes of localized spatial sound (with volumes that change based on the proximity of the individual and their movement). Authentic sound, physically, could involve “the identity of sound pressures in the ear canal (binaural technology) or the identity of sound fields in an extended spatial area (sound field synthesis)” (Brinkmann & Weinzierl, 2023, p. 149). The technologies to enable full sound field authenticity does not exist presently, so sound authenticity refers more to a psychological sense (Brinkmann & Weinzierl, 2023) in the listener. “Basic Audio Quality” (BAQ) refers to ‘all aspects of the sound quality being assessed’, such as ‘timbre, transparency, stereophonic imaging, spatial presentation, reverberance, echoes, harmonic distortions, quantisation noise, pops, clicks and background noise” (ITU-R BS.1284-2, 2019, p. 7, as cited in Brinkmann & Weinzierl, 2023, p. 147). The subjective perception of the listener is important given the focus also on the “Overall Listening Experience” (OLE) (Brinkmann & Weinzierl, 2023, p. 148).

The objects in the scene and the scene itself may be interactive. Text may be part of the AR, but these have to be readable and legible (perhaps based on outlining the text or offering a background on which the text can reside). The lighting in AR is often artificial (sometimes mixed with natural light), and some can adapt to the environment (interior light, exterior or natural or mixed natural-artificial light). Some systems have built-in intelligence and smart technologies for enhanced experiential features. For example, deep learning is applied in AR for object detection in some systems (Ghasemi, Jeong, Choi, Park, & Lee, 2022). Building AR to outdoor spaces is more difficult because of the spaciousness, the natural light, the natural elements, and other factors. Matching 3d LiDAR point clouds to 2d spaces is another challenge (Liu, Lai, Wang, Bian, Yang, Xia, … & Liu, Mar. 2020, p. 654).

General Types of Augmented Reality (1)

There is not a formal consensus-based typography of AR types. In older writing, augmented reality (AR) referred to web conferencing and email and remoting in to work computers (De Michelis, De Paoli, Pluchinotta, & Susani, April 2000, p. 82). In the present day, augmented reality refers to audiovisual overlays of virtual objects and scenes over a physical space. In some cases, the multimedia augments or enriches the physical space. In other cases, the mediated reality may suppress or diminish parts of the physical space, in order to create particular sensory impressions (often sight, often sound, sometimes touch, and others).] One study described the setup of a synaesthesia AR, which combines multiple perceptual senses:

In this application, users can visualize colors corresponding to each unique note in the 12-tone equal-temperament tuning system, and the auditory input can be selected from audio files or real-time microphone. A gestural hand-tracking interface allows users to paint the world space in visualized synesthetic colors. (Shashaank & Feiner, Mar. 2022, p. 874)

Some AR types are marker-based, and these require camera-acquired visual codes or symbols or other visual trackers, such as Quick Response or QR codes to trigger the painting-in of the AR audiovisuals. Markers may also be built into physical objects that may be moved by the user. A "vision-haptic visualization" enables users to view the 3d model on a marker which can be manipulated by hand (Santos, Chen, Taketomi, Yamamoto, Miyazaki, & Kato, 2013, p. 41). Markerless AR refers to 3d audiovisuals that spawn without the presence of visual triggers but start with users being at particular locations and starting an AR app to start the AR experience. In other cases, being in a particular interior or exterior locale is enough.

Thinking about AR as (1) small, (2) medium, (3) large, (4) global scale, and (5) galaxy-scale may also be helpful.

(1) Small-scale AR may be something at book size, maybe tabletop size.

Perhaps a (2) medium-sized AR may be room-sized. Various works do suggest that scale affects various learning experiences and simulations. A de-escalation training in an augmented virtuality space benefits from the regular sizes of depicted people (in terms of real-sizing) (Hughes & Ingraham, March 2016). Interestingly, a study found that there is some support for the idea that "room-scale conditions may improve learning outcomes related to spatial updating regardless of form factor since participants were able to walk around the full space…in AR" (Craig, Willemsen, Downs, Lover, & Barber, Mar. 2022, p. 893). The size of the AR display matters for teaching and learning, but more research will be needed to better understand the size phenomenon.

A (3) large one may involve multiple room interiors…or the equivalent as an exterior space (or perhaps even park-size). A wide-area AR uses "wireless tags" and "visible light communication projector(s)" (including moving ones). The respective framerates and timing are coordinated to create visual effects and perhaps superimpose visuals with visual accuracy (Hiyama, Fujino, Kashiwagi, & Hirose, Sept. 2011).

A (4) global or terra-scale size may be the world itself, mapped with 3d, 4d, and various wonders.

AR experiences may be acquired through "coarse localization" using geospatial navigation through global navigation satellite systems (Rambach, Pagani, & Stricker, 2023, p. 59) snf "feature matching" for particular landmarks p. 60), and others.

A (5) galaxy-scale AR is not yet known to exist per se.

In terms of so-called "heterogeneous" AR (Hill, Barba, MacIntyre, Gandy, & Davidson, July 2011, p. 9), geocoded locations may be explored at terra-scale. With so much geo-tagged in the physical world, people have been creating a "terra-scale, heterogeneous augmented reality *mirror world*" to bring the cyber and physical together (Hill, Barba, MacIntyre, Gandy, & Davidson, July 2011, p. 9). They explain this phenomenon:

Mirror worlds are a structuring of the virtual world that aligns closely with the physical world, allowing both localized in-situ users and non-local users to interact through a heterogeneous mixture of augmented and virtual reality. Our interest is specifically in mirror world systems having three main qualities: a) inherent massively multiuser online (MMO) scale and persistence, b) technology and affordances to support facile transitions between augmented reality (AR) and virtual reality (VR) on heterogeneous platforms, and c) data formats that support individual authoring and distribution of content much like that of the modern web. (Hill, Barba, MacIntyre, Gandy, & Davidson, July 2011, p. 9)

People collaborate around such works "via full virtual reality systems, browser based 3D environments, mixed reality systems and ubiquitous computing installations" (Hill, Barba, MacIntyre, Gandy, & Davidson, July 2011, p. 10). Cell connectivity, the Internet infrastructure, specifically the "existing commercial communication network," may be used to enable distributed augmented reality" for ubiquitous learning (Cahyadi, Santoso, Bandung, & Langi, Apr. 2012, p. 1). [Some forms of AR can be lightweight.]

Some require head-mounted displays or particular glasses to evoke. Some locales may have external AR displays, based on projectors, speakers, and a mix of other technologies, which do not require anything but physical presence to experience. Some AR experiences are portable and location-agnostic, but others require particular physical locations to activate.

There are some terms for particular AR systems, such as the Multi-Object Oriented Augmented Reality (MOOAR) system (Chang & Tan, Dec. 2010, p. 20), which is a location-based adaptive mobile learning environment. A Mobile Augmented Reality System (MARS) is another (Chang & Tan, Dec. 2010, p. 20). Many other such terms likely exist in pockets, but wide adoption for such terms does not seem to have been adopted per se.

Various devices may be involved in the consuming or experiencing of AR. There may be head-mounted displays, special glasses, mobile devices, or various combinations of equipment and devices. In some cases, whole backpacks of equipment and smart wearables may be necessary for a full and complex AR experience.

People may communicate with the AR displays through hand gestures, body positioning, voice, and other inputs along with various devices and tangibles / manipulatives (such as those with tangible augmented reality interfaces). For example, one AR setup enables users to hold a "spray can" that allows viewing of an artwork by "infrared, ultraviolet, x-ray, the back of the painting, and illumination from the left, right, bottom, and top" for different explorations (Kolstee & Van Eck, Oct. 2011, p. 51). Input devices are highly varied. For example, users may input text in AR environments through virtual displayed keyboards using haptic gloves or hand-held controllers (Frutos-Pascual, Gale, Harrison, Creed, & Williams, (Aug. 2021, p. 480). [Some non-QWERTY keyboard alternatives are being explored, too.] AR interfaces refer to various designed AR planes, buttons, dashboards, tables of contents, and other elements that enable users to engage with the audiovisual elements.

An interface is "a space for the focusing of attention" (Erofeeva & Klowait, May 2021, p. 3). Some AR displays include multiple interfaces, requiring users to switch between them. Some interfaces may be invisible, engaged with through gestures to cameras.

Ambiguity of focus may also occur when users of AR are engaging the technologies to describe, for example, where they may want to place a digital object. One application "allows users to intuitively arrange virtual furniture in a virtual room using a combination of speech and gestures from a real paddle" (Irawati, Green, Billinghurst, Duenser, & Ko, Oct. 2006, p. 183). In this AR multimodal interface, people use their voices (and the technology uses semantic techniques for interpretation) and physical gesturing with a physical tactual paddle to move virtual furniture. Some AR technologies use gaze, facial expressions, movements, gestures, voice, and a combination of inputs.

Researchers are working towards different frameworks to categorize AR. One team writes:

The variety of approaches and definitions in AR requires classification. We define two intrinsic characteristics of AR systems, task focus and nature of augmentation. Based on these two characteristics, we identify four classes of AR systems. (Dubois & Nigay, Apr. 2000, p. 165)

One metanalysis uses learning strategies in terms of AR technologies. The researchers identified four main learning methodologies using AR: "learning based on interaction, learning based on game, learning based on collaboration and learning based on practical approach" with the most commonly reported one "learning based on interaction" with the virtual materials (Yadav & Aalam, Oct. 2021, p. 227). The most common learning was learner engagement with "unreal things which are merged in the actual world" (Yadav & Aalam, Oct. 2021, p. 224). As yet, though, there does not seem to be an accepted general framework.

Pedagogical Rationales for the Uses of AR for Formal (Accredited), Nonformal (Unaccredited Courses), and Informal (Non-Learning Contexts) Learning (2)

A common rationale for going with augmented reality in learning involves the capture of learner attention and motivation. AR is seen to increase "concentration, interest, and efficiency of learning" (Chen, Liu, Hsieh, Huang, Wang, & Nien, May 2017, p. 373), with some AR including gamification aspects. One AR game involves learners moving physically to collect virtual objects, which "allows them to attempt multiple choice questions, to test their knowledge" (Saritha, Mankad, Venkataswamy, & Bapu, Dec. 2018, p. 4). AR enables experiential learning, with learners able to experience nano-scale atomic-scale simulations (microbial agents, nano technologies, "invisible phenomena", and micro-worlds), macro-scale simulations [solar system learning (Salazar, Pacheco-Quispe, Cabeza, Salazar, & Cruzado, Oct. 2020)]; dynamic weather systems over 3d topographic maps (Chiou & Barrnaki, Mar. 2019, p. 1369); simulating weather in an AR geoscience sandbox (Kundu, Muhammad, & Sattar, Dec. 2017); travels in time (past, present, and future), the imagination (imaginary spaces and ideas), and others. Whole "atmospheres" are created by harnessing AR with "constellations of objects" that evoke enriched surrounds (Krogh, Apr. 2000, p. 136). There are depictions of less commonly explored spaces, such as underwater (Blum, Broll, & Müller, 2009). AR enables users to zoom into the inner structure of the depicted object, for example, so transcending physical materiality in many cases. One example of invisible phenomena involves electromagnetic radiation, which is not seeable with the naked (unaided) human eye; in this study, university students experienced "moderate spatial presence, low simulator sickness and high levels of acceptance and satisfaction" (Vrellis, Delimitros, Chalki, Gaintatzis, Bellou, & Mikropoulos, July 2020, p. 333). One research team points to AR/VR as complementary tools to enhance education. They suggest that AR/VR may be used for historical re-enactments, foreign travel, space travel, and other depictions. AR/VR may depict places where no humans can go, such as within the inner mantle of the Earth (Elkoubaiti & Mrabet, May 2018, p. 2).

AR was used to recreate various historical and cultural objects that had been looted and burned but which bore cultural value to present-day citizens (Wei, Weng, Liu, & Wang, Mar. 2016, p. 307). The AR objects were used to enhance park tours and to recall history.

AR can enable "advanced spatial visualization and interaction" for some types of "superior learning" environments and experiences (Billinghurst & Duenser, 2012, p. 56). AR enables people to transport to different times "to explore and touch the past, present and the future" (Shanmugam, Sudha, Lavitha, Venkatesan, & Keerthana, Mar. 2019, p. 1). Another team writes: "Technologies on the mixed reality spectrum…can be used to immerse a user in the living experiences of other entities" such as "a robotic ant which lives inside a natural ecosystem with other ants, or to a bacteria (sic) which travels through the respiratory system of a larger organism" (Radu & Antle, Mar. 2017, p. 2).

The physics of objects may be reconfigured in the AR space, with different behaviors and enablements. There has to be some care about negative or false learning though, given that the "free wills of machines can break the (in-world physical) common sense" (Zhang, Nov. 2020, p. 275). The researcher writes:

Physical common sense is the intuitive knowledge that can be obtained from the physical world. But the common sense will be broken in symmetrical reality because of the integration of the physical world and the virtual world. (Zhang, Nov. 2020, p. 275)

AR may change people's "physical common sense" in symmetrical realities (Zhang, Nov. 2020, p. 275).

The phenomenon of bidirectional control with the physical world acting on the virtual through "forward control" but also the virtual world and its virtual agents exercising "inverse control." The researcher writes:

The so-called forward control is the form that humans are using in daily life…Contrary to the forward control, the inverse control is conducted by virtual agents. Virtual agents can control the virtual worlds and the physical worlds in two ways. The way to control the virtual objects (e.g., grasp a virtual cup) is similar to the humans in controlling physical objects, because the virtual agents and the virtual objects come from the same space. The way to control physical objects is more complicated. If the virtual agent wants to control a physical object, it is required to find an appropriate physical embodiment (e.g., a mechanical arm) to physically contact the target object, and the physical embodiment is directly controlled by the virtual agent. (Zhang, Nov. 2020, p. 275)

There may be risks in designing and developing for users socialized into the multi-billion-dollar electronic gaming industry who may have outsized senses of AR objects in a higher education context. After all, many users have been acculturated into symmetrical realities well prior to experiencing AR in a learning context. Then, there is also the physiological reality:

Producing high-quality VR content is difficult, because our eyes are very good at distinguishing between what is and isn't real. For example, the binocular stereoscopy of human eyes is largely missing in tradition 360-degree panoramic video-capture solutions. More advanced imaging systems, such as ones equipped with depth cameras, can recover certain aspects of 3D geometry to generate stereoscopic pairs. However, partial 3D is still insufficient to provide motion parallax, which is essential for providing a realistic viewing experience. In addition to stereo and motion parallax, human eyes also achieve 3D vision through refocusing, where only the object in the focal plane is clear and objects at other distances are blurry. The real world presents extremely high-dimensional data, comprising geometry, lighting, surface reflectance, and so on. We must record every piece of information in this high-dimensional dataset to faithfully reproduce reality. (Yu, 2017, p. 104)

In a sense, AR/VR designers are working with a sophisticated vision and image processing system.

Human beings acquire most of their information about the world through their eyes. Shaped by physiological evolution and extensive daily training, the human eye has cultivated an effective mechanism to perceive the external world, and this mechanism of perception is ultra-sensitive. For example, the human eye is very sensitive to depth information, which is perceived through clues such as binocular parallax, motion parallax, occlusion, and convergence. (Yu, 2017, p. 104)

That said, augmented reality is used for the following: declarative knowledge, practical knowledge, sequential processes, procedural knowledge, programming, communications, concepts, systems thinking, and a range of other applied learning. To actualize the learning requires deep subject matter expertise. For example, "complex concept visualization" is needed to enhance understanding using AR and reciprocal teaching strategies in mobile learning (Noorasura & Sazilah, June 2011, p. 717).

Educational Theorizing and AR

Kolb's Experiential Learning cycle describes four steps: experiencing, reflecting, thinking, and acting (or "concrete experience," "reflective observation," "abstract conceptualization," and "active experimentation"). AR enables engagement visually, textually, auditorially, tactually, and in embodied and kinesthetic ways.

Where there may be risks in engaging real objects, AR-based ones may be used in their stead for safety and re-experiencing without higher risks or costs (Bourguet & Romero-Gonzalez, May 2021). Another researcher shows risk reduction in going virtual (where it is possible to model in-world physics and chemistry and others) vs. real world interactions in labs (El Kabtane, Mourdi, El Adnani, & Sadgal, Mar. 2015, p. 363).

Some AR tools enable sculpting that emulates physical materiality. Inputs may be intuitive hand motions and voice (Scotto, 2022, p. 91). Sculpting is "a complex craft that relies on the synergy of multiple factors" requiring "makers' dexterity, material properties and environmental conditions" for effective sculpting (Scotto, 2022, p. 91).

Tangible objects—those that may be held and handled—may also be built into the AR experience. Some simple tangibles may be marked cards used to spawn AR visuals (Costa, Queiroz, Miranda, de Freitas, dos Santos, & Meiguins, July 2019, p. 52). Other tangibles can be any physical object on which are mapped AR behaviors and / or markers.

Also, some works describe the scripting of automated synthetic agents or non-playable characters (NPCs) that can interact with the human learner(s). AR can be used in face-to-face (F2F) contexts among learners, or it can be an individual learner type of experience (social vs. asocial), including self-administered autonomous learning. The sociality may be technologically mediated, with people in different physical locations. AR/VR are seen to "improve student learning, motivation, and...teamwork and group cooperation" (Kaviyaraj & Uma, Jan. 2022, p. 1221) and create a "student-centered environment" (pp. 1221 – 1222).

The learning may be a one-off designed one, or it may be part of a series. It may be a fully built-out space, with opportunities for exploration. It may be a directed-path in-physical space experience.

Figure 2. Sociality in AR spaces

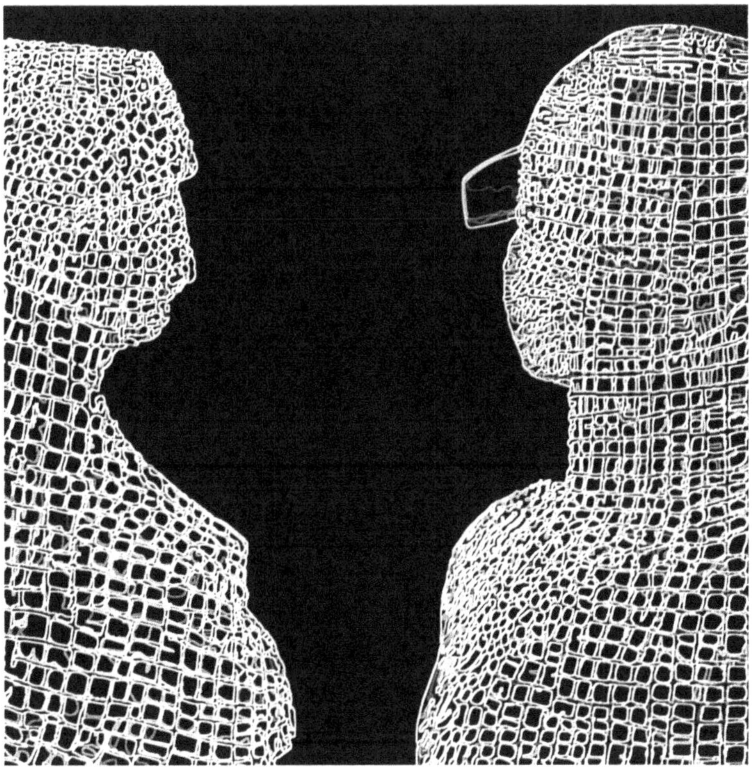

The layers of Bloom's Taxonomy, from the base to the top, place human learning on a dependencies-based hierarchy: remember, understand, apply, analyze, evaluate, and create. This approach may be useful to describe the types of learning enabled with AR builds.

Authentic and applied learning theories may apply to some contexts, given the learning-by-doing (virtually). Some refer to kinesthetic learning theories. Constructivism and even "radical constructivism" has been cited in one work (Collins, Regenbrecht, & Lanalotz, Oct. 2018, p. 45).

Formal, Nonformal, and Informal Learning and AR

In the learning space, there are three general types of learning. Formal learning refers to accredited learning at various levels, from high school through university typically, where credits are earned and agencies provide oversight to the learning. Nonformal learning refers to unaccredited learning, which are courses offered by various organizations and entities but which do not convey credit. Informal learning refers to incidental learning that occurs outside of courses but occur as part of regular life experiences, perhaps like conversations, like media consumption, and others.

In the research literature, AR has been used for K-12 through university learning. It covers formal courses, nonformal courses and trainings (especially in healthcare), and informal learning such as through game apps, through museum visits, through entertainment, through artful expression, and other cases.

Formal Accredited Learning

AR has been applied to the fields of "mathematics, physics, chemistry, history and in many other domains" (Maqableh & Sidhu, Mar. 2010, p. 184). AR enables visualization of structures common to the "studies and research in chemistry, biochemistry, and structural biology" (Rodríguez, Dal Peraro, & Abriata, 2022, p. 1).

AR is an attractive option for the STEM and STEAM fields, with their harnessing for virtual and hybrid labs, dedicated designs for particular virtualized experiments and virtual "field work," and others. In the science, technology, engineering, math, and art fields, there is plenty of inquiry-based and exploratory types of learning. Engineering focuses on learning by doing as a common learning approach (Kaur, Mantri, & Horan, 2020, p. 881). [AR enables virtual and some physical hands-on learning.] There is a need to identify problems, conceptualize them, conduct research, capture data, design solutions, test the solutions, and effectively evaluate what works optimally (Nguyen & Dang, Oct. 2017, p. 315), approaches which can be strengthened by AR. Inquiry and exploration may be supported:

Learning to do inquiry includes a set of skills that students need to master to 'do science', but it also goes beyond mere process skills. Learning to do inquiry also means combining these processes with scientific knowledge, reasoning and critical thinking to development scientific knowledge. Learning about inquiry is about knowing how scientific knowledge is developed through inquiry approaches. (Creane, Crotty, & Farren, 2015, p. 393)

In another, robots are built into a mixed reality training simulation that involves a "personalized and immersive learning experience" to strengthen defined problem solving, in a science, technology, engineering, and math (STEM) context (Doswell & Mosley, July 2006, p. 864). High-tech is used to teach about the Internet of Things (IoT), ultimately to make IoT more attractive and to raise awareness of this Panessai, Iksan, Zahari, Abdulbaqi, Modi Lakulu, Husin, ... & Wahyudiono, Mar. 2021). Inan earlier work, AR and robotics are combined "to introduce computers and information technology students to some fundamental concepts, through the use of simulation, experiments on real robots and design of robotic creatures in virtual environments" (Buiu, Buga, & Coman, Nov. 2013, p. 71).

In a chemistry teaching context, learners engage "a direct manipulation user interface" (it looks like a hand-length plastic device with a cube square on the end and black-and-white QR codes on 5 sides of the cube (Maier & Klinker, Sept. 2013, p. 164). The researchers write that "a direct manipulation 3D user interface" can enable learners to "literally grasp the spatial structure" (Maier & Klinker, Sept. 2013, p. 165). Finally, in science learning, for those with intellectual disabilities, instructors had different preferences on whether to use AR or VR or some other approach depending on the instructional objectives and strategies as applied to each student based on their academic profiles and particular intellectual disabilities (Iatraki, Delimitros, Vrellis, & Mikropoulos, July 2021, p. 381).

In the engineering space, a VAR (virtual and augmented reality) has been used to teach assembly design. This is "a virtual instruction based pedagogical tool which integrates virtual models and visual cues to teach engineering design," with learners taking on practical assembly design challenges. Learners interact with real and virtual machine part objects in the presence of interactive and guided support (Adas, Shetty, & Hargrove, Oct. 2013, p. 696) . VARs and other spaces can be dedicated ones for particular applications, or they may be general exploratory ones.

A fractography lab simulates what happens to various materials when they are fractured with differing amounts of pressure. In this case, the team made the AR experience as "tangible as possible, allowing students to hold a material (or an object representing the material) in their hand and to trigger a fracture by selecting a stress force and a stress point on the material's surface" (Bourguet & Romero-Gonzalez, May 2021, p. 2).

A different AR lab enables the harnessing of "a real-world surface in a virtual lab" (Ahmed, Lataifeh, Alhamarna, Alnahdi, & Almansori, Sept. 2021, p. 1). This lab enables real-time synchronous interactions for collaboration virtually (Ahmed, Lataifeh, Alhamarna, Alnahdi, & Almansori, Sept. 2021, p. 4).

One AR program motivates learners to think visually and to practice sketching. This app was found to be more helpful for the non-art participants than those with some art training already and perhaps served as "some kind of obstruction to their intrinsic skills" (Liao & Kuo, Nov. 2020, p. 97). In another work, AR was used to teach guitar-playing, with an AR hand model about how to hold the strings, and also a segment to learn the parts of a guitar (Motokawa & Saito, Oct. 2006). Another AR app supports piano playing based on 3d performance animations on a head-mounted display (HMD) device, with demonstrations and instructions (Guo, Cui, Zhao, Li, & Hao, Mar. 2021, p. 436). Yet another app supports appreciation for ancient Chinese poetry; this was built from AR and machine learning for entertainment, learning, and culture (Yang, Caballero, & Juanatas, 2022, p. 285). Learners study the workings of light and shade in art education (Nathanasit & Wongta, Feb. 2018, p. 71), in another application. There is an AR for learning dance given spatio-temporal multimedia (Davcev, Trajkovic, Kalajdziski, & Celakoski, Aug. 2003).

Another AR application projects human anatomy on a learner's body to help facilitate the "mental mapping compared to traditional teaching paradigms" (Ienaga, Bork, Meerits, Mori, Fallavollita, Navab, & Saito, Sept. 2016, p. 294). An older work shows health systems, like the digestive and circulatory systems (Pérez-López, Contero, & Alcaniz, July 2010). A Spatial Augmented Reality on Person (SARP) system may enable self-referential encoding which lets learners see visualizations applied over their own bodies (Johnson & Sun, Mar. 2013, p. 59), as a form of AR-based embodied learning of anatomical structures (p. 60). Researchers found that this approach resulted in reductions in "…incorrect identifications…during successive iterations" (Johnson & Sun, Mar. 2013, p. 60).

Yet another uses a motion sensing visual device to depict a learner in an edutainment medical AR app. Here, the learner can fit human bones to a representation of a person based on their own body size. A bioscience app enables the study of frog anatomy and the various organs of the frog, as well as a virtual microscope simulation (Chang & Yu, May 2017, o, 1674). Another AR system allows users to use "a mobile terminal that took a picture of a microscope from a textbook and then displayed the structure and functions of the instruments" (Zhou, Tang, Lin, & Han, 2020, p. 316).

Another AR application offers a virtual playground for improving the learning of English:

A student that can see some virtual elements through a device would give instructions to another student that can not (sic) see these same elements. The author of the idea illustrated the concept by sketching an interaction in which a student with the device can see a virtual snake and give instructions so the other student can escape or survive. (Pereira, da Silva, Roberto, Teichrieb, & Cavalcante, Nov. 2020, p. 86)

AR enables language learners to be surrounded by "the culture and community of the target language" as a learning context, which enables situated learning (Yang, Liao, & Shih, July 2013, p. 439).

There can be in-situ labeling of various objects and phenomena in the AR to promote learning (Huynh, Orlosky, & Höllerer, Mar. 2019).

One mobile AR game has students collecting "virtual radiation data" about radiological contamination on an imaginary campus. The learners take measurements at various campus locations. They interview virtual characters on campus. As they engage, the learners acquire socio-scientific reasoning skills, among other lessons. (Chang, Yu, Wu, & Hsu, July 2016)

Augmented reality learning environments (ARLEs) are designed to encourage exploration, sociality, and sensory and psychological immersion (Santos, Chen, Taketomi, Yamamoto, Miyazaki, & Kato, 2013, p. 42). These are built out using various metaphors for the spaces, such as as displays, as "mirrors," as special "glasses" (Santos, Chen, Taketomi, Yamamoto, Miyazaki, & Kato, 2013, p. 43). Some are depicted as portals into other worlds. ARLEs are seen as "being especially educationally engaging for otherwise academically challenged students" (Drljević, Wong, & Botički, 2017, p. 419), so they may be harnessed for accessibility. Various ARLEs may be instructor-led with high-touch presence, but others may not. Where teachers are present, they often have technologies that enable their awareness of goings-ons in the ARLE, while protecting against excessive "orchestration load" (Drljević, Wong, & Botički, 2017, p. 422).

One research work describes an ARLE used to help high school students learn 3d geometry with an app that works on both Android and iOS platforms (Gargrish, Mantri, & Kaur, 2020, p. 1039).

Studies of students' e-learning experiences via AR-learning applications (AR-LRP) have found various benefits. Researchers write:

Uses and gratifications theory was proposed as a theoretical foundation of the current study's conceptual model. Four dimensions of UGT benefits were proposed as key antecedents of the students' experience with AR.LRP: personal interactive benefits, social interactive benefits, affective benefits, and cognitive benefits. The model was also extended by considering the role of telepresence. Further, technostress was proposed on the current study to moderate the relationship between the aspects of UGT and e-learning experience. (Baabdullah, Alsulaimani, Allamnakhrah, Alalwan, Dwivedi, & Rana, 2022, p. 1)

The research results found that there were personal interactive benefits, affective benefits, and cognitive benefits, and telepresence…with AR-LRP (Baabdullah, Alsulaimani, Allamnakhrah, Alalwan, Dwivedi, & Rana, 2022). "Technostress was also found to significantly moderate the relationship between UGT dimensions and student experience with AR.LRP" (Baabdullah, Alsulaimani, Allamnakhrah, Alalwan, Dwivedi, & Rana, 2022, p. 1). They also found a statistically significant relationship between "UGT dimensions and student experience with AR.LGP and students' learning performance" (Baabdullah, Alsulaimani, Allamnakhrah, Alalwan, Dwivedi, & Rana, 2022, p. 1).

Learners Building the AR

In several mentioned cases, learners use various technology tools to build AR themselves, including children building games in AR (Billinghurst & Duenser, 2012, p. 59). Another AR build focuses on the teaching and practice of assembly tasks, to help students build AR/VR course contents for handheld devices (Del Gallego, Nov. 2020, p. 111). One work describes an AR environment for computer programming: a "natural interaction method for inputting, revising, fixing code, and viewing concurrent virtual information" (Resnyansky, Billinghurst, & Lee, Mar. 2022, p. 662). Another work uses AR for computer programming, too: their system "allows students to freely assemble puzzle cards to compare various 3D animated programming results" (Kao & Ruan, 2022, p. 1). This study found that the AR "helped the students improve their programming achievements, gain higher learning motivation, reduce their cognitive load, and acquire a high degree of technology acceptance" (Kao & Ruan, 2022, p. 1). They suggest that it was not the AR part that encouraged learner motivation but the "high interactive design such as 'puzzle cards'" as critical for higher learner motivation (Kao & Ruan, 2022, p. 1).

In one collaborative AR setup, learners may engage in remote design critique of digital artifacts through the technology. They write of the setup:

...a mobile augmented reality application that combines KinectFusion and ARKit to allow users to 1) scan artifacts and share the resulting 3D models, 2) view the model simultaneously in a shared virtual environment from remote physical locations, and 3) point to and draw on the model to aid communication. (Li, Hicks, Lages, Lee, Sharma, & Bowman, Mar. 2021, p. 585)

This setup enables learners to use a smart phone to capture an image, turn it into a 3d model, and upload it to a cloud server, where others may experience the object in AR format (p. 586). They are able to collaborate around each other's creations.

In yet another case, children engage in collaborative authoring via AR, to learn more about AR technology:

Through a model view, it turns AR concepts such as surface planes and images into interactive objects... It supports collaborative cross-device authoring by synchronizing a model view and AR view...It incorporates familiar elements from the user's own world with references to shops and institutions from their own neighbourhood. (Lunding, Grønbæk, Bilstrup, Sørensen, & Petersen, Apr. 2022, p. 1)

This is an approach to harness computational thinking as regards AR for children.

Teachers and instructors play important roles in leading AR-based learning. In such cases, teachers need to be able to direct learner attention in clear ways. They need to enable "a change of the participation framework" (Erofeeva & Klowait, May 2021, p. 3). Sometimes, desynchronization may occur in such contexts (like hybrid classrooms), where different learners are focused on different things, and they are not aligned with the instructor's approach. A "common focus of attention" is needed for effective group learning (Erofeeva & Klowait, May 2021, p. 4); "participants...must expend more effort to manage attention when AR is used along with the interactive whiteboard" (p. 4). Instructors and learners have to practice to enable "mutual visibility" in an AR-enhanced classroom or shared space (p. 5).

Nonformal Unaccredited Learning (Including Trainings) (b)

In a healthcare context, extended reality (XR) is seen to evoke "perceptions of realism and deep immersion, and enables visualization, interactive learning, enhancement of skills and repeated practice within a safe learning environment, consequently bettering skills, learning/knowledge and learner satisfaction" (Gasteiger, van der Veer, Wilson, & Dowding, Mar. 2022, p. 734). XR enables a "realist review" (Gasteiger, van der Veer, Wilson, & Dowding, Mar. 2022, p. 735).

Another example of nonformal learning from AR are guided tours, both indoors and outdoors. One research work describes the "caching" digital objects for "educaching" based on tags and / or GPS technologies (Perez-Sanagustin, Hernández-Leo, Santos, Kloos, & Blat, 2014, p. 119).

Informal Learning (c)

One work described an AR teaching app about a historic building, with an intention of showing how prior cultures influenced later ones in terms of historic buildings (Chin, Hou, Wang, & Lee, July 2017, p. 87). Having an AR overlay of the historic buildings can provide "a deeper understanding of the building structure, features, historical references and era influence while simultaneously exploring the historic site through the interaction effect that combines the virtual and the real" (Chin, Hou, Wang, & Lee, July 2017, p. 87). The researchers had to include relevant background historical and architectural data to create their app effectively. AR is used to promote local creative industries and long-term historical culture as well as contemporary tourism such as to the Hainan part of China with the Li people (Liying, Weng, Liyao, Maozheng, & Xiaoping, Dec. 2021, p. 295). AR enables modelers to not have to create the entire environment but only virtual parts that enable the perception of the "world as an organic whole" to enhance the learning (Liying, Weng, Liyao, Maozheng, & Xiaoping, Dec. 2021, p. 298).

AR is a common communications tool for museums. A meta-analytic review on incorporating virtual and augmented reality in museum learning found that AR was used for declarative knowledge, analytical problem solving, emotional experience, behavioral impacts, procedural practical knowledge, and others Zhou, Chen, & Wang, 2022, p. 5). This research team found "a significant positive effect of AR and VR on visitors' measured gains in knowledge and skills" based on 13 evaluated studies (Zhou, Chen, & Wang, 2022, p. 11).

In the formal, nonformal, and informal learning spaces, various electronic books (e-books) also use AR. Augmented books resemble print ones…but "their pages have virtual graphics superimposed on them" (Billinghurst & Duenser, 2012, p. 57). AR is seen to benefit young readers with their "reading comprehension and in understanding spatial data, especially for those with low reading ability" (Billinghurst & Duenser, 2012, p. 61), if such works are purposefully designed. Another children's e-book is a bilingual text (English and Bangla) built on a platform that enables readers to be creative and interactive as optimal (Hossain, Barman, & Haque, Oct. 2019, p. 2568). Children may make decisions as they navigate the digital book.

AR may be built onto print materials like print posters, billboards, flyers, and handouts. Users of an AR math book were found to be "more motivated in learning math especially in the attention and satisfaction subscales" (Chen, June 2013, p. 1). The researcher writes:

Participants in the AR group had a more positive attitude towards attention and satisfaction than those in the non-AR group. It reveals that AR is more attractive, easy to use, convenient, and interesting to them. Although participants in the AR group may not regard AR integrated course materials to be more relevant to or be more confident in their learning, AR improved their level of satisfaction, interaction, and willingness to use AR in the education field. (Sun, et al., 2008, as cited in Chen, June 2013, p. 5).

An AR-based interactive textbook can be used as assistive technology for students with learning disabilities. This textbook looks the same as a regular book, and is without "any special markers" or "identifiers" but "once the children focus on a text, the 3D images, audio and videos that explain the text more graphically will be augmented on that page" (Vinumol, Chowdhury, Kambam, & Muralidharan, May 2013, p. 232). [It is unclear if the AR aligns with accessibility guidelines in terms of the images, the audio, or the video, among others. It is unclear how much control users have to drive the augmented reality.] The AR textbook is designed to support "an inquiry-based and experiential learning approach" (Vinumol, Chowdhury, Kambam, & Muralidharan, May 2013, p. 233). The "miniature exhibits" help learners better engage dynamically with the focal information, especially for children with limited attention spans (Vinumol, Chowdhury, Kambam, & Muralidharan, May 2013, p. 232 and 235).

One study focused on the need for keeping social connections during the SARS-CoV-2 / COVID-19 pandemic. The researcher shot various storytelling videos in her apartment while "sheltering in place" and included 3d versions of her family members even though they were a continent away (Kumar & Kumar, 2021). Artists may use AR as a remote collaboration tool given the power of "in-camera, real-time compositing."

AR instantiates in many objects and spaces used for learning. Indeed, there are AR books, AR virtual writing, AR drawing boards, AR games, AR tours, AR ecosystems, AR exploratory spaces, and other variants.

AR for Learning: Design, Development, and Deployment

Designing augmented reality for learning requires a wide range of knowledge, skills, and attitudes (and abilities) or KSAs. It is important to understand how the human perceptual systems work, for sight, sound, smell, taste, and touch. The most important senses for VR and AR are visual, acoustic, and haptic (Doerner & Steinicke, 2022). Various depth cues may be strong or weak, depending on the visualization: shape size, horizon lines, occlusion, texture modeling, lighting, and others. Movement may indicate distances. The depiction of motion parallax shows "the light stimuli from near objects move faster across the retina than those from farther away" (Doerner & Steinicke, 2022, p. 47). The researchers explain: "Through movement, objects suddenly become occluded or reappear behind the objects that are obscuring them. This change, called *accretion*, also gives cues to the spatial arrangement of the objects" (Doerner & Steinicke, 2022, p. 47). Latencies for spawning or painting in should be below 20 milliseconds where possible (Doerner & Steinicke, 2022, p. 61).

Sensory inputs from the world are perceived and processed differently by different people. There are subjectivities in perception based on the person, the physiology, the personality, the prior experiences, and other factors:

The visual system combines, amplifies, filters out or recombines responses to external stimuli originating from the sensory cells during the complex process of perception. (Doerner, Broll, Jung, Grimm, Göbel, & Kruse, 2022, p. 2)

There is "no fixed, unambiguous and objective connection between (1) reality with the light stimuli it exerts on a human being and (2) the visual perception by the human being of this reality" (Doerner, Broll, Jung, Grimm, Göbel, & Kruse, 2022, p. 3). Changes to the inputs do not have a one-to-one correlation with what people may perceive. Given people's cognitive biases and other limits, people may be prone to illusions and misapprehensions and self- and other- delusions. AR may harness various types of perceptions since it draws from both digital and real: auditory perception, olfactory perception, gustatory, perception, haptic perception, tactile perception, vestibular perception, proprioception, thermoception, and nociception (Doerner, Broll, Jung, Grimm, Göbel, & Kruse, 2022, p. 4), and enteroception, in an alternate world. Haptic perception may be understood in multi-dimensional ways:

The senses that contribute to haptic perception are divided into: tactile perception (element of surface sensitivity), kinesthetic perception/proprioception (depth sensitivity) and temperature and pain perception. (Doerner & Steinicke, 2022, p. 49)

Some challenges in using haptic devices involve the breaking of the sense of the world. One researcher explains:

In AR, the challenge in using haptics is that the display typically occludes real objects the user might want to interact with. Also, in OST (optical see-through) displays, the haptic device is still visible behind virtual objects rendered on the display. (Grubert, 2023, p. 114)

AR enables telepresence and physical presence simultaneously, depending on the design. Traditionally, near-perceptions include the senses of smell, taste, and touch; far-perceptions include vision and hearing. In AR, however, vision and hearing are close-in given the need for mobile devices, head-mounted displays, and features of digital visuals and sounds. In some contexts, given that see-through displays have lower resolution, the visual perception thresholds for AR requiring physical navigation of the user over physical distances requires some adaptation. Different route guidance systems to help with people's navigating through AR spaces. For example, arrows may serve as visual direction indicators close-in. HMD devices may be set with "a large focal depth" (Tönnis, Klein, & Klinker, Sept. 2008, p. 189). AR for indoor navigation (inside buildings) has been found to offer a better user experience than 2d or paper maps (Verma, Agrawal, & Sarasvathi, Feb. 2020, p. 58). To design effective AR, it is important to consider "the scene illumination, the distance to the target and the ambient noise" as some core variables (Ghouaiel, Cieutat, & Jessel, Apr. 2014, p. 1). It is important to be aware of different effects on human visual perception based on the technologies and designs.

One study about touch in VR explored whether such experiences enable heightened senses of presence and also learning. This study found that touch enhanced the sense of presence, but it was "unclear as-yet what the impacts may be on the learning (Zhao, Forte, & Kopper, Mar. 2018, p. 741). The touch was created based on "different floor materials and physical artifact props" (Zhao, Forte, & Kopper, Mar. 2018, p. 741), with touch information being captured through research participants' hands and feet.

Beyond sensory perception, it is important to know how people learn. It helps to know what is effective for teaching. It is important to understand technologies. One study explored multi-faceted aspects of VR and AR applications in education, including the following factors: educational purpose, learner or user experience, delivery technology, back-end technology, user interaction, system interaction, production technology, and type of gamification (Motejlek & Alpay, 2021, pp. 420-423). This work was informed by extant competing taxonomies of educational praxis. This systemic formalization may be applied for the analysis of complex systems, for deeper understandings, for cost analyses, and other usages (Motejlek & Alpay, 2021, p. 425).

One study suggests that individual's spatial abilities benefit their learning with AR. "Spatial ability" is defined here as "the ability of manipulating visual patterns" and is "an important component of human intelligence" (Liao, Yu, & Wu, Apr. 2015, p. 221). A more recent work found the importance of "higher mental rotation abilities" for AR learning (Krüger, Palzer, & Bodemer, 2022, p. 1). As to learning from AR and 3d, the researchers found the following:

As expected, learners who received the 3D AR presentation had higher resulting spatial relations knowledge about the object, but not higher resulting general knowledge about the topic. (Krüger, Palzer, & Bodemer, 2022, p. 14)

Finally, those with "low mental rotation abilities" did not benefit from 3D presentations in terms of higher resulting knowledge whereas those with high mental rotation abilities did benefit (Krüger, Palzer, & Bodemer, 2022, p. 14). Visual-spatial thinking can be improved with practice as well.

AR itself is multimodal and often audiovisual. It may have an effect on sensorimotor processes, such as goal-directed reaching towards particular visual illusions. One study explored three conditions in education and training contexts: unmediated reality (UR), AR, and VR. The research team assessed the "speed-accuracy relationship of reaching movements in different mediation conditions (and found that it) was modulated by contextual information surrounding a target" (Resch, Manzone, Welsh, Nitsche, & Mazalek, July 2021, p. 398). This finding was an effect in terms of VR, but "not in the UR or AR conditions"; said another way, the movements in VR "are generated by different sensorimotor processes than in UR (unmediated reality) and AR (augmented reality)" (Resch, Manzone, Welsh, Nitsche, & Mazalek, July 2021, p. 398).

Human perception and movement seem to be affected by the mediated information and digital augmentations. One study found that people's object location memory is affected by engaging in the AR/VR space. One study explored different location techniques, based on input devices (joystick), pointing-and-teleporting, and walking-in-place to see how these might affect object location learning. Their results "indicate that the average placement error, or distance between original and recalled object location, is approximately 20cm for all locomotion technique conditions" (Xu, Murcia-López, & Steed, Mar. 2017, p. 315).

AR Alone Not Necessarily Beneficial for Learning

Augmented reality does not automatically benefit learning, as multiple studies have found. One study found that research participants took approximately half the time to solve the tutorial in the desktop version than the mobile one even as there was "no statistically significant difference…for information recall scores between the two versions" (Arce-Lopera, Gomez, & Montoya, Nov. 2019, p. 194).

One study suggests that the learner's sense of spatial presence inside a mediated environment may require "the allocation of limited processing resources, potentially inhibiting the processing of other information" (Ahn, Nowak, & Bailenson, 2022, p. 1). The Limited Capacity Model of Motivated Mediated Message Processing (LC4MP) (Ahn, Nowak, & Bailenson, 2022, p. 1) may speak to this issue, as well as the cognitive theory of multimedia learning. High spatial presence reduces learning recall. To address this issue, some have hypothesized that segmenting VR content may lower the cognitive processing load for participants; however, an empirical study found that while "modality features and individual differences drove user experiences of spatial presence, which negatively impacted recall, but segmentation of VR content had no effect on learning outcomes" (Ahn, Nowak, & Bailenson, 2022, p. 1).

Another study explored four modalities of learning surrounding a memory task. They describe their findings: We compare time and number of attempts to successfully complete a memory matching game across virtual reality, augmented reality, a large touchscreen table-top display and a real environment. The results indicate that participants took more time to complete the task in both the augmented reality and real conditions" as compared to the two fastest ones in VR and table-top touch display conditions. (Willemsen, Jaros, McGregor, Downs, Berndt, & Passofaro, Mar. 2018, p. 723). For the particular task, AR and real conditions were more time-consuming than VR and table-top touch display conditions.

A different study found a learner preference for desktop scenario-based training vs. an AR scenario. Researchers found that "Desktop was perceived as more efficient, corroborated by the significantly higher number of mistakes made in AR" (Gonzalez, Koh, Kapalo, Sottilare, Garrity, Billinghurst, & LaViola, Oct. 2019, p. 1199).

Besides learning inefficacies, there have been reports of "simulator sickness" from VR, AR, and gameplay (Wang, Liang, Monteiro, Xu, Chen, & Chen, Nov. 2020, p. 247). One study concluding that "60 – 80% of users of a VR application show symptoms of cybersickness" (Lawson, 2015, as cited in Doerner & Steinicke, 2022, p. 62). Demographic dimensions are a factor. Females are more prone to this than males to simulator sickness; age variability also exists, with cybersickness peaking in childhood, and declining between 12 and 21 and then "declining more slowly until about age 50" (Vrellis, Delimitros, Chalki, Gaintatzis, Bellou, & Mikropoulos, July 2020, p. 335). Prior exposures to AR/VR may also affect cybersickness. Because of this phenomenon, the amount of time spent in the application is something to consider (Doerner & Steinicke, 2022, p. 60).

The senses of nausea and cybersickness come from various ways that technologies are used to partially emulate the world's light field. One research team writes:

Depth cues can also be wrong, e.g., the image blur might not be displayed correctly because it is difficult to determine the exact point the observer fixates on. While in reality the depth cues are consistent, they can be contradictory in VR... Contradictory depth cues not only have consequences such as a misjudgment of the spatial arrangement of objects in space or the loss of presence because the virtual world appears unnatural; other negative consequences can include eye stress, exhaustion and headaches" based on the "vergence-focus conflict" or "accommodation-convergence discrepancy" or "vergence-accommodation conflict." (Doerner & Steinicke, 2022, p. 56)

The high performance of the human eye can identify discrepancies in sizes, distances, motion, lighting, and other visual aspects. The discrepant visual inputs may result in feelings of sickness and disorientation:

Users of a VR/AR application may experience undesirable side effects: headaches, cold sweat, paleness, increased salivation, nausea and even vomiting, ataxia (disturbance of movement coordination), drowsiness, dizziness, fatigue, apathy (listlessness) or disorientation. (Doerner & Steinicke, 2022, p. 60)

Researchers write that factors such as "image contrast and associated flicker, refresh rate, tracking errors, quality of system calibration and use of stereo displays" may trigger cybersickness; the larger the field of view (and the more peripheral vision is involved), the more frequently the occurrence of cybersickness is observed" (Doerner & Steinicke, 2022, p. 61).

To design effective AR learning, it helps to consider the ergonomics of device and fatigue from the constant holding or wearing (Ancient & Teeuw, July 2020, p. 402). It is important to consider cognitive load needs, by avoiding informational overload (Ancient & Teeuw, July 2020, p. 403) and minimizing task switching (p. 404), which may be distractive. If designed well, AR may enable a "VR like immersive experience without losing any surrounding awareness or feeling nauseous" (Tripathi, Oct. 2019, p. 66).

Various wearables and devices may be uncomfortable to use. One study compared 3d presentation technologies: "a handheld PC and a head-mounted display" with the finding that the handheld PC "was more suitable" for presenting augmented instructions (Asai, Kobayashi, & Kondo, July 2005, p. 213).

Some studies have found that the experimental group that used AR for their learning showed greater improvement in performance in their post test (vs. the control group) (Salazar, Pacheco-Quispe, Cabeza, Salazar, & Cruzado, Oct. 2020, p. 4). Such works are case-based though, and there have not yet been generalizable works that have necessarily shown this improved learning performance. In a study of an immersive virtual diorama in a natural science museum, the researcher found two statistically significant correlations between the AR app features and "*actual* learning outcomes: Story…and Plant Info" (Harrington, June 2020, p. 77). Another study involving an AR/VR chemistry lab found high rates of learning engagement in terms of "flow" and high learner "acceptance" as well in this empirical study (Hou & Lin, July 2017, p. 1005).

GETTING STARTED WITH AUGMENTED REALITY (AR) IN ONLINE TEACHING AND LEARNING IN HIGHER EDUCATION: AN EXTENDED ENVIRONMENTAL SCAN FOR PEDAGOGICAL DESIGN LEADS

The steps to designing AR for learning is conceptualized in three main phases: design, development, and deployment, with testing interspersed. A general and iterative workflow is implied in Table 2. The table, "Building AR Objects, Scenarios, and Experiences for Learning in Higher Education," includes some complexity and perhaps more staffing than any real time would ever have. The focus here is on a wide range of considerations, to err more on being inclusive and perhaps comprehensive.

Table 2. Building AR objects, scenarios, and experiences for learning in higher education

1. Design	
Grant writing / funding / budgeting	• Write the grant(s) • Acquire funding • Ensure a reasonable budget
Research (primary, secondary, tertiary, and others)	• Conduct relevant research (primary, secondary, tertiary, and others) • Document research • Assess the research for decision-making
Technologies	• Assess potential technologies • Test technologies for usability • Test technologies for ruggedness • Test technologies for quality outputs • Test technologies for interoperability

continues on following page

Table 2. Continued

Review of the authorizing document Review of the project aims	• What are the various defined goals of the project? Implied goals? • Who are the target learners? • What sorts of AR experiences may be desirable? • Will the AR be in-situ (situated in a physical space) or mobile? • What sorts of technologies will users have? • What does the general budget look like? • What is the available equipment, software, and other technologies? Are other resources available? • Who are those leading the work? What are their interests? Skills? • What is the timeline of the project? • How do the deadlines break down to a reasonable calendar?
Seating of the cross-functional collaborative team members (or functionalities)	Various capabilities and skills would benefit an AR project. This does not suggest that all the roles will be filled. Certainly, individuals may meet several functional requirements. Others may contribute their skills as available. • Subject matter expert(s)/ content expert(s) • Grant writer(s) Researcher • Researcher(s) • Scout(s) • Instructional designer(s) (stylebook, sketching, storyboarding, prototyping) • Photographer(s) • Scanner(s) • Writer(s), documenter(s) • 3d designer(s) / programmer(s) / art director(s) • Character designer(s) • Digital artist(s) / wireframer(s) • Sound engineer(s) / designer(s) • Motion (animation) designer(s) • Multimedia / audiovisual designer(s) • Interface designer(s) • Location scout(s) (location design, spatial design, scene design) • Experience designer(s) • Alpha (α) tester(s) • Accessibility expertise (in 2d, in 3d, 4d, in assistive devices, in digital learning systems, and others) • Beta (β) tester(s) • Usability expertise • Legal counsel (for reference)
Setup of consensus stylebook (by the cross-functional team)	• Set up shared understandings • Define common professional terminology • Describe standards for the team's work • Define project aesthetics • Set expectations for the types of files (still imagery, audio, video, animation, and others) • Ensure proper documentation • Ensure clear deadlines • Ensure legal rights to all the raw files • Ensure rights releases for all video recordings, photos, sound recordings, and other content from talent
Initial bodystorming, "programming by demonstration," brainstorming, drafting, storyboarding, and planning	• "Bodystorm" • "Programming by demonstration" (for non-programmer expression of interactivity) • Brainstorm • Draft • Storyboard • Plan • Set up work (assignments) • Set up schedules and timelines • Organize the budget

continues on following page

Table 2. Continued

Paper prototyping	• Design scenes (and express as prototypes / drafts / storyboards / scenarios) • Design characters • Design looks-and-feels, aesthetics, art • Design functions • Design objects • Design interfaces • Design interactions • Design sociality • Create lightweight or low-fidelity models • Create semi-functional wireframes • Document the ideas
Decision-making	• Evaluate prototypes • Revise prototypes
Redesign	• Rework paper prototypes • Design new requisite objects as needed (and go through the evaluation cycle, the decision-making, and further redesign as needed)
2. Development	
Reconnaissance of various "place" and "spatial" locations for in-situ designs	• Capture photos • Capture scans • Capture sketches • Capture journaling • Capture voice memos • Other captures of other observations
Research (and documentation)	• Conduct additional research as needed • Analyze data • Make additional decisions
Writing	• Create learning contents • Storyboard / sketch / draft
Creation of 3d digital objects (with behaviors, with motions, with sound)	• May include objects from scratch (lines, primitives, polygons, and others)… • May include pre-builts (open-source, commercial, or others) • May include various types of physical materiality and related in-world physics • Ensure accessibility (such as through universal design, in which there are designs for everyone, not just for the "average" person) • Ensure usability
Creation of 3d phenomena	• Create particulate phenomena (liquid flows, for example) • Create weather systems • Create non-rigid (vs. rigid) objects • Ensure accessibility (such as through universal design) • Ensure usability
Creation of the interface	• Design interface • Ensure accessibility (such as through universal design) • Ensure usability
Compositing and layout of scenes	• Place 2d, 3d, and 4d objects into a scene • Apply proper scaling of 2d, 3d, and 4d objects effectively into the scene • Enable interrelations of the various objects in the scene • Design the coherence of the scene • Ensure coherence between scenes (if there are multiple scenes)
Creation of a coherent experience	• Enabling an entry • Enabling an exit (or conclusion or wrap-up) to the AR experience
Assignment designs	• Design assignments
Social collaboration designs	• Design social collaboration among learners

continues on following page

Table 2. Continued

Development of assessments	• Design assessments
Alpha (α) testing	• Test for technological functionality (across all contexts and devices) • Test for accessibility (in 2d, in 3d, in 4d) • Test for legality • Test for copyright • Test for rights releases • And others
Beta (β) testing	• Test for user adoption • Test for usability
3. Deployment	
Training of teachers (subject matter experts or "SMEs," content experts or "CEs")	• Set up workshops to read teachers into the usage of AR learning contents • Support the technology adoption • Support the change in pedagogy
Lead-up / lead-in learning to the AR segments	• Deploy the lead-up learning for the AR segments
Lead-away learning from the AR segments	• Deploy the lead-away learning for the AR segments • Create notes for pre-, during-, post-AR experience usage (to reinforce the learning); create analog (printable) leave-behinds on the Web and Internet • Create digital leave-behinds (handouts, notes, and others) on the Web and Internet
Public launch	• Launch the AR learning with all lead-up and lead-away contents o There may be a soft launch to a particular target group as an earlier trial rollout. o There may be a hard launch as a public and high-profile rollout. The hard launch usually follows a soft launch.
Publicity	• Market the AR approach (as needed)
Archival of project materials	• Archive raw files, notes, rights releases, finished files, unfinished files, and any other relevant documentation • Ensure the ability to return to project files for revisions
Continuing alpha and beta testing	• Learn from the usage of the AR materials • Revise and update as relevant
Primary research on AR-supported teaching efficacy	• Conduct solid research on teaching with AR o Scholarship of Teaching and Learning or "SoTL" o Action research o And others • Write up • Publish
Primary research on AR-supported learning efficacy	• Conduct solid research on learning with AR o Eye-tracking research o Learning performance research o Survey research (learner reportage) o And others • Write up • Publish

The work itself is glossed over in Table 2. The process may be clearer with a sequence of design questions about the AR experience for learning:

1. What does the AR scene depict of the world?
2. What is the user's role in the world? Roles? (What is the setup?)

3. What powers do the learners have and why? (From where do they have this power?)
4. Is there more information that they can acquire? How, and why?
5. How is the scene designed to indicate desired action? (visual / textual / auditory calls to action)
6. What relevant thing does the learner's action or actions do?
    a. Does it start a process?
    b. Does it involve decision-making? (higher level of user control)
    c. Does it involve different sequences? (such as through branching logic)
7. What are the various possible paths through the interaction?
8. What is learned through the interaction?
    a. What are possible types of learning through the interaction?
    b. What are the mechanics of the interaction?
9. What are the effects in the real?
10. What are the effects in the virtual/ The augmentation layer?
11. What are the effects in the melded real and melded virtual?

Some additional elaboration is included here.

(1) Design

When people think of augmented reality for learning, many focus first on the 3d and 4d digital artifacts and scene. Instead of thinking multi-modally, many may just think visually and leave out sound, touch, and accompanying effects in the physical world. It is important to include "non-visual aspects of our physical reality…when creating AR scenarios" (Schraffenberger & van der Heide, Nov. 2016, p. 1). The researchers observe: "…visual content can take non-visual and multimodal forms" (Schraffenberger & van der Heide, Nov. 2016, p. 6). It may also help to think about interaction effects between the various virtual AR objects:

The illusion of virtual and real objects being part of the same space might be affected by whether virtual and real objects influence one another—both in visual and in non-visual ways. Consequently, we should broaden the traditional understanding of multimodal interaction, which focuses on the interaction between a user and a system and also focus on the multimodal influences between the virtual content and its real surroundings. (Schraffenberger & van der Heide, Nov. 2016, p. 6)

For all the complexity, visuals in AR are often representational instead of high-fidelity photorealistic. The various objects in AR are not only visual, though. Many have various behavioral characteristics, such as to enable interactions with learners and the creation of illusion of in-world physics. Researchers write:

There are three principal components in interaction in AR systems: the user, the user interface and the virtual content. (Ghazwani & Smith, Feb. 2020, p. 39)

The designed AR interactions should align with designer needs "while also contributing to the enhancement of user experience" (Ghazwani & Smith, Feb. 2020, p. 39).

Much more goes into a design than the actual AR parts. Early steps in thinking about how to approach a design task may involve efforts such as "body-storming, storyboarding, and mocking up prototypes using a variety of materials" (Maguire, July 2020, p. 470). Bodystorming is described here:

Bodystorming is a technique used to quickly generate and evaluate design ideas that are vague or too early stage to prototype. The design team members act out scenes imagined in an AR or VR application. The purpose is to ideate quickly and efficiently by encouraging participants to think spatially. (Maguire, July 2020, p. 472)

Another approach is "programming by demonstration" described as a method for non-programmers to "describe interactivity by performing examples of the expected behavior," which has been integrated into AR design. (Leiva, Grønbæk, Klokmose, Nguyen, Kazi, & Asente, Oct. 2021, p. 626)

Then, the ideas are documented in various forms: digital [written / textual, mathematical, visual sketch, audiovisual, wireframing, and others), and analog ["paper, cardboard, sticky tape, straws, pin-boards, Lego bricks," and others] (Maguire, July 2020, p. 470), and mixed forms. These are low-fidelity prototypes that are not costly to make but capture an idea to enable its sharing with others for evaluation and critique and development.

The objects in the AR should be consistent:

Consistency refers to having similar operations and elements for achieving similar tasks to provide the user with a smooth, clean experience. Thus, for example, text labels and text sizes should be consistent throughout the AR application. (Maguire, July 2020, p. 476)

The quality of the various objects—including labels—should align with how they are used by people and with empirical findings of what is efficacious. Researchers write:

In an augmented reality system, labelling technique is a very useful assistant technique for browsing and understanding unfamiliar objects or environments, through which the superimposed virtual labels or words or pictures on the real scene provide convenient information to the viewers, expand the recognition to area of interests and promote the interaction with real scene. How to design the layout of labels in user's field of view, keep the clarity of virtual information and balance the ratio between virtual information and real scene information is a key problem in the field of view management. (Li, Liu, & Wang, Dec. 2018, p. 1)

This study used a survey to explore the following elements: "length of leader line, orientation of leader line, occlusion between labels, occlusion between leader line and label, occlusion between leader lines, all of (the) occlusion(s), movement speed of labels, information explanation, scene expansion, clutter of view plane, (and) overall labelling layout" (Li, Liu, & Wang, Dec. 2018, p. 5) to understand what is most efficacious.

The instructional design requires consideration of the learning. Experiential design considers what learners experience as they proceed through an AR learning experience. At minimum, it is important to avoid a "poor, cluttered experience" (Drljević, Wong, & Botički, 201de7, p. 430). Every element in an AR experience should have a learning purpose. The experience should be "minimalist" and focused

(Drljević, Wong, & Botički, 201de7, p. 431). A research team has created a STAR-ARLE rubric (Student Teacher Assessment Rubric – Augmented Reality Learning Experience).

It helps to think about the learner's experience in the AR experience. What is their first view as they enter the AR? What are they asked to do? How are they prepared for the task sequence? What will they do in the AR space (View objects? Analyze objects? Move objects purposefully? Engage in a work process? Acquire and communicate information? Analyze a scene? Read text? Collaborate with a peer other or peer group? Collaborate? Design? Present? Move through a physical space? Etc.)

Suffice it to say that serious professional skills are required above. There are professional standards for the work. Ensuring that various technologies work of-a-piece is already a challenge. Programming in 2d, 3d, and 4d is difficult, with many programs requiring mathematical understandings to model 3d spaces (Doerner, 2022) and motion design thinking required for 4d.

One study describes an interdisciplinary process model for how to build AR contents as part of a collaborative team.

The development of Augmented Reality (AR) applications still poses several challenges for research and development. Apart from the complex modeling of interaction concepts comprising physical and virtual objects, the collaboration of different actors within the development process is particularly demanding. In AR development, authoring tools facilitate the modeling of User Interfaces (UI) and special frameworks simplify the implementation of AR-specific functionalities, but collaborative processes between UI designers and software developers are still underrepresented. (Börsting, Shulikina, & Gruhn, Sept. 2021, p. 178)

This is a practically usable model that does not require prior knowledge but does seem to require use of a shared technology. They write:

The novelty and the core characteristics of the technology lead to challenges, which span over every phase and role within the development process. When considering development phases individually, it becomes apparent that, for example, the UI design process is hindered by a lack of standards and explicit guidelines… as well as by the complex modeling of 3D content and interactions. The implementation phase poses further challenges, such as non-standardized hardware…or the complex integration of tracking methods that usually lack localization accuracy. (Börsting, Shulikina, & Gruhn, Sept. 2021, p. 178)

The technology includes some designed source code templates.

(2) Development

Three-dimensional scene reconstruction is used for complex information capture and display. Researchers write:

Three-dimensional…scene reconstruction is one of the key techniques in Augmented Reality (AR), which is related to the integration of image processing and display systems of complex information. Stereo matching is a computer vision based approach for 3-D scene reconstruction. (Nie, Liu, Wang, Liu, & Wang, Mar. 2019, p. 1100)

The mapping of physical spaces is nontrivial even with working cameras and 3d scanners to capture point clouds to represent physical spaces (Wientapper, Wuest, & Kuijper, May 2011, p. 140). There is a tool and process for capturing a remote environment with a LiDAR-equipped tablet and creating an AR experience from that location and then enabling the experiencing of the AR at that remote site (Wang, Nguyen, Asente, & Dorsey, May 2021, p. 1). Various visualizations may be made from that capture, including a "bird's eye view" and others. Technologies enable the knitting together of "photorealistic composite images using captured images" (Wang, Nguyen, Asente, & Dorsey, May 2021, p. 1). Various tools require transcoding in complex ways to enable the digital files to intercommunicate.

The authoring tools for AR are not so complex as in the past. In prior times, creating contents for AR required programming skills and was a deterrent for a large swath of the educating population (Cubillo, Martin, Castro, Diaz, Colmenar, & Botički, Oct. 2014, p. 1). Many required understandings of math and geometry (Doerner, 2022, p. 404). Now, there are low-code, visual-coding, and no-code authoring tools (dedicated and general software development kits or "SDKs," game engines, scripting tools, and others). Some development platforms enable building once into a master project file and then versioning out various AR displays to different platforms. One team observes about AR development:

Authoring processes need to be carefully planned so that authors can collaborate efficiently and without any frictional losses using tools, APIs (application programming interfaces) and SDKs (software development kits). (Broll, Weidner, Schwandt, Weber, & Doerner, 2022, p. 372)

Plug-ins may add additional functionalities, such as creating tangible interactions.

All AR authoring tools provide the core functionalities of tracking and rendering by using low-level libraries and frameworks. Currently, to author tangible interactions for AR, designers use plug-in tools or stand-alone tools that allow for interaction authoring through scripting. However, visual programming can be a more efficient method for non-programmers to author tangible interactions while developing TAR design representations for usability training. (Jain & Choi, July 2020, p. 50)

Building AR is not just about technologies, but it is critical to consider instructional design. One research team defines this as "a special curriculum…to carefully integrate the use of AR and its various accompanying devices into classroom use" (Santos, Chen, Taketomi, Yamamoto, Miyazaki, & Kato, 2013, p. 45). The designed AR-based learning may align with how people learn and think:

People store much more information than what is presented to them. Aside from the concepts to be remembered, we also generate associations that help us make sense of, and thus remember, information. Elaboration is the creation of such additional associations. There are two kinds of elaboration: imprecise elaboration and precise elaboration.

Imprecise elaboration is the creation of additional associations unrelated to remembered information. Whereas precise elaboration is the creation of additional material closely related to remembered material. When learning, students sometimes take advantage of elaborative rehearsal: a memory technique that involves thinking about the meaning of the term to be remembered. Aside from this semantic processing, the use of visual imagery and haptic information can also be a powerful form of elaboration of knowledge. (Santos, Chen, Taketomi, Yamamoto, Miyazaki, & Kato, 2013, p. 48)

Those who author VR and AR require various skills, including "programming skills, knowledge of real-time computer graphics and image processing, human-machine interface design skills and usability know-how" (Broll, Weidner, Schwandt, Weber, & Doerner, 2022, p. 371). It is also important to understand how various algorithms work (p. 371). AR technologies have been full of promise, but the full adoption of AR in games has been "substantially hindered by technical glitches and limitations" (Alha, Leorke, Koskinen, & Paavilainen, 2023, p. 342), leaving the potential of AR "firmly in a perpetual near-future" (p. 343).

Assessments of such objects should include the learning takeaways from the experience.

In terms of the alpha and beta testing, it helps to have all necessary functions tested for as well as all legal considerations included. In the academic literature, researchers have created and validated a user experience usability heuristic checklist to "assess and inform design changes that influence the user experience of an AR or MR application and/or device" (Derby & Chaparro, 2022, p. 165). This checklist has 11 heuristics and 94 checklist items of usability for AR and MR technologies (as emerging ones) (Derby & Chaparro, 2022, p. 165). Is the technology easy to set up? Is there accessible help and documentation information for the app? Does the design enable control for cognitive overload and does it avoid "unnecessary clutter"? (Derby & Chaparro, 2022, p. 170) Are the visual elements easy to identify? Is there clarity between the visual elements which are visual only and others which are "interactable"? Are the various objects accessible for the completion of learner tasks, or are they occluded or hidden or blocked? Has the application been built with "consistency & standards" (Derby & Chaparro, 2022, pp. 170 - 171)? Is there clear differentiation between what AR content is public and what is private (viewable only to particular users or devices)? Is there sufficient feedback so users know what is going on? Are there design elements to minimize user discomfort? Are the visual elements designed for the recognition of objects without the need for direct recall (which adds to the cognitive load of working memory)? A copy of this heuristic has been included in the Appendices.

Usability testing after the creation of the AR contents as learning media is *de rigueur* (Kurniawan, Purwanto, & Mansur, Nov. 2019, p. 89).

Then, too, in terms of accessibility, it helps to consider both the physical real and the virtual. In a physical location, is it sufficiently well lit? Is it wheelchair accessible? Are there benches so that people do not have to continually stand? One research study suggests that universal design is needed in the building of eXtended reality for education. The disability categories in a review of the literature about extended reality include the following: "cognition, senses (seeing, hearing, touch), voice, physical (mobility, motor)" (Simon-Liedtke & Baraas, 2022, p. 128). Input methods to engage with AR require multiple channels, so as to accommodate those with mobility issues, whose with vocal disabilities, and other challenges (Simon-Liedtke & Baraas, 2022). There is a need for proper pacing and pauses between interactions, so that users of AR do not become fatigued (Simon-Liedtke & Baraas, 2022). Various AR text should be clear:

Augmented elements such as labels, text boxes and highlighting should be clear and readable on the device on which the AR application is running at a normal viewing distance. It should be clear what elements the annotations relate to. (Maguire, July 2020, p. 475)

Every element of the physical and digital spaces and objects have to be accessible.

For digital accessibility in augmented reality, there are a range of issues:

- Is color of sufficient value and contrast (dark vs. light)? In 2d, in 3d, in 4d?
- Is color used as the only informational channel?
- Are objects or shapes occluded?
- Is it easy to orientate to the scene?
- Are there poor viewing angles that have not been made more accessible?
- What sorts of elements are there in the AR audiovisual scene visually? Textually? Auditorially? Audio-visuals?
- Is information offered in multiple forms?
- If (textual) labels are used, are they readable? (Are they lined for legibility? Is there a sufficient high-contrast between the text and its placed background? Or real-world background?) Are they consistently placed in 3d space? Are they available pre- and post- motion? Is the textual information available in non-textual formats (like audio)? Are there multiple channels for the textual information to be communicated effectively?
- Are there multiple ways to navigate? To move through the space?
- Is there wheelchair accessibility?
- Safety and security aspects to ensure the physical safety of all?
    - Are there indicators about how to progress?
    - Are there clear ways to know if one has missed something?
- Is there an ability to control for sound in the physical space? The virtual space? The AR space? How is 360-degree sound handled?
    - How is ambient sound handled as the soundtrack of the AR space?
    - How is spatial or locational-based sound handled in the AR space? Does the sound work location-wise in terms of heightened and less-heightened sound?
- If there are animations (and videos), can the user control the speed of the animations? Is the pacing sufficiently timed to enable perception and learning, given the challenges of transience in motion and changes over time (and the cognitive load of such experiences)?
    - Can the user pause?
    - Can the user speed up the animation as needed?
    - Can the user stop all animations and motions and videos? (particularly for those triggered in sensory and cognitive ways)
- Are there ways to replay or re-experience the entire AR sequences?
- Are any strobe effects included? [These may trigger seizures and other negative health effects, so they should not be.]
- If there is a lot of busyness (color, motion) in the AR visuals, are there ways to tone down or quiet the visuals? Are there ways to manage for cognitive overload? For split attention? For cognitive neurodivergence?
- How are sensitive or controversial topics addressed? Are these set up in non-triggering ways?
- Are there clear ways to exit at any time at the convenience of the individual? The groups?
- Is it clear how to use the AR interface? Any tangible interfaces? Mixes of interfaces in the AR and the real?
    - Are there ways to move through the interface back to any desirable point (or juncture)?
- Is it clear how to interact with the various objects? The various characters? Other people?
- Is it clear how to be telepresent?
- Is it clear how to interact with other live (and telepresent) people in the AR space?

- Are there alternative learning experiences outside of the AR? For those who choose not to participate, are there ways that they may acquire equivalent learning?
- Is the storytelling in the AR effective?
- Is the learning in the AR effective? What about for various learning audiences?
- Are there stereotyped depictions of people? Exclusionary messages? Discriminatory messages? Avoid these at all costs. All people should be treated with dignity and respect.
- Others?

Researchers are working at how to ensure full accessibility in the AR space. Some of the above is from current digital standards for accessibility in digital instructional design. Indeed, there are a variety of ways to innovate solutions.

There can be specific instruments for usability testing of a particular AR experience or object. One work includes a list of questions asked of students who used the learning object:

Could you clearly visualize and understand the different parts of the membrane reactor that was taught earlier in the classroom?

Do you believe that the VR interface improved your understanding of the membrane reactor when compared to the real reactor in the laboratory?

Do you feel that audio narration would improve the learning during the self-guided tour?

Did you experience any sort of physical discomforts such as nausea, headache, or eye strain while using the VR hardware?

Do you think that VR can be used as an alternative mode of education…?

Do you believe that a hybrid model involving traditional classroom learning, hands-on experiments, and VR exercises would be the best possible approach for education? (Kumar, Carberry, Beenfeldt, Andersson, Mansouri, & Gallucci, 2021, p. 151)

Targeted surveys such as that above may result in unique insights to a particular case-based context.

(3) Deployment

Learners do not automatically know how to benefit from AR learning contexts. There need to be instructional support, so teachers need to be read into the context.

Preliminary testing of both versions revealed that users were interested in AR technology but did not intuitively understand how to better utilize the system in comparison with a static video. Moreover, in spite there was not a statistically significant difference between information understanding between both conditions, the mobile application was rated significantly lower than the desktop application in user engagement for collaborative environments. (Arce-Lopera, Gomez, & Montoya, Nov. 2019, p. 193)

Ideally, the instructors using the technology would be "at the table" at the beginning, so their expertise and insights may be used in the design, the development, and the deployment.

Usability testing is critical to understand how would-be users of the AR materials perceive it. Immersion, for example, is a subjective and psychological property, not an objective measurable variable alone per se:

It is important to state that approaching immersion as an objective property fails to consider the perceptual limits, context, and individual factors such as mood, preference, expertise, and expectations. It has been established that an improvement in the technical specifications of the system does not necessarily lead to a proportional perceptual change (evident by non-linear psychophysical curves). Limiting immersion to the physical domain removes the sensory and cognitive filters that play an active part in determining the overall experience. It has been appropriately suggested that the term system immersion should be used when referring to this perspective on immersion. (Agrawal & Bech, 2023, pp. 324-325)

Immersion is measured by including three main areas—the physical, the perceptual, and the affective (Agrawal & Bech, 2023, p. 325). Systems may be said to have "immersive potential" to elicit deep mental involvement by its users (Agrawal & Bech, 2023, pp. 327 - 328). While people may have different immersive tendencies, as predispositions, this was not found to directly influence their "immersion ratings" (Agrawal & Bech, 2023, p. 344). This study found that immersion is better measured in gradations than as a binary (Agrawal & Bech, 2023, p. 343). Also, the "quality of experience" (QoE) is important. This QoE variable…

Is the degree of delight or annoyance of a person whose experience involves an application, service, or system. It results from the person's evaluation of the fulfillment of his or her expectations and needs with respect to the utility and/or enjoyment in the light of the person's context, personality, and current state. (Agrawal & Bech, 2023, p. 329)

Knowledge transfer may occur in full dimensionality, which may make this approach to learning "attractive" (Bahuguna, Verma, & Raj, Feb. 2018, p. 1).

After the AR deployment for learning, various forms of research may be conducted about the teaching and learning. In the AR/VR space, machine learning is also being applied to find data patterns using "a progressing calculative algorithm field in which algorithms are created to imitate human behavior" (Angra, Sharma, & Sharma, Apr. 2022, p. 2601). While schools are natural spaces for *in vivo* research, there has to be a "duty of care" when working with children in the research (Southgate & Smith, Mar. 2017, p. 3), as it is so with vulnerable and other populations in human subject's research. This work also advises: "Don't underestimate the time or level of engagement needed, even for pilot studies" (Southgate & Smith, Mar. 2017, p. 3). One study broke apart different learning assets on a Mobile AR Learning Environment to understand their respective contributions to the learning (Durairaj & Aurelia, July 2017, p. 1112).

There have been some efforts to standardize some of the research into mixed reality for empirical research. One approach proposes focusing on digital narratives and storytelling and integrated psychophysiological methods (Bruni, Dini, & Simonetti, July 2021, p. 3). As yet, there is not a consensus around how to conduct research in this space for more sharable insights and generalizability. Indeed, those active in this space have shown plenty of creativity in their research approaches, including using bio-safe and remote means to conduct AR app evaluation during the pandemic (Teixeira, Lahm, Peres, Mauricio, & Teixeira, 2021, p. 147).

Discussion

A back-of-the-napkin estimate for setting up an Augmented Reality Shop at a university would include funding multiple professional positions (AR programmers, audiovisual experts, instructional designers, and others), the purchase of expensive technologies and their maintenance, funds to pay subject matter experts and content experts to support the pedagogical applications, access to various physical spaces, and others. This work will require thorough planning. It will require time.

Institutions with academic departments that can benefit from AR may be able to actualize the funding. Smaller institutions will likely go with third-party companies that do the design-development-deployment work. Some institutions may have angel investors and grant funds to access to actualize this, if there is strong leadership and vision. [As a side note, it is one thing to consider setting up AR willy-nilly, without sufficient considerations, and think about conducting teaching-and-learning efficacy research as a pie-in-the-sky endeavor. To paraphrase a famous saying: "Amateurs talk strategy; professionals talk logistics." To actualize the work will require more than imagination and pretend. Administrators who cannot get past amateur hour engage a lot of cheap talk and try to pressure others to take on unfunded mandates, but they do not advance progress in the real.]

To test the waters, the Midwestern university may start with a project or two with particular subject matter experts. Perhaps some AR objects may be made to standard and deployed, for the learning value and for staff to acquire some practice. Early "small wins" and proofs-of-concept can stand to benefit more complex efforts in terms of AR. Handling projects without high-pressure external deadlines may allow for more room to learn. From early steps, next steps may be defined.

A light and brief inclusive learning "use case." As to inclusion using AR, such as for immigrant learners at any phase of their learning, certainly, various cultural overlays may be applied. These may be intercultural overlays, cross-cultural overlays, and multi-cultural overlays, too. Perhaps labels (single-lingual label or multi-lingual label) may be added to AR spaces for faster non-native language uptake. Perhaps other AR overlays may be done to enhance the experiential learning in-situ with the real and the digital. Some AR spaces may be designed to enable learners to build out their own spaces, as mentioned prior. Immigrant and other learners may express their voices and creativity in their own rich-modality ways.

FUTURE RESEARCH DIRECTIONS

AR is seen as a conduit for people to access "rapidly flowing information which becomes meaningful and 'alive' as it is embedded in the appropriate spatial and time framework" (Lampropoulos, Keramopoulos, & Diamantaras, 2020, p. 32). It is a sign of the digitization and datafication of daily modern life. How AR evolves and manifests depends on various factors. As it changes, it will affect what people can do with it for teaching and learning.

Higher education does not have a sufficient amount of augmented reality (AR) curriculum for either industry or academia. Higher education is "struggling to keep abreast of its development and to train specialists quickly, providing few courses which sufficiently align with the needs of industry" (Fominykh, Wild, Klamma, Billinghurst, Costiner, Karsakov, ... & Smolic, 2020, p. 131). The courses that do exist are seen as weak in addressing "the formative foundations of AR education" (Fominykh, Wild, Klamma, Billinghurst, Costiner, Karsakov, ... & Smolic, 2020, p. 131). A review of the available courses shows different bureaucratic placements of the courses. Finally, this research team has created a model AR curriculum based on four dimensions: "skills, lesson plan, course format, and assessment regime" in order to align with the needs of industry (particularly 'hard' and technical skills") (Fominykh, Wild, Klamma, Billinghurst, Costiner, Karsakov, ... & Smolic, 2020, p. 139). They list the necessary abilities:

AR development skills, platform-specific development skills, specific programming / markup language skills, advanced computing skills, computer vision skills, computer graphics skills, advanced data analysis and AI skills, audio engineering skills, interaction technology skills, design and rapid prototyping skills, hardware and hardware-related skills, (and) user evaluation skills. (Fominykh, Wild, Klamma, Billinghurst, Costiner, Karsakov, ... & Smolic, 2020, p. 140)

They propose a curriculum with "units of lectures and practical tutorials" (Fominykh, Wild, Klamma, Billinghurst, Costiner, Karsakov, ... & Smolic, 2020, p. 141), and a mix of theory and hands-on practices.

A knowledge mapping in publishing related to virtual reality, augmented reality, mixed reality, and extended reality suggest particular foci. These include the following: "cognitive load, learning environment, knowledge acquisition, training, gamification, assessment, children education, engineering education, and higher medical education" (Zhang, Cui, Shan, Qu, Zhang, Tu, & Wang, June 2020, p. 215). "VR, AR, and MR" all face "many challenges with respect to technology, infrastructure, teaching, learning, etc." (Zhang, Cui, Shan, Qu, Zhang, Tu, & Wang, June 2020, p. 218). This work lays some basic groundwork for what to consider when setting up an AR project or shop in higher education. It provides some applied structure for how this shop may be set up and how workflows may be engaged.

Follow-on work may describe how others have set up actual AR shops, at varying levels of budgets. One team cited "cost for virtual reality hardware; cost for virtual reality software; human resource costs" and others (Kumar, Carberry, Beenfeldt, Andersson, Mansouri, & Gallucci, 2021, p. 150). There are high-end technologies that may be used to capture light fields with high geometric and photometric accuracy, for example, but these may be expensive in the university context. Perhaps there may be writings from both the Global North and the Global South.

Much more work is needed on pedagogical theories and modeling as applied to AR teaching and learning. More work may be done on setting up one-off ARs and sequential ones. Narrative AR could be developed in more depth.

There are many extant questions. There is much room for more teaching and learning cases using AR. The accessibility personas created for other contexts have some applicability, but perhaps the set of personas may be broadened to ensure AR application. The real world is full of people with varying mixes of lived experiences, lived contexts, and mixed abilities (both visible and invisible). Designing to include those in "edge cases" may ensure broader usage and more enriched AR experiences.

Is there room for modular designs and archival of shared 3d and 4d digital learning objects? What are ways to design AR learning for those learners at different developmental phases? In different learning fields?

How can an AR learning sequence be versioned? How can branches be made (based on customized learner needs)? [One research team has observed that "...designing authoring workflows and learning paths can be different in these environments as the transfer of design ideas can affect the quality of the learning experiences" (Hensen & Klamma, July 2020, p. 319).]

What are some practical insights for planning AR installations in certain locations (indoor and outdoor)?

Given the "slow fires" of paper and the "fast fires" of digital contents, what are ways that the augmented reality artifacts may be protected into the future, for usage across different platforms?

Some suggest that future workplace trainings will be based on AR. Certainly, AR is used to define activity scripts in the workplace, with supports for decisions, work guidance, and other processes (Wild, 2016). If so, future employees would benefit from exposures to AR.

As yet, there are no known automated or other tests for AR accessibility. These may be built into some AR systems. A sensor may be used to assess some aspects of accessibility for AR. This is another area ripe with possibilities.

CONCLUSION

Using AR "on learning material" can make the experience of learning "impressive and fun" (Pranoto & Panggabean, 2019, p. 506). While there are AR benefits for learning (Knyazev & Cheremukhina, May 2022, p. 37), it is not the only available tool on the market. There are strengths and weaknesses to using any technology and pedagogical approach. AR, if not built well, can be exclusionary and inaccessible. If the technologies are used, though, the AR environment has to be as open as possible to the widest ranges of users. A social model of disability suggests the following: "The environment is disabled, not the person." In this sense, the responsibility is on those making such environments to make them as accessible and warm and welcoming and effective as possible. It can be an expensive endeavor.

This chapter explored the research literature, common instructional design practice, and other elements to consider how a university may begin to think about setting up an augmented reality shop for the creation of customized digital learning contents. The staffing, equipment, software, physical spaces, and such, are not low-cost. The skillsets required are high-end and demanding ones.

This work does not take a pedagogical theory approach although several theories are mentioned. In these early stages, a theory-agnostic approach may be more effective. This is not to say that there are not some educational theories that may apply here, such as TPACK and the multimedia theory of learning and others. Rather, for now, the initial focus is on applied AR in teaching and learning.

REFERENCES

Adas, H. A., Shetty, S., & Hargrove, S. K. (2013, October). *Virtual and augmented reality based assembly design system for personalized learning. In 2013 Science and Information Conference*. IEEE.

Agrawal, S. R., & Bech, S. (2023). Immersion in audiovisual experiences. In *Sonic Interactions in Virtual Environments* (pp. 319–351). Springer. doi:10.1007/978-3-031-04021-4_11

Ahmed, N., Lataifeh, M., Alhamarna, A. F., Alnahdi, M. M., & Almansori, S. T. (2021, September). LeARn: A collaborative learning environment using augmented reality. In *2021 IEEE 2nd International Conference on Human-Machine Systems (ICHMS)* (pp. 1-4). IEEE. 10.1109/ICHMS53169.2021.9582643

Ahn, S. J. G., Nowak, K. L., & Bailenson, J. N. (2022). Unintended consequences of spatial presence on learning in virtual reality. *Computers & Education*, *186*, 104532. doi:10.1016/j.compedu.2022.104532

Al-Azawi, R. (2018, April). Embedding augmented and virtual reality in educational learning method: present and future. In *2018 9th International Conference on Information and Communication Systems (ICICS)* (pp. 218-222). IEEE. 10.1109/IACS.2018.8355470

Alalwan, N., Cheng, L., Al-Samarraie, H., Yousef, R., Alzahrani, A. I., & Sarsam, S. M. (2020). Challenges and prospects of virtual reality and augmented reality utilization among primary school teachers: A developing country perspective. *Studies in Educational Evaluation*, *66*, 100876. doi:10.1016/j.stueduc.2020.100876

Alha, K., Leorke, D., Koskinen, E., & Paavilainen, J. (2023). Augmented play: An analysis of augmented reality features in location-based games. *Convergence (London)*, *29*(2), 342–361. doi:10.1177/13548565231156495

Aljowaysir, N., Ozdemir, T. O., & Kim, T. (2019, June). Differentiated learning patterns with mixed reality. In *2019 IEEE Games, Entertainment, Media Conference (GEM)* (pp. 1-4). IEEE.

Allal-Chérif, O. (2022). Intelligent cathedrals: Using augmented reality, virtual reality, and artificial intelligence to provide an intense cultural, historical, and religious visitor experience. *Technological Forecasting and Social Change*, *178*, 121604. doi:10.1016/j.techfore.2022.121604

Ancient, C., & Teeuw, R. (2020, July). Augmented reality interface design to support visualisation of 'risk landscapes'. In *International Conference on Human-Computer Interaction* (pp. 391-408). Springer. 10.1007/978-3-030-49760-6_28

Angra, S., Sharma, B., & Sharma, K. D. (2022, April). Amalgamation of virtual reality, augmented reality and machine learning: A review. In *2022 2nd International Conference on Advance Computing and Innovative Technologies in Engineering (ICACITE)* (pp. 2601-2604). IEEE. 10.1109/ICACITE53722.2022.9823716

Apostolakis, K. C., Margetis, G., & Stephanidis, C. (2020, November). Pleistocene Crete: A narrative, interactive mixed reality exhibition that brings prehistoric wildlife back to life. In *2020 IEEE International Symposium on Mixed and Augmented Reality Adjunct (ISMAR-Adjunct)* (pp. 237-240). IEEE. 10.1109/ISMAR-Adjunct51615.2020.00069

Arce-Lopera, C., Gomez, A., & Montoya, C. (2019, November). User engagement for collaborative learning on a mobile and desktop augmented reality application. In *2019 International Conference on Virtual Reality and Visualization (ICVRV)* (pp. 193-195). IEEE. 10.1109/ICVRV47840.2019.00045

Asai, K., Kobayashi, H., & Kondo, T. (2005, July). Augmented instructions-a fusion of augmented reality and printed learning materials. In *Fifth IEEE International Conference on Advanced Learning Technologies (ICALT'05)* (pp. 213-215). IEEE. 10.1109/ICALT.2005.71

Azuma, R., Baillot, Y., Behringer, R., Feiner, S., Julier, S., & MacIntyre, B. (2001). Recent advances in augmented reality. *IEEE Computer Graphics and Applications*, *21*(6), 34–47. doi:10.1109/38.963459

Azuma, R. T. (1997). A survey of augmented reality. *Presence (Cambridge, Mass.)*, *6*(4), 355–385. doi:10.1162/pres.1997.6.4.355

Baabdullah, A. M., Alsulaimani, A. A., Allamnakhrah, A., Alalwan, A. A., Dwivedi, Y. K., & Rana, N. P. (2022). Usage of augmented reality (AR) and development of e-learning outcomes: An empirical evaluation of students' e-learning experience. *Computers & Education*, *177*, 104383. doi:10.1016/j.compedu.2021.104383

Bahuguna, Y., Verma, A., & Raj, K. (2018, February). Smart learning based on augmented reality with android platform and its applicability. In *2018 3rd International Conference on Internet of Things: Smart Innovation and Usages (IoT-SIU)* (pp. 1-5). IEEE. 10.1109/IoT-SIU.2018.8519853

Bichlmeier, C., Wimmer, F., Heining, S. M., & Navab, N. (2007). Contextual anatomic mimesis: Hybrid in-situ visualization method for improving multi-sensory depth perception in medical augmented reality. IEEE. 1 – 10.

Billinghurst, M., & Duenser, A. (2012). Augmented reality in the classroom. *Computer*, *45*(7), 56–63. doi:10.1109/MC.2012.111

Blum, L., Broll, W., & Müller, S. (2009). Augmented reality under water. In *SIGGRAPH'09* (pp. 1–1). Posters.

Börsting, I., Shulikina, E., & Gruhn, V. (2021, September). Interdisciplinary Collaboration in augmented reality development—A process model. In *International Conference on Augmented Reality, Virtual Reality and Computer Graphics* (pp. 178-194). Springer, Cham. 10.1007/978-3-030-87595-4_14

Bouaziz, R., Alhejaili, M., Al-Saedi, R., Mihdhar, A., & Alsarrani, J. (2020, December). Using marker based augmented reality to teach autistic eating skills. In *2020 IEEE International Conference on Artificial Intelligence and Virtual Reality (AIVR)* (pp. 239-242). IEEE. 10.1109/AIVR50618.2020.00050

Bourguet, M. L., & Romero-Gonzalez, M. (2021, May). Work-In-Progress-Teaching invisible phenomena and virtual experiments: Immersion or augmentation? In *2021 7th International Conference of the Immersive Learning Research Network (iLRN)* (pp. 1-3). IEEE.

Bourguet, M. L., Ye, W., & Romero-Gonzalez, M. (2022, May). Work-In-Progress—Developing materials science experiments using augmented reality: How much reality is needed? In *2022 8th International Conference of the Immersive Learning Research Network (iLRN)* (pp. 1-3). IEEE.

Brinkmann, F., & Weinzierl, S. (2023). Audio quality assessment for virtual reality. In *Sonic Interactions in Virtual Environments* (pp. 145–178). Springer. doi:10.1007/978-3-031-04021-4_5

Broll, W. (2022). Augmented reality. In *Virtual and Augmented Reality (VR/AR)* (pp. 291–329). Springer. doi:10.1007/978-3-030-79062-2_8

Broll, W., Weidner, F., Schwandt, T., Weber, K., & Doerner, R. (2022). Authoring of VR/AR applications. In *Virtual and Augmented Reality (VR/AR)* (pp. 371–400). Springer. doi:10.1007/978-3-030-79062-2_10

Bruni, L. E., Dini, H., & Simonetti, A. (2021, July). Narrative cognition in mixed reality systems: Towards an empirical framework. In *International Conference on Human-Computer Interaction* (pp. 3-17). Springer. 10.1007/978-3-030-77599-5_1

Buiu, C., Buga, A., & Coman, A. M. (2013, November). Teaching robotics and virtual reality in a synergistic approach. In *2013 7th IEEE International Conference on e-Learning in Industrial Electronics (ICELIE)* (pp. 71-75). IEEE. 10.1109/ICELIE.2013.6701275

Cahyadi, E., Santoso, H. A., Bandung, Y., & Langi, A. Z. (2012, April). Augmented reality Virtual Class Box for digital learning services. In *2012 International Conference on Cloud Computing and Social Networking (ICCCSN)* (pp. 1-4). IEEE. 10.1109/ICCCSN.2012.6215754

Calle-Bustos, A. M., Juan, M. C., Abad, F., & Mollá, R. (2019, July). An augmented reality app for therapeutic education and suitable for mobile devices with different features. In *2019 IEEE 19th International Conference on Advanced Learning Technologies (ICALT)* (Vol. 2161, pp. 337-339). IEEE. 10.1109/ICALT.2019.00106

Carreras, A., & Sora, C. (2009, October). Coupling digital and physical worlds in an AR magic show performance: Lessons learned. In *2009 IEEE International Symposium on Mixed and Augmented Reality-Arts, Media and Humanities* (pp. 25-28). IEEE. 10.1109/ISMAR-AMH.2009.5336729

Chang, H. Y., Yu, Y. T., Wu, H. K., & Hsu, Y. S. (2016, July). The impact of a mobile augmented reality game: Changing students' perceptions of the complexity of socioscientific reasoning. In *2016 IEEE 16th International Conference on Advanced Learning Technologies (ICALT)* (pp. 312-313). IEEE.

Chang, R. C., & Yu, Z. S. (2017, May). Application of augmented reality technology to promote interactive learning. In *2017 International Conference on applied system Innovation (ICASI)* (pp. 1673-1674). IEEE. 10.1109/ICASI.2017.7988257

Chang, W., & Tan, Q. (2010, December). Augmented reality system design and scenario study for location-based adaptive mobile learning. In *2010 13th IEEE International Conference on Computational Science and Engineering* (pp. 20-27). IEEE. 10.1109/CSE.2010.66

Chen, J. Y., Liu, C. H., Hsieh, C. H., Huang, S. Y., Wang, W. K., & Nien, B. H. (2017, May). Kinect augmented reality gear game design. In *2017 International Conference on Applied System Innovation (ICASI)* (pp. 373-375). IEEE. 10.1109/ICASI.2017.7988429

Chen, Y. C. (2013, June). Learners' motivation in an augmented reality E-learning system. In *2013 International Conference on Engineering, Technology and Innovation (ICE) & IEEE International Technology Management Conference* (pp. 1-6). IEEE. 10.1109/ITMC.2013.7352609

Chen, Z. Y., Li, Y. J., Wang, M., Steinicke, F., & Zhao, Q. (2021, October). A reinforcement learning approach to redirected walking with passive haptic feedback. In *2021 IEEE International Symposium on Mixed and Augmented Reality (ISMAR)* (pp. 184-192). IEEE. 10.1109/ISMAR52148.2021.00033

Chin, K. Y., Hou, C. X., Wang, C. S., & Lee, K. F. (2017, July). Using augmented reality technology for the development of historic building teaching application: A Mackay Culture Course. In *2017 IEEE 17th International Conference on Advanced Learning Technologies (ICALT)* (pp. 87-88). IEEE. 10.1109/ICALT.2017.7

Chiou, Y. M., & Barrnaki, R. (2019, March). [DC] learning tornado formation via collaborative mixed reality. In *2019 IEEE Conference on Virtual Reality and 3D User Interfaces (VR)* (pp. 1369-1370). IEEE. 10.1109/VR.2019.8798339

Collins, J., Regenbrecht, H., & Lanalotz, T. (2018, October). Back to the future: Constructivist learning in virtual reality. In *2018 IEEE International Symposium on Mixed and Augmented Reality Adjunct (ISMAR-Adjunct)* (pp. 45-46). IEEE. 10.1109/ISMAR-Adjunct.2018.00030

Costa, I. V., Queiroz, V. F., Miranda, B. P., de Freitas, A. A., dos Santos, C. G. R., & Meiguins, B. S. (2019, July). A card-based interaction to design visualizations in augmented reality environments. In *2019 23rd International Conference in Information Visualization??? Part II* (pp. 52-55). IEEE.

Craig, P., Willemsen, P., Downs, E., Lover, A., & Barber, W. (2022, March). Learning environments in AR: Comparing tablet and head-mounted augmented reality devices at room and table scale. In *2022 IEEE Conference on Virtual Reality and 3D User Interfaces Abstracts and Workshops (VRW)* (pp. 892-893). IEEE. 10.1109/VRW55335.2022.00297

Creane, S., Crotty, Y., & Farren, M. (2015). A proposed use of virtual and augmented reality for supporting inquiry based learning. *Proceedings of the 2015 International Conference on Interactive Mobile Communication Technologies and Learning,* 393 – 395.

Cubillo, J., Martín, S., Castro, M., Diaz, G., Colmenar, A., & Botički, I. (2014, October). A learning environment for augmented reality mobile learning. In 2014 IEEE Frontiers in Education Conference (FIE) Proceedings (pp. 1-8). IEEE. doi:10.1109/FIE.2014.7044039

Daher, S. (2017, March). *Optical see-through vs. spatial augmented reality simulators for medical applications. In 2017 IEEE Virtual Reality (VR).* IEEE.

Davcev, D., Trajkovic, V., Kalajdziski, S., & Celakoski, S. (2003, August). Augmented reality environment for dance learning. *International Conference on Information Technology: Research and Education, 2003 Proceedings. ITRE2003,* 189–193.

De Backer, P., Simoens, J., Creemers, H., Vermijs, S., Matthys, R., Bravi, C. A., Sarchi, L., Piazza, P., Paciotti, M., Farinha, R., Debbaut, C., Desender, L., Van Praet, C., Mottrie, A., & Decaestecker, K. (2022). Augmented reality instrument detection: Enabling 3D model-instrument interaction through deep learning. *European Urology Open Science, 44,* S406. doi:10.1016/S2666-1683(22)02254-6

De Michelis, G., De Paoli, F., Pluchinotta, C., & Susani, M. (2000, April). Weakly augmented reality: Observing and designing the work-place of creative designers. In *Proceedings of DARE 2000 on Designing Augmented Reality Environments* (pp. 81-91). 10.1145/354666.354675

Del Gallego, N. P. (2020, November). A proposed learning content for teaching handheld augmented reality in a classroom setting. In *2020 22nd Symposium on Virtual and Augmented Reality (SVR)* (pp. 111-118). IEEE. 10.1109/SVR51698.2020.00030

Derby, J. L., & Chaparro, B. S. (2022). The development and validation of an augmented and mixed reality usability heuristic checklist. In *International Conference on Human-Computer Interaction* (pp. 165-182). Springer. 10.1007/978-3-031-05939-1_11

Doerner, R. (2022). Mathematical Foundations of VR/AR. In *Virtual and Augmented Reality (VR/AR)* (pp. 401–412). Springer. doi:10.1007/978-3-030-79062-2_11

Doerner, R., Broll, W., Jung, B., Grimm, P., Göbel, M., & Kruse, R. (2022). Introduction to virtual and augmented reality. In *Virtual and Augmented Reality (VR/AR)* (pp. 1–37). Springer. doi:10.1007/978-3-030-79062-2_1

Doerner, R., & Horst, R. (2022). Overcoming challenges when teaching hands-on courses about Virtual Reality and Augmented Reality: Methods, techniques and best practice. *Graphics and Visual Computing*, *6*, 200037. doi:10.1016/j.gvc.2021.200037

Doerner, R., & Steinicke, F. (2022). Perceptual aspects of VR. In *Virtual and Augmented Reality (VR/AR)* (pp. 39–70). Springer. doi:10.1007/978-3-030-79062-2_2

Doswell, J. T. (2008). Pedagogy play: Virtual instructors for wearable augmented reality during hands-on learning and play. *Second IEEE International Conference on Digital Game and Intelligent Toy Enhanced Learning,* 215 – 216.

Doswell, J. T., & Mosley, P. H. (2006, July). Robotics in mixed-reality training simulations: augmenting STEM learning. In *Sixth IEEE International Conference on Advanced Learning Technologies (ICALT'06)* (pp. 864-868). IEEE. 10.1109/ICALT.2006.1652579

Drljević, N., Wong, L. H., & Botički, I. (2017). Where does my Augmented Reality Learning Experience (ARLE) belong? A student and teacher perspective to positioning ARLEs. *IEEE Transactions on Learning Technologies, 10*(4), 419–435. doi:10.1109/TLT.2017.2690426

Dubois, E., & Nigay, L. (2000, April). Augmented reality: which augmentation for which reality? In *Proceedings of DARE 2000 on Designing Augmented Reality Environments* (pp. 165-166). 10.1145/354666.354695

Durairaj, M., & Aurelia, P. S. (2017, July). A modernistic and contemporary mobile augmented reality erudition system. In *2017 International Conference on Computing Methodologies and Communication (ICCMC)* (pp. 1109-1112). IEEE. 10.1109/ICCMC.2017.8282645

El Kabtane, H., Mourdi, Y., El Adnani, M., & Sadgal, M. (2015, March). The integration of augmented reality in the virtual learning environment for practical activities. In *2015 International Conference on Electrical and Information Technologies (ICEIT)* (pp. 363-368). IEEE. 10.1109/EITech.2015.7162960

Elkoubaiti, H., & Mrabet, R. (2018, May). A generic architecture of augmented and virtual reality in classrooms. In *2018 6th International Conference on Multimedia Computing and Systems (ICMCS)* (pp. 1-4). IEEE. 10.1109/ICMCS.2018.8525976

Erofeeva, M., & Klowait, N. O. (2021, May). The impact of virtual reality, Augmented reality, and interactive whiteboards on the attention management in secondary school STEM teaching. In *2021 7th International Conference of the Immersive Learning Research Network (iLRN)* (pp. 1-5). IEEE.

Fominykh, M., Wild, F., Klamma, R., Billinghurst, M., Costiner, L. S., Karsakov, A., ... Smolic, A. (2020). Model augmented reality curriculum. In *Proceedings of the Working Group Reports on Innovation and Technology in Computer Science Education* (pp. 131-149). 10.1145/3437800.3439205

Frutos-Pascual, M., Gale, C., Harrison, J. M., Creed, C., & Williams, I. (2021, August). Character input in augmented reality: An evaluation of keyboard position and interaction visualisation for head-mounted displays. In *IFIP Conference on Human-Computer Interaction* (pp. 480-501). Springer. 10.1007/978-3-030-85623-6_29

Gao, Y. F., Wang, H. Y., & Bian, X. N. (2016, July). Marker tracking for video-based augmented reality. In *2016 International Conference on Machine Learning and Cybernetics (ICMLC)* (Vol. 2, pp. 928-932). IEEE. 10.1109/ICMLC.2016.7873011

Gargrish, S., Mantri, A., & Kaur, D. P. (2020). Augmented reality-based learning environment to enhance teaching-learning experience in geometry education. *Procedia Computer Science*, *172*, 1039–1046. doi:10.1016/j.procs.2020.05.152

Garzotto, F., Torelli, E., Vona, F., & Aruanno, B. (2018, December). HoloLearn: Learning through mixed reality for people with cognitive disability. In *2018 IEEE International Conference on Artificial Intelligence and Virtual Reality (AIVR)* (pp. 189-190). IEEE. 10.1109/AIVR.2018.00042

Gasteiger, N., van der Veer, S. N., Wilson, P., & Dowding, D. (2022, March). Exploring how, for whom and in which contexts extended reality training 'works' in upskilling healthcare workers: A realist review. In *2022 IEEE Conference on Virtual Reality and 3D User Interfaces Abstracts and Workshops (VRW)* (pp. 734-735). IEEE. 10.1109/VRW55335.2022.00218

Geroimenko, V. (2022). *Augmented reality art* (3rd ed.). Springer. doi:10.1007/978-3-030-96863-2

Ghasemi, Y., Jeong, H., Choi, S. H., Park, K. B., & Lee, J. Y. (2022). Deep learning-based object detection in augmented reality: A systematic review. *Computers in Industry*, *139*(103661), 1–15. doi:10.1016/j.compind.2022.103661

Ghazwani, Y., & Smith, S. (2020, February). Interaction in augmented reality: Challenges to enhance user experience. In *Proceedings of the 2020 4th International Conference on Virtual and Augmented Reality Simulations* (pp. 39-44). 10.1145/3385378.3385384

Ghouaiel, N., Cieutat, J. M., & Jessel, J. P. (2014, April). Adaptive augmented reality: plasticity of augmentations. In *Proceedings of the 2014 Virtual Reality International Conference* (pp. 1-4). Academic Press.

Ghulamani, S., & Zareen, S. (2018, March). Educating students in remote areas using augmented reality. In *2018 International Conference on Computing, Mathematics and Engineering Technologies (iCoMET)* (pp. 1-6). IEEE. 10.1109/ICOMET.2018.8346350

Gonzalez, A. V., Koh, S., Kapalo, K., Sottilare, R., Garrity, P., Billinghurst, M., & LaViola, J. (2019, October). A comparison of desktop and augmented reality scenario based training authoring tools. In *2019 IEEE International Symposium on Mixed and Augmented Reality (ISMAR)* (pp. 1199 - 1200). IEEE. 10.1109/VR.2019.8797973

Grubert, J. (2023). Mixed Reality Interaction Techniques. In *Springer Handbook of Augmented Reality* (pp. 109–129). Springer International Publishing. doi:10.1007/978-3-030-67822-7_5

Gundala, D. S. A., Alamuri, S. S., Firdaus, A., & Kumar, G. K. (2022, February). Implementing augmented reality using OpenCV. In 2022 IEEE Delhi Section Conference (DELCON) (pp. 1-4). IEEE.

Guo, R., Cui, J., Zhao, W., Li, S., & Hao, A. (2021, March). Hand-by-hand mentor: An AR based training system for piano performance. In *2021 IEEE Conference on Virtual Reality and 3D User Interfaces Abstracts and Workshops (VRW)* (pp. 436-437). IEEE. 10.1109/VRW52623.2021.00100

Harrington, M. C. (2020, June). Connecting user experience to learning in an evaluation of an immersive, interactive, multimodal augmented reality virtual diorama in a natural history museum & the importance of story. In *2020 6th International Conference of the Immersive Learning Research Network (iLRN)* (pp. 70-78). IEEE. 10.23919/iLRN47897.2020.9155202

Hensen, B., & Klamma, R. (2020, July). Comparing authoring workflows and learning paths in Web & mixed reality environments. In *2020 IEEE 20th International Conference on Advanced Learning Technologies (ICALT)* (pp. 319-321). IEEE. 10.1109/ICALT49669.2020.00102

Hill, A., Barba, E., MacIntyre, B., Gandy, M., & Davidson, B. (2011, July). Mirror worlds: experimenting with heterogeneous AR. In *2011 International Symposium on Ubiquitous Virtual Reality* (pp. 9-12). IEEE. 10.1109/ISUVR.2011.28

Hiyama, A., Fujino, H., Kashiwagi, G., & Hirose, M. (2011, September). Ubiquitous augmented reality: expanding augmented reality environment with wireless tags and visible light communication projector. In *Proceedings of the 13th International Conference on Ubiquitous Computing* (pp. 597-598). 10.1145/2030112.2030231

Hossain, M. F., Barman, S., & Haque, A. B. (2019, October). Augmented reality for education; AR children's book. In TENCON 2019-2019 IEEE Region 10 Conference (TENCON) (pp. 2568-2571). IEEE.

Hou, H. T., & Lin, Y. C. (2017, July). The development and evaluation of an educational game integrated with augmented reality and virtual laboratory for chemistry experiment learning. In *2017 6th IIAI International Congress on Advanced Applied Informatics (IIAI-AAI)* (pp. 1005-1006). IEEE. 10.1109/IIAI-AAI.2017.14

Hughes, C. E., & Ingraham, K. M. (2016, March). *De-escalation training in an augmented virtuality space. In 2016 IEEE Virtual Reality (VR)*. IEEE.

Huynh, B., Orlosky, J., & Höllerer, T. (2019, March). In-situ labeling for augmented reality language learning. In *2019 IEEE Conference on Virtual Reality and 3D User Interfaces (VR)* (pp. 1606-1611). IEEE. 10.1109/VR.2019.8798358

Iatraki, G., Delimitros, M., Vrellis, I., & Mikropoulos, T. A. (2021, July). Augmented and virtual environments for students with intellectual disability: design issues in Science Education. In *2021 International Conference on Advanced Learning Technologies (ICALT)* (pp. 381-385). IEEE. 10.1109/ICALT52272.2021.00122

Ienaga, N., Bork, F., Meerits, S., Mori, S., Fallavollita, P., Navab, N., & Saito, H. (2016, September). First deployment of diminished reality for anatomy education. In *2016 IEEE International Symposium on Mixed and Augmented Reality (ISMAR-Adjunct)* (pp. 294-296). IEEE. 10.1109/ISMAR-Adjunct.2016.0099

Interactive Design Foundation. (2020). *Augmented reality—The past, the present and the future*. Retrieved Dec. 19, 2022, from https://www.interaction-design.org/literature/article/augmented-reality-the-past-the-present-and-the-future

Iqbal, M. Z., Mangina, E., & Campbell, A. G. (2019, October). Exploring the use of augmented reality in a kinesthetic learning application integrated with an intelligent virtual embodied agent. In *2019 IEEE International Symposium on Mixed and Augmented Reality Adjunct (ISMAR-Adjunct)* (pp. 12-16). IEEE. 10.1109/ISMAR-Adjunct.2019.00018

Irawati, S., Green, S., Billinghurst, M., Duenser, A., & Ko, H. (2006, October). " Move the couch where?": developing an augmented reality multimodal interface. In *2006 IEEE/ACM International Symposium on Mixed and Augmented Reality* (pp. 183-186). IEEE. 10.1109/ISMAR.2006.297812

Jain, K., & Choi, Y. M. (2020, July). Authoring interactions for tangible augmented reality. In *International Conference on Human-Computer Interaction* (pp. 43-50). Springer.

Jang, J., Ko, Y., Shin, W. S., & Han, I. (2021). Augmented reality and virtual reality for learning: An examination using an extended technology acceptance model. *IEEE Access : Practical Innovations, Open Solutions*, *9*, 6798–6809. doi:10.1109/ACCESS.2020.3048708

Johnson, A. S., & Sun, Y. (2013, March). *Exploration of spatial augmented reality on person. In 2013 IEEE Virtual Reality (VR)*. IEEE.

Kao, G. Y. M., & Ruan, C. A. (2022). Designing and evaluating a high interactive augmented reality system for programming learning. *Computers in Human Behavior*, *132*, 107245. doi:10.1016/j.chb.2022.107245

Kaur, D. P., Mantri, A., & Horan, B. (2020). Enhancing student motivation with use of augmented reality for interactive learning in engineering education. *Procedia Computer Science*, *172*, 881–885. doi:10.1016/j.procs.2020.05.127

Kaviyaraj, R., & Uma, M. (2022, January). Augmented reality application in classroom: An immersive taxonomy. In *2022 4th International Conference on Smart Systems and Inventive Technology (ICSSIT)* (pp. 1221-1226). IEEE.

Kiat, L. B., Ali, M. B., Abd Halim, N. D., & Ibrahim, H. B. (2016, October). Augmented reality, virtual learning environment and mobile learning in education: A comparison. In *2016 IEEE Conference on e-Learning, e-Management and e-Services (IC3e)* (pp. 23-28). IEEE. 10.1109/IC3e.2016.8009034

Klippel, A., Wallgrün, J. O., Masrur, A., Zhao, J., & LaFemina, P. (2019, March). Warping space and time-xR reviving educational tools of the 19th Century. In *2019 IEEE Conference on Virtual Reality and 3D User Interfaces (VR)* (pp. 1022-1023). IEEE. 10.1109/VR.2019.8797897

Knyazev, A., & Cheremukhina, J. (2022, May). Regulatory and methodological support for the mixed reality technology in education. In *2022 2nd International Conference on Technology Enhanced Learning in Higher Education (TELE)* (pp. 37-39). IEEE. 10.1109/TELE55498.2022.9801029

Kolstee, Y., & Van Eck, W. (2011, October). The augmented Van Gogh's: Augmented reality experiences for museum visitors. In *2011 IEEE International Symposium on Mixed and Augmented Reality-Arts, Media, and Humanities* (pp. 49-52). IEEE. 10.1109/ISMAR-AMH.2011.6093656

Krogh, P. G. (2000, April). Interactive rooms—augmented reality in an architectural perspective. In *Proceedings of DARE 2000 on Designing Augmented Reality Environments* (pp. 135-137). 10.1145/354666.354681

Krüger, J. M., Palzer, K., & Bodemer, D. (2022). Learning with augmented reality: Impact of dimensionality and spatial abilities. *Computers and Education Open*, *3*, 100065. doi:10.1016/j.caeo.2021.100065

Kumar, A., & Kumar, S. (2021). A new normal. *In the Proceedings of SIGGRAPh '21 Immersive Pavilion,* 1 – 2.

Kumar, V. V., Carberry, D., Beenfeldt, C., Andersson, M. P., Mansouri, S. S., & Gallucci, F. (2021). Virtual reality in chemical and biochemical engineering education and training. *Education for Chemical Engineers*, *36*, 143–153. doi:10.1016/j.ece.2021.05.002

Kundu, S. N., Muhammad, N., & Sattar, F. (2017, December). Using the augmented reality sandbox for advanced learning in geoscience education. In *2017 IEEE 6th International Conference on Teaching, Assessment, and Learning for Engineering (TALE)* (pp. 13-17). IEEE. 10.1109/TALE.2017.8252296

Kurniawan, M. P., Purwanto, A., & Mansur, M. F. (2019, November). Augmented Reality of Android-based learning media of sun and earth structure. In *2019 4th International Conference on Information Technology, Information Systems and Electrical Engineering (ICITISEE)* (pp. 85-90). IEEE. 10.1109/ICITISEE48480.2019.9003985

Lakshmiprabha, N. S., Santos, A., Mladenov, D., & Beltramello, O. (2014, September). [Poster] An augmented and virtual reality system for training autistic children. In *2014 IEEE International Symposium on Mixed and Augmented Reality (ISMAR)* (pp. 277-278). IEEE. 10.1109/ISMAR.2014.6948448

Lampropoulos, G., Keramopoulos, E., & Diamantaras, K. (2020). Enhancing the functionality of augmented reality using deep learning, semantic web and knowledge graphs: A review. *Visual Informatics*, *4*(1), 32–42. doi:10.1016/j.visinf.2020.01.001

Lang, T., Maclntyre, B., & Zugaza, I. J. (2008, March). *Massively multiplayer online worlds as a platform for augmented reality experiences. In 2008 IEEE Virtual Reality Conference*. IEEE.

Lee, W., Jeong, P., Choi, H., Kim, J., & Moon, B. (2022). Online illumination learning for interactive global illumination in augmented reality. *IEEE Access : Practical Innovations, Open Solutions*, *10*, 109498–109509. doi:10.1109/ACCESS.2022.3214516

Leiva, G., Grønbæk, J. E., Klokmose, C. N., Nguyen, C., Kazi, R. H., & Asente, P. (2021, October). Rapido: Prototyping Interactive AR Experiences through Programming by Demonstration. In *The 34th Annual ACM Symposium on User Interface Software and Technology* (pp. 626-637). ACM.

Li, G., Liu, Y., & Wang, Y. (2018, December). An empirical evaluation of labelling method in augmented reality. In *Proceedings of the 16th ACM SIGGRAPH International Conference on Virtual-Reality Continuum and its Applications in Industry* (pp. 1-9). 10.1145/3284398.3284422

Li, X. Z., Chen, C. C., & Kang, X. (2022, July). Research on Intangible cultural heritage education inheritance based on augmented reality technology. In *2022 IEEE International Conference on Consumer Electronics-Taiwan* (pp. 49-50). IEEE. 10.1109/ICCE-Taiwan55306.2022.9869146

Li, Y., Hicks, D., Lages, W. S., Lee, S. W., Sharma, A., & Bowman, D. A. (2021, March). ARCritique: Supporting remote design critique of physical artifacts through collaborative augmented reality. In *2021 IEEE Conference on Virtual Reality and 3D User Interfaces Abstracts and Workshops (VRW)* (pp. 585-586). IEEE. 10.1109/VRW52623.2021.00175

Liao, S. C., & Kuo, M. J. (2020, November). An analysis for motivating sketching practice with augmented reality in Da Vinci Eye. In *2020 International Symposium on Computer, Consumer and Control (IS3C)* (pp. 95-97). IEEE. 10.1109/IS3C50286.2020.00032

Liao, Y. T., Yu, C. H., & Wu, C. C. (2015, April). Learning geometry with augmented reality to enhance spatial ability. In *2015 International Conference on Learning and Teaching in Computing and Engineering* (pp. 221-222). IEEE. 10.1109/LaTiCE.2015.40

Lichty, P. (2020). Making inside the augment: Augmented reality and art/design education. In *Augmented Reality in Education* (pp. 261–278). Springer. doi:10.1007/978-3-030-42156-4_15

Liu, W., Lai, B., Wang, C., Bian, X., Yang, W., Xia, Y., ... Li, J. (2020, March). Learning to match 2d images and 3d lidar point clouds for outdoor augmented reality. In *2020 IEEE Conference on Virtual Reality and 3D User Interfaces Abstracts and Workshops (VRW)* (pp. 654-655). IEEE. 10.1109/VRW50115.2020.00178

Liying, F., Weng, N. G., Liyao, M., Maozheng, F., & Xiaoping, Q. (2021, December). Research on the application of augmented reality technology in the transformation and development of cultural and creative industries. In *International Conference on Intelligent Technologies for Interactive Entertainment* (pp. 295-308). Springer.

Lunding, M. S., Grønbæk, J. E. S., Bilstrup, K. E. K., Sørensen, M. L. S. K., & Petersen, M. G. (2022, April). ExposAR: Bringing augmented reality to the computational thinking agenda through a collaborative authoring tool. In *CHI Conference on Human Factors in Computing Systems* (pp. 1-14). 10.1145/3491102.3517636

Maguire, M. (2020, July). An exploration of low-fidelity prototyping methods for augmented and virtual reality. In *International Conference on Human-Computer Interaction* (pp. 470-481). Springer. 10.1007/978-3-030-49760-6_33

Maier, P., & Klinker, G. (2013, September). Augmented chemical reactions: An augmented reality tool to support chemistry teaching. In *2013 2nd Experiment@ International Conference (exp. at'13)* (pp. 164-165). IEEE.

Mangina, E. (2017, October). 3D learning objects for augmented/virtual reality educational ecosystems. In *2017 23rd International Conference on virtual system & Multimedia (VSMM)* (pp. 1-6). IEEE.

Maqableh, W. F., & Sidhu, M. S. (2010, March). From boards to augmented reality learning. In *2010 International Conference on Information Retrieval & Knowledge Management (CAMP)* (pp. 184-187). IEEE. 10.1109/INFRKM.2010.5466920

Mikropoulos, T. A., Delimitros, M., Gaintatzis, P., Iatraki, G., Stergiouli, A., Tsiara, A., & Kalyvioti, K. (2020, June). Acceptance and user experience of an augmented reality system for the simulation of sensory overload in children with autism. In *2020 6th International Conference of the Immersive Learning Research Network (iLRN)* (pp. 86-92). IEEE. 10.23919/iLRN47897.2020.9155113

Milgram, P., & Kishino, F. (1994). A taxonomy of mixed reality visual displays. *IEICE Transactions on Information and Systems*, *77*(12), 1321–1329.

Mohamed, B., & Mohamed, B. (2012, July). Proposition of a 3d pattern for e-learning augmented reality applications based on artoolkit library. In *International Conference on Education and e-Learning Innovations* (pp. 1-4). IEEE. 10.1109/ICEELI.2012.6360672

Molnár, G., & Sik, D. (2019, October). Smart devices, smart environments, smart students-A review on educational opportunities in virtual and augmented reality learning environments. In *2019 10th IEEE International Conference on Cognitive Infocommunications (CogInfoCom)* (pp. 495-498). IEEE. 10.1109/CogInfoCom47531.2019.9089984

Motejlek, J., & Alpay, E. (2021). Taxonomy of virtual and augmented reality applications in education. *IEEE Transactions on Learning Technologies*, *14*(3), 415–429. doi:10.1109/TLT.2021.3092964

Motokawa, Y., & Saito, H. (2006, October). Support system for guitar playing using augmented reality display. In *2006 IEEE/ACM International Symposium on Mixed and Augmented Reality* (pp. 243-244). IEEE. 10.1109/ISMAR.2006.297825

Murodillaevich, N. F., Eshpulatovich, G. U., & Kuvondik, K. (2020, November). Improve teaching and learning approach 3D primitives with Virtual and Augmented Reality. In *2020 International Conference on Information Science and Communications Technologies (ICISCT)* (pp. 1-7). IEEE. 10.1109/ICISCT50599.2020.9351418

Nanthanasit, A., & Wongta, N. (2018, February). Approach augmented reality real-time rendering for understanding light and shade in art education. In *2018 International Conference on Digital Arts, Media and Technology (ICDAMT)* (pp. 71-74). IEEE. 10.1109/ICDAMT.2018.8376498

Nguyen, V. T., & Dang, T. (2017, October). Setting up virtual reality and augmented reality learning environment in unity. In *2017 IEEE International Symposium on Mixed and Augmented Reality (ISMAR-Adjunct)* (pp. 315-320). IEEE. 10.1109/ISMAR-Adjunct.2017.97

Nie, G. Y., Liu, Y., Wang, C., Liu, Y., & Wang, Y. (2019, March). Exploring stereovision-based 3-D scene reconstruction for augmented reality. In *2019 IEEE Conference on Virtual Reality and 3D User Interfaces (VR)* (pp. 1100-1101). IEEE. 10.1109/VR.2019.8797778

Noorasura, A. D., & Sazilah, S. (2011, June). A model of mobile learning object design for concept comprehension using reciprocal teaching strategies and augmented reality. In *2011 IEEE International Conference on Computer Science and Automation Engineering* (Vol. 3, pp. 717-720). IEEE. 10.1109/CSAE.2011.5952775

Norouzi, N., Kim, K., Bruder, G., Bailenson, J. N., Wisniewski, P., & Welch, G. F. (2022). The advantages of virtual dogs over virtual people: Using augmented reality to provide social support in stressful situations. *International Journal of Human-Computer Studies*, *165*, 102838. doi:10.1016/j.ijhcs.2022.102838

Ortiz, J. S., Guevara, B. S., Espinosa, E. G., Santana, J., Tamayo, L. R., & Andaluz, V. H. (2020, June). 3D virtual content for education applications. In *2020 15th Iberian Conference on Information Systems and Technologies (CISTI)* (pp. 1-5). IEEE.

Osato, Y., & Koizumi, N. (2020). Compact optical system displaying mid-air images movable in depth by rotating light source and mirror. *Computers & Graphics*, *91*, 290–300. doi:10.1016/j.cag.2020.08.006

Oswald, P., Tost, J., & Wettach, R. (2014, November). The real augmented reality: real-time game editor in a spatial augmented environment. In *Proceedings of the 11th Conference on Advances in Computer Entertainment Technology* (pp. 1-4). 10.1145/2663806.2663853

Panessai, I. Y., Iksan, N., Zahari, S. A., Abdulbaqi, A. S., Modi Lakulu, M. M. B., Husin, M. R., . . . Wahyudiono, P. H. (2021, March). Learning Internet of Things by using augmented reality. In *2021 the 5th International Conference on Virtual and Augmented Reality Simulations* (pp. 17-20). 10.1145/3463914.3463926

Patil, S., Prabhu, C., Neogi, O., Joshi, A. R., & Katre, N. (2016, August). E-learning system using Augmented Reality. In *2016 International Conference on Computing Communication Control and automation (ICCUBEA)* (pp. 1-5). IEEE.

Pereira, L. F., da Silva, M. M., Roberto, R. A., Teichrieb, V., & Cavalcante, P. S. (2020, November). Virtual playground: An augmented reality application to improve English learning. In *2020 22nd Symposium on Virtual and Augmented Reality (SVR)* (pp. 83-91). IEEE.

Pérez-López, D., Contero, M., & Alcaniz, M. (2010, July). Collaborative development of an augmented reality application for digestive and circulatory systems teaching. In *2010 10th IEEE International Conference on Advanced Learning Technologies* (pp. 173-175). IEEE. 10.1109/ICALT.2010.54

Perez-Sanagustin, M., Hernández-Leo, D., Santos, P., Kloos, C. D., & Blat, J. (2014). Augmenting reality and formality of informal and non-formal settings to enhance blended learning. *IEEE Transactions on Learning Technologies*, *7*(2), 118–131. doi:10.1109/TLT.2014.2312719

Pranoto, H., & Panggabean, F. M. (2019). Increase the interest in learning by implementing augmented reality: Case studies studying rail transportation. *Procedia Computer Science*, *157*, 506–513. doi:10.1016/j.procs.2019.09.007

Radu, I., & Antle, A. (2017, March). Embodied learning mechanics and their relationship to usability of handheld augmented reality. In *2017 IEEE Virtual Reality Workshop on K-12 Embodied Learning through Virtual & Augmented Reality (KELVAR)* (pp. 1-5). IEEE. 10.1109/KELVAR.2017.7961561

Rambach, J., Pagani, A., & Stricker, D. (2023). Principles of Object Tracking and Mapping. In *Springer Handbook of Augmented Reality* (pp. 53–84). Springer International Publishing. doi:10.1007/978-3-030-67822-7_3

Resch, G., Manzone, J., Welsh, T., Nitsche, M., & Mazalek, A. (2021, July). Goal-directed reaching in real, augmented, and virtual environments. In *2021 International Conference on Advanced Learning Technologies (ICALT)* (pp. 398-400). IEEE. 10.1109/ICALT52272.2021.00127

Resnyansky, D., Billinghurst, M., & Lee, G. (2022, March). A tangible augmented reality programming learning environment for textual languages. In *2022 IEEE Conference on Virtual Reality and 3D User Interfaces Abstracts and Workshops (VRW)* (pp. 662-663). IEEE. 10.1109/VRW55335.2022.00182

Rodríguez, F. C., Dal Peraro, M., & Abriata, L. A. (2022). Online tools to easily build virtual molecular models for display in augmented and virtual reality on the web. *Journal of Molecular Graphics & Modelling*, *114*, 108164. doi:10.1016/j.jmgm.2022.108164 PMID:35325844

Rozinaj, G., Vančo, M., Vargic, R., Minárik, I., & Polakovič, A. (2018, June). Augmented/virtual reality as a tool of self-directed learning. In *2018 25th International Conference on Systems, Signals and Image Processing (IWSSIP)* (pp. 1-5). IEEE.

Salazar, J. L. H., Pacheco-Quispe, R., Cabeza, J. D., Salazar, M. J. H., & Cruzado, J. P. (2020, October). *Augmented reality for solar system learning. In 2020 IEEE ANDESCON*. IEEE.

Santos, M. E. C., Chen, A., Taketomi, T., Yamamoto, G., Miyazaki, J., & Kato, H. (2013). Augmented reality learning experiences: Survey of prototype design and evaluation. *IEEE Transactions on Learning Technologies*, *7*(1), 38–56. doi:10.1109/TLT.2013.37

Saritha, R. C., Mankad, U., Venkataswamy, G., & Bapu, S. B. (2018, December). An augmented reality ecosystem for learning environment. In *2018 IEEE International Conference on Advanced Networks and Telecommunications Systems (ANTS)* (pp. 1-6). IEEE. 10.1109/ANTS.2018.8710093

Saßmannshausen, S. M., Radtke, J., Bohn, N., Hussein, H., Randall, D., & Pipek, V. (2021, June). Citizen-Centered Design in Urban Planning: How Augmented Reality can be used in Citizen Participation Processes. In *Designing Interactive Systems Conference 2021* (pp. 250-265). 10.1145/3461778.3462130

Schraffenberger, H., & van der Heide, E. (2016, November). Multimodal augmented reality: The norm rather than the exception. In *Proceedings of the 2016 Workshop on Multimodal Virtual and Augmented Reality* (pp. 1-6). 10.1145/3001959.3001960

Scotto, F. (2022). Sculpting in augmented reality. In *International Conference on Human-Computer Interaction* (pp. 91-107). Springer.

Shanmugam, M., Sudha, M., Lavitha, K., Venkatesan, V. P., & Keerthana, R. (2019, March). Research opportunities on virtual reality and augmented reality: a survey. In *2019 IEEE International Conference on System, Computation, Automation and Networking (ICSCAN)* (pp. 1-6). IEEE. 10.1109/ICSCAN.2019.8878796

Shashaank, N., & Feiner, S. (2022, March). Synesthesia AR: Creating sound-to-color synesthesia in augmented reality. In *2022 IEEE Conference on Virtual Reality and 3D User Interfaces Abstracts and Workshops (VRW)* (pp. 874-875). IEEE.

Shen, S., Xu, K., Sotiriadis, M., & Wang, Y. (2022). Exploring the factors influencing the adoption and usage of augmented reality and virtual reality applications in tourism education within the context of COVID-19 pandemic. *Journal of Hospitality, Leisure, Sport and Tourism Education*, *30*, 100373. doi:10.1016/j.jhlste.2022.100373 PMID:35069015

Simon-Liedtke, J. T., & Baraas, R. C. (2022). The Need for Universal Design of eXtended Reality (XR) Technology in Primary and Secondary Education. In *International Conference on Human-Computer Interaction* (pp. 121-141). Springer. 10.1007/978-3-031-06015-1_9

Southgate, E., & Smith, S. P. (2017, March). Designing and conducting research using immersive technologies in schools: Seven observations. In *2017 IEEE Virtual Reality Workshop on K-12 Embodied Learning through Virtual & Augmented Reality (KELVAR)* (pp. 1-3). IEEE. 10.1109/KELVAR.2017.7961564

Stefan, P., Wucherer, P., Oyamada, Y., Ma, M., Schoch, A., Kanegae, M., & Navab, N. (2014, March). *An AR edutainment system supporting bone anatomy learning. In 2014 IEEE Virtual Reality (VR)*. IEEE.

Sun, R., Haraldsson, H., Zhao, Y., & Belongie, S. (2019, October). Anon-Emoji: An optical see-Through augmented reality system for children with autism spectrum disorders to promote understanding of facial expressions and emotions. In *2019 IEEE International Symposium on Mixed and Augmented Reality Adjunct (ISMAR-Adjunct)* (pp. 448-450). IEEE. 10.1109/ISMAR-Adjunct.2019.00052

Teixeira, N., Lahm, B., Peres, F. F. F., Mauricio, C. R. M., & Teixeira, J. M. (2021). Augmented reality on museums: The Ecomuseu Virtual Guide. *Proceedings of the SVR '21*, 147 – 156.

Tönnis, M., Klein, L., & Klinker, G. (2008, September). Perception thresholds for augmented reality navigation schemes in large distances. In *2008 7th IEEE/ACM International Symposium on Mixed and Augmented Reality* (pp. 189-190). IEEE. 10.1109/ISMAR.2008.4637360

Tripathi, S. (2019, October). Integration of virtual reality and augmented reality for immersive gaming and learning. In *2019 2nd International Conference on Power Energy, Environment and Intelligent Control (PEEIC)* (pp. 63-66). IEEE. 10.1109/PEEIC47157.2019.8976608

Uribe, J., Harmon, D., Laguna, B., & Courtier, J. (2022). Augmented-reality Enhanced Anatomy Learning (A-REAL): Assessing the utility of 3D holographic models for anatomy education. *Annals of 3D Printed Medicine*, 100090.

Vertucci, R., D'Onofrio, S., Ricciardi, S., & De Nino, M. (2023). History of Augmented Reality. In *Springer Handbook of Augmented Reality* (pp. 35–50). Springer International Publishing. doi:10.1007/978-3-030-67822-7_2

Vinumol, K. P., Chowdhury, A., Kambam, R., & Muralidharan, V. (2013, May). Augmented reality based interactive text book: An assistive technology for students with learning disability. In *2013 XV Symposium on Virtual and Augmented Reality* (pp. 232-235). IEEE. 10.1109/SVR.2013.26

Vrellis, I., Delimitros, M., Chalki, P., Gaintatzis, P., Bellou, I., & Mikropoulos, T. A. (2020, July). Seeing the unseen: User experience and technology acceptance in Augmented Reality science literacy. In *2020 IEEE 20th International Conference on Advanced Learning Technologies (ICALT)* (pp. 333-337). IEEE.

Wang, J., Liang, H. N., Monteiro, D. V., Xu, W., Chen, H., & Chen, Q. (2020, November). Real-time detection of simulator sickness in virtual reality games based on players' psychophysiological data during gameplay. In *2020 IEEE International Symposium on Mixed and Augmented Reality Adjunct (ISMAR-Adjunct)* (pp. 247-248). IEEE. 10.1109/ISMAR-Adjunct51615.2020.00071

Wang, Z., Nguyen, C., Asente, P., & Dorsey, J. (2021, May). DistanciAR: Authoring site-specific augmented reality experiences for remote environments. In *Proceedings of the 2021 CHI Conference on Human Factors in Computing Systems* (pp. 1-12). 10.1145/3411764.3445552

Wei, X., Weng, D., Liu, Y., & Wang, Y. (2016, March). *A tour guiding system of historical relics based on augmented reality. In 2016 IEEE Virtual Reality (VR).* IEEE.

Wientapper, F., Wuest, H., & Kuijper, A. (2011, May). Reconstruction and accurate alignment of feature maps for augmented reality. In *2011 International Conference on 3D Imaging, Modeling, Processing, Visualization and Transmission* (pp. 140-147). IEEE. 10.1109/3DIMPVT.2011.25

Wild, F. (2016). The future of learning at the workplace is augmented reality. *Computer*, *49*(10), 96–98. doi:10.1109/MC.2016.301

Willemsen, P., Jaros, W., McGregor, C., Downs, E., Berndt, M., & Passofaro, A. (2018, March). Memory task performance across augmented and virtual reality. In *2018 IEEE Conference on Virtual Reality and 3D User Interfaces (VR)* (pp. 723-724). IEEE. 10.1109/VR.2018.8446457

Xu, M., Murcia-López, M., & Steed, A. (2017, March). *Object location memory error in virtual and real environments. In 2017 IEEE Virtual Reality (VR).* IEEE.

Yadav, S., & Aalam, Z. (2021, October). Meta-analysis of learning strategies in teaching using: Augmented reality technology. In *2021 4th International Conference on Recent Developments in Control, Automation & Power Engineering (RDCAPE)* (pp. 224-229). IEEE.

Yang, F., Caballero, J. M., & Juanatas, R. A. (2022). Designing of Chinese ancient poetry app based on iOS platform augmented reality and machine learning. *Proceedings of the 2022 7th International Conference on Business and Industrial Research,* 285 – 288.

Yang, M. T., Liao, W. C., & Shih, Y. C. (2013, July). VECAR: Virtual English classroom with markerless augmented reality and intuitive gesture interaction. In *2013 IEEE 13th International Conference on Advanced Learning Technologies* (pp. 439-440). IEEE.

Yount, Z. F., Kass, S. J., & Arruda, J. E. (2022). Route learning with augmented reality navigation aids. *Transportation Research Part F: Traffic Psychology and Behaviour*, *88*, 132–140. doi:10.1016/j.trf.2022.05.019

Yu, J. (2017). A light-field journey to virtual reality. *IEEE MultiMedia*, *24*(2), 104–112. doi:10.1109/MMUL.2017.24

Zhang, H., Cui, Y., Shan, H., Qu, Z., Zhang, W., Tu, L., & Wang, Y. (2020, June). Hotspots and trends of virtual reality, augmented reality and mixed reality in education field. In *2020 6th International Conference of the Immersive Learning Research Network (iLRN)* (pp. 215-219). IEEE. 10.23919/iLRN47897.2020.9155170

Zhang, Z. (2020, November). Understanding physical common sense in symmetrical reality. In *2020 IEEE International Symposium on Mixed and Augmented Reality Adjunct (ISMAR-Adjunct)* (pp. 275-276). IEEE. 10.1109/ISMAR-Adjunct51615.2020.00077

Zhao, Y., Forte, M., & Kopper, R. (2018, March). VR touch museum. In *2018 IEEE Conference on Virtual Reality and 3D User Interfaces (VR)* (pp. 741-742). IEEE. 10.1109/VR.2018.8446581

Zhou, X., Tang, L., Lin, D., & Han, W. (2020). Virtual & augmented reality for biological microscope in experiment education. *Virtual Reality & Intelligent Hardware*, *2*(4), 316–329. doi:10.1016/j.vrih.2020.07.004

Zhou, Y., Chen, J., & Wang, M. (2022). A meta-analytic review on incorporating virtual and augmented reality in museum learning. *Educational Research Review*, *36*, 100454. doi:10.1016/j.edurev.2022.100454

Zuo, T., Spek, E. D., Hu, J., & Birk, M. V. (2021, December). Investigating the motivational effect of fantasy and similarity through avatar identification in AR game-based learning. In *International Conference on Intelligent Technologies for Interactive Entertainment* (pp. 279-294). Springer, Cham.

KEY TERMS AND DEFINITIONS

2D: Two-dimensional space, often specified on a flat plane with x (horizontal) and y (vertical) axes and a coordinate system to indicate location on the plane.

3D: Three-dimensional space, often specified as comprised of the x, y, and z axes; volumetric space representing with higher fidelity the actual world (in theory).

4D: 2D or 3D visuals including motion (with motion as the fourth dimension).

Artificial Lighting: The illusion of a light field (whether natural or artificial or other) using digital illumination techniques (and algorithms enabling light interactions with various surface types and varying real-world shapes).

Augmented Reality (AR): The uses of digital virtual objects in physical space to annotate or enrich human perception in the physical space (or may require a headset to engage an augmented world in a physical space).

Augmented Reality Learning Experience (ARLE): The subjective and objective learning experience from designed augmented reality scenarios and scenes and interactions.

Augmented Reality Learning Object (ARLO): A base unit of an AR digital learning object.

Augmented Reality Virtual Reality (AR/VR): The inclusion of both VR and AR as a mixed reality solution for particular objectives (including for learning).

Authoring Tool: Software used for the creation and editing of digital objects of various types (with particular technical standards).

Bodystorming: A pre-prototype walk-through of a scene or scenario for augmented reality or virtual reality in order to enable quick ideation through spatial interactions (Maguire, July 2020, p. 472); an idea somewhat related to "brainstorming" albeit with a focus on embodied creativity or innovation.

Contour: An outline, often of a shape, and often in reference to a curved line; the general form or structure of a thing.

Contrast: The difference between the lightness and darkness of particular colors (based on particular lighting conditions).

Curve: A non-linear line, a line or stroke or outline with curvature.

Digital Learning Object: A discrete designed entity used for learning, including augmented reality (AR) learning objects or "AR-LOs."

Diminished Reality: The removal of parts of physical reality from the observer view in real time through digital occlusion (but not considered part of "augmented reality" but rather part of "mediated reality" (Broll, 2022, p. 321); taking away real-world light information instead of adding digital objects per se, introducing the illusion of "negative space" in some senses).

Disembodied Learning: Incorporeal learning; non-physically present sorts of learning (historically applied to distance or remote learning); learning through symbols and not direct experience with the actual depicted object; indirect non-experiential learning.

Edge: The outside limit of an area or object; a line; a stroke.

Embodied Learning: Experiencing the learning through the senses and proprioception (awareness of the body's positioning, from within) and interoception / enteroception (awareness of the body's internal state, through the unconscious, subconscious, and conscious) through the body.

Extended Reality (XR): A term which includes "virtual reality" and "augmented reality" and "mixed reality"; sometimes "eXtended reality."

Feature Map: The connecting of particular variables to matched values or dimensions or qualities.

Haptic Devices: Input and / or output devices that use touch (perhaps include pressure, temperature, and other factors).

Haptic Gloves: Wearable interactive device to simulates actual touch through haptic sensors, an input and output device.

Head-Mounted Device (HMD): Immersive VR or AR headset, sometimes head-mounted display.

Illumination: The lighting, available light.

Immersive AR (IAR): The blending of the real and the virtual for a full-sensory embodied experience that is perceive as full-surround and engaging.

Immersive VR or AR Headset: Head-mounted display, head-mounted device.

Line: A stroke, which may be continuous or broken, varying or consistent in weight (width), and with other features.

Marker: A visual indicator that situates or positions the virtual object in 3D space.

Markerlessness: A type of AR that does not require a marker (such as a QR code) to be scanned in order to appear; such AR requires the launch of an app or web-based AR in a location (and some without a need for a location) to show the digital elements.

Mesh: An interlaced overlay of columns and rows representing the external geometric shape for modeling (may be in 2d or 3d), by adjusting mesh points, handle points, textures, gradients, applied colors, and other aspects.

Mid-Air Images: Imaging technologies that show moving computer graphics (CGs) in real space.

Mixed Reality (MR): A term which refers to the combination of the physical-real and the augmented or diminished or virtual real (based on technical and other mediation).

Mobile Augmented Reality Learning Systems (MARLS): Systems designed for learning through mobile augmented reality (using mobile devices to project the digital augmentations).

Mobile Augmented Reality System (MARS): AR mapped to mobile settings (Chang & Tan, Dec. 2010, p. 20).

Mobile Learning: A form of ubiquitous "anytime anywhere" learning using mobile devices to access the learning materials, activities, interactivity, and other features.

Model: A visual representation of an object, phenomena, event, scene, person, or some combination.

Motion: Movement, changes over time.

Multi-Object-Oriented Augmented Reality (MOOAR) System: A system that enables the building and deployment of a location-based adaptive mobile learning environment for the setup of augmented reality scenarios and objects (for people's experiences).

Node (Nodes): Vertex, a point at which lines start or end or bend; a point in space; a point at which lines intersect.

Non-Playable Characters (NPC): Scripted synthetic agents that spawn in an AR scene and "interact" with human users (at somehow perform or communicate to the human users).

Occlusion: The blocking or obstructing of one object with another, with the closest object to a viewer blocking what is behind.

Point-of-View (POV): Perspective, line-of-sight, angle-of-view.

Polygon: A 2D or 3D closed shape (in geometry).

Position: The location of an AR or virtual object in relation to another object or floor.

Pre-Rendering: Adding color, texture, and details to a 2d or 3d wireframe for evocative images on a screen or in ambient space—done ahead of time of the actual viewing or consumption.

Primitive: A core shape or polygon or element that is used to build more complex objects and forms and virtual or augmented environments.

QR (Quick Response) Code: "A machine-readable code consisting of an array of black and white squares, typically used for storing URLs or other information for reading by the camera on a smartphone" (per Google dictionary).

QR (Quick Response) Marker: A two-dimensional machine-readable code that may be used by an augmented reality program to display particular designed artifacts or other elements based on the embedded information there.

Registration: The accurate recognition of an object with a smartphone camera or other device.

Rendering: Adding color and texture to a 2d or 3d wireframe to create visuals on a screen or in ambient space, sometimes referred to as "painting in" or "spawning."

Segmented Reality: The combination of real and virtual reality to create a sense of different and "divided" elements that come together in a more coherent experience (without a full emulation of reality) (De Michelis, De Paoli, Pluchinotta, & Susani, April 2000, p. 82).

Self-Referential Encoding: Learning new information such as about the human body by seeing AR visualizations projected on their own bodies (in a form of embodied learning).

Simulator Sickness: A sense of nausea or dizziness from engaging in virtual reality or augmented reality or mixed reality (or some combination).

Sound Design: The planning for sound effects, voice overs, and other sound effects for a 3d or 4d sequence.

Spatial Augmented Reality (SAR): The overlay of digitally projected visuals on physical objects and scenes (vs. using mobile devices, monitors, head-mounted displays, hand-helds, or other such objects).

Spatial Augmented Reality on Person (SARP): The overlay of digitally projected visuals on people's physical bodies (such as skeletons, organs, and other representations of the internal physical state).

Strong Augmented Reality Paradigm: An approach involving changing "the space perception of its inhabitants so that they cannot distinguish the physical base of their place from its virtual extension" (De Michelis, De Paoli, Pluchinotta, & Susani, April 2000, p. 82).

Tabletop Display: The projection or display of augmented reality scenes and objects on a table surface

Tangible Augmented Reality (TAR): Virtual components are registered to physical ones, and the virtual elements may be "manipulated by interacting with physical components in the real world" (Jain & Choi, July 2020, p. 43).

Texture: A visual pattern indicating the surface feel of a substance.

UV Mapping: A spatio-physical mapping from 3d to 2d (and vice versa) in which the x-axis is "U" and the vertical y-axis is the "Y" (in order to enable proper application of texturing to a 3d shape at the level of granularity and focus that makes visual sense) ("UV mapping," Nov. 23, 2022); has been replaced by some other technologies and approaches, such as tri-planar mapping.

UV Position: The mapping of 3D to 2D and vice versa to enable the painting of textures and colors on a 3d surface in a way that is visually appropriate for the 3d shape or object or environment.

VAR: Virtual and augmented reality.

Virtual Reality (VR): A 3D simulated environment or immersive virtual world that evokes a space, personages, physics, and objects, among others; VR may be passive or interactive.

Virtual Reality Augmented Reality (VR/AR): The inclusion of both VR and AR as a mixed reality solution for particular objectives (including for learning).

Weak Augmented Reality Paradigm: An approach involving inducing "people to behave as if their place were transformed even if the physical space where they are located does not seem changed" such as remoting into a workstation or remote lab (De Michelis, De Paoli, Pluchinotta, & Susani, April 2000, p. 82); a partial AR experience that does not change the full perceptual surround of the individual or group in the AR experience.

XR (Extended Reality): A term which includes "virtual reality" and "augmented reality" and "mixed reality"; sometimes "eXtended reality."

Z-Axis: The axis on which the third-dimension depends indicating physical depth.

APPENDICES

NOTE: The review of the literature involved various brand names for technologies related to augmented reality (AR), including hardware (head-mounted displays, projectors, computers, and others), software (software development kits, plug-ins, and others), and various techniques for designing, developing, and deploying AR contents. Given the state of the field, the changes are fast, and the validity of more specific information seems fairly out-of-date for this work, so the information is not included. Likewise, technological specifications are in flux. The various types of AR and their respective capabilities also vary.

Derby and Chaparro AR and MR Usability Heuristic Checklist

An augmented reality and mixed reality usability heuristic checklist may be valuable for readers, so the Derby & Chaparro checklist is included here verbatim and in its entirety.

Unboxing & Set-up

1. Is the unboxing process a positive experience?
2. When the user interacts with the device for the first time, are they introduced to the user interface, basic interaction methods, and basic features/content?
3. Is a quick start guide available with the device?
4. Is a call to action (QR code, instructions to use AR, etc.) clearly marked in the physical space?

Help & Documentation

5. Is there the option of a tutorial upon first use of the device and/or application?
6. Does the tutorial explain all of the necessary actions/mechanics to use the device and/or application?
7. Is the tutorial easy to understand?
8. Are required interactions easy to learn?
9. Is help or documentation easily accessible for the application?
10. Are instructions easy to understand?
11. Do instructions provide actionable feedback?
12. If auditory instructions are given, do these instructions match what the user is seeing in the application?
13. Are error messages easy to understand?
14. Do error messages provide actionable feedback?
15. Does the device's user interface and / or application avoid irreversible errors?
16. Is there a way for the user to report errors or crashes to the developer?

Cognitive Overload

17. Is the user eased into the virtual environment?
18. Does the device's user interface and / or application avoid clutter, as appropriate?
19. Does the device's user interface and / or application avoid large amounts of text? (Derby & Chaparro, 2022, p. 182)

What the Bard AI Suggests for Applications of Augmented Reality in Learning

Finally, as a nod to the times, it may be beneficial to elicit feedback from a text- and image-based generative AI, Bard, by Google. The prompt was the following: "what sorts of particular learning is augmented reality using mobile devices good for?"

The response is as follows presented verbatim:

"Augmented reality (AR) is a technology that superimposes a computer-generated image on a user's view of the real world, thus providing a composite view. AR can be used in a variety of learning applications, including:

- Science and math: AR can be used to visualize complex concepts in science and math, such as the solar system or the circulatory system. For example, an AR app could allow students to see a 3D model of the solar system orbiting around the sun, or to see a virtual heart beating inside a human chest.
- History and geography: AR can be used to bring historical events and places to life. For example, an AR app could allow students to see a Roman legionnaire marching through the streets of ancient Rome, or to see a virtual map of the American Civil War battlefield at Gettysburg.
- Language learning: AR can be used to help students learn new languages by providing them with real-world context for the words and phrases they are learning. For example, an AR app could allow students to see a virtual Spanish-speaking shopkeeper or a virtual French-speaking restaurant waiter.
- Art and design: AR can be used to help students learn about art and design by providing them with interactive tools that allow them to create their own artworks. For example, an AR app could allow students to design their own virtual sculptures or to paint their own virtual landscapes.
- Engineering and manufacturing: AR can be used to help students learn about engineering and manufacturing by providing them with interactive simulations that allow them to design and build their own virtual products. For example, an AR app could allow students to design their own virtual car or to build their own virtual house.

"AR is a powerful tool that can be used to enhance learning in a variety of ways. By providing students with a more interactive and engaging learning experience, AR can help them to learn more effectively.

"Here are some of the benefits of using AR in learning:

- Engagement: AR can be very engaging for students, as it allows them to interact with the content in a more realistic and interactive way.
- Retention: AR can help students to retain information better, as they are more likely to remember something that they have seen and interacted with.
- Transference: AR can help students to transfer their learning to real-world situations, as they are able to see how the concepts they are learning apply to the real world.
- Collaboration: AR can be used to facilitate collaboration between students, as they can work together to create and explore AR content.

"If you are looking for a way to make your learning more engaging, effective, and memorable, then AR is a great option to consider."

Chapter 4
Enhancing E-Orientation Platform Usage via the Metaverse:
An Extended TAM Approach for Moroccan University Students

Rachida Ihya
https://orcid.org/0009-0009-2098-9657
Faculty of Sciences Ben M'Sick, Hassan II University, Casablanca, Morocco

Mohammed Ait Daoud
https://orcid.org/0000-0002-8627-4429
Faculty of Sciences Ben M'Sick, Hassan II University, Casablanca, Morocco

Tarek Ihya
https://orcid.org/0009-0001-7263-3478
Faculty of Sciences Ben M'Sick, Hassan II University, Casablanca, Morocco

ABSTRACT

This chapter seeks to foster e-orientation platform acceptance among Moroccan students within the context of the evolving Metaverse. The authors focused on the Faculty of Sciences Ben M'Sick, employing meta-analytic methods to gather quantitative data through a student questionnaire survey. The analyses, performed using Python, revealed that perceived ease of use, usefulness, quality, and trust significantly impact the intention to use an e-orientation platform in the Metaverse. These insights guided the authors to design an extended technology acceptance model (TAM) specifically tailored to e-orientation platforms in the Metaverse, aiming to meet the needs and expectations of students, parents, and guidance counselors. The study underscores the potential of the Metaverse in addressing the inherent challenges of e-orientation systems and highlights the importance of user perception in the effective design and acceptance of e-orientation platforms.

DOI: 10.4018/979-8-3693-1034-2.ch004

1. INTRODUCTION

The evolution of Information and Communication Technologies (ICT) has catalyzed a transformation in how we approach educational guidance and counseling. One major shift is the emergence of the "E-orientation" concept, which has transitioned traditional academic and professional orientation from an in-person process to an online one, using various digital tools. This movement aligns with the needs and preferences of young individuals who demand modern, innovative tools to facilitate their educational choices and aid in strategic development (Boulahcen, 2005).

One such innovative tool currently gaining considerable attention in the field of ICT is the metaverse. Although not a novel concept, the metaverse had a significant surge in popularity and interest when Mark Zuckerberg announced Facebook's Metaverse project in October 2021. This announcement stimulated intense curiosity among educators, students, and researchers, who saw the potential of the metaverse to enhance the social aspects of learning and teaching, creating immersive and interactive virtual environments (García-Pazo, Lopez, Coll, Moreno, & Brogi, 2023; Ripka, Tiede, Grafe, & Latoschik, 2020; Wiederhold, 2022).

The term "metaverse" combines the prefix "meta", signifying transcendence, with "universe", referring to a virtual environment parallel to and interconnected with the physical world (L.-H. Lee et al., 2021). It represents an ecosystem that fuses both physical and virtual worlds, facilitating immersive experiences, collaboration, and interactive social experiences. This fusion creates a new paradigm that could dramatically reshape the e-orientation landscape.

However, implementing the metaverse and other ICT tools in the e-orientation process presents unique institutional and methodological challenges. At an institutional level, the requirement for training to master these innovative tools may not be fully acknowledged or supported by major education stakeholders like the Ministry of National Education. This gap in support and perception can hamper the successful integration of these tools into the e-orientation system.

Methodologically, the validation of information contained within these digital platforms presents another hurdle. Current e-orientation platforms may overwhelm students with an abundance of information, leading to potential misdirection in their orientation choices. With scant validation studies conducted on these platforms, the relevance of the information they offer remains uncertain, adding to the complexity of the orientation process (Abouhanifa, Benmadani, Khalfaoui, Hanini, & Kabbaj, 2008).

Today, the current research on the acceptance of Moroccan electronic guidance systems are relate to the "Meta-model of e-orientation platforms" and "Modernization of a domain e-orientation meta-model" (Guerss et al., 2015; zahra, Mohammed, Khadija, Mohammed, & Abdelouahed, 2015). However, a few research that focused on the acceptance prediction model for the electronic guidance systems has been conducted before (Ihya, Aitdaoud, Namir, Guerss, & Haddani, 2020; Ihya, Namir, Elfilali, Guerss, & Daoud, 2019; Ihya, Namir, Filali, Daoud, & Guerss, 2019).

Our research aims to address these challenges by developing an extended Technology Acceptance Model (TAM). The TAM is designed to predict and explain the usage intentions of e-orientation platforms, incorporating variables such as perceived usefulness, perceived ease of use, and intent to use. We aim to extend this model to include factors such as socio-demographic and social aspects, system and information quality, experience, risk, and other significant variables affecting platform acceptance.

In our study, we specifically focus on enhancing the user experience and acceptance of e-orientation platforms through the integration of the metaverse. We believe that the immersive and interactive features of the metaverse could serve as a major factor in improving user acceptance and satisfaction, thereby revolutionizing the e-orientation system.

We evaluate these hypotheses using the Moroccan e-orientation platform, orientation-chabab.com. This platform was chosen based on a previous comparative study between Moroccan e-orientation platforms (Fatima-zahra & Khadija, 2016).The data for our study was gathered through a questionnaire distributed to a sample of 608 students from the Ben M'Sick Faculty of Sciences, allowing us to gauge their perception and acceptance of this platform.

The subsequent steps in our research involve the preparation and analysis of data, followed by testing the extended TAM model. We aim to validate the proposed relationships between the various factors and user acceptance, which will allow us to understand the role of the metaverse in improving the e-orientation system.

The incorporation of the Metaverse into the e-orientation system presents a promising opportunity to revolutionize the way students make educational and career decisions. As we delve into the factors influencing the acceptance of Moroccan electronic guidance systems and the potential of the metaverse, we aim to provide valuable insights to enhance the e-orientation experience for students and contribute to the broader development of efficient, effective e-orientation systems.

2. LITERATURE REVIEW

The literature extensively examines various theoretical models of technology acceptance that have been widely employed in information systems research to explain individuals' acceptance of new technologies. One prominent model among these is the Technology Acceptance Model (TAM), which is recognized as the most commonly used and suitable model for elucidating the acceptance of information systems by individuals (Davis, 1989a; Legris, Ingham, & Collerette, 2003).

The TAM, initially proposed by Davis in 1985, provides an explanation and prediction of the usage of information technologies, drawing upon the Theory of Reasoned Action (TRA). It encompasses two main influencing variables that determine an individual's acceptance of information technology: perceived usefulness (PU) and perceived ease of use (PEOU).

Perceived usefulness refers to the extent to which an individual believes that utilizing a particular system would enhance their job performance. On the other hand, perceived ease of use pertains to the degree to which an individual believes that using a particular system would be effortless. These two factors play a crucial role in shaping an individual's acceptance of information technology according to the TAM.Figure 1 illustrates the Technology Acceptance Model (TAM) (Davis, 1985) (Hill, Fishbein, & Ajzen, 1977).

The TAM has been extensively applied in numerous studies to predict users' intention to accept new technologies across various sectors. As identified in the review conducted by (Yousafzai, Foxall, & Pallister, 2007a, 2007b), the TAM serves as a valuable model for identifying gaps in understanding and providing guidelines for implementing effective management strategies.

However, according to Bagozzi (Bagozzi, 2007), the extension of the theoretical foundations of the TAM is considered to be too limited. As a result, a multitude of models, derived from the TAM, have been proposed that incorporate additional external and moderating variables. These models range from TAM2, as depicted in the above figure, to the more recent UTAUT2 Unified Model. These extended models aim to provide a more comprehensive understanding of technology acceptance by incorporating various factors beyond the original TAM framework.

The advent of the Metaverse, a new and immersive form of technology that merges physical and virtual realities, prompts an extension of these models to explore its acceptance. The concept of Metaverse, once a theme in science fiction, is now increasingly associated with educational and social applications (Duan et al., 2021, 2021; Knox, 2022; Ning et al., 2023; Wiederhold, 2022). The integration of Metaverse technologies into e-orientation platforms, for example, provides opportunities for more immersive and interactive learning experiences. Yet, empirical studies on the acceptance of the Metaverse, particularly in the context of e-orientation platforms, are limited.

Figure 1. Final version of the technology acceptance model (Venkatesh & Davis, 1996a)

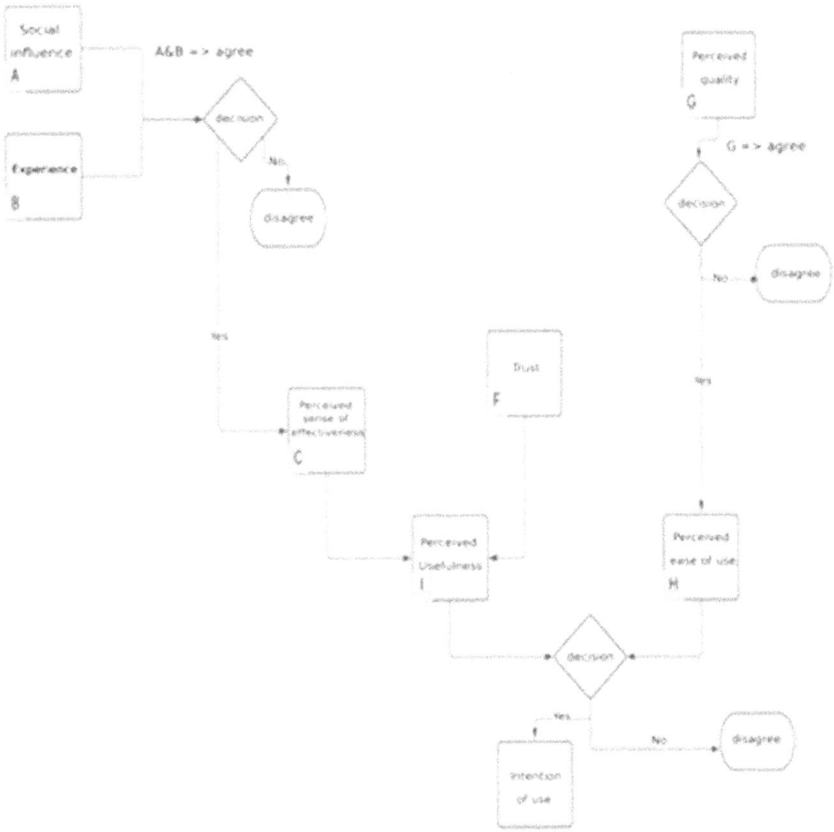

3. HYPOTHETICAL MODEL OF OUR RESEARCH (EXTENDED TAM)

Davis' Technology Acceptance Model (TAM) is a widely recognized tool for comprehending technology acceptance, emphasizing perceived usefulness and perceived ease of use as pivotal determinants for accepting new technologies (Davis, 1985). To understand individuals' behavior towards orientation systems, it's critical to examine factors influencing the acceptance of these systems. Our extended model, which includes extra external variables, provides a more thorough understanding of electronic orientation system acceptance (Davis, 1989a).

Understanding individuals' behavior towards new technologies requires considering the social aspect's significant impact. Social influence involves how others' actions shape an individual's behavior (Hu, Lin, & Chen, 2005; Yi & Hwang, 2003). Other research confirms the role of social influence in technology acceptance (Bonn, Kim, Kang, & Cho, 2015; EL-Shinnawy, Badawi, & Nassar, 2010), emphasizing its effect on perceived ease of use.

Trust is increasingly viewed as a key barrier preventing students from embracing e-guidance platforms. Trust influences technology's perceived usefulness and the behavioral intention to adopt it (Koufaris & Hampton-Sosa, 2004; Pavlou, 2003). Therefore, establishing trust is paramount for effective e-guidance platform utilization.

Individuals' responses to new technologies like E-orientation platforms are influenced by their prior experiences (Legris et al., 2003). This highlights the significance of prior experience in understanding attitudes towards E-orientation platform adoption.

Our research fills a gap by investigating perceived quality and perceived risk's impact on the intention to use the E-orientation platform (Cox & Rich, 1964). Additionally, we explore how perceived efficiency influences users' acceptance of the platform, an aspect previously less examined within the TAM framework (Downey et al., 2006; Strong, 2006).

In conclusion, our study expands the TAM by incorporating additional variables such as experience, social influence, perceived risk, perceived quality, and trust. This new model enhances our understanding of technology acceptance factors.

4. RESEARCH METHODS

In our study, we employed a meta-analytical approach, choosing the Faculty of Sciences Ben M'Sick as our research site due to its substantial post-baccalaureate student population and lack of an integrated orientation platform. We gathered data via interviews with volunteer students across all years, providing insights into e-orientation system acceptance. The qualitative data was subsequently analyzed using Python, employing descriptive and inferential methods.

4.1 Sample

The selection of the Faculty of Sciences Ben M'Sick as the study field was based on several factors. Firstly, the faculty has a substantial population of new post-baccalaureate students, which presents an excellent opportunity to conduct a comprehensive study encompassing a diverse range of participants. Additionally, the absence of an integrated orientation platform within the faculty makes it an ideal setting to examine the acceptance of the e-orientation system.

4.2 Data Collection

To gather data for our research, we conducted interviews with students in their first, second, and third years of study at the Ben M'Sick Faculty of Science. These students willingly volunteered to participate in the experiment, contributing valuable insights into their perceptions and acceptance of the e-orientation system.

By employing this methodology, we aim to obtain a deeper understanding of the factors influencing the acceptance of the e-orientation system among students at the Ben M'Sick Faculty of Sciences.

We selected the survey method as the primary approach for data collection, utilizing an applied questionnaire among students at the Ben M'Sick Faculty of Sciences. The questionnaire was administered in two formats:

- Online Distribution: We distributed a link to the questionnaire through "Facebook" and "WhatsApp" groups composed of students. Respondents were directed to a web page hosting the questionnaire, where they provided their answers using check boxes and drop-down buttons. The questionnaire was accompanied by a cover letter explaining the research purposes and objectives. Upon completion, respondents clicked the "Submit" button, and their answers were automatically received and stored in our site's database. A thank you message was displayed immediately to prevent multiple submissions.
- Individual Interviews: In addition to the online survey, we conducted individual interviews with each participant. These interviews were carried out by members of our research team. The questionnaire served as a guide for the interviews, ensuring consistency in the data collected. On average, the completion time for the questionnaire was approximately 18 minutes per respondent.

By employing both online distribution and individual interviews, we aimed to gather comprehensive data on the acceptance of the e-orientation system from students at the Ben M'Sick Faculty of Sciences. The combination of these methods allowed us to collect a wide range of perspectives and insights.

The survey was conducted during the registration period for first-year, second-year, and third-year students in 2022 and 2023. A total of 622 students participated in the survey. However, 14 responses were deemed incomplete and were subsequently excluded from the analysis. As a result, a final sample of 608 respondents was selected for the study.

4.3 Data Analysis

Our final sample consists of 608 students: 306 men (50.3%) and 302 women (49.7%). Men are slightly more numerous than women (46%) distributed respectively: 477 single (78.5%), 123 married (20.2%),3 widowers (0.5%), and 5 divorced (0.8%) whose ages varies between 18 and 35 with an average age of 26.5 and a standard deviation 0.943. We note that 40.3% of respondents are between the ages of 25 and 35.

Table 1 shows the presentation of participants by age and educational level. The age of the participants reflects that normally expected of first-year students: 42 of the students under the age of 18,85 of the students aged 18 to 20 (except for less than 0.2% of the students aged 21 to 24). As for second-year students: 216 responded to our survey, 43 of them are aged 18 to 20 and 173 students aged 21 to 24. In contrast, there are 211 in the third year aged 21 to 24 and 34 between 25 and 35.

Table 1. Age educational level*

		Education Level			Total
		First Year	Second Year	Third Year (Bachelor)	
Age	Under 18 years	42	0	0	42
	From 18 to 20 years	85	43	0	128
	21 to 24 years	20	173	211	404
	25 to 35 years	0	0	34	34
Total		147	216	245	608

5. RESULTS

After collecting the data for our extended TAM model, the next step involves a two-stage methodology to analyze the collected data. Initially, we engage in exploratory activities including data cleaning and questionnaire unidimensionality verification. This phase involves assessing the reliability index of items through Cronbach α computation (Amirrudin, Nasution, & Supahar, 2021), we perform a confirmatory analysis to ascertain the impact of independent variables on dependent ones.

The questionnaire, comprising 31 statements, uses a 5-point Likert scale where respondents signify their agreement or disagreement to provided assertions. Other items are measured on a scale ranging from "Unimportant" to "Very Important." Cronbach's alpha index, symbolized by "α," gauges the internal coherence (reliability) by calculating the average correlation between items.

To evaluate the reliability of the confidence items, we first computed Cronbach's alpha coefficient. The result, $\alpha = 0.772$, is moderately satisfactory. Upon eliminating item CONF1, the alpha value significantly improved to $\alpha = 0.932$, thus revealing this item's minor influence on the model's dependent variables.

The questionnaire demonstrated satisfying metric qualities with Cronbach α index exceeding .7, and ranging between .772 and 1. The strong correlation between the items within each scale reflects a high degree of internal consistency. The perceived quality questionnaire, in particular, exhibits superior internal consistency (α =.987 and KMO=.905).

The confirmatory phase of our study leverages Python software to investigate the relationships between independent and dependent variables, aiming to validate hypotheses and determine the significance of these relationships. Python's extensive libraries and packages, which streamline data analysis and hypothesis testing, contribute to its popularity in scientific research (Courant et al., 2013). We utilized Python version 3.8.0, a major release that incorporates numerous enhancements and features.

Pearson's correlation coefficient (r) serves as our primary estimator, aligning with common practices in TAM studies. Pearson's correlation coefficient is easy to interpret and ranges from -1 to 1. A value of -1 signifies a perfect negative linear relationship, 1 denotes a perfect positive linear relationship, and 0 signifies no linear relationship (Glass & Evans, 1981).

In the scope of statistical analysis, Cohen's guidelines help interpret the practical significance of the relationship between independent and dependent variables (Cohen & Ross, 1977). Effect size is a measure of the strength or magnitude of a relationship or difference between variables. Cohen suggested using Cramer's V statistic to evaluate effect size and provided thresholds to interpret weak, moderate, and strong effects. These guidelines facilitate the understanding of the significance and impact of the relationships in the study.

The data analysis process encompasses three phases. The first phase presents the results of the bivariate correlation analysis, offering insights into relationships within the extended TAM framework. The second phase describes the correlations between each pair of variables in terms of their magnitude, statistical significance, and strength of association. The final phase entails performing the chi-square test, specifically the Turkey test, to evaluate the formulated hypotheses.

We examine correlations between the independent variables—"Perceived Ease of Use," "Experience," "Social Influence," "Perceived Sense of Effectiveness," "Perceived Risk," and "Trust"—and the dependent variable, "Perceived usefulness," to further the understanding of interdependencies among these variables.

- Analysis of correlations between "Perceived Usefulness" and "Perceived Ease of Use"

According to the data on Table 2, there is a positive correlation between the perceived usefulness and perceived ease of use. All of the tested variables are significantly linked, and the test value is highly significant. The Cramer V association measure indicates the strength of the relationship between perceived usefulness and perceived ease of use. Similarly, Karahanna and Straub (Karahanna & Straub, 1999) also explored the connection between perceived usefulness and perceived ease of use, revealing that the usefulness of new technology is influenced by its perceived ease of use. The alternative hypothesis that the two variables are dependent is confirmed, while the null hypothesis is rejected.

Table 2. Analysis of correlation between perceived usefulness (PU) and perceived ease of use (PEU)

Dependent Variables	Independent Variables	Pearson r Coefficient	Test $\div^2$	p-Value	Cramer's V
PU 1	PEU1	0.999	502.195	2.244734e-107	0.454
	PEU2	0.997	502.339	2.089091e-107	0.454
	PEU3	0.997	500.007	6.676243e-107	0.453
PU 2	PEU1	0.999	502.339	2.244734e-107	0.454
	PEU2	0.997	500.007	2.089091e-107	0.454
	PEU3	0.997	501.615	6.676243e-107	0.453
PU 3	PEU1	0.998	501.615	2.996645e-107	0.454
	PEU2	0.997	501.759	2.789597e-107	0.454
	PEU3	0.997	499.453	8.797325e-107	0.453
PU 4	PEU1	0.999	502.195	2.244734e-107	0.454
	PEU2	0.997	502.339	2.089091e-107	0.454
	PEU3	0.997	500.007	6.676243e-107	0.453

- Analysis of correlations between "Perceived Usefulness" and "Experience"

The hypothesis test in Table 3 shows that the experiment has a moderately significant impact on the perceived usefulness following a potential use of an e-orientation platform (p0.05). Additionally, the results of the Cramer V measure indicate a weak relationship between the two variables, falling within the interval of >=0.10 and =0.20, indicate a weak relationship between the two variables. Therefore, there is no strong correlation between the two variables.

Table 3. Analysis of the correlation between perceived usefulness (PU) and experience variables

Dependent Variables	Independent Variables	Pearson r Coefficient	Test $\div^2$	p-Value	Cramer's V
PU1	Experience1	0.286	45.673	2.879761e-09	0.137
	Experience2	0.299	50.261	3.184354e-10	0.143
PU2	Experience1	0.286	45.673	2.879761e-09	0.137
	Experience2	0.299	50.261	3.184354e-10	0.143
PU3	Experience1	0.284	45.063	3.857150e-09	0.136
	Experience2	0.297	49.489	3.857150e-09	0.142
PU4	Experience1	0.286	45.673	2.879761e-09	0.137
	Experience2	0.299	50.261	3.184354e-10	0.143

- Analysis of correlations between "Perceived Usefulness" and "Social Influence"

According to Table 4 provided, the perceived usefulness of a guidance platform is greatly affected by social influence. The Pearson coefficient values ranging from 0.291 to 0.319 and a P-value less than 0.05, coupled with low values of V of cramer between 0.10 and 0.20, indicate that the opinions of family, friends, and other important people can influence how useful e-orientation platforms are perceived to be. This finding corroborates the results of previous studies such as Peng et al. (2016) and Bonn et al. (2015), which both suggest that social influence has a significant impact on Perceived usefulness in various technological applications (Bonn et al., 2015; Peng & Dredze, 2016). Therefore, it can be concluded that social influence is a crucial factor in shaping people's perceptions of the usefulness of guidance platforms.

The study's participants have concluded that social influence has an impact on Perceived usefulness. This leads to the validation of the alternative hypothesis and the rejection of the null hypothesis.

Table 4. Analysis of the correlation between "perceived usefulness" (PU) and "social influence" (SI) variables

Dependent Variables	Independent Variables	Pearson r Coefficient	Test $\div^{2}$	p-Value	Cramer's V
	SI 1	0.319	49.090	5.591078e-10	0.142
	SI 2	0.293	48.917	6.075505e-10	0.141
PU1	SI 3	0.309	47.266	1.341711e-09	0.139
	SI 4	0.317	48.967	5.929952e-10	0.141
	SI 5	0.303	48.900	6.123604e-10	0.141
	SI 1	0.319	49.090	5.591078e-10	0.142
	SI 2	0.293	48.917	6.075505e-10	0.141
PU2	SI 3	0.309	47.266	1.341711e-09	0.139
	SI 4	0.317	48.967	5.929952e-10	0.141
	SI 5	0.303	48.967	6.123604e-10	0.141
	SI 1	0.316	49.170	5.379913e-10	0.142
	SI 2	0.291	48.970	5.379913e-10	0.141
PU3	SI 3	0.307	47.143	1.423294e-09	0.139
	SI 4	0.315	48.721	6.675321e-10	0.141
	SI 5	0.301	48.846	6.286750e-10	0.141
	SI 1	0.319	49.090	5.591078e-10	0.142
	SI 2	0.293	48.917	6.075505e-10	0.141
PU4	SI 3	0.309	47.266	1.341711e-09	0.139
	SI 4	0.317	48.967	5.929952e-10	0.141
	SI 5	0.303	48.900	6.123604e-10	0.141

- Analysis of correlations between "Perceived usefulness" and "Perceived sense of Effectiveness"

The results of the hypothesis test in Table 5 revealed a significant impact of perceived efficiency on the perceived usefulness of using an e-orientation platform, with an average level of intensity. In other words, when users perceive the platform to be more efficient in achieving their goals, they also perceive it to be more useful in helping them with their orientation needs. Therefore, the alternative hypothesis, which suggests a relationship between perceived effectiveness and perceived usefulness, was supported, while the null hypothesis was rejected. This finding highlights the importance of perceived efficiency in shaping users' perceptions of the usefulness of the e-orientation platform.

Table 5. Analysis of the correlation between perceived usefulness (PU) and perceived sense of effectiveness (PE) variables.

Dependent Variables	Independent Variables	Pearson r Coefficient	Test $\div^2$	p-Value	Cramer's V
PU1	PE1	0.380	69.061	3.581065e-14	0.168
	PE2	0.386	69.061	4.663751e-14	0.167
	PE3	0.363	60.524	2.250985e-12	0.157
	PE4	0.337	53.396	7.037993e-11	0.148
PU2	PE1	0.380	69.061	3.581065e-14	0.168
	PE2	0.386	68.518	4.663751e-14	0.167
	PE3	0.363	60.524	2.250985e-12	0.157
	PE4	0.337	53.396	7.037993e-11	0.148
PU3	PE1	0.380	69.113	3.492634e-14	0.168
	PE2	0.387	68.573	4.539635e-14	0.167
	PE3	0.364	60.594	2.175752e-12	0.157
	PE4	0.338	53.441	6.888863e-11	0.148
PU4	PE1	0.380	69.061	3.581065e-14	0.168
	PE2	0.386	68.518	4.663751e-14	0.167
	PE3	0.363	60.524	2.250985e-12	0.157
	PE4	0.337	53.396	7.037993e-11	0.148

- Analysis of correlations between "Perceived usefulness" and "Perceived Risk"

The results of Table 6 determine that there is no significant impact of perceived risk on perceived usefulness. The correlation between these two variables is weak and lacks statistical significance ($p > 0.05$). As a result, the null hypothesis of independence between the variables was accepted. This finding aligns with previous research by Pavlou (2003), which suggests that trust and perceived risk have a stronger association with consumer acceptability in e-commerce compared to the perceived usefulness of the platform. It indicates that while perceived risk may not directly affect the perceived usefulness of the e-orientation platform, other factors such as trust and perceived risk may play a more influential role in determining its acceptance among users(Pavlou, 2003).

- Analysis of correlations between "Perceived usefulness" and "Trust"

The Table 7 displayed above presents the outcomes of the correlation test conducted between trust variables and perceived usefulness. The results reveal that trust significantly affects the perceived usefulness of the e-orientation platform (with a value of $p < 0.05$) and an average intensity (V=>0.10), which leads to the rejection of the null hypothesis and confirmation of the alternative hypothesis. This finding is consistent with previous research (Gefen, Karahanna, & Straub, 2003), which demonstrated a positive correlation between trust and perceived usefulness. Similarly, it was observed that trust has a positive impact on perceived usefulness (Eriksson, Kerem, & Nilsson, 2005).

Table 6. Correlation analysis between perceived usefulness (PU) and perceived risk (PR) variables

Dependent Variables	Independent Variables	Pearson r Coefficient	Test ÷²	p-Value	Cramer's V
PU1	PR1	0.149	18.529	9.721768e-04	0.087
	PR2	0.156	19.528	6.186450e-04	0.089
	PR3	0.165	19.528	2.419513e-04	0.094
PU2	PR1	0.149	18.529	9.721768e-04	0.087
	PR2	0.156	19.528	9.721768e-04	0.089
	PR3	0.165	21.588	2.419513e-04	0.094
PU3	PR1	0.150	18.704	8.980977e-04	0.087
	PR2	0.157	19.700	5.720968e-04	0.090
	PR3	0.165	21.758	2.238880e-04	0.094
PU4	PR1	0.149	18.529	9.721768e-04	0.087
	PR2	0.156	19.528	6.186450e-04	0.089
	PR3	0.165	21.588	2.419513e-04	0.094

Table 7. Analysis of perceived usefulness (PU) and trust variables

Dependent Variables	Independent Variables	Pearson r Coefficient	Test ÷²	p-Value	Cramer's V
PU1	Trust2	0.606	186.88	2.469734e-39	0.277
	Trust3	0.670	266.018	2.301328e-56	0.330
PU2	Trust2	0.606	186.889	2.377746e-18	0.277
	Trust3	0.670	266.018	2.301328e-56	0.330
PU3	Trust2	0.605	186.653	186.653e-39	0.277
	Trust3	0.669	265.844	2.509232e-56	0.330
PU4	Trust2	0.606	186.889	2.469734e-39	0.277
	Trust3	0.670	186.889	2.301328e-56	0.330

- Analysis of the correlations between " Perceived Ease of Use " and "Experience"

Based on the statistical analysis conducted in Table 8 on both the independent variable (experience) and the dependent variable (perceived ease of use), it was found that experience has a significant impact on the perceived ease of use ($p < 0.05$). Although the correlation between the two variables is not very strong, the result supports our alternative hypothesis, suggesting that experience influences how users perceive the ease of use of the e-orientation platform. This finding contradicts the null hypothesis, which proposed no relationship between experience and perceived ease of use. Therefore, it can be concluded that prior experience with similar technologies plays a role in shaping users' perceptions of how easy the platform is to use.

Table 8. Correlation analysis between perceived ease of use (PEU) and experience variables

Dependent Variables	Independent Variables	Pearson r Coefficient	Test $\div^{2}$	p-Value	Cramer's V
PEU1	Expérience1	0.284	45.559	3.042132e-09	0.136
	Expérience2	0.298	49.961	3.678179e-10	0.143
PEU2	Expérience1	0.286	45.605	2.974788e-09	0.136
	Expérience2	0.299	50.204	3.272460e-10	0.143
PEU3	Expérience1	0.289	46.494	1.943468e-09	0.138
	Expérience2	0.302	51.456	1.792255e-10	0.145

- Analysis of correlations between "Perceived Ease of Use" and "Social Influence"

As shown in Table 9, the analysis of the variables related to social influence and perceived ease of use reveals predominantly positive correlations, with a P-value less than 0.05, indicating that participants who perceive the e-orientation platform as easy to use also tend to be positively influenced by the opinions of their family and colleagues. This finding suggests a significant relationship between perceived ease of use and social influence, which has been consistently observed in previous studies focusing on online learning and the impact of social pressure on students' perceptions of ease of use. Researchers, further support this notion by explaining how social influence affects individuals' perceptions of technology's ease of use(Shen, Laffey, Lin, & Huang, 2006).

Table 9. Correlation analysis between perceived ease of use (PEU) and social influence (SI) variables

Dependent Variables	Independent Variables	Pearson r Coefficient	Test $\div^{2}$	p-Value	Cramer's V
PEU1	SI 1	0.318	48.758	6.556872e-10	0.141
	SI 2	0.292	48.401	7.782949e-10	0.141
	SI 3	0.307	48.401	2.092234e-09	0.138
	SI 4	0.315	47.975	9.549758e-10	0.140
	SI 5	0.302	48.497	7.433954e-10	0.141
PEU2	SI 1	0.322	50.250	3.200503e-10	0.143
	SI 2	0.296	49.934	3.726157e-10	0.143
	SI 3	0.310	47.480	1.210861e-09	0.139
	SI 4	0.318	49.185	5.341670e-10	0.142
	SI 5	0.306	50.042	3.537008e-10	0.143
PEU3	SI 1	0.323	49.945	3.706342e-10	0.143
	SI 2	0.296	49.885	3.815221e-10	0.143
	SI 3	0.296	49.885	3.815221e-10	0.143
	SI 4	0.319	49.284	5.093734e-10	0.142
	SI 5	0.307	49.830	3.917002e-10	0.143

Therefore, it can be concluded that individuals who perceive the e-orientation platform as easy to use are more likely to be influenced by social factors, such as the opinions of their family and colleagues. As a result, the null hypothesis is rejected.

- Analysis of correlations between "Perceived Ease of Use" and "Perceived Quality"

The results of the correlation test between perceived quality and perceived ease of use are presented in the Table 10. The data reveals a statistically significant correlation between the two variables, with a correlation coefficient (r) falling within the range of 1< r <1 and a p-value less than 0.05. The strength of the relationship is found to be moderate, indicating that there is a meaningful association between perceived ease of use and perceived quality.

Table 10. Correlation analysis between perceived ease of use (PEU) and perceived quality (PQ) variables

Dependent Variables	Independent Variables	Pearson r Coefficient	Test ÷^{2}	p-Value	Cramer's V
PEU1	PQ1	0.589	181.769	3.108440e-38	0.273
	PQ2	0.557	166.238	6.710288e-35	0.261
	PQ3	0.584	178.826	1.332287e-37	0.271
	PQ4	0.574	188.959	8.868722e-40	0.278
	PQ5	0.584	181.058	4.417408e-38	0.272
	PQ6	0.579	175.667	6.350432e-37	0.268
PEU2	PQ1	0.588	181.332	3.858862e-38	0.273
	PQ2	0.557	165.911	3.858862e-38	0.261
	PQ3	0.583	178.404	1.641415e-37	0.270
	PQ4	0.573	188.649	1.033849e-39	0.278
	PQ5	0.583	180.619	5.490250e-38	0.272
	PQ6	0.578	175.223	7.911328e-37	0.268
PEU3	PQ1	0.588	180.544	5.696522e-38	0.272
	PQ2	0.558	166.486	5.934220e-35	0.261
	PQ3	0.583	177.612	2.427635e-37	0.270
	PQ4	0.573	187.787	1.583816e-39	0.277
	PQ5	0.582	179.862	7.981242e-38	0.271
	PQ6	0.577	174.470	1.147845e-36	0.267

These findings provide support for the alternative hypothesis, suggesting that perceived ease of use and perceived quality are indeed dependent on each other. It implies that individuals who perceive the e-orientation platform as easy to use are more likely to perceive it as having higher quality. This result aligns with previous research that has highlighted the connection between ease of use and perceived quality in various technological contexts.

- Analysis of correlations between "Perceived ease of use" and "Perceived Sence of Effectiveness".

Agarwal and Karahanna(Agarwal & Karahanna, 2000) have identified "Perceived Sense of Effectiveness" as a significant factor influencing the perceived ease of use in the context of technology acceptance. Their findings suggest that a higher level of perceived effectiveness is associated with greater perceived ease of use, supporting our alternative hypothesis. Consistent with this, our results in Table 13 indicate a significant correlation between perceived ease of use and perceived effectiveness (with p<0.05). This finding aligns with Venkatesh's study on the new technology adoption mode l(Venkatesh & Davis, 2000), which emphasizes the role of the "Perceived Sense of Effectiveness" variable in shaping the perception of ease of use.

Table 11. Correlation analysis between perceived ease of use (PEU) and perceived sense of effectiveness (PE) variables

Dependent Variables	Independent Variables	Pearson r Coefficient	Test ÷²	p-Value	Cramer's V
PEU1	PE1	0.380	501.473	3.216503e-107	0.454
	PE2	0.387	69.126	3.470624e-14	0.168
	PE3	0.387	69.126	2.182568e-12	0.157
	PE4	0.338	53.522	6.625910e-11	0.148
PEU2	PE1	0.379	68.966	3.750680e-14	0.168
	PE2	0.386	68.521	4.657144e-14	0.167
	PE3	0.386	60.454	4.657144e-14	0.167
	PE4	0.386	53.428	6.933010e-11	0.148
PEU3	PE1	0.380	499.728	7.669035e-107	0.453
	PE2	0.387	69.176	3.387650e-14	0.168
	PE3	0.364	60.657	2.110760e-12	0.157
	PE4	0.334	52.412	1.130828e-10	0.146

The observed relationship between perceived ease of use and perceived effectiveness underscores the notion that when individuals perceive a technology to be more effective in achieving desired outcomes, they are more likely to perceive it as easy to use. This finding has important implications for the design and implementation of e-orientation platforms, as it suggests that enhancing perceived effectiveness can contribute to improving the perceived ease of use and subsequent acceptance of the platform by users.

- Analysis of correlations between "Perceived Sense of Effectiveness" and "Social Influence"

The data presented in Table 12 above reveals a significant correlation between Perceived Sense of Effectiveness and social influence, with a statistical significance level of less than 0.05. This result supports the alternative hypothesis that one's perception of effectiveness towards an e-orientation platform is influenced by social factors. It is consistent with the perspective put forth by Bandura (Bandura,

2003), who posits that an individual's beliefs about their own abilities are shaped by various sources of information, including verbal persuasion and social influence. Bandura emphasizes the significance of close forms of social influence in fostering a sense of personal efficacy.

Table 12. Correlation analysis between perceived sense of effectiveness (PE) and social influence (SI) variables

Dependent Variables	Independent Variables	Pearson r Coefficient	Test ÷²	p-Value	Cramer's V
PE1	SI 1	0.277	43.717	7.345476e-09	0.134
	SI 2	0.277	41.636	1.984207e-08	0.130
	SI 3	0.297	41.636	7.999463e-09	0.133
	SI 4	0.303	45.486	3.149266e-09	0.136
	SI 5	0.303	45.862	2.630313e-09	0.137
PE2	SI 1	0.265	38.655	8.205147e-08	0.126
	SI 2	0.265	35.929	2.992039e-07	0.121
	SI 3	0.265	30.350	4.152878e-06	0.111
	SI 4	0.265	31.912	1.993812e-06	0.114
	SI 5	0.265	31.912	1.872336e-06	0.114
PE3	SI 1	0.269	37.553	1.385184e-07	0.124
	SI 2	0.269	33.925	7.717100e-07	0.118
	SI 3	0.260	34.421	6.105224e-07	0.118
	SI 4	0.273	37.877	1.187896e-07	0.124
	SI 5	0.266	37.390	1.496746e-07	0.123
PE4	SI 1	0.269	38.992	6.991609e-08	0.126
	SI 2	0.269	36.347	2.454419e-07	0.122
	SI 3	0.287	41.372	2.250559e-08	0.130
	SI 4	0.287	43.165	9.559360e-09	0.133
	SI 5	0.287	37.739	1.268253e-07	0.124

- Analysis of correlations between "Perceived Sense of Effectiveness" and "Experience"

According to our research (see Table 13), we have found a statistically significant relationship between the perception of effectiveness and experience ($p=0.05$). This finding supports our hypothesis that experience has an impact on the perception of effectiveness, although the correlation between the two variables is weak ($0.10 \leq V \leq 0.20$). However, previous studies on the acceptance of new technology and information communication suggest that vicarious experiences, where individuals observe the skills of others and compare them to their own, can influence beliefs about effectiveness (Bandura, 1997). Positive experiences that provide contextualized knowledge and empower students can contribute to the development of a positive self-efficacy belief.

Table 13. Correlation analysis between perceived sense of effectiveness (PE) and experience variables

Dependent Variables	Independent Variables	Pearson r Coefficient	Test ÷^{2}	p-Value	Cramer's V
PE1	Experience1	0.229	40.587	3.271787e-08	0.129
	Experience2	0.229	41.897	3.271787e-08	0.131
PE2	Experience1	0.227	35.201	4.223565e-07	0.120
	Experience2	0.235	37.737	1.269353e-07	0.124
PE3	Experience1	0.231	33.399	9.895266e-07	0.117
	Experience2	0.266	31.146	2.857447e-06	0.113
PE4	Experience1	0.188	33.399	9.895266e-07	0.117
	Experience2	0.178	31.146	2.857447e-06	0.113

- Analysis of correlations between "Trust" and "Perceived Quality"

Our analysis (see Table 14) reveals a strong and positive relationship between the perceived quality variables and confidence, with a p-value below 0.05. This aligns with the research conducted by Hernandez-Ortega (Hernandez-Ortega, 2011), which suggests that trust in technology is contingent upon its perceived reliability and functionality, also known as conceptual quality. This result provides further support to the notion that trust and perceived quality are interconnected, reinforcing our hypothesis.

Table 14. Correlation analysis between trust and perceived quality (PQ) variables

Dependent Variables	Independent Variables	Pearson r Coefficient	Test ÷^{2}	p-Value	Cramer's V
Trust 2	PQ1	0.660	228.639	2.590802e-48	0.306
	PQ2	0.617	209.476	3.442980e-44	0.293
	PQ3	0.654	224.357	2.163817e-47	0.303
	PQ4	0.638	243.795	1.412306e-51	0.316
	PQ5	0.650	225.357	1.317695e-47	0.304
	PQ6	0.658	227.418	4.745292e-48	0.305
Trust 3	PQ1	0.593	190.216	4.762763e-40	0.279
	PQ2	0.547	172.715	2.733205e-36	0.266
	PQ3	0.587	187.006	2.330237e-39	0.277
	PQ4	0.577	209.687	3.101181e-44	0.293
	PQ5	0.585	189.306	7.471277e-40	0.278
	PQ6	0.590	189.321	7.414320e-40	0.279

- Analysis of correlations between "Trust" and "Perceived Risk"

The test of significance conducted on the relationship between trust and perceived risk in Table 15 yielded the following results: (p <= .05 with V < 0.140). These findings indicate that there is no significant impact of perceived risk on trust in the use of an e-orientation platform, aligning with the research conducted by Deutsch and Sheppard & Sherman (Deutsch, 1958; Sheppard & Sherman, 1998).However, it is worth noting that in another study by (Ayo, Mbarika, & Oni, 2015),a statistically significant negative impact of perceived risks on trust was observed .

Table 15. Correlation analysis between trust and perceived risk (PR) variables

Dependent Variables	Independent Variables	Pearson r Coefficient	Test $\div^{2}$	p-Value	Cramer's V
Trust2	PR1	0.070	4.989	2.884030e-01	0.045
	PR2	0.077	6.364	1.735193e-01	0.051
	PR3	0.074	6.596	1.588145e-01	0.052
Trust3	PR1	0.057	6.626	1.569949e-01	0.052
	PR2	0.065	7.664	1.046679e-01	0.056
	PR3	0.062	8.472	7.571400e-02	0.059

In the context of using an e-orientation platform, our results suggest that the perceived risk perceived by respondents does not appear to influence their confidence in using the platform. This indicates that the variables of trust and risk are not interdependent in the context of the e-orientation platform.

- Analysis of correlations between "Trust" and "Experience"

The Table 16 presents the results of the chi-square test, indicating a significant relationship between trust and experience with a p-value of less than 0.001. This suggests that as the number of experiences increases, there is a high level of user confidence. However, the strength of this relationship, as indicated by Cramer's V, is weak.

Table 16. Correlation analysis between trust and experience variables

Dependent Variables	Independent Variables	Pearson r Coefficient	Test $\div^{2}$	p-Value	Cramer's V
Trust2	Experience1	0.305	51.827	1.499066e-10	0.145
	Experience2	0.294	51.870	1.467906e-10	0.146
Trust3	Experience1	0.267	40.024	4.278911e-08	0.128
	Experience2	0.254	39.524	5.428429e-08	0.127

These findings are consistent with previous studies, such as Nooteboom (Nooteboom, 2000),which emphasize that confidence is primarily built through hands-on experience with technology . Additionally, Degeratu (Degeratu, Rangaswamy, & Wu, 2000) highlight that improved experience can enhance confidence in using a website.Therefore, we reject the null hypothesis.

- Analysis of correlations between "Perceived Quality" and "Experience"

Table 17 shows that the link between "Perceived Quality" and "Experience" is significant ***(0<r<=1 withp<0.001)***. This finding is consistent with the study by (Zeithaml, 1988) which confirms that perceived quality refers to the consumer's subjective assessment of the superiority of a product(Zeithaml, 1988).

Table 17. Correlation analysis between perceived quality (PQ) and experience variables

Dependent Variables	Independent Variables	Pearson r Coefficient	Test $\div^2$	p-Value	Cramer's V
PQ1	Experience1	0.289	45.579	3.013032e-09	0.136
	Experience2	0.288	46.499	1.938972e-09	0.138
PQ2	Experience1	0.260	37.049	1.759575e-07	0.123
	Experience2	0.258	37.372	1.509659e-07	0.123
PQ3	Experience1	0.288	45.341	3.376948e-09	0.136
	Experience2	0.284	45.601	2.980764e-09	0.136
PQ4	Experience1	0.277	41.260	2.373938e-08	0.130
	Experience2	0.274	43.590	7.803092e-09	0.133
PQ5	Experience1	0.285	44.125	6.042698e-09	0.134
	Experience2	0.296	48.858	6.248016e-10	0.141
PQ6	Experience1	0.280	43.310	8.922447e-09	0.133
	Experience2	0.279	44.434	5.212554e-09	0.135

The study suggests that perceived quality is an individual characteristic influenced by the accumulated experience. Similarly, Otto and Ritchie (Otto & Ritchie, 1995),describe perceived quality as a broad concept that encompasses the emotional aspects of the experience . Therefore, our findings support the alternative hypothesis, indicating a significant relationship between experience and perceived quality.

- Analysis of correlations between "Perceived Risk" and "Experience"

Table 18 reveals a non-significant correlation between perceived risk and experience in using an e-orientation platform, indicated by a near-zero Pearson value (with $p < 0.05$). The variable "Perceived risk" seems unconnected with experience, contradicting previous research by NAN et LIER(NAN^{TEL} & ^{TEL}LIER, 1992) suggesting that computer experience reduces perceived risk. Conversely, (Salkin, 1999) notes that internet familiarity doesn't necessarily lessen user fear, with experienced users more aware of potential risks. Therefore, according to the findings, experience does not reduce perceived risk in using e-orientation platforms, leading to the rejection of the alternative hypothesis.

Table 18. Correlation analysis between perceived risk (PR) and experience variables

Dependent Variables	Independent Variables	Pearson r Coefficient	Test ÷²	p-Value	Cramer's V
PR1	Experience1	0.027	0.967	0.914	0.019
	Experience2	0.045	3.843	0.427	0.039
PR2	Experience1	0.043	2.060	0.724	0.029
	Experience2	0.058	5.460	0.243	0.047
PR3	Experience1	0.047	1.519	0.823	0.024
	Experience2	0.061	4.409	0.353	0.042

- Link between "Intent of Use", "Perceived Usefulness", "Perceived Ease of Use", "Perceived Quality", "Trust", "Social Influence" and "Experience"

The analysis highlights positive correlations between the "Intention of Use" variable and others including "Perceived Usefulness", "Perceived Ease of Use", "Perceived Quality", "Trust", "Social Influence", and "Experience" ($p<0.05$) (Chen et al., 2014; Leduc et al., 2013). The strongest relationships with "Intention of Use" are exhibited by "Perceived usefulness" and "Perceived Ease of Use", indicated by a Cramer's V over 0.30, as also emphasized in prior studies (Garača & others, 2011; Maaloul & Mezghani, 2003; Seymour et al., 2007; Venkatesh & Davis, 1996b). Understanding these connections aids in designing efficient, user-friendly e-orientation platforms.

6. DISCUSSION

Our research extends the Technology Acceptance Model (TAM) presented by (Venkatesh & Davis, 1996a) by examining the relationship between various elements such as perceived usefulness, perceived usability, intention of use, experience, trust, perceived quality, perceived risk, and perceived sense of efficiency within an e-orientation platform context. We developed a questionnaire using existing scales from the scientific literature and found high reliability indexes and item correlations, confirming the internal consistency of our eight scales.

We then tested the relationships between these constructs using correlation analysis, hypothesis testing, and Cramer's V analysis to validate or reject null hypotheses. The usefulness of the platform strongly influenced its intended use, supporting the findings of (J.-S. Lee, Cho, Gay, Davidson, & Ingraffea, 2003) who stressed the importance of perceived usefulness of the educational platform in its acceptance by learners. Thus, a learner who understands the value and potential improvements of an e-orientation platform is more likely to use it.

Our study also found that the platform's ease of use significantly impacts acceptance, influencing user intention and satisfaction. Contrary to (Venkatesh & Davis, 2000), we found that perceived usefulness had an equivalent impact on the intention to use an e-orientation platform as perceived ease of use, suggesting the importance of both for adoption.

Perceived quality was found to directly impact intention to use, indicating that users who find the e-orientation platform navigable and informative are more likely to use it, a concept prevalent in studies of online purchasing, banking, and e-government systems (Chang & Tung, 2008; H.-H. Lee & Kim, 2008) but underexplored in education.

We also observed that prior experiences with the e-orientation platform positively influenced its acceptability (Brangier & Barcenilla, 2003), as did trust in the technology, in line with (Saparudin, Rahayu, Hurriyati, & Sultan, 2020) study. Overall, perceived quality, trust in technology, experience, and social influence were significant factors in using the e-orientation platform, with ease of use and perceived usefulness being the most crucial.

In addition, our study introduced perceived sense of efficiency and perceived risk as new variables in our extended TAM model. We found that perceived efficiency positively impacted perceived usefulness and ease of use, in line with (Stylianou & Jackson, 2007) findings. Perceived risk had a significant effect on perceived usefulness and trust in technology, indicating that lower perceived risk leads to higher perceived usefulness and confidence in the e-orientation platform. However, the impact of risk on perceived usefulness was less significant than its impact on trust, leading us to reject the hypothesis linking perceived risk and perceived usefulness.

Social influence also had a significant effect on perceived usefulness and ease of use, corroborating (Davis, 1989b) emphasis on the role of social influence in IT acceptance and usage, and reinforcing the importance of communication among users in technology acceptance (Barreto & Ellemers, 2015). Lastly, our study found that user experience positively influenced the perceived usefulness and usability of the e-orientation platform (Shin, Biocca, & Choo, 2013), further underscoring the importance of previous experience in technology adoption.

In the Figure 2 we present our model Acceptance model prediction's of the E-orientation Moroccan platform.

Figure 2. Acceptance model prediction's of the e-orientation Moroccan platform

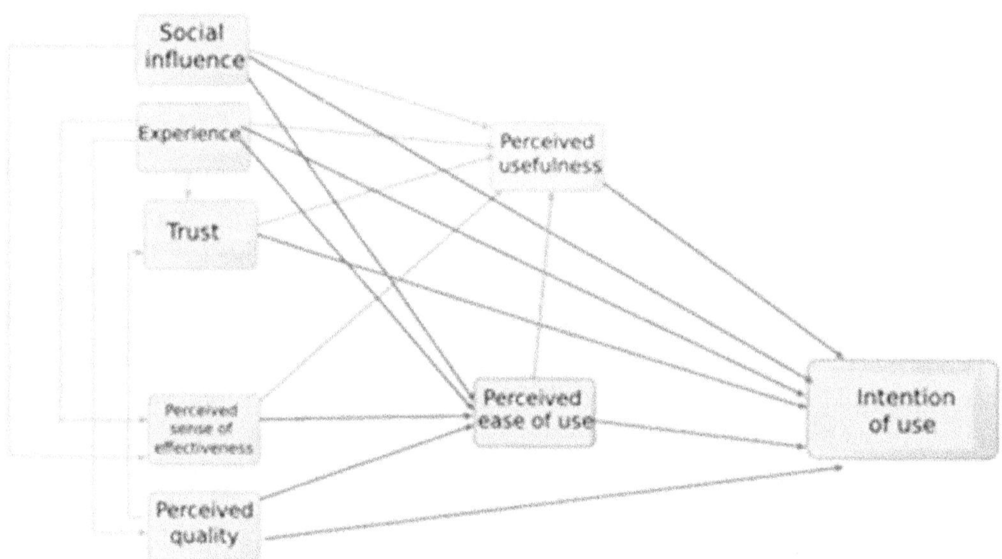

Our findings reveal the impact of various factors on the perceived usefulness of an e-orientation platform. Primarily, the perceived ease of use greatly influences its usefulness; if users deem the platform easy to use, they're unlikely to abandon it. Trust, experience, and social influence also have a direct effect on perceived usefulness, with trust originating from previous use and perceived quality of the platform. However, perceived risk can hinder this trust. Notably, "perceived quality" has a greater impact on "perceived ease of use" than "perceived efficiency," "experience," and "social influence." Users are more inclined to use a platform that offers high-quality navigation and information. We depict our model in an algorithm and a flowchart for clearer implementation guidance.

Figure 3. Flowchart of our algorithm for prediction's of the e-orientation Moroccan platform

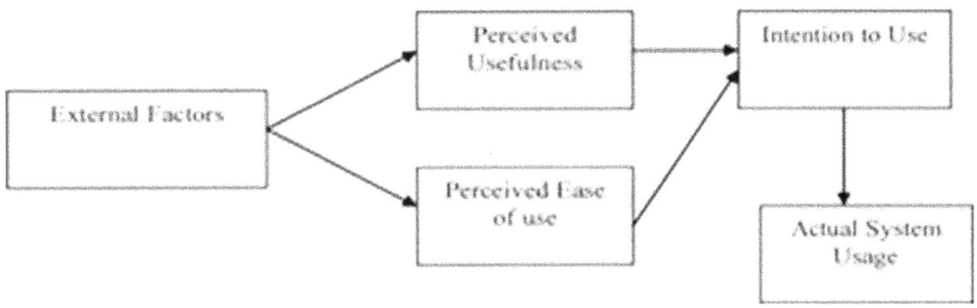

We developed a Python algorithm predicting user intention to use an e-orientation platform. The algorithm considers factors such as social influence, experience, perceived sense of effectiveness, and perceived quality, all linked to perceived usefulness and perceived ease of use, dictating the user's intention. The algorithm determines user intention by assessing perceived usefulness and ease: if both are positive, the user is likely to use the platform. However, if both are negative, the user is unlikely to adopt the platform. This approach provides a clear indication of the user's intention based on their perceptions of the platform's usefulness, ease of use, social influence, experience, and perceived quality.

7. CONCLUSION

This study aimed to explore the acceptance of e-orientation platforms among Moroccan students by developing a research model considering the needs of students, parents, and counselors. We concentrated on the "Orientation-chabab.com" platform due to its extensive features and dependable information.

Adapting and expanding the Technology Acceptance Model (TAM), we integrated individual, social, and technical factors to improve its predictive capabilities. We conducted a survey at the Faculty of Sciences Ben M'Sick and received 608 responses.

The analysis underscored the significant influence of perceived ease of use and usefulness on the intention to use an e-orientation platform. The perceived quality and trust in the platform emerged as crucial for guiding students' choices, emphasizing the importance of a user-friendly interface, reliable information, and positive social influence for the platform's success.

Furthermore, factors like perceived efficiency, quality, and experience, along with social influence, positively affected perceived ease of use. This indicates the user's experience, the platform's technical standards, and social influence as critical determinants of ease of use. Notably, prior experience with e-orientation platforms boosts perceived efficiency and helps alleviate perceived risks, mitigating potential platform rejection.

Looking forward, the exploration and potential incorporation of the Metaverse into e-orientation platforms add an intriguing aspect to this research. The Metaverse's immersive and interactive nature could revolutionize students' engagement with e-orientation platforms, offering a new and promising approach to educational technology.

Our study enriches the understanding of e-orientation platform adoption among students and provides valuable insights for educators, policy makers, and developers about the factors driving platform acceptance. This research lays the groundwork for future platform enhancements, setting the stage for more immersive and engaging educational experiences in the Metaverse era.

However, our study didn't explore the emotional acceptability of technology adoption due to its complexity. Future research should investigate this aspect and the potential impacts of Metaverse integration to deepen our understanding of e-orientation platform acceptance. This could contribute to developing more user-centric and immersive platform designs.

REFERENCES

Abouhanifa, S., Benmadani, M., Khalfaoui, M., Hanini, M., & Kabbaj, M. (2008). *L'outil informatique : Analyse des obstacles qui entravent son utilisation efficace en classe du secondaire*. Association EPI.

Agarwal, R., & Karahanna, E. (2000). Time flies when you're having fun : Cognitive absorption and beliefs about information technology usage. *Management Information Systems Quarterly*, *24*(4), 665–694. doi:10.2307/3250951

Amirrudin, M., Nasution, K., & Supahar, S. (2021). Effect of variability on Cronbach alpha reliability in research practice. *Jurnal Matematika, Statistika dan Komputasi, 17*(2), 223-230.

Ayo, C. K., Mbarika, V., & Oni, A. A. (2015). The influence of trust and risk on intention to use e-democracy in Nigeria. *Mediterranean Journal of Social Sciences*, *6*(6), 477–486. doi:10.5901/mjss.2015.v6n6s1p477

Bagozzi, R. P. (2007). The legacy of the technology acceptance model and a proposal for a paradigm shift. *Journal of the Association for Information Systems*, *8*(4), 3. doi:10.17705/1jais.00122

Bandura, A. (1997). *The anatomy of stages of change*. Academic Press.

Bandura, A. (2003). Social cognitive theory for personal and social change by enabling media. In *Entertainment-education and social change* (pp. 97–118). Routledge.

Barreto, M., & Ellemers, N. (2015). Detecting and experiencing prejudice : New answers to old questions. *Advances in Experimental Social Psychology*, *52*, 139–219. doi:10.1016/bs.aesp.2015.02.001

Bonn, M. A., Kim, W. G., Kang, S., & Cho, M. (2015). Purchasing Wine Online : The Effects of Social Influence, Perceived Usefulness, Perceived Ease of Use, and Wine Involvement. *Journal of Hospitality Marketing &amp\mathsemicolon. Journal of Hospitality Marketing & Management, 25*(7), 841–869. doi:10.1080/19368623.2016.1115382

Boulahcen, A. (2005). Le processus d'orientation scolaire au Maroc. *Revue internationale d'éducation de Sèvres*, (38), 25-34. doi:10.4000/ries.1427

Brangier, É., & Barcenilla, J. (2003). *Concevoir un produit facile à utiliser*. Paris: Editions d'organisation.

Chang, S.-C., & Tung, F.-C. (2008). An empirical investigation of students' behavioural intentions to use the online learning course websites. *British Journal of Educational Technology, 39*(1), 71–83. doi:10.1111/j.1467-8535.2007.00742.x

Chen, M., Mao, S., & Liu, Y. (2014). Big data : A survey. *Mobile Networks and Applications, 19*(2), 171–209. doi:10.1007/s11036-013-0489-0

Courant, J., de Falco, M., Gonnord, S., Filliâtre, J.-C., Conchon, S., Dowek, G., & Wack, B. (2013). *Informatique pour tous en classes préparatoires aux grandes écoles : Manuel d'algorithmique et programmation structurée avec Python*. Eyrolles.

Cox, D. F., & Rich, S. U. (1964). Perceived Risk and Consumer Decision-Making—The Case of Telephone Shopping. *JMR, Journal of Marketing Research, 1*(4), 32–39. doi:10.1177/002224376400100405

Davis, F. D. (1985). *A technology acceptance model for empirically testing new end-user information systems : Theory and results* [PhD Thesis]. Massachusetts Institute of Technology.

Davis, F. D. (1989a). Perceived Usefulness, Perceived Ease of Use, and User Acceptance of Information Technology. *Management Information Systems Quarterly, 13*(3), 319. doi:10.2307/249008

Davis, F. D. (1989b). Perceived Usefulness, Perceived Ease of Use, and User Acceptance of Information Technology. *Management Information Systems Quarterly, 13*(3), 319. doi:10.2307/249008

Degeratu, A. M., Rangaswamy, A., & Wu, J. (2000). Consumer choice behavior in online and traditional supermarkets : The effects of brand name, price, and other search attributes. *International Journal of Research in Marketing, 17*(1), 55–78. doi:10.1016/S0167-8116(00)00005-7

Deutsch, M. (1958). Trust and suspicion. *The Journal of Conflict Resolution, 2*(4), 265–279. doi:10.1177/002200275800200401

Downey, G. L., Lucena, J. C., Moskal, B. M., Parkhurst, R., Bigley, T., Hays, C., Jesiek, B. K., Kelly, L., Miller, J., Ruff, S., Lehr, J. L., & Nichols-Belo, A. (2006). The globally competent engineer : Working effectively with people who define problems differently. *Journal of Engineering Education, 95*(2), 107–122. doi:10.1002/j.2168-9830.2006.tb00883.x

Duan, H., Li, J., Fan, S., Lin, Z., Wu, X., & Cai, W. (2021). Metaverse for social good : A university campus prototype. *Proceedings of the 29th ACM international conference on multimedia*, 153-161. 10.1145/3474085.3479238

El-Shinnawy, A. H., Badawi, A. H., & Nassar, A. M. (2010). Two-step scheduling algorithm for IEEE802.16 wireless networks. In *2010 IEEE 12th International Conference on Communication Technology*. IEEE. 10.1109/ICCT.2010.5688935

Eriksson, K., Kerem, K., & Nilsson, D. (2005). Customer acceptance of internet banking in Estonia. *International Journal of Bank Marketing*, *23*(2), 200–216. doi:10.1108/02652320510584412

Fatima-zahra, G., & Khadija, D. (2016). Modernization of a domain E-orientation metamodel. In *2016 11th International Conference on Intelligent Systems: Theories and Applications (SITA)*. IEEE. 10.1109/SITA.2016.7772308

Garača, Ž., & ... (2011). Factors related to the intended use of ERP systems. *Management*, *16*(2), 23–42.

García-Pazo, P., Lopez, F. P., Coll, A. B., Moreno, C., & Brogi, L. (2023). Low cost 360 degree virtual reality video creation for nursing intensive care unit practices: A descriptive study. *EDULEARN23 Proceedings*, 6957-6957.

Gefen, D., Karahanna, E., & Straub, D. W. (2003). Trust and TAM in online shopping : An integrated model. *Management Information Systems Quarterly*, *27*(1), 51–90. doi:10.2307/30036519

Glass, I., & Evans, T. L. (1981). A period–luminosity relation for Mira variables in the Large Magellanic Cloud. *Nature*, *291*(5813), 303–304. doi:10.1038/291303a0

Guerss, F., Aitdaoud, M., Douzi, K., Guemmat, K., Namir, A., & Talbi, M. (2015). *Towards a new ontology of the Moroccan Post-baccalaureate learner profile for the E-orientation system "MMSyOrientation"*. Academic Press.

Hernandez-Ortega, B. (2011). The role of post-use trust in the acceptance of a technology : Drivers and consequences. *Technovation*, *31*(10-11), 523–538. doi:10.1016/j.technovation.2011.07.001

Hill, R. J., Fishbein, M., & Ajzen, I. (1977). Belief, Attitude, Intention and Behavior : An Introduction to Theory and Research. *Contemporary Sociology*, *6*(2), 244. doi:10.2307/2065853

Hu, P. J.-H., Lin, C., & Chen, H. (2005). User acceptance of Intelligence and Security Informatics technology : A study of COPLINK. *Journal of the American Society for Information Science and Technology*, *56*(3), 235–244. doi:10.1002/asi.20124

Ihya, R., Aitdaoud, M., Namir, A., Guerss, F. Z., & Haddani, H. (2020). Using Machine Learning Algorithms to Predict the E-orientation Systems Acceptancy. In *Innovations in Smart Cities Applications* (3rd ed., pp. 117–130). Springer International Publishing. doi:10.1007/978-3-030-37629-1_10

Ihya, R., Namir, A., Elfilali, S., Guerss, F. Z., & Daoud, M. A. (2019). Modeling the Acceptance of the E-Orientation Systems by Using the Predictions Algorithms. In *Learning and Analytics in Intelligent Systems* (pp. 27–31). Springer International Publishing. doi:10.1007/978-3-030-36778-7_3

Ihya, R., Namir, A., Filali, S. E., Daoud, M. A., & Guerss, F. Z. (2019). J48 algorithms of machine learning for predicting user's the acceptance of an E-orientation systems. In *Proceedings of the 4th International Conference on Smart City Applications*. ACM. 10.1145/3368756.3368995

Karahanna, E., & Straub, D. W. (1999). The psychological origins of perceived usefulness and ease-of-use. *Information & Management, 35*(4), 237–250. doi:10.1016/S0378-7206(98)00096-2

Knox, J. (2022). The Metaverse, or the Serious Business of Tech Frontiers. *Postdigital Science and Education, 4*(2), 207–215. doi:10.1007/s42438-022-00300-9

Koufaris, M., & Hampton-Sosa, W. (2004). The development of initial trust in an online company by new customers. *Information &amp\mathsemicolon. Information & Management, 41*(3), 377–397. doi:10.1016/j.im.2003.08.004

Leduc, S., Vallery, G., Bellhari, S., & Gaston, S. (2013). *Ergonomie des interfaces logicielles : Recommandations pour la conception, le développement et l'évaluation des applications*. Hermès.

Lee, H.-H., & Kim, J. (2008). The effects of shopping orientations on consumers' satisfaction with product search and purchases in a multi-channel environment. *Journal of Fashion Marketing and Management, 12*(2), 193–216. doi:10.1108/13612020810874881

Lee, J.-S., Cho, H., Gay, G., Davidson, B., & Ingraffea, A. (2003). Technology acceptance and social networking in distance learning. *Journal of Educational Technology & Society, 6*(2), 50–61.

Lee, L.-H., Braud, T., Zhou, P., Wang, L., Xu, D., Lin, Z., ... Hui, P. (2021). All One Needs to Know about Metaverse : A Complete Survey on Technological Singularity, Virtual Ecosystem, and Research Agenda. *ArXiv, abs/2110.05352*.

Legris, P., Ingham, J., & Collerette, P. (2003). Why do people use information technology? A critical review of the technology acceptance model. *Information & Mathsemicolon. Information & Management, 40*(3), 191–204. doi:10.1016/S0378-7206(01)00143-4

Maaloul, I., & Mezghani, L. (2003). L'implantation des ERP et ingénierie du changement : Les déterminants de la satisfaction des utilisateurs d'un ERP dans les entreprises tunisiennes. *XIIème Conférence de l'Association Internationale de Management Stratégique*.

Nantel, J.-A., & Tellier, C. (1992). L'achat par services télématisés : Qui en sont les utilisateurs et pourquoi? *Technologies de l'Informatique et Société, 4*(3), 333-350.

Ning, H., Wang, H., Lin, Y., Wang, W., Dhelim, S., Farha, F., ... Daneshmand, M. (2023). A Survey on the Metaverse : The State-of-the-Art, Technologies, Applications, and Challenges. *IEEE Internet of Things Journal*.

Nooteboom, B. (2000). *Trust as a governance device. In Cultural factors in economic growth*. Springer.

Otto, J. E., & Ritchie, J. B. (1995). Exploring the quality of the service experience: A theoretical and empirical analysis. *Advances in Services Marketing and Management, 4*(1), 37-61.

Pavlou, P. A. (2003). Consumer acceptance of electronic commerce : Integrating trust and risk with the technology acceptance model. *International Journal of Electronic Commerce, 7*(3), 101–134. doi:10.1080/10864415.2003.11044275

Peng, N., & Dredze, M. (2016). Improving named entity recognition for chinese social media with word segmentation representation learning. *arXiv preprint arXiv:1603.00786*. doi:10.18653/v1/P16-2025

Ripka, G., Tiede, J., Grafe, S., & Latoschik, M. E. (2020). *Teaching and Learning Processes in Immersive VR – Comparing Expectations of Preservice Teachers and Teacher Educators*. Academic Press.

Salkin, S. (1999). Fear of buying. *Logistics Management and Distribution Report*, *8*(5), 101–104.

Saparudin, M., Rahayu, A., Hurriyati, R., & Sultan, M. A. (2020). Exploring the role of trust in mobile-banking use by Indonesian customer using unified theory of acceptance and usage technology. *International Journal of Financial Research*, *11*(2), 51–60. doi:10.5430/ijfr.v11n2p51

Seymour, L., Makanya, W., & Berrangé, S. (2007). End-users' acceptance of enterprise resource planning systems : An investigation of antecedents. *Proceedings of the 6th annual ISOnEworld conference*, 1-22.

Shen, D., Laffey, J., Lin, Y., & Huang, X. (2006). Social influence for perceived usefulness and ease-of-use of course delivery systems. *Journal of Interactive Online Learning*, *5*(3), 270–282.

Sheppard, B. H., & Sherman, D. M. (1998). The grammars of trust : A model and general implications. *Academy of Management Review*, *23*(3), 422–437. doi:10.2307/259287

Shin, D.-H., Biocca, F., & Choo, H. (2013). Exploring the user experience of three-dimensional virtual learning environments. *Behaviour & Mathsemicolon Information Technology, 32*(2), 203-214. doi:10.1080/0144929X.2011.606334

Strong, S. (2006). *Early childhood education and care*. Organization for Economic Co-operation and Development.

Stylianou, A. C., & Jackson, P. J. (2007). A comparative examination of individual differences and beliefs on technology usage : Gauging the role of IT. *Journal of Computer Information Systems*, *47*(4), 11–18.

Venkatesh, V., & Davis, F. D. (1996). A Model of the Antecedents of Perceived Ease of Use : Development and Test. *Decision Sciences*, *27*(3), 451–481. doi:10.1111/j.1540-5915.1996.tb01822.x

Venkatesh, V., & Davis, F. D. (2000). A Theoretical Extension of the Technology Acceptance Model : Four Longitudinal Field Studies. *Management Science*, *46*(2), 186–204. doi:10.1287/mnsc.46.2.186.11926

Wiederhold, B. K. (2022). *Ready (or Not) player one : Initial musings on the metaverse*. Mary Ann Liebert, Inc.

Yi, M. Y., & Hwang, Y. (2003). Predicting the use of web-based information systems : Self-efficacy, enjoyment, learning goal orientation, and the technology acceptance model. *International Journal of Human-Computer Studies*, *59*(4), 431–449. doi:10.1016/S1071-5819(03)00114-9

Yousafzai, S. Y., Foxall, G. R., & Pallister, J. G. (2007). Technology acceptance : A meta-analysis of the TAM: Part 1. *Journal of Modelling in Management*, *2*(3), 251–280. doi:10.1108/17465660710834453

Zahra, G. F., Mohammed, A., Khadija, D., Mohammed, T., & Abdelouahed, N. (2015). Implementation of a Computerized System for the Orientation of the Moroccan Student in the University. *Procedia - Social and Behavioral Sciences, 182*, 381-387. doi:10.1016/j.sbspro.2015.04.797

Zeithaml, V. A. (1988). Consumer Perceptions of Price, Quality, and Value : A Means-End Model and Synthesis of Evidence. *Journal of Marketing*, *52*(3), 2–22. doi:10.1177/002224298805200302

Chapter 5
Exploring the Emerging Potential of the Metaverse in Education:
Gamification, Advantages, and Limitations

Marco Yamba-Yugsi
Universidad Católica de Cuenca, Ecuador

Ruth S. Contreras-Espinosa
https://orcid.org/0000-0002-9699-9087
Universitat de Vic, Spain & Universitat Central de Catalunya, Spain

Jose Luis Eguia-Gomez
Universitat Politécnica de Catalunya, Spain

ABSTRACT

This chapter explores the transformative integration of virtual worlds, particularly the Metaverse, into the field of education. It delves into the evolving pedagogical strategies that capitalize on immersive, interactive learning experiences, catering to the preferences of today's digitally native students. These virtual environments enable educators to craft dynamic, personalized curricula and empower students to become active participants in their educational journey. The chapter also highlights the importance of digital proficiency for both educators and students in navigating these virtual realms. While the benefits of the Metaverse in education are evident, challenges related to infrastructure, privacy, security, and ethics are addressed. In general, this chapter compressively provides an analysis of the evolving landscape of education within the Metaverse.

DOI: 10.4018/979-8-3693-1034-2.ch005

1. INTRODUCTION

The digital era has initiated a profound transformation, intricately integrating internet connectivity into our daily lives. From smartphones and tablets to laptops and smart devices, our reliance on the digital domain has advanced to a degree where access to the internet is considered a fundamental requirement, introducing a novel dimension to our hierarchy of necessities (Lengsfeld, 2019). This digital-era framework, inspired by Maslow's hierarchy, encompasses four essential domains: (1) basic needs, symbolized by digital infrastructure; (2) psychological needs, manifested through social networks; (3) self-fulfillment, embracing career growth and skill development, and (4) societal needs, encompassing interconnectedness and the digital economy (Tabach & Trgalová, 2020). This unique dimension is vividly depicted in Figure 1, where artificial intelligence (AI), deep learning (DL), and knowledge integration (KI) play pivotal roles. Revisiting and adapting Maslow's models in this digital context offers valuable insights, exemplified by their integration into the Digital Society Index (DSI) inquiries, ensuring that the hierarchy's fundamental structure is preserved to provide a holistic framework for addressing digital needs and societal considerations (Kaddoura & Al Husseiny, 2023).

Within this rapidly evolving digital landscape, one concept stands out as a beacon of innovation and change: the Metaverse. The Metaverse, often described as a collective virtual shared space, presents an intriguing vision of the future, promising to redefine the very nature of teaching and learning. As educators and learners increasingly immerse themselves in this digital domain, it becomes abundantly clear that the Metaverse offers a vast reservoir of untapped potential for the evolution of education.

At the heart of this monumental shift lies the dynamic concept of gamification, a pedagogical methodology that artfully interweaves game-like elements into conventional learning contexts, aiming to enhance engagement and motivation among learners (Swacha, 2021). This fusion of the Metaverse with the principles of gamification ushers in an educational renaissance, marking a profound paradigm shift. Its ushers in an era characterized by dynamic, interactive, and deeply personalized learning experiences meticulously tailored to resonate with the preferences and expectations of today's tech-savvy learners.

Traditionally, education has been tethered to the physical confines of classrooms, ensnared by standardized curricula that cater to the masses. However, the convergence of the Metaverse with gamification obliterates these age-old boundaries, effectively emancipating the educational process from its traditional moorings. Within this evolving educational landscape, learning undergoes a metamorphosis, transforming into an immersive odyssey. Students embark on quests, traverse intricate virtual realms, and engage with educational content in ways that were once relegated to the realm of science fiction.

Furthermore, this transformative amalgamation empowers educators with a versatile toolkit to craft engaging and innovative learning experiences. They cease to be mere transmitters of information, ascending instead to the roles of architects and storytellers within these virtual realms. The Metaverse, in this context, unfolds as an expansive canvas upon which educators artfully weave educational narratives that captivate, challenge, and inspire learners.

This chapter will investigate the transformative potential of the Metaverse in reshaping educational paradigms, focusing on how it enhances engagement, interactivity, and personalized learning experiences. We will analyze the role of gamification as a pedagogical strategy within the Metaverse, exploring how it can motivate learners, facilitate immersive learning environments, and adapt to diverse student needs. Here, we will showcase real-world practical examples of educational institutions successfully implementing the Metaverse and gamification, along with the lessons learned and best practices. Additionally, we will anticipate future developments and viewpoints concerning incorporating the Metaverse into education, the progression of gamification, and the changing responsibilities of educators, encompassing the necessity for ongoing professional development.

In this section, we will explore the educational opportunities presented by the Metaverse, placing a particular emphasis on the integration of gamification to enhance the quality of learning interactions. The chapter's structure is as follows: first, we will delve into the Foundations of the Metaverse in Education, which involves defining its context and examining its emerging applications within the educational domain. Second, we will thoroughly investigate the significance of gamification in the educational context of the Metaverse. Third, we will examine practical examples where educational institutions have effectively implemented Metaverse and gamification techniques, conducting an analysis of the lessons learned and best practices. Finally, the chapter will conclude with a series of relevant reflections.

Figure 1. Emerging technology based on Marlow's law (Kaddoura & Al Husseiny, 2023)

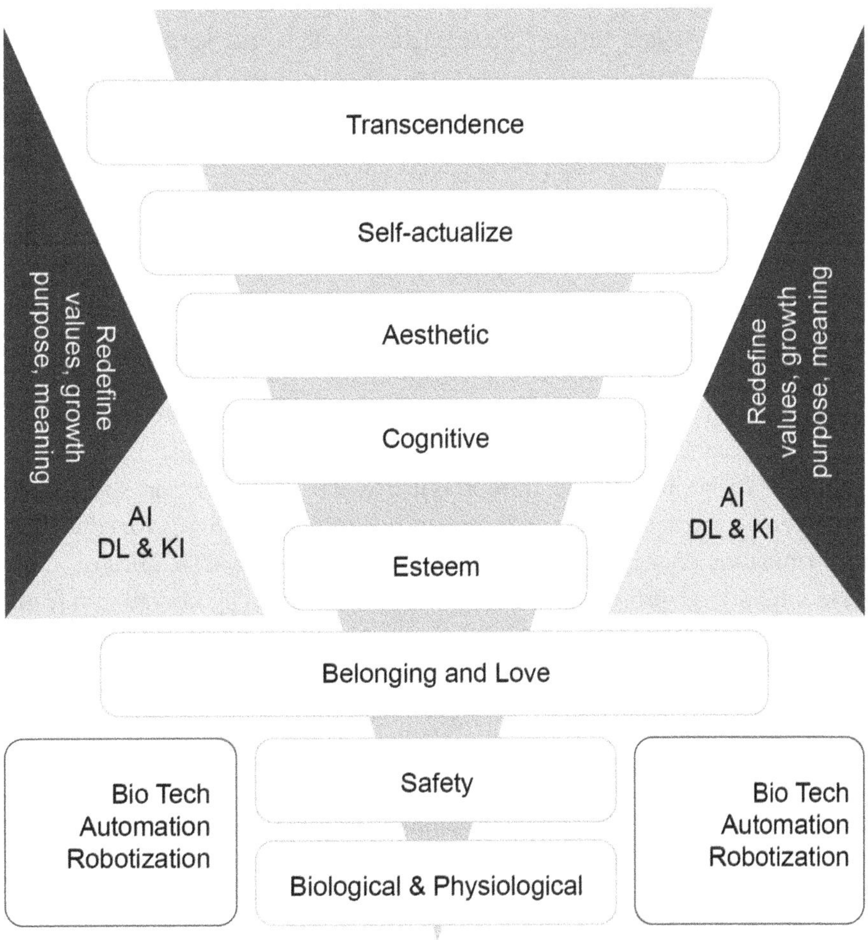

2. FUNDAMENTALS OF THE METAVERSE IN EDUCATION

The term "Metaverse," formed by merging "meta" and "universe," introduces an innovative concept that transcends conventional boundaries, reshaping our interactions with digital and physical realms (Richter & Richter, 2023). It goes beyond jargon, representing a growing digital universe with the potential to revolutionize our lives, workplaces, and education. We must explore the definition and context to comprehend the Metaverse's potential and impact fully. The Metaverse is a shared virtual realm, an interconnected digital cosmos blurring the lines between the tangible world and virtual spaces (Richter & Richter, 2023). It results from the convergence of advanced technologies, including virtual reality (VR), augmented reality (AR), artificial intelligence (AI), and blockchain, creating a persistent multi-user environment for unprecedented interactions, collaborations, and engagements with digital content.

The origins of the Metaverse find their roots in the realm of science fiction, particularly as envisioned by authors like Neal Stephenson. These authors conceived expansive virtual realms where individuals could interact, socialize, and conduct business beyond the physical world's limitations. What began as speculative fiction has since matured into a tangible technological landscape with practical applications in the real world. A defining characteristic of the Metaverse lies in its enduring nature. In contrast to isolated applications or platforms, the Metaverse exists as an ever-evolving, constantly accessible digital realm where experiences, interactions, and content persist over time. This persistence facilitates various activities, encompassing virtual social interactions, entertainment, commercial transactions, and educational endeavors (Ghamya et al., 2023).

With the relentless march of technology, the Metaverse's pragmatic uses are steadily broadening, especially within the sphere of education. The growing accessibility and user-friendliness of virtual reality systems are paving the way for incorporating Metaverse-driven tools and platforms into educational settings. This transition has substantial potential, promising a wealth of immersive and interactive learning opportunities that can benefit educators and students.

The Metaverse's capacity to revolutionize education is nothing less than profound. With technological progress and the growing accessibility of virtual reality systems, the feasibility of adapting virtual reality glasses and peripherals for prolonged and comfortable use is rising. This marks a crucial advancement in developing Metaverse-centric hardware and software customized explicitly for educational objectives, potentially transforming the pedagogical landscape as we know it (Swacha, 2021).

The Metaverse introduces a profound transformation in education by liberating it from conventional confines. Traditional education, characterized by physical classrooms and standardized curricula, has frequently restricted the breadth of learning encounters. In the Metaverse, these limitations dissolve, ushering in an immersive and interactive learning era. Here, students transcend their traditional roles as passive knowledge recipients, actively engaging in and shaping their educational odysseys.

Envision a history class where students do not simply read about ancient civilizations but immerse themselves in virtual recreations of historical environments. They interact with historical figures and directly observe events. In the Metaverse, learning transforms into an adventure, with students embarking on quests, navigating complex virtual realms, and connecting with educational material in unprecedented ways (Domingo & Bradley, 2018).

Educators assume a central role in this evolution. They shift from being mere transmitters of knowledge to becoming designers and narrators within these virtual domains. The Metaverse equips educators with various inventive instruments to construct engaging and customized educational stories. It evolves into a platform where they can shape experiences that fascinate, test, and motivate learners.

The immersive and interactive characteristics of the Metaverse perfectly resonate with the inclinations and anticipations of contemporary tech-savvy students. These learners are accustomed to interacting with digital material in vibrant and engaging manners, rendering the Metaverse an optimal arena for nurturing their inquisitiveness, inventiveness, and analytical capabilities. It ushers fresh prospects for project-centered education, cooperative troubleshooting, and hands-on learning experiences.

The significance of incorporating gamification into Metaverse-based education cannot be emphasized enough. Gamification introduces a revolutionary method that seamlessly incorporates gaming elements into non-gaming settings. When employed within the Metaverse, it elevates immersive learning encounters to an entirely new echelon.

Central to the educational promise of the Metaverse lies the notion of involvement. In conventional educational scenarios, sustaining student engagement can be demanding, but gamification offers a remedy. Through the integration of gaming elements like scores, achievements, progression tiers, rankings, and interactive tasks, gamification harnesses humanity's inherent yearning for success, acknowledgment, and rivalry (Manzano-León et al., 2021).

In the realm of the Metaverse, this engagement takes on heightened significance. Students cease to be passive receptors of knowledge; they evolve into dynamic participants in their educational odysseys. Gamification prompts them to traverse virtual realms, fulfill quests, cooperate with peers, and partake in friendly competition within a motivational setting. This dynamic pedagogical approach harmonizes seamlessly with the immersive essence of the Metaverse, effectively transforming education into an exhilarating expedition rather than a mundane task.

Furthermore, gamification adeptly accommodates the diverse array of learning styles and preferences found among students. In conventional classrooms, standardized teaching methods might not sufficiently cater to the unique needs of every learner. However, within the expansive realm of the Metaverse, gamification empowers the crafting of tailor-made educational journeys. Here, students possess the agency to select their educational paths, establish personal objectives, and advance at their preferred tempo. Such a high degree of personalization bolsters motivation and ensures learners are profoundly engaged in their educational pursuits (Manzano-León et al., 2021).

Additionally, the Metaverse presents a distinctive platform for collaborative learning, and gamification augments its collaborative potential. Students can assemble into teams, collectively tackle challenges, and compete with other groups within virtual realms. This collaborative facet nurtures teamwork and exposes learners to a rich tapestry of viewpoints and diverse problem-solving methodologies.

Moreover, gamification fosters the cultivation of vital 21st-century competencies such as critical thinking, creativity, problem-solving, and adaptability. Within the Metaverse, students confront intricate challenges that demand astute critical and creative thinking for triumph. They acquire the ability to acclimatize to novel circumstances and nurture resilience when confronted with obstacles (Palomino et al., 2019).

Fundamentally, the incorporation of gamification into the educational domain of the Metaverse reshapes pedagogical paradigms. It leverages involvement, individualization, cooperation, and competency enhancement dynamics, culminating in an all-encompassing and revolutionary educational journey. As we explore deeper into the educational realms of the Metaverse, it becomes progressively clear that gamification stands as a pivotal element in unlocking its complete capacity to transform education.

3. GAMIFICATION IN THE METAVERSE

The integration of gamification as an educational strategy within the Metaverse signifies a dynamic amalgamation of two formidable educational frameworks. The Metaverse, with its immersive digital realm, inherently fosters the incorporation of gamification elements, forging a potent synergy that drives profound transformations in the realm of learning experiences.

Within the Metaverse, gamification surpasses conventional learning approaches by infusing educational tasks with game-like mechanisms like points, badges, levels, leaderboards, and interactive challenges. These components operate as stimulants, propelling students to immerse themselves in educational content and partake in many virtual encounters. As an illustration, students might amass points upon accomplishing assignments, earn badges signifying mastery of particular skills, or ascend through levels by showcasing their expertise. These mechanisms deliver prompt feedback and acknowledgment, capitalizing on students' innate drive for accomplishment and intrinsic motivation (Jovanović & Milosavljević, 2022).

Gamification in Metaverse learning environments offers exciting possibilities for immersive education. One striking implementation is quest-based learning, where students assume roles and embark on educational adventures. They make choices that impact historical events, delve into scientific experiments within virtual laboratories, or participate in interactive storytelling experiences. These quests excite learning, encouraging students to actively explore and apply knowledge (Nadi-Ravandi & Batooli, 2022).

Another implementation is Virtual laboratories; within the Metaverse, it provides a gamified space for scientific exploration. Students conduct experiments, record observations, and conclude in a safe, virtual setting. This approach enhances scientific understanding and nurtures curiosity and experimentation skills (Oliveira et al., 2018).

Interactive storytelling is another implementation that transports literature and language arts into the Metaverse. Students become characters in narratives, making decisions that shape the storyline. This improves reading comprehension and fosters creativity and critical thinking as they navigate the plot's twists and turns (Nadi-Ravandi & Batooli, 2022).

These are only a few examples that illustrate how gamification breathes life into Metaverse-based education. By merging immersive technology with game-inspired elements, educators create engaging and interactive learning environments that captivate students and facilitate deep understanding. These gamified experiences open doors to personalized learning, skill development, and collaborative exploration, marking a significant advancement in modern pedagogy.

Gamification within Metaverse education brings many benefits and advantages, transforming how we approach teaching and learning. Firstly, it enhances engagement and motivation. The gamified elements within the Metaverse captivate students' interest, making learning more exciting and enjoyable. When students actively participate in quests, solve challenges, and earn rewards, they are more motivated to delve into educational content. Secondly, gamification fosters personalized learning experiences. Within the Metaverse, students can choose their paths, explore topics of interest, and set their learning pace. This autonomy caters to diverse learning styles and promotes a sense of ownership over one's education (Pisano, 2018).

Moreover, it nurtures critical skills. Gamified experiences in the Metaverse often require problem-solving, decision-making, and creativity. These challenges cultivate essential 21st-century skills, preparing students for the demands of the future workforce. Furthermore, it encourages collaboration. Many gamified Metaverse environments involve teamwork, where students collaborate to achieve common goals. This collaborative learning builds communication and cooperation skills essential in today's interconnected world. Additionally, it provides instant feedback. Students receive immediate feedback on their actions and decisions in gamified Metaverse scenarios. This feedback loop facilitates a deeper understanding of concepts and encourages iterative learning. Finally, it makes learning memorable. Gamification leverages storytelling, simulations, and interactive experiences, which tend to stick in learners' minds. This results in better retention of knowledge and a more profound understanding of complex subjects (Pisano, 2018).

The Metaverse, comprising Augmented Reality, Lifelogging, Mirror World, and Virtual Reality, represents a convergence point between the physical and virtual realms. Virtual Reality stands out as the most actively engaged modality in education, fostering collaboration and content creation. Each of the four Metaverse categories holds distinct traits and educational implications, offering diverse opportunities.

Figure 2. The four elements of Metaverse and their educational implications (Kaddoura & Al Husseiny, 2023)

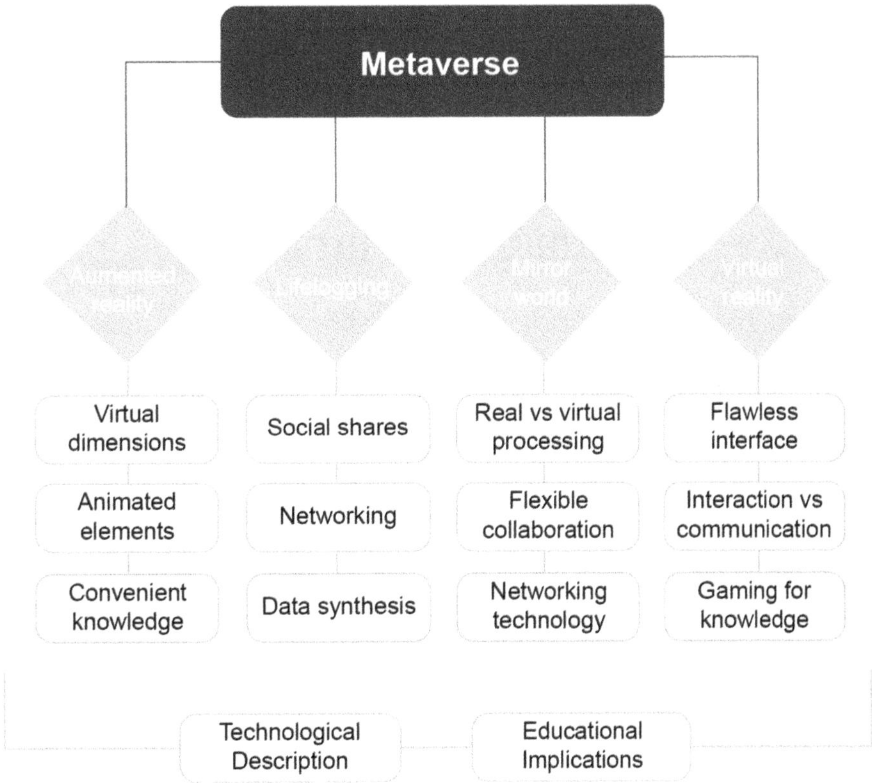

4. ADVANTAGES OF METAVERSE IN EDUCATION

As illustrated in Figure 3, the emergence of the Metaverse has transformed 3D virtual worlds, originally designed for gaming and recreation, into educational platforms. This fusion of education and entertainment enhances student engagement, making the Metaverse a promising space for educational activities. However, it faces inherent challenges and limitations (Stanoevska-Slabeva, 2022).

Figure 3. Advantages of Metaverse in education (adapted from Kaddoura & Al Husseiny, 2023, with additional elements by authors)

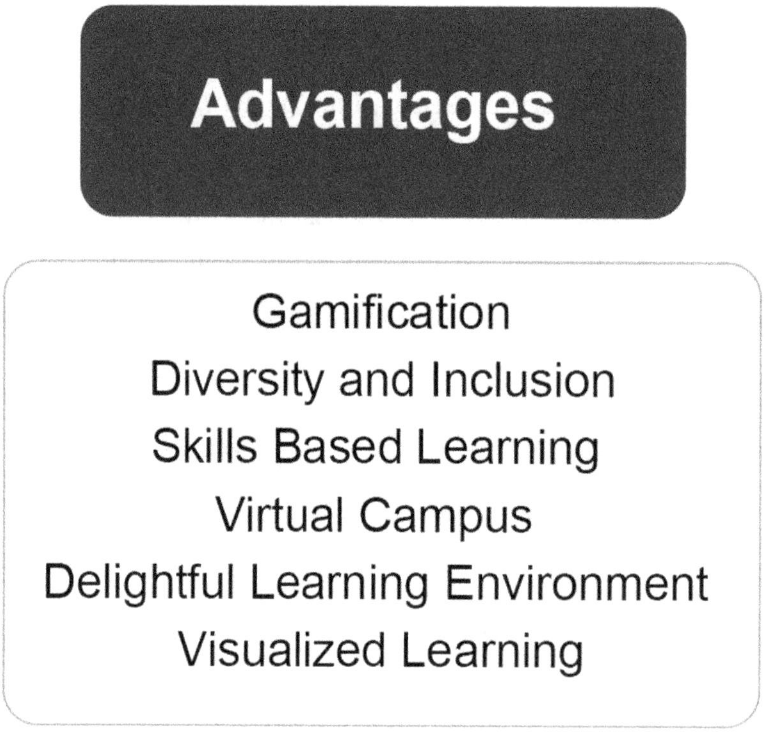

Creating an active learning environment is crucial for improving students' cognitive abilities, especially critical thinking and active participation in online learning. Despite its importance, further exploration and novel frameworks are needed to enhance learning competencies and online performance.

4.1 Gamification

Integration of gamification into the Metaverse has several advantages, especially in education. As Generation Z, born after 1995, becomes the primary users of the Metaverse, gamification becomes crucial due to their preference for game-like experiences (Park & Kim, 2021). Gamification incorporates elements like points, badges, levels, and leaderboards into educational activities within the Metaverse, making learning more engaging and interactive. Active participation increases motivation and improves learning outcomes (Kim et al., 2018).

In the Metaverse, students can explore virtual worlds tailored to their learning preferences and strengths, allowing personalized learning experiences catering to diverse styles and paces. These experiences simulate real-world scenarios, promoting critical thinking and problem-solving skills. Gamification elements also enable continuous progress tracking, enhancing the quality of education by providing timely feedback. Furthermore, gamification fosters positive attitudes toward learning and boosts learner motivation (Kim et al., 2018). Additionally, as the Metaverse becomes more integrated into society, students gain valuable digital literacy skills, better preparing them for the digital age's demands.

4.2 Diversity and inclusion

Integrating the Metaverse into educational settings facilitates the convergence of students from diverse backgrounds within a unified learning environment (Park & Min, 2022). Diversity, equity, and inclusion principles have assumed a pronounced significance within the contemporary socio-economic landscape across various sectors. The availability of technology and services has engendered an essential foundation for social equity, catalyzing advancing diversity, equity, and inclusion agendas (Zallio & Clarkson, 2022).

The Metaverse presents a compelling prospect for mitigating numerous challenges experienced in the physical world. These challenges encompass physical disabilities, constrained access to specific locations, social isolation from limited exposure to diverse demographics, and the provision of novel sensory experiences tailored to individuals with sensory or cognitive impairments (Zallio & Clarkson, 2022).

4.3 Skill-Based Learning

Learning in the Metaverse offers a unique opportunity to develop various skills, allowing learners to practice and refine them extensively, aligning with a skill-based learning approach (Han et al., 2023). Augmented reality within mobile media can enhance cognitive development and create innovative learning experiences. However, it's essential to validate the effectiveness of self-directed education and its impact on academic performance, especially considering the lack of prior training for educators and students (Lin et al., 2022). Educators must adapt to digital communication channels, and students must enhance their technological proficiency to remain competitive in the global job market. To succeed in the global marketplace, students must develop a versatile skill set, including critical thinking, problem-solving, communication, collaboration, and digital literacy.

4.4 Virtual Campus

The World Bank Group, using its Open Learning Campus, emphasizes various educational benefits associated with the Metaverse. These advantages encompass the establishment of a realistic virtual campus to facilitate learner connectivity, the enhancement of real-world competencies in hybrid and virtual environments, the exploration of diverse realms through immersive storytelling and visualization, the augmentation of human capabilities in both social and challenging contexts, the formulation of inclusive solutions tailored to learners with disabilities, and the amplification of overall learning performance (Kaddoura & Al Husseiny, 2023).

Predominantly, ongoing endeavors to create a campus Metaverse are centered on virtual environments and virtual reality modalities. In contrast, an Augmented Reality (AR) Metaverse affords the unique capacity for situated interaction within specific physical spaces, bridging the divide between physical campus infrastructure and digital content. This distinctive feature of an AR campus Metaverse presents a rare opportunity to seamlessly amalgamate digital content with physical infrastructure, rendering situated services accessible to campus users (Hussain, 2023).

4.5 Delightful Learning Environment

Deploying a Metaverse within an educational context necessitates considering its social implications. Within the framework of an educational scenario, four fundamental constituents come to the forefront, namely, educators, learners, educational resources, and the educational milieu (Sá & Serpa, 2023). In the context of an educational Metaverse, the virtual learning environments exhibit a remarkable degree of fluidity, subject to replication and modification by any or all individuals inhabiting these spaces. This dynamic feature facilitates robust interaction between students and available educational resources and environments (Stanoevska-Slabeva, 2022).

Furthermore, the Metaverse is a pivotal conduit bridging the real and virtual realms, fostering experiential learning and immersion and ultimately providing learners with realistic and enriching educational experiences. An inherent virtue of the Metaverse is its capacity to significantly augment tangible learning, a coveted attribute within instructional contexts. This mode of instruction engages students' sensory faculties, encompassing visual, auditory, and tactile modalities, thereby engendering a conducive and gratifying learning milieu (Inceoglu & Ciloglugil, 2022).

4.6 Personalization

In the context of the metaverse, the avatars can be individualized, representing cultural, physical, and social. These avatars possess the ability to interact with other entities, collaborating in the achievement of specific goals. In addition to this aspect, it is crucial to emphasize that in the metaverse, an avatar or an AI-based virtual agent has the capacity to provide highly personalized feedback and motivation, thereby enhancing the effectiveness of interventions aimed at fostering behavioral change (Petrigna & Musumeci, 2022).

4.7 Visualized Learning

The rapid progress in computer vision and graphics technology has engendered Metaverse environments characterized by pronounced visual richness and impact. Within an effective educational Metaverse setting, it becomes imperative for educators and learners to navigate realistic virtual landscapes seamlessly, fostering a highly organic interaction between pedagogical actions and the digital environment (Zonaphan et al., 2022). Consequently, the development of natural interaction technologies assumes paramount significance within the educational Metaverse, complementing the concurrent evolution of visual experiential technologies.

4.8 Data Analytics and Feedback

Metaverse platforms can collect student interactions and performance data, allowing educators to track progress and provide timely feedback. This data-driven approach can help identify areas where students may need extra support (Lee et al., 2021).

5. LIMITATIONS AND CHALLENGES

In addition to their higher cost than conventional educational tools such as computers and textbooks, XR technologies often demand a robust and high-speed internet connection for optimal functionality. Furthermore, creating content within XR environments entails elevated expenses, necessitating specialized tools, and proficiencies essential for developing interactive virtual settings conducive to effective learning (Figure 4).

Figure 4. Disadvantages of Metaverse in education (adapted from Kaddoura & Al Husseiny, 2023, with additional elements by authors)

5.1 Expensive Infrastructure

In addition to their higher cost than conventional educational tools such as computers and textbooks, XR technologies often demand a robust and high-speed internet connection for optimal functionality. Furthermore, creating content within XR environments entails elevated expenses, necessitating specialized tools and proficiencies for developing interactive virtual settings conducive to effective learning (Stanoevska-Slabeva, 2022).

5.2 Absence of Legislative Restrictions

The Metaverse, being a relatively recent concept, currently exists within an unconventional framework devoid of established legal regulations on a national or international scale. Consequently, the imperative of formulating legal frameworks to govern this nascent realm becomes evident, potentially piquing the interest of both national and international educational stakeholders. Notably, the Metaverse operates within a decentralized internet landscape, raising concerns regarding its computer security integrity (Kaddoura & Al Husseiny, 2023).

5.3 Cultural Biases

The extensive adoption of Information and Communication Technology (ICT) has sparked apprehensions regarding the potential exacerbation of social and economic disparities, as it has the potential to marginalize further individuals belonging to the less skilled and technologically unversed segments of economically disadvantaged communities. Within virtual reality, pre-existing inequalities manifest in reality can be magnified manifold. In this context, the Metaverse presents an avenue through which the reformation and restructuring of regulations about social equity can be contemplated (Monaco & Sacchi, 2023).

5.4 Usability and Accessibility Issues

Contemporary XR technologies may pose challenges for a significant portion of the population. For example, individuals with limited hand dexterity may encounter difficulties in effectively operating controls, while using head-mounted displays (HMD) can be cumbersome for those who wear glasses. Moreover, equitable access to certain technologies remains elusive for individuals from diverse backgrounds and identities. For instance, some head coverings, like religious head coverings or natural Black hairstyles, may not be compatible with headphones (Wang et al., 2022).

Due to its attributes, XR particularly lends itself to the instruction of skills, competencies, beliefs, and attitudes that may not be effectively assessed through conventional multiple-choice learning evaluations. This is due to its capacity to provide a personalized and less structured learning environment. Nevertheless, despite the wealth of user data that XR can collect, encompassing aspects such as movement and eye tracking, an as-yet-unrealized potential exists in harnessing this data for meaningful learning assessments.

5.5 Time Constraints

The utilization of Motion Devices (MDs) within Virtual Reality (VR) and Mixed Reality (MR) contexts can exhibit diminishing effects over time, potentially resulting in user discomfort or nausea within as short a timeframe as 10 to 15 minutes. Therefore, it is advisable to employ such devices judiciously rather than relying on them as the predominant educational modality throughout an entire course. For extended-duration interventions, alternative technologies such as computer-based applications, augmented reality on mobile devices, or low-tech solutions may be more suitable and sustainable options (Prabadevi et al., 2023).

5.6 Expertise Deficiency

The concept of perceived compatibility within the context of a learner's perspective pertains to their assessment of how technology aligns with their background, existing standards, and prior experiences. In essence, perceived compatibility signifies how students perceive the benefits of technology utilization. This concept is in harmony with the broader idea of compatibility, which posits that individuals are more inclined to embrace novel technological innovations when they align with their established norms and expectations (Zhang et al., 2022).

5.7 Device Challenges

The Metaverse, with its growing user base and reliance on cloud-based platforms, requires significant computing power to sustain its operations. This includes processing, storage, and data transfer capabilities. As the Metaverse evolves, its complexity and power consumption continuously increase, driven by innovative business models and cloud technologies (Lin et al., 2022).

However, challenges exist regarding the cost of VR headsets and other required technologies, which may hinder the adoption of the Metaverse. Some demographic groups could face exclusion based on education, socioeconomic status, age, and disabilities (Mystakidis, 2022).

The Metaverse generates large amounts of data, including sensor data, virtual space for user interactions, and high-resolution video feeds, demanding substantial network capacity. While 5G technology theoretically offers high speeds, it may only partially meet the Metaverse's requirements. Peer-to-peer (P2P) communication methods are a potential solution, with user devices combining content from various sources to provide a cohesive virtual environment (Aslam et al., 2023).

Low latency is crucial for the user experience, but achieving it across geographically dispersed Metaverse users takes much work. Like those in haptic and extended reality (XR) headsets, sensors in the Metaverse require extremely low latency. Remote rendering of virtual content at the network edge is a potential strategy to address this latency issue (Lin et al., 2022).

5.8 Network Security and Privacy Concerns

The intrinsic connection between one's genuine identity and the Metaverse has been notably emphasized. In a manner reminiscent of previous network environments, the Metaverse finds itself confronted with the imperative of meticulously addressing concerns about data privacy protection as it lays the foundations for a new era of networking.

As apprehensions surrounding security within immersive educational platforms mount, the vulnerability of head-mounted display (HMD) devices to potential attacks becomes a pertinent issue, as these attacks could potentially disorient users through the superimposition or alteration of visual content within their field of view (Jagatheesaperumal et al., 2022). Indeed, the exigencies of privacy and security within the Metaverse demand our unwavering attention.

Although our empirical analysis has corroborated the utilization of secure communication protocols for safeguarding transmitted data on commercial social VR platforms, the Metaverse remains susceptible to a gamut of security concerns, including the exposure of user-identifying information. Given the imperative of headset access, users are often compelled to verify their identities by providing biometric data, rendering them susceptible to potential security breaches (Di Pietro & Cresci, 2021).

Furthermore, the digital twins that inhabit the Metaverse warrant our diligent protection. In this context, many intricate machine-learning models underpin digital twins, exerting tangible influence over real-world entities. Consequently, breaches targeting these models could precipitate unforeseen ramifications within the physical realm.

Moreover, user-worn headsets consistently amass personal data, encompassing biometric information and user activity, to enhance the Quality of Experience (QoE). However, this practice has raised profound privacy concerns. One plausible avenue to explore entails blockchain storage for the digital twins inhabiting the Metaverse and for housing biometric data (Chen et al., 2022).

Nonetheless, it is imperative to underscore that users engaging with the Metaverse should primarily be attuned to the pronounced privacy risks at hand, given that the privacy-enhancing mechanisms hitherto presented remain insufficient in grappling with this distinctive challenge. We must acknowledge that technology, albeit capable of providing some privacy protection, operates within inherent constraints that necessitate astute consideration.

The Metaverse confronts a formidable challenge and ethical dilemma concerning privacy. Protocols governing the acquisition and dissemination of personally identifiable information remain subjects of ongoing debate. Given the colossal volume of data poised for collection, analysis, categorization, commodification, and monetization, datafication and privacy constitute the bedrock of the Metaverse. In commerce, the intrinsic value of data transcends its tangible form, residing instead in its capacity to forge connections with databases and analytical tools (Sun et al., 2022).

The advent of networked digital technologies, which have permeated the fabric of everyday existence, has ushered smart cities into an unprecedented era characterized by datafication and algorithmization. This surge in data processing raises profound concerns regarding privacy infringement. Within the ethical considerations surrounding intelligent urban landscapes, Calvo (2020) investigates the moral consequences of urban society's datafication and algorithmization.

From a legal and informational practice standards perspective, justice issues loom large, posing substantial impediments to privacy safeguards within the Metaverse. Equity is a paramount concern concerning the Metaverse's utilization of profiling and behavioral and social classification of individuals in the virtual realm. The Metaverse ought to prioritize algorithmic fairness across its design framework. Consequently, procedural justice should persist as a governing principle, as it necessitates a high level of openness for users and outcome control methods (Lee et al., 2021). Nevertheless, it is crucial to acknowledge that algorithmic governance may inadvertently perpetuate unfairness and inequality, mirroring the broader concerns of data justice across diverse demographic groups, with the potential for adverse repercussions (Jauhiainen et al., 2022).

Despite the difficulties faced by technological illiteracy, manipulative behavior, cognitive dissonance, and the privacy paradox, issues and risks associated with privacy infringement do not appear to deter the youth demographic from engaging in daily social media activities. A similar pattern of acceptance may emerge among this demographic about the Metaverse. Conversely, the adult population exhibits heightened concerns regarding privacy. Consequently, devising verifiable privacy safeguards is a paramount challenge the Metaverse must address to garner societal acceptance (Lee et al., 2021).

5.9 Physical and Mental Health

The Metaverse's problematic application and the associated issue of user addiction represent formidable challenges necessitating careful consideration and remediation efforts. The protracted implications of the COVID-19 pandemic on urban lifestyles and work dynamics further exacerbate these challenges. Recent scholarly inquiry has extensively demonstrated that sustained engagement with these virtual environments may yield further complications regarding excessive internet usage and addictive behaviors. This is particularly salient in light of the crisis's societal transition, which has shifted from traditional face-to-face interactions and social meetings to virtual counterparts (Kaddoura & Al Husseiny, 2023).

Recent empirical data and findings substantiate the emergence of mental health issues and addictive tendencies associated with virtual reality, accounting for a substantial 47% of the risks associated with the Metaverse among global internet users in 2021 (Statista, 2022). The prospect of overreliance on the

Metaverse due to its immersive experiences raises concerns about physical and mental health ramifications, potentially resulting in users neglecting their daily responsibilities.

Indeed, the extensive utilization of Metaverse offerings has given rise to a dependency on immersive technology, encouraging active dialogues among scientists, technologists, and physicians. This subject matter is expected to become increasingly fertile ground for further investigation, discourse, and critical examination, with many perspectives poised to be explored (Bojic, 2022). Consequently, formulating and implementing evidence-based strategies and recommendations for policymakers are expected to pose substantial challenges.

Furthermore, the assertion made by Meta, purporting that individuals can engage in various activities within the Metaverse, encompassing social interactions, work, recreation, education, commerce, and creative pursuits, with a focus on enhancing the purposefulness of online engagement, paradoxically conflicts with the likely trajectory of cyberspace utilization, especially among younger cohorts. The evolving landscape of the Metaverse, with its diverse array of engaging activities, may entice young users into protracted and aimless online interactions. This discrepancy underscores the intricate interplay between immersive technologies and psychological states; peak experiences, optimal attention span restoration, and great emotional experiences are all intrinsically linked to individuals' engagement with natural environments in virtual or augmented reality settings.

The discourse surrounding the ethical dimensions of the Metaverse has gained unprecedented prominence, aligning with the historical precedence of ethical considerations accompanying novel technologies. Many ethical concerns necessitate comprehensive examination and resolution to establish the Metaverse as a secure virtual realm capable of surmounting contemporary communication and equity challenges.

6. PRACTICAL EXAMPLES

The metaverse, a 3D virtual environment still in development, has already begun to yield promising success stories in the realm of education. The following examples showcase how the metaverse is being utilized to enhance learning experiences, fostering engagement and skill development.

Corporate Training in the Metaverse: Several companies, including Roblox, have begun to offer courses aimed at their users and collaborators. In this context, Roblox offers specializations that cover a variety of topics, such as 'Blender + Roblox,' 'Graphic Narrative of Video Games,' and 'Creating Popular Games in Roblox,' among others (Roblox Corporation, 2023). The fact that Roblox has millions of users clearly demonstrates the potential of the metaverse in corporate training.

Higher Education in Virtual Worlds: Universities are also exploring the metaverse as a platform for higher education. The Parsons School of Design, for instance, offers a fashion design course on Roblox. This innovative approach has received positive feedback from students who appreciate the interactive and engaging nature of learning in virtual environments (Roblox Corporation, 2022).

Professional Training in the Metaverse: Beyond traditional education, companies like Udemy are providing professional training courses within the metaverse. For instance, Udemy offers a programming course in The Sandbox metaverse. This course has gained popularity among students seeking to acquire new skills, highlighting the metaverse's potential for professional development (Udemy, 2023).

VoRtex: Is an innovative platform designed to support collaborative learning in virtual environments, aligning with educational standards and serving as an open-source solution based on metaverse concepts and modern technology. This gamification strategy promotes teamwork, positive behavior, and motivation, fostering active participation in the learning process (Jovanović & Milosavljević, 2022).

These are just a few examples of the success stories emerging from educational initiatives in the metaverse. As this technology continues to evolve, it is highly likely that we will witness even more innovative applications in education, with a growing body of research and practical examples providing valuable insights into the metaverse's educational potential.

6.1 Integration With Metaverse and Gamification Education

The integration of gamification and immersive virtual environments is in alignment with the educational potential of the Metaverse (Tayal et al., 2022). The growing reputation of the Metaverse heralds the dawn of a more immersive online interaction for users, where they have the opportunity to harness multiple advantages:

- They showcase how virtual worlds, like those within the Metaverse, can provide engaging and immersive learning experiences.
- Gamification principles, such as active participation, motivation, and collaboration, are evident in these cases, demonstrating the effectiveness of game elements in education.
- The cases emphasize the importance of educators adapting to these new learning environments, aligning with the discussion about the evolving role of educators in the Metaverse.

6.2 Lessons Learned and Good Practices

These real-world examples yield valuable insights for educators and institutions:

- **Engagement and Enjoyment**: Incorporating gamification and the Metaverse into education has the potential to render learning not only more captivating but also more pleasurable. This approach ensures that students become active participants in their learning, resulting in heightened curiosity and fervor for the subjects.
- **Improved Learning Outcomes**: The efficacy of gamification and the Metaverse in enhancing student engagement, motivation, and learning outcomes has been consistently demonstrated. These innovative tools stimulate students to assume responsibility for their educational voyage.
- **Inclusivity**: Leveraging gamification and the Metaverse can foster a more inclusive educational environment. It caters to various learning styles and requirements, accommodating a broader spectrum of students.
- **Predicting Future Issues**: Educators can employ these technologies to anticipate forthcoming societal issues by closely tracking student engagement and performance. Timely intervention can aid in tackling academic and behavioral challenges.
- **Enhanced Assessment**: Gamification and the Metaverse equip educators with advanced instruments for assessing the efficiency of their teaching approaches. Insights derived from data enable ongoing enhancements in instructional strategies.
- **Non-Didactic Learning**: These technologies promote experiential learning. Students actively explore, experiment, and collaborate, nurturing a sense of independence and curiosity. These real-world instances highlight the transformative capacity of gamification and the Metaverse in

education, providing a sneak peek into a future where learning is not just efficient but also an exhilarating journey.

7. FUTURE OF THE METAVERSE IN EDUCATION

The educational potential of the Metaverse's future is brimming with promise, guided by pivotal trends that will sculpt its trajectory. The Metaverse's capacity to deliver immersive encounters is on the brink of expansion thanks to advancing technology. The refinement of virtual reality and augmented reality technologies is poised to enable students to delve further into educational content, surpassing the confines of conventional learning methods (McHaney et al., 2018).

Personalization is another fundamental pillar in the future of education within the Metaverse. Systems powered by artificial intelligence are poised to flexibly adjust content to cater to the unique requirements of each student, fundamentally transforming the efficacy and involvement in education. This customized approach to educational experiences promises to substantially improve learning results (Schlemmer & Backes, 2018).

Furthermore, the inherently global character of the Metaverse will cultivate international collaborations. Pupils from diverse corners will engage in joint ventures, enriching cultural interchange and nurturing a broader global outlook. This globalized educational approach can dismantle geographical confines and champion diversity within the realm of learning.

Simultaneously, educational establishments will increasingly acknowledge the significance of imparting Metaverse technology proficiency to educators. Prioritizing professional development in this regard will prove pivotal in harnessing the complete capabilities of the Metaverse within educational settings, guaranteeing that educators possess the necessary skills to navigate this ever-evolving educational milieu effectively.

7.1 Evolution of Gamification in Education

Gamification will persist as a potent educational catalyst within the Metaverse, adapting to harmonize with the evolving demands of learners. A notable progression is the advent of customized gamified learning trajectories, furnishing students with personalized educational odysseys. These trajectories encompass quests, trials, and encounters meticulously crafted to resonate with each student's passions and proficiencies, stimulating engagement and fostering motivation (Rabah et al., 2018).

The fusion of AI with gamification promises to usher in a profound transformation. AI will furnish instantaneous feedback and calibrate challenges to harmonize with the diverse learning proclivities of students, thereby accentuating the personalized essence of Metaverse education. Furthermore, gamification will introduce inventive methodologies for evaluating student progress and acknowledging milestones, with digital accolades, certifications, and leaderboards evolving into increasingly intricate and sophisticated forms of recognition (Rabah et al., 2018).

Crucially, gamification's influence will transcend conventional classrooms, serving as a bedrock for lifelong learning. Working professionals will immerse themselves in ongoing skill enhancement via interactive, gamified encounters, cementing that education is an enduring, lifelong voyage.

Educators stand at the forefront of the Metaverse's assimilation into education, where continuous training becomes paramount. Competency in Metaverse technologies and gamification is imperative for educators to craft captivating and immersive learning journeys (McHaney et al., 2018).

Within the Metaverse, educators will assume innovative roles as architects of virtual learning landscapes. Their task will be constructing educational narratives and encounters that transcend conventional pedagogical approaches. A fundamental facet of their role will involve fostering collaboration among students in virtual endeavors and engagements (McHaney et al., 2018).

Furthermore, educators must commit to lifelong learning, continuously updating their knowledge of technological advances and pedagogical breakthroughs. As they navigate students through the Metaverse, educators will simultaneously embark on their learning journeys, adjusting to the perpetually shifting educational terrain.

8. CONCLUSIONS AND RECOMMENDATIONS

The infusion of virtual environments into education signifies a profound transformation, delivering custom-tailored learning encounters to a cohort of digitally savvy learners. This transformation has introduced pioneering pedagogical strategies that underscore active engagement by students and the cultivation of collaborative learning. With technological progress, these virtual realms have grown in scalability and adaptability, enabling their utilization across various domains, ranging from scholarly investigations to interactive simulations.

Mastery of virtual world navigation is essential for educators and students, with digital proficiency among students being a valuable asset. Educators can craft a cohesive curriculum that integrates virtual experiences with traditional teaching, becoming facilitators of knowledge and critical thinking. Meanwhile, students' digital adeptness empowers them to actively participate in their learning journey, preparing them for a technology-centric job market.

Designing proficient virtual learning environments demands meticulous attention to user interfaces, navigational aspects, accessibility, and interactivity. User-friendly interfaces and accessibility features ensure an inclusive educational experience, while interactivity is crucial for engaging and immersive virtual learning.

However, the Metaverse in education presents distinct challenges. Infrastructure limitations, such as unequal access to high-speed internet and computing devices, must be addressed to ensure equitable access to virtual education. Privacy and security concerns arise as copious data is generated in virtual realms, necessitating robust data security protocols. Ethical considerations related to digital identities and online behavior require educators to promote responsible digital citizenship and address ethical dilemmas within virtual environments.

In conclusion, integrating virtual worlds into education has fundamentally transformed pedagogical approaches, emphasizing active learning and collaboration. The scalability and versatility of virtual environments offer diverse applications, while digital proficiency among students and educators enhances their ability to navigate and create within these spaces. Careful design is essential for creating engaging virtual learning environments. However, challenges related to infrastructure, privacy, security, and ethics must be systematically addressed to unlock the full potential of the Metaverse in education. As we navigate this transformative journey, the future of education shines with vibrant opportunities for growth and innovation.

REFERENCES

Aslam, A. M., Chaudhary, R., Bhardwaj, A., Budhiraja, I., Kumar, N., & Zeadally, S. (2023). Metaverse for 6G and Beyond: The next revolution and deployMent ChallenGes. *IEEE Internet of Things Magazine*, *6*(1), 32–39. doi:10.1109/IOTM.001.2200248

Bojic, L. (2022). Metaverse through the prism of power and addiction: What will happen when the virtual world becomes more attractive than reality? *European Journal of Futures Research*, *10*(1), 1–24. doi:10.1186/s40309-022-00208-4

Calvo, P. (2020). The ethics of Smart City (EoSC): Moral implications of hyperconnectivity, algorithmization and the datafication of urban digital society. *Ethics and Information Technology*, *22*(2), 141–149. doi:10.1007/s10676-019-09523-0

Chen, Z., Wu, J., Gan, W., & Qi, Z. (2022). Metaverse security and privacy: An overview. In *2022 IEEE International Conference on Big Data (Big Data)* (pp. 2950-2959). IEEE.

Di Pietro, R., & Cresci, S. (2021). Metaverse: security and privacy issues. In *2021 Third IEEE International Conference on Trust, Privacy and Security in Intelligent Systems and Applications (TPS-ISA)* (pp. 281-288). IEEE.

Domingo, J. R., & Bradley, E. G. (2018). Education student perceptions of virtual reality as a learning tool. *Journal of Educational Technology Systems*, *46*(3), 329–342. doi:10.1177/0047239517736873

Ghamya, K., Yadav, C. C., Pranav, D. V. S., Reddy Madhavi, K., & Patel, A. (2023). Metaverse: The Potential Threats in the Virtual World. In *Proceedings of Fourth International Conference on Computer and Communication Technologies: IC3T 2022* (pp. 59-67). Singapore: Springer Nature Singapore.

Han, J., Liu, G., & Gao, Y. (2023). Learners in the Metaverse: A systematic review on using Roblox in learning. *Education Sciences*, *13*(3), 296. doi:10.3390/educsci13030296

Hussain, S. (2023, April). Metaverse for education–Virtual or real? *Frontiers in Education*, *8*, 1177429. doi:10.3389/feduc.2023.1177429

Inceoglu, M. M., & Ciloglugil, B. (2022). Use of Metaverse in education. In *International conference on computational science and its applications* (pp. 171-184). Cham: Springer International Publishing.

Jagatheesaperumal, S. K., Ahmad, K., Al-Fuqaha, A., & Qadir, J. (2022). Advancing education through extended reality and internet of everything enabled metaverses: applications, challenges, and open issues. *arXiv preprint arXiv:2207.01512.*

Jauhiainen, J. S., Krohn, C., & Junnila, J. (2022). Metaverse and Sustainability: Systematic Review of Scientific Publications until 2022 and Beyond. *Sustainability (Basel)*, *15*(1), 346. doi:10.3390/su15010346

Jovanović, A., & Milosavljević, A. (2022). VoRtex Metaverse platform for gamified collaborative learning. *Electronics (Basel)*, *11*(3), 317. doi:10.3390/electronics11030317

Kaddoura, S., & Al Husseiny, F. (2023). The rising trend of Metaverse in education: Challenges, opportunities, and ethical considerations. *PeerJ. Computer Science*, *9*, e1252. doi:10.7717/peerj-cs.1252 PMID:37346578

Kim, S., Song, K., Lockee, B., Burton, J., Kim, S., Song, K., & Burton, J. (2018). *What is gamification in learning and education?* Springer International Publishing. doi:10.1007/978-3-319-47283-6

Lee, L. H., Braud, T., Zhou, P., Wang, L., Xu, D., Lin, Z., . . . Hui, P. (2021). All one needs to know about metaverse: A complete survey on technological singularity, virtual ecosystem, and research agenda. *arXiv preprint arXiv:2110.05352.*

Lengsfeld, J. (2019). *Digital era framework.* Academic Press.

Lin, H., Wan, S., Gan, W., Chen, J., & Chao, H. C. (2022). Metaverse in education: Vision, opportunities, and challenges. In *2022 IEEE International Conference on Big Data (Big Data)* (pp. 2857-2866). IEEE.

Manzano-León, A., Camacho-Lazarraga, P., Guerrero, M. A., Guerrero-Puerta, L., Aguilar-Parra, J. M., Trigueros, R., & Alias, A. (2021). Between level up and game over: A systematic literature review of gamification in education. *Sustainability (Basel), 13*(4), 2247. doi:10.3390/su13042247

McHaney, R., Reiter, L., & Reychav, I. (2018). Immersive simulation in constructivist-based classroom e-learning. *International Journal on E-Learning, 17*(1), 39–64.

Monaco, S., & Sacchi, G. (2023). Travelling the metaverse: Potential benefits and main challenges for tourism sectors and research applications. *Sustainability (Basel), 15*(4), 3348. doi:10.3390/su15043348

Mystakidis, S. (2022). Metaverse. *Metaverse. Encyclopedia, 2*(1), 486–497. doi:10.3390/encyclopedia2010031

Nadi-Ravandi, S., & Batooli, Z. (2022). Gamification in education: A scientometric, content and co-occurrence analysis of systematic review and meta-analysis articles. *Education and Information Technologies, 27*(7), 10207–10238. doi:10.1007/s10639-022-11048-x PMID:35431599

Oliveira, T. A., Marranghello, N., Silva, A. C. R., & Pereira, A. S. (2018). Virtual laboratories development using 3D environments. In *Virtual and augmented reality: Concepts, methodologies, tools, and applications* (pp. 733–758). IGI Global. doi:10.4018/978-1-5225-5469-1.ch035

Palomino, P. T., Toda, A. M., Oliveira, W., Cristea, A. I., & Isotani, S. (2019). Narrative for gamification in education: why should you care? In *2019 IEEE 19th International Conference on Advanced Learning Technologies (ICALT)* (Vol. 2161, pp. 97-99). IEEE. 10.1109/ICALT.2019.00035

Park, S., & Kim, S. (2022). Identifying world types to deliver gameful experiences for sustainable learning in the metaverse. *Sustainability (Basel), 14*(3), 1361. doi:10.3390/su14031361

Petrigna, L., & Musumeci, G. (2022). The Metaverse: A New Challenge for the Healthcare System: A Scoping Review. *Journal of Functional Morphology and Kinesiology, 7*(3), 63. doi:10.3390/jfmk7030063 PMID:36135421

Pisano, S. (2018). *Students' experiences with games and their academic potential: An interpretative phenomenological analysis* [Doctoral dissertation]. Northeastern University.

Prabadevi, B., Deepa, N., Victor, N., Gadekallu, T. R., Maddikunta, P. K. R., Yenduri, G., . . . Liyanage, M. (2023). Metaverse for Industry 5.0 in NextG Communications: Potential Applications and Future Challenges. *arXiv preprint arXiv:2308.02677.*

Rabah, J., Cassidy, R., & Beauchemin, R. (2018). Gamification in education: Real benefits or edutainment. In *17th European Conference on e-Learning, Athens, Greece* (pp. 489-497). Academic Press.

Richter, S., & Richter, A. (2023). What is novel about the Metaverse? *International Journal of Information Management, 73*, 102684. doi:10.1016/j.ijinfomgt.2023.102684

Roblox Corporation. (2022, November 1). *The New School's Parsons School of Design and Roblox Partner to Educate on Digital Fashion Design and Trends.* Roblox Corporation. Available at: https://corp.roblox.com/2022/11/01/the-new-schools-parsons-school-of-design-and-roblox-partner-to-educate-on-digital-fashion-design-and-trends/

Roblox Corporation. (2023, August 28). *Curiosity.* Roblox Corporation. Available at: https://www.robloxschool.com/

Sá, M. J., & Serpa, S. (2023). Metaverse as a learning environment: Some considerations. *Sustainability (Basel), 15*(3), 2186. doi:10.3390/su15032186

Schlemmer, E., & Backes, L. (2018). The Real Virtuality of Metaverses. In Virtual and Augmented Reality: Concepts, Methodologies, Tools, and Applications (pp. 47-64). IGI Global. doi:10.4018/978-1-5225-5469-1.ch003

Stanoevska-Slabeva, K. (2022). Opportunities and challenges of metaverse for education: a literature review. *EDULEARN22 Proceedings*, 10401-10410. 10.21125/edulearn.2022.2527

Statista. (2022, November 28). *Metaverse - Statistics & Facts.* Statista. Available at: https://www.statista.com/topics/8652/metaverse

Stephenson, N. (2003). *Snow crash: A novel.* Spectra.

Sun, J., Gan, W., Chao, H. C., & Yu, P. S. (2022). Metaverse: Survey, applications, security, and opportunities. *arXiv preprint arXiv:2210.07990.*

Swacha, J. (2021). State of research on gamification in education: A bibliometric survey. *Education Sciences, 11*(2), 69. doi:10.3390/educsci11020069

Tabach, M., & Trgalová, J. (2020). Teaching mathematics in the digital era: Standards and beyond. *STEM teachers and teaching in the digital era: Professional expectations and advancement in the 21st century schools*, 221-242.

Tayal, S., Rajagopal, K., & Mahajan, V. (2022). Virtual reality based metaverse of gamification. In *2022 6th International Conference on Computing Methodologies and Communication (ICCMC)* (pp. 1597-1604). IEEE. 10.1109/ICCMC53470.2022.9753727

Udemy. (2022, November 1). *Metaverse Masterclass: Learn Everything About the Metaverse*. Udemy. Available at: https://www.udemy.com/course/metaverse-masterclass-learn-everything-about-the-metaverse/

Wang, Y., Su, Z., Zhang, N., Xing, R., Liu, D., Luan, T. H., & Shen, X. (2022). A survey on metaverse: Fundamentals, security, and privacy. *IEEE Communications Surveys and Tutorials*.

Zallio, M., & Clarkson, P. J. (2022). Designing the metaverse: A study on inclusion, diversity, equity, accessibility and safety for digital immersive environments. *Telematics and Informatics*, *75*, 101909. doi:10.1016/j.tele.2022.101909

Zhang, X., Chen, Y., Hu, L., & Wang, Y. (2022). The metaverse in education: Definition, framework, features, potential applications, challenges, and future research topics. *Frontiers in Psychology*, *13*, 6063. doi:10.3389/fpsyg.2022.1016300 PMID:36304866

Zonaphan, L., Northus, K., Wijaya, J., Achmad, S., & Sutoyo, R. (2022). Metaverse as A Future of Education: A Systematic Review. In *2022 8th International HCI and UX Conference in Indonesia (CHIuXiD)* (Vol. 1, pp. 77-81). IE. 10.1109/CHIuXiD57244.2022.10009854

KEY TERMS AND DEFINITIONS

Artificial Intelligence (AI): Artificial Intelligence involves the development of computer systems that can perform tasks that typically require human intelligence, such as problem-solving, learning, and decision-making

Augmented Reality (AR): Augmented Reality overlaps digital information, such as images, videos, or 3D models, onto real-world devices like smartphones or AR glasses.

Cultural Biases: This context refers to pre-existing prejudices and inequalities that can be amplified in virtual reality and the Metaverse, particularly concerning disadvantaged communities, highlighting the need for reconsidering regulations related to social equity.

Extended Reality: Refers to a group of immersive technologies that create digital environments for displaying and visualizing data.

Gamification: Gamification incorporates game-like elements and mechanics into various contexts, with particular benefits evident when integrated into the Metaverse, particularly in fields such as education.

Inclusion: Refers to integrating the Metaverse in educational settings, promoting a unified learning environment for students from diverse backgrounds.

Lifelong Learning: Lifelong learning is the continuous pursuit of knowledge and skills throughout one's life, often beyond formal education.

Marlow's Pyramid: It facilitates recognizing our needs in the digital field.

Metaverse: The Metaverse refers to a collective, virtual shared space that combines physical reality with digital virtuality. It's a space where users can interact with each other and digital objects in real time, often through avatars, and it can encompass various immersive technologies like virtual reality (VR) and augmented reality (AR).

Network Security: In this context, it encompasses individuals' well-being in both their physical and psychological aspects. It refers to the potential challenges and risks associated with the extensive use of the Metaverse, including addiction, excessive internet usage, mental health issues, neglect of daily life responsibilities, and the need for strategies and recommendations to address these concerns.

Skill-Based Learning: Learning in the Metaverse provides a unique opportunity for skill development, emphasizing critical thinking, problem-solving, communication, collaboration, and digital literacy.

Usability and Accessibility Issues: It refers to the challenges people face, particularly those with limited skills.

Virtual Campus: Refers to a digital environment within the Metaverse that offers various educational benefits, including realistic virtual spaces.

Virtual Reality (VR): Virtual Reality is a technology that creates immersive, computer-generated environments that users can interact with as if they were in the physical world.

Chapter 6

Teachers and Schools Navigating Virtual Worlds and the Metaverse for Enhanced E-Learning:

Evaluating an E-Capacity Model Approach

Richard Adade
https://orcid.org/0000-0001-8006-1302
University of South Africa, South Africa

Leila Goosen
https://orcid.org/0000-0003-4948-2699
University of South Africa, South Africa

ABSTRACT

The purpose of the study reported on in this chapter is evaluating teachers' and schools' capacities to integrate technologies into a new educational curriculum using an e-capacity model approach. Against the background of navigating virtual worlds and the metaverse for enhanced e-learning, the chapter will discuss issues with regard to effective strategies and policies for digital integration in education and training, societal issues (social inequality and the digital divide, etc.), legal and ethical issues (intellectual property legislation, etc.), the hybridization of training (hybrid, Hy Flex, co-modal, etc.), simulations, artificial intelligence (AI) for training, the educational metaverse, and information and communication technologies (ICTs).

INTRODUCTION

This section will describe the general perspective of the chapter and end by specifically stating the aim and objectives.

DOI: 10.4018/979-8-3693-1034-2.ch006

Navigating Virtual Worlds and the Metaverse for Enhanced E-Learning

Artificial Intelligence and Blockchain for Training

The revitalizing power of '*digital learning*' stems from the wide range of digital tools that it provides and that training professionals must master. As a result, educational players today have unprecedented opportunities to capitalize on collaborative platforms, *blockchain for training*, deep learning, serious games, learning analytics, rapid learning, virtual classes/videoconferencing, mobile learning, and educational technologies being used for an Information and Communication Technologies for Development (ICT4D) Massive Open Online Course (MOOC) in the 21st century or growing innovative e-schools as part of a community engagement project. The digital transformation of education is accelerating thanks to these digital tools, and teaching is now investing in the educational metaverse. Because of the effects of technological advancements (Ansu-Kyeremeh & Goosen, 2022), learners can be immersed in appropriate environments that will aid in their learning processes. In line with the goal of this book, that of the chapter is to contribute as researchers to share their experiences with *Artificial Intelligence* (AI) *for training* and the metaverse, digital learning, the tools it provides, as well as new practices to adopt.

Evaluating Teachers and Schools Integrating Technologies into a New Educational Curriculum Using an E-Capacity Model Approach

Information and communications technologies (ICTs) had been delineated from completely different viewpoints. ICTs describe the methods, equipment and software used in the production, storage, processing, transmission, and management of information. It includes a range of digital instruments, connections, and devices that make information collection, organization, distribution and utilization easier (International Society for Technology in Education (ISTE), 2023). With ICTs, complex and difficult content had been made easy to understand, and through group or collaborative learning experiences, students grasp and master concepts with ease. As a result, current reforms in education demand that teachers and schools must implement some sort of technology in their classrooms by integrating it into their pedagogies during lessons. However, both schools and teachers find it difficult "to do so due to inadequate ICT facilities" (Mwenisongole, 2021, p. 215) in schools (Radwan, Razak, & Ghavifekr, 2019). Additionally, the scarcity of continuous professional development for teachers is also considered to be a barrier to classroom implementation of such educational reforms (Polikoff & Porter, 2014).

In accordance with a report by Wallet and Melgar (2015) for the United Nations Educational Scientific and Cultural Organization (UNESCO) Institute for Statistics, ICTs significantly affect how many organizations go about their everyday business, promoting efficiency, communication, and innovation across a range of industries. In the current digital era, it had developed into a crucial component for organizational accomplishment. The combination of data processing and communicational technologies will help schools and teachers towards coming up with and developing instructional technologies (Manichander, 2015).

According to Talukder, Alam and Apu (2015), ICTs assist the user to obtain access to a lot of information easily through interactions with mobile devices and other advanced technologies. It encompasses the internet, as well as internet technologies like Wi-Fi, projectors, cell phones, and other mediums for communication. ICTs also include personal computers, operating systems and application software, storage devices and mediums, audio-visual media and custom-made software that gives user the chance to contact, search, transfer, and manage personal data.

Over time, there had been significant improvement in ICT development. Social media platforms, which are used mainly for information dissemination, are essential for learners. Emerging trends related to the Web2.0 era had amplified the way knowledge is acquired and shared, compared to how information was transferred in the 'olden days' (Voccia, 2011). Information can now be shared globally because the internet had made the world a global community; pictures, videos and posts, both motivational and educational; thoughts can be easily shared, even including jobs advertisements. With the evolution in technologies, all these things mentioned can be done by learners in any place, at their own convenience, be on smart devices, like mobile phones, laptops, palmtops, iPads, tablets, or personal computers. Computer lecturers are therefore using their institutional Learning Management System (LMS) for ICT education in the cyber world (Goosen & Naidoo, 2014).

From a broad perspective, social media platforms encompass all web-based technologies like YouTube, instant messaging services, personal blogs, micro-blogs, such as Instagram, and social networking services (Facebook, Messenger and the WhatsApp platform).

Many nations have had to use information and communication technologies as an intermediary for teaching the abilities and expertise learners require to thrive in the technological society today with the goal to close this gap and give every student an opportunity to experience of equity instructional methods (Buabeng-Andoh, 2012). ICTs are accepted in all corners of the world as a futuristic medium or strategies that teachers use to tweak their teaching methods to improve students' enabled learning and achievements. In a broader context, ICTs cover digital information and electronic information storage, retrieval, manipulation, transmission, or reception. In fact, Goosen (2018b) showed how information and communication technologies broaden students' access to an ICT4D MOOC and education.

"The integration of ICT into education", particularly in the classroom setting, is of utmost importance as learners are accustomed to technology usage and thrive in a technology-rich environment (Pondiwa, El Nabahany, & Phiri, 2022, p. 135). This is because technology in education offers valuable pedagogical benefits, and the application of ICTs can lead to effective and successful learning with the support and assistance of its various "elements and components. It is" accurate to claim that with technology-based tools and equipment, students may study practically all subject areas more efficiently, beginning with sciences, mathematics, choosing the 'best' from various programming languages, performing arts, and other key topics (Shah, 2022, p. 134).

ICTs aid in the transformation of teacher-cantered lessons into learner-cantered ones (Sanchez & Alemán, 2011). Therefore, ICTs provide both students and educators with numerous educational resources and opportunities. Likewise, instructors' skill sets need to be strengthened for successful ICT integration. In order to raise educational standards and enhance teaching and learning results, the education sector has also embraced ICTs. ICTs had drawn more attention in recent years as a monitoring tool for efficient delivery of instruction in high schools. The focus is on utilizing laptops and other technology devices as tools for instruction rather than merely as a complement to the instructor when using ICTs for education (Bolaji & Adeoye, 2022). This idea was supported by Banerjee (2019), who exposed the influence of constructive thinking in global society as a result of the integration of ICTs into the pedagogy of teacher education.

Target Audience

Like that of the book that it proposes to form part of, the intended target audience of this chapter will be digital learning professionals and researchers, such as instructional designers, multimedia developers, user experience (UX) specialists, e-learning managers, learning data analysts, learning systems managers (LSM), and e-learning project managers. Furthermore, like the book, this chapter will include information on innovative pedagogical methods and emerging trends regarding technologies that promote learner engagement and success.

Recommended Topics

From the recommended topics suggested for this book, the chapter will especially focus on:

- Effective strategies and policies for digital integration in education and training
- Training systems and professional development for teachers in the era of Education 4.0
- Societal issues (social inequality and digital divide, etc.)
- Legal and ethical issues (intellectual property legislation, etc.)
- Digital identity, well-being and educational inclusion
- Hybridization of training (hybrid, Hy Flex, co-modal, etc.)
- Simulations
- Artificial intelligence for training
- Educational metaverse

Aim and Objectives

As part of this book, the chapter aims to provide relevant theoretical frameworks university partnerships promoting continued support of e-schools, as well as the most recent empirical research findings in the field of digital learning. It will be aimed at professionals, teachers, doctoral students, and anyone else, who wants to improve their understanding of the benefits and limitations of using digital technologies at various levels of education and training, such as collaborative platforms, deep learning, serious games, learning analytics, rapid learning, virtual classes/videoconferencing, mobile learning, MOOCs, and the educational metaverse.

The aim of the study reported on in this chapter is to use the e-capacity model approach to evaluate teachers and schools integrating technologies in the new education curriculum in the Asante Akim central municipality, Ghana. Specifically, the objectives of the research are to (Ahenkora, Adubofour, Osei, & Ibrahim, 2023):

1. Investigate the key *school improvement conditions* in relation to ICT integration into the new curriculum in the Asante Akim central municipality.
2. Determine ICT-related school conditions that influence the integration of ICTs in educational practices in the classroom.
3. Investigate the factors regarding ICT-related teacher conditions that contribute to the effective integration of ICTs into the new curriculum in the Asante Akim central municipality.
4. Determine the extent to which teachers actually use ICTs in their instructional practices.

The study reported on in this chapter does have some similarities to one, which investigated the status of ICT infrastructure towards the inclusion of ICTs in the new curriculum in the Hohoe municipality, Ghana (Adade, 2022).

BACKGROUND

This section of the chapter will provide broad definitions and discussions of the topic on teachers and schools navigating virtual worlds and the metaverse for enhanced e-learning by evaluating an e-capacity model approach, and incorporate the views of others (in the form of a literature review) into the discussion to support, refute, or demonstrate the authors' position on the topic.

Hybridization of Training (Hybrid, Hy Flex, Co-Modal, etc.)

In Morocco, the COVID-19 pandemic context had "functioned as a force to change the realm of digital learning, prompting numerous organizations that had previously been unwilling to take the jump" to change their perceptions of the outcomes related to co-modal education (Chafiq, Elimadi, Talbi, & Ghazouani, 2023, p. 295), as well as the role of educators as agents and conveyors for positive change in global education.

In the proceedings of the *Europe, Middle East, and North Africa conference on Information Systems and Technologies to support Learning (EMENA-ISTL 2018)*, Chafiq, Housni and Moussetad (2019, p. 118) indicated that in "the Moroccan context, universities have put digital transformation at the heart of their projects of development thanks to a wide range of hybrid learning" towards a dynamics of techno-pedagogical *innovation* within the university in a case study of the Hassan II University of Casablanca.

Towards the design of innovative and social hybrid learning based on Social, Mobile, Analytics and Cloud (SMAC) technologies, Chafiq and Housni (2019, p. 126), in the same proceedings, pointed out that blended "learning is currently part of the higher education scene, but with significant variations between teachers, institutions and even countries."

Ngugi and Goosen (2019, p. 90) also looked at aspects of *innovation* within the university context. Towards smart *innovation* for information systems, literature "identified multiple factors, which promote Innovative Behavior (IB) among employees. The problem stated" was "that facilitating the development of IB among undergraduate" technology students needed modelling motivation, metacognition and affective aspects of learning.

The purpose of the paper presented by Goosen (2019, p. 134) at *EMENA-ISTL 2018* was "introducing how Information Systems (IS) and technologies are opening new worlds for learning to children with Autism Spectrum Disorders (ASDs)."

The study purpose described by Gouws and Goosen (2019, p. 144) "was exploring *emerging technologies* in community engagement, inspiring students' interest in Science, Engineering and Technology in South Africa."

Simulations

An online international journal article on *emerging technologies* in learning by Lahlali, Chafiq, Radid,Moundy and Srour (2023, p. 193) investigated the effect of integrating interactive simulations on the development of students' motivation, engagement, interaction and school results, as the "concept of chemical bonding and related concepts are essential topics for the fundamental understanding of chemistry courses by secondary school students."

"Following the suspension of classes in Morocco due to the health crisis related to COVID-19, an adaptation of the pedagogical intervention of teaching" was required (Moundy, Chafiq, & Talbi, 2021, p. 1). Against the background of education sciences, distance learning featured as part of a c Comparative analysis of student engagement in digital textbook use during quarantine.

In terms of methodology, Hannoun, Chafiq, Raji, Elkouali and Razine (2023, p. 1) reported on "a descriptive transversal study of physicians practicing in Morocco. The data were collected using a questionnaire that included questions on" e.g., reliability. Physicians' perceptions of health topics covered by traditional media and the opinions of physicians as consumers of media were described in the latter journal article on public health in Africa.

Another article in the latter journal discussed a cross-sectional study in Kankan, Guinea, which necessitated "a thorough grasp of the" level of knowledge, attitudes, and practices toward COVID-19 among the general population in order to implement "decisive and effective infection prevention and control measures" (Demba, et al., 2023, p. 1).

"Communally popularized in the year 2002 with the start of Amazon web services, *cloud computing* has transformed the way" Information Technology (IT) "services and resources are furnished to" clients (M'Rhaouarh, Moutamanni, Labzai, Namir, & Chafiq, 2021, p. 4411). Mathematical modeling and optimal control of abstaining attitudes related to cloud computing adoption was therefore related in a journal article on mathematical and computational science.

M'rhaouarh, Namir and Chafiq (2021, p. 36) narrated cloud computing as "a developed technology which can transform the manner how traditional companies work. It becomes crucial in the IT industry. In addition," cloud computing enabled the use of the performance measures of a queuing model to optimize profit in a *cloud computing* environment in an international journal article on computer science and information security.

The research in an international journal article on advanced computer science and applications presented practices with regard to "online assessment in a digital device in the context of university training, aimed at improving their practices with emerging" trends in technologies based on the case of Hassan II university (Mrisse, Chafiq, Talbi, & Moundy, 2023, p. 450).

Data analytics and a Cumulative Accuracy Profile (CAP) approach were used by Housni, Namir, Talbi and Chafiq (2019, p. 17) in the real-time maintenance of instructional design models, as in "a constantly changing climate, professors find themselves" in an environment with pressing demands for them "to tailor their ways in schooling, according to the needs of the market and students."

MAIN FOCUS OF THE CHAPTER

Issues, Controversies, Problems

This section of the chapter will present the authors' perspective on the issues, controversies, problems, etc., as these relate to the main theme of Navigating Virtual Worlds and the Metaverse for Enhanced E-Learning and arguments supporting the authors' position on teachers and schools navigating virtual worlds and the metaverse for enhanced e-learning by evaluating an e-capacity model approach. It will also compare and contrast with what has been, or is currently being, done as it relates to the specific topic of the chapter.

One disadvantage of incorporating technology into schools is that the younger generation had grown up in an era dominated by mobile technologies and the internet. Today, it is common for children to engage in activities such as following YouTube channels, playing games, and creating and sharing videos using smartphones. However, this increased exposure to mobile devices may pose challenges for students' attention and concentration during traditional lectures. To address this issue, educators should aim to incorporate modern technologies into their teaching, actively engaging students and *leveraging* technologies to enhance the learning experience (Stecuła, 2022). *Leveraging* ethical standards in artificial intelligence technologies was suggested as a guideline for responsible teaching and learning applications (Uunona & Goosen, 2023). According to research by Shatri (2020), "parents play a crucial role in" their children's education, often monitoring their activities on smartphones, the internet, and other devices (Fitri, Siahaya, Nugraha, & Arief, 2022, p. 353). However, there are instances where parents neglect their responsibility and fail to exercise control over their children's digital usage. Both teachers and parents hold the primary responsibility in ensuring that children have appropriate access to information technologies. Sometimes, parents may reprimand their children for the improper positioning of the computer, which may be perceived as excessive and unwarranted.

A lack of support from administration runs counter to the findings of a significant body of research that highlighted the significance of the coordinator's "leadership in the ICT implementation in schools" (Rodríguez-Miranda, Pozuelos-Estrada, & León-Jariego, 2014, p. 262), coupled with the support that they provide to instructors to resolve these issues (Tondeur, Cooper, & Newhouse, 2010).

In educational research, compared to using either qualitative or quantitative approaches, combining the two research methodologies might potentially provide a more thorough knowledge of study phenomena. A mixed-methods approach enables the fusion and synergy of several data sources, allowing for a more thorough investigation of complicated issues (Poth & Munce, 2020).

According to a journal article on mixed methods research expanding on a brief history and range of mixed methods research by Maxwell (2016), another persuasive justification "for combining qualitative and quantitative methods is the" acknowledgment that each form of research possesses intrinsic worth and, in specific aspects, these mutually enhance one another (Johnson, 1990). Consequently, there is an added benefit in combining these methods. A researcher may seek to enhance the validity of their research findings by directly comparing the outcomes derived "from one method (qualitative or quantitative)" with "those obtained from another (quantitative or qualitative)" to identify areas of convergence or divergence (Chukwu, 2021, p. 118). This comparison allows for a more comprehensive understanding of the research **issue** (Plano Clark & Ivankova, 2015).

The benefits of mixed methods research include the ability to provide a more thorough and nuanced understanding of research **issues**, going beyond the drawbacks of one technique, and make it easier to triangulate and agree on results. But it also requires thorough preparation and consideration of methodological precision, data integration strategies, and the researcher's abilities and competence (Creswell & Creswell, 2018). In a guidebook published by Conroy, Houchins, Hitchcock and Anderson (2023), the application of a mixed methods approach in the field of social sciences is extensively addressed and thoroughly discussed. According to Creswell and Plano Clark (2017), after a study has been designed and while using a mixed methods approach, specific procedures must be carried out. The first step in doing this is gathering the necessary quantitative and qualitative data. In order to respond to the survey questions, the study then analyze this data. The results of the analysis are integrated using the rationale chosen for the study after the data have been analyzed.

Interviewing, according to Javeed, et al. (2022) is a crucial "qualitative method of data collection that" may be utilized to explore and describe issues and practices in education (Sefala, 2021, p. 14). Interviews are a crucial component of qualitative data collecting in educational research because these enable researchers to explore and explain a wide range of educational-related themes and practices. Researchers may obtain profound insights into the experiences, viewpoints, and behaviors of people participating in the educational setting via interviews, which allow them to examine the complexity and subtleties of educational phenomena. Researchers may capture the specifics of educational procedures, regulations, and relationships using this technique since it provides a singular chance to collect rich and thorough information. Through the use of interviews, researchers may glean insightful qualitative information that advances knowledge of educational phenomena and informs educational theory, practice, and *policy*.

A following chapter on data collection, analysis and discussion will present the findings of the study, including the analysis and interpretation of the collected data. The data will be organized and presented in relation to specific categories and themes, supported by various sources and a comprehensive literature review. The primary objective of that chapter will be to compare, validate, and discuss the findings, examining their consistency and addressing any potential discrepancies or **controversies** that may arise.

Societal Issues (Social Inequality and the Digital Divide, etc.)

"In the educational system, the different parental resources of university students are linked to social inequality through distinct mechanisms"; these are reproduced and legitimized in an international journal article on engineering pedagogy looking at the effect of parental social status in academia in a comparative case of the public/private university in Morocco (Aamro, Chafiq, Radid, & Talbi, 2023, p. 80).

Legal and Ethical Issues (Intellectual Property Legislation, etc.)

Information and Communication Technology Policy Planning

A number of issues, including legal and *policy* ones, as well as those related to infrastructure, educational resources, training for teachers, curricula, and evaluation, have an impact on ICTs in education (Tay, Lim, & Lim, 2015). In the same context, Tairab and Ronghuai (2017) showed that ICT *policy* is one of the key elements that can propel educational advancement in K–12 system of Sudan.

Teachers claim that parents' or communities' initiatives help schools use ICT infrastructure (Chapelle & Li, 2011). Technical problems have become more prevalent, causing frustration amongst staff members and pupils, as well as impeding instruction and education. If there is no technical help or repairs, teachers cannot use their personal computer for a while (Jamieson-Proctor, et al., 2013). Because they will not get assistance with the issue, teachers will not use computers out of fear that the technology will break down. The study by Tũrel and Johnson (2012) found that technological issues are a great setback for teachers. Unreliable internet connectivity, computer virus attacks, as well as broken printers are some of these challenges. Instructors should be provided with training sessions to learn more about incorporating ICTs in the education process. Peer tutoring programs, however, were used at many educational institutions. In order to prepare for teaching and learning, a teacher with more ICT experience would guide and mentor a teacher with less ICT experience. A number of variables enable the incorporation of

ICT for learning and instruction in classroom settings. ICT support policies should come first, followed by all the ICT tools plus software, and lastly, an evaluation of the instructor's readiness and capacity to incorporate these into the educational curriculum (Agbatogun, 2012).

Educational Metaverse

Against the background of *Influencer Marketing Applications Within the Metaverse*, the chapter by Chafiq, Elimadi, Ghazouani and Talbi (2023, p. 87) considered the relationships between the commercial metaverse and the customer, as well as asking what the realities, challenges, and perspectives are for brands? The metaverse had "made customer experience personalization a top priority ever since it was founded. Users can customize their avatars and live experiences to create something" appealing.

When merging Big Data with the metaverse, Ghazouani, Chafiq, Zaher, Azouazi and Chakir (2023, p. 263) proposed an architecture with multiple layers: "A shared virtual universe called a metaverse is produced when various virtual worlds and augmented reality settings collide."

Data Collection Procedure

Pilot research will be carried out to identify any issues that could complicate the execution of the study before the final questionnaire is sent out. The questionnaire and interview guide will first be made available to subject matter experts who have sufficient knowledge on how to employ ICT in teaching and learning, as well as research in general. Konongo-Odumasi senior high school will serve as the site of the pilot study, because the respondents have comparable difficulties in the Akim central municipality. The pilot study will be based on simple random sampling, utilizing a total of 16 teachers.

Data Analysis and Interpretation

Data interpretation, according to Miles, Huberman, and Saldana (2019), is the act of making meaning of the gathered data by spotting patterns, themes, and linkages. It entails deriving meaning and knowledge from the data via analysis, followed by producing inferences or interpretations based on the analysis. Data interpretation seeks to obtain deeper insight and interpretations from the data than basic descriptions. Coding and categorizing the data, looking for recurrent patterns, and creating explanatory frameworks or hypotheses to explain the events being studied are often involved. In qualitative research, data interpretation is a crucial phase that enables researchers to draw meaningful conclusions and advance knowledge of the study issue.

Rational for the Study

The purpose of the study is to use an e-capacity model approach to evaluate teachers and schools integrating technologies in a new education curriculum in the Asante Akim central municipality. This is regarded to be a problem because the new educational reform demands that teachers and schools have additional technological skills and infrastructure in other to implement this reform. Teachers may feel burdened with added responsibilities, and students affected academically, if teachers lack the knowledge and skills to integrate ICTs during the reform. This problem may be one that hinders some teachers and schools if they lack the needed ICT infrastructure and ICT support, which could affect the implementation process.

Statement of the Problem

Digital Identity, Well-Being, and Educational Inclusion

The Ghanaian government introduced a revised curriculum in September 2019 with the aim of addressing shortcomings in the previous curriculum and fostering various essential skills and competencies (GhanaWeb, 2019). The new curriculum emphasizes the development of teamwork, problem-solving, critical thinking, creativity, innovation, interpersonal skills, leadership abilities, effective communication, collaboration, cultural identity, global citizenship, and digital literacy (National Council for Curriculum and Assessment (NCCA), 2020). Moreover, it aimed at enhancing the teaching and learning process across all subjects by prioritizing learner-centered pedagogies, integrating ICTs as a teaching tool, and promoting pedagogies that prioritize equity and *educational inclusion.*

In order to facilitate the preparation of lessons, instruction, and educational outcomes, the vice president of the Republic of Ghana, Bawumia, in collaboration with the teacher unions and "KA Technologies Ghana Limited, a" local ICT company that manufactures laptops, launched the 'One Teacher, One Laptop' initiative (Jin & Schmidt-Crawford, 2017). Every teacher in a public school, from kindergarten to senior high, would get a laptop computer as part of this plan. The government would cover seventy percent of the laptop cost, with each instructor footing the remaining thirty percent (Ghana National Association of Teachers, 2021).

After success in the implementation of the new educational reform, it is crucial that the teachers, who play a central role in implementing the curriculum, possess the skills to integrate technologies into education. The success of the new curriculum is closely linked to teachers' ability to incorporate technologies effectively. "The Ministry of Education and National" Teaching Council (NTC) should gather data on teachers' level of readiness and capacity for ICT integration. This information will enable stakeholders to identify and address any gaps in knowledge or skills that need to be addressed.

In light of this context, this study seeks to evaluate teachers' and schools' capacity to integrate technologies in the new education curriculum in Asante Akim municipality.

SOLUTIONS AND RECOMMENDATIONS

This section of the chapter will discuss solutions and recommendations in dealing with the issues, controversies or problems presented in the preceding section.

Solutions

In an effort to uncover solutions to support Palestinian secondary schools in efficiently integrating technologies into teaching, Barham, Chavas, Fitz, Salas and Schechter (2014) concluded that technology integration in Palestinian schools is still geared toward a traditional approach. Principals that are able to implement technologies in their schools should conduct themselves in a supervisory role (Demski, 2012).

In the cont4ext of Big Data and a smart digital environment, adaptivity, "personalization and recommendation techniques are classic solutions recommended by many specialists for providing successful learning experiences by offering" a recommender system for videos suggestion in a Small Private Online

Course (SPOC) in terms of a proposed personalized learning method (Belarbi, Chafiq, Talbi, Namir, & Benlahmar, 2019b, p. 92).

Recommendations

School Improvement Conditions

Recommendations regarding variables in terms of *school improvement conditions* as being favorable for the successful improvement of innovative reform make up the first layer of the e-capacity model.

ICT support is the term used to describe the help and services offered to people or organizations in connection to their usage of ICTs. It includes providing technical assistance, troubleshooting, direction towards ensuring that ICT systems and tools are operating, setting up and configuring both software and hardware, resolving technical problems, providing instruction regarding ICT tools and applications, and making recommendations on best practices for utilizing ICTs.

FUTURE RESEARCH DIRECTIONS

This section of the chapter will discuss future and emerging trends and provide insight about the future of the theme of Navigating Virtual Worlds and the Metaverse for Enhanced E-Learning, from the perspective of the chapter focus on teachers and schools navigating virtual worlds and the metaverse for enhanced e-learning by evaluating an e-capacity model approach. The viability of a paradigm, model, implementation issues of proposed programs, etc., may also be included in this section. Future research directions within the domain of the topic will finally be suggested.

The impact of emerging mobile technology trends "is being felt in several sectors" these days, including education. In their international journal article on advanced computer science and applications, Belarbi, Namir, Talbi and Chafiq (2020, p. 473) presented "an analysis of the development of the mobile dimension" in a small private online course through a multi-objectives optimization.

"Cloud computing is one of the" most popular emerging trends being "utilized these days. It is the upcoming technology provisioning resources to" customers (M'rhaouarh, Chafiq, & Namir, 2021, p. 733). In *the proceedings of the international conference on smart city applications*, the latter authors were moving toward using cloud computing at universities in developing countries considering the COVID-19 crisis.

In the context of international journal articles on emerging trends regarding technologies for learning online, Moundy, Chafiq and Talbi (2022a, p. 240) indicated that following the adoption by the Moroccan educational system of "a blended learning approach vis-à-vis the circumstances of the" COVID-19 pandemic, which required an adaptation of digital textbooks and flipped classrooms, there had been some experimentation with the self-learning method based on the development of soft skills and disciplinary knowledge. "The digital transformation of institutions renovates universities to strengthen the integration of *educational technologies* with a focus on the *quality* of learning." According to Goosen (2018a), sustainable and inclusive *quality* education can be achieved through research-informed practice on information and communication technologies. The objective of another article by Moundy, Chafiq and Talbi (2022b, p. 296) was to discuss a model for scripting and designing a digital textbook, while in their article, Belarbi, Chafiq, Talbi, Namir and Benlahmar (2019a, p. 110) addressed a method for the construction of "a structured user profile in a Small Private Online Course ... based on user's video clickstream analysis".

Educational technologies can also be used in distance education to take learning programming beyond the horizon (Goosen & Van Heerden, 2017).

Manichander (2015) discussed emerging trends and issues in education.

Effective Strategies and Policies for Digital Integration in Education and Training

In addition, Information Technology helps teachers create interesting teaching materials that will motivate learners to participate actively in their own learning. According to earlier research (Dudeney, 2010), incorporating ICTs into the classroom can increase student involvement and speed up instruction. Education might well be revolutionized by research on technology-supported learning and teaching methods for educators, but this would require rigorous planning and *policy* creation. The future approach must be understood by both policymakers and researchers on an equal footing. National ICT policies can serve a number of crucial goals. These help the overall population of a nation, as well as instructors, parents, and pupils. ICTs offer a rationale, a list "of goals, and an illustration of how educational institutions would" function if ICTs were incorporated into the process of instruction and learning (Ornstein, Levine, Gutek, & Vocke, 2016). A national ICT policy can accomplish a number of significant goals. National ICT policies, according to Makoza (2022), are dynamic instruments that need to be modified often to stay up to date and in step with regional, global, and technical advancements. The latter author highlighted how policy is now the main driver of ICT development and how it may transform a country, improve social and economic lives, and enhance the standard of living for its population.

CONCLUSION

This section of the chapter will provide a discussion of the overall coverage and concluding remarks.

The study reported on in this chapter is focused on the evaluation of teachers and schools integrating technologies into the new educational curriculum using an e-capacity model approach. The chapter included a literature/scholarship review and the applicable theoretical framework as background, as well as some details on the applicable research methodology in terms of the data collection procedure, data analysis and interpretation, and finally, this conclusion (Li, 2023).

REFERENCES

Aamro, E. H., Chafiq, N., Radid, M., & Talbi, M. (2023). The Effect of Parental Social Status in Academia: Comparative Case of the Public/Private University in Morocco. *International Journal of Engineering Pedagogy*, *13*(3), 80–99. doi:10.3991/ijep.v13i3.33973

Adade, R. (2022, December). Status of ICT Infrastructure towards the inclusion of ICT in the new curriculum in the Hohoe Municipality, Ghana. *International Journal of Research in Engineering and Science*, *10*(12), 568–572.

Agbatogun, A. O. (2012). Investigating Nigerian primary school teachers' preparedness to adopt personal response system in ESL classroom. *International Electronic Journal of Elementary Education*, *4*(2), 377–394.

Ahenkora, S., Adubofour, E. B., Osei, E. G., & Ibrahim, A. (2023). Technology Use Among Ghanaian Junior High School Mathematics Teachers in the Ahafo-Ano South District. *Journal of Education and Training Studies*, *11*(3), 78–87. doi:10.11114/jets.v11i3.6066

Ansu-Kyeremeh, E. K., & Goosen, L. (2022). Exploring the Socioeconomic Facet of Online Inclusive Education in Ghana: The Effects of Technological Advancement in Academia. In M. Garcia (Ed.), *Socioeconomic Inclusion During an Era of Online Education* (pp. 47–66). IGI Global. doi:10.4018/978-1-6684-4364-4.ch003

Banerjee, I. (2019). Integration of ICT in pedagogy of teacher education: Influence of constructive thinking in global society. *International Journal of Scientific Research and Review*, *7*(6), 130–136.

Barham, B. L., Chavas, J. P., Fitz, D., Salas, V. R., & Schechter, L. (2014). The roles of risk and ambiguity in technology adoption. *Journal of Economic Behavior & Organization*, *97*, 204–218. doi:10.1016/j.jebo.2013.06.014

Belarbi, N., Chafiq, N., Talbi, M., Namir, A., & Benlahmar, E. (2019a, January 17). User profiling in a SPOC: A method based on user video clickstream analysis. *International Journal of Emerging Technologies in Learning*, *14*(1), 110–124. doi:10.3991/ijet.v14i01.9091

Belarbi, N., Chafiq, N., Talbi, M., Namir, A., & Benlahmar, H. (2019b, February 22). A recommender system for videos suggestion in a SPOC: A proposed personalized learning method. In *Big Data and Smart Digital Environment* (pp. 92–101). Springer International Publishing. doi:10.1007/978-3-030-12048-1_12

Belarbi, N., Namir, A., Talbi, M., & Chafiq, N. (2020). A Multi-Objectives Optimization to Develop the Mobile Dimension in a Small Private Online Course (SPOC). *International Journal of Advanced Computer Science and Applications*, *11*(1), 473–480. doi:10.14569/IJACSA.2020.0110158

Bolaji, H. O., & Adeoye, M. A. (2022). Accessibility, Usability, and Readiness Towards ICT Tools for Monitoring Educational Practice in Secondary Schools in Ilorin Metropolis. *Indonesian Journal of Multidiciplinary Research*, *2*(2), 257–264.

Buabeng-Andoh, C. (2012). Factors influencing teachers' adoption and integration of information and communication technology into teaching: A review of the literature. *International Journal of Education and Development using ICT, 8*(1), 136-155.

Chafiq, N., Elimadi, I., Ghazouani, M., & Talbi, M. (2023). Commercial Metaverse and the Customer: What Are the Realities, Challenges, and Perspectives for Brands? In Influencer Marketing Applications Within the Metaverse (pp. 87-101). IGI Global.

Chafiq, N., Elimadi, I., Talbi, M., & Ghazouani, M. (2023). Comodal Education in a COVID-19 Pandemic Context: Perceptions and Outcomes. In *The Role of Educators as Agents and Conveyors for Positive Change in Global Education* (pp. 295–314). IGI Global. doi:10.4018/978-1-6684-7869-1.ch013

Chafiq, N., & Housni, M. (2019). Towards the Design of an Innovative and Social Hybrid Learning Based on the SMAC Technologies. In *Information Systems and Technologies to Support Learning: Proceedings of EMENA-ISTL 2018* (pp. 126-133). Springer.

Chafiq, N., Housni, M., & Moussetad, M. (2019). Towards a dynamics of techno-pedagogical innovation within the university: Case study Hassan II University of Casablanca. In *Information Systems and Technologies to Support Learning: Proceedings of EMENA-ISTL 2018* (pp. 118-125). Springer International Publishing.

Chapelle, O., & Li, L. (2011). An empirical evaluation of Thompson sampling. *Advances in Neural Information Processing Systems*, *24*, 2249–2257.

Chukwu, O. L. (2021). *Neoliberalism and the University: An Analysis of Patterns of Transformation within Nigerian Private and Public Institutions*. University of York.

Conroy, M., Houchins, D., Hitchcock, J., & Anderson, J. (2023). Use of Mixed Methods in Emotional/Behavioral Disorders Intervention Research. *Behavioral Disorders*, *48*(3), 163–173. doi:10.1177/01987429231160283

Creswell, J. W., & Creswell, J. D. (2018). *Research design: qualitative, quantitative, and mixed methods approaches* (5th ed.). SAGE.

Creswell, J. W., & Plano Clark, V. L. (2017). *Designing and conducting mixed methods research*. Sage publications.

Demba, M., Kapasa, R. L., Camara, T., Halabi, N., Abdelaziz, H., Oumnia, B., ... Coppieters't Wallant, Y. (2023). Knowledge, attitudes, and practices toward COVID-19 among the general population: A cross-sectional study in Kankan, Guinea. *Journal of Public Health in Africa*, *14*(3). Advance online publication. doi:10.4081/jphia.2023.2231 PMID:37197262

Demski, J. (2012). Rebuilding the LMS for the 21st Century. *Campus Technology*, *25*(8), 34–37.

Dudeney, G. (2010). *The Internet and the language classroom* (Vol. X). Cambridge University Press.

Fitri, E. Y., Siahaya, J., Nugraha, A., & Arief, I. (2022). Analysis of the role of parents in online learning in the covid-19 pandemic. *International Journal of Demos*, *4*(1), 352–363. doi:10.37950/ijd.v4i1.210

Ghana National Association of Teachers. (2021). *One Laptop, One Teacher, Kick Start*. Retrieved from https://www.ghanateachers.com/news-media/gnat-news/one-laptop-one-teacher

GhanaWeb. (2019). *New Schools' Curriculum Starts in September 2019*. Retrieved from https://www.ghanaweb.com/GhanaHomePage/NewsArchive/New-schools-curriculum-starts-in-September-2019-766446

Ghazouani, M., Chafiq, N., Zaher, N., Azouazi, M., & Chakir, A. (2023). Merging Big Data With the Metaverse: A Proposed Architecture With Multiple Layers. In Influencer Marketing Applications Within the Metaverse (pp. 263-287). IGI Global. doi:10.4018/978-1-6684-8898-0.ch017

Goosen, L. (2018a). Sustainable and Inclusive Quality Education Through Research Informed Practice on Information and Communication Technologies in Education. In L. Webb (Ed.), *Proceedings of the 26th Conference of the Southern African Association for Research in Mathematics, Science and Technology Education (SAARMSTE)* (pp. 215 - 228). Gabarone: University of Botswana.

Goosen, L. (2018b). Ethical Information and Communication Technologies for Development Solutions: Research Integrity for Massive Open Online Courses. In C. Sibinga (Ed.), *Ensuring Research Integrity and the Ethical Management of Data* (pp. 155–173). IGI Global. doi:10.4018/978-1-5225-2730-5.ch009

Goosen, L. (2019). Information Systems and Technologies Opening New Worlds for Learning to Children with Autism Spectrum Disorders (Á. Rocha, & M. Serrhini, Eds.). Smart Innovation, Systems and Technologies, 111, 134-143. doi:10.1007/978-3-030-03577-8_16

Goosen, L., & Naidoo, L. (2014). Computer Lecturers Using Their Institutional LMS for ICT Education in the Cyber World. In C. Burger, & K. Naudé (Ed.), *Proceedings of the 43rd Conference of the Southern African Computer Lecturers' Association (SACLA)* (pp. 99-108). Port Elizabeth: Nelson Mandela Metropolitan University.

Goosen, L., & Van Heerden, D. (2017). Beyond the Horizon of Learning Programming with Educational Technologies. In U. I. Ogbonnaya, & S. Simelane-Mnisi (Ed.), *Proceedings of the South Africa International Conference on Educational Technologies* (pp. 78 - 90). Pretoria: African Academic Research Forum.

Gouws, P., & Goosen, L. (2019). Technologies to Inspire Education in Science, Engineering and Technology Through Community Engagement in South Africa. *Smart Innovation, Systems and Technologies, 111*, 144–153.

Hannoun, A., Chafiq, N., Raji, M., Elkouali, M. H., & Razine, R. (2023). Physicians' perception of health topics covered by traditional media in Morocco: Opinion of physicians as consumers of the media. *Journal of Public Health in Africa, 14*(5). Advance online publication. doi:10.4081/jphia.2023.2275 PMID:37441121

Housni, M., Namir, A., Talbi, M., & Chafiq, N. (2019). Applying Data Analytics and Cumulative Accuracy Profile (CAP) Approach in Real-Time Maintenance of Instructional Design Models. In Lecture Notes in Real-Time Intelligent Systems (pp. 17-25). Springer.

International Society for Technology in Education (ISTE). (2023). *ISTE Standards: Educators*. Retrieved from https://www.iste.org/standards/iste-standards-for-teachers

Jamieson-Proctor, R., Albion, P., Finger, G., Cavanagh, R., Fitzgerald, R., Bond, T., & Grimbeek, P. (2013). Development of the TTF TPACK Survey Instrument. *Australian Educational Computing, 27*(3), 26–35.

Javeed, F., Shahzad, B., Shaikh, A., Reshan, A., Saleh, M., Ahmad, S., ... Rajab, K. (2022). Strengthening Software Make vs. Buy Decision: A Mixed-Method Approach. *Intelligent Automation & Soft Computing, 32*(1), 193–205. Advance online publication. doi:10.32604/iasc.2022.021769

Jin, Y., & Schmidt-Crawford, D. A. (2017). Parents' perceptions of the first-year implementation of a one-to-one laptop initiative in a Midwestern high school. *Computers in the Schools, 34*(1-2), 73–87. doi:10.1080/07380569.2017.1293470

Johnson, E. R. (1990). *Psychological adjustment of mainstream adolescents: physically disabled and nondisabled*. Arizona State University.

Lahlali, A., Chafiq, N., Radid, M., Moundy, K., & Srour, C. (2023). The Effect of Integrating Interactive Simulations on the Development of Students' Motivation, Engagement, Interaction and School Results. *International Journal of Emerging Technologies in Learning, 18*(12), 193–207. doi:10.3991/ijet.v18i12.39755

Li, M. (2023). Chinese mathematics teachers' TPACK and attitudes toward ICT integration in the post-pandemic era. *Eurasia Journal of Mathematics, Science and Technology Education, 19*(7), em2301. Advance online publication. doi:10.29333/ejmste/13346

M'rhaouarh, I., Chafiq, N., & Namir, A. (2021, November). Toward Using Cloud Computing at Universities in Developing Countries Considering the Covid-19 Crisis. *The Proceedings of the International Conference on Smart City Applications* (pp. 733-743). Cham: Springer International Publishing.

M'Rhaouarh, I., Moutamanni, H., Labzai, A., Namir, A., & Chafiq, N. (2021). Mathematical modeling and optimal control of abstaining attitude of could computing adoption. *Journal of Mathematical and Computational Science, 11*(4), 4411–4427.

M'rhaouarh, I., Namir, A., & Chafiq, N. (2021). The use of the performance measures of queuing model to optimize profit in a Cloud Computing environment. *International Journal of Computer Science and Information Security, 19*(11). Advance online publication. doi:10.5281/zenodo.5831851

Makoza, F. (2022). A Review of Critical Studies on National ICT Policy in the Context of Africa. *International Journal of Information Systems and Social Change, 13*(1), 1–22. doi:10.4018/IJISSC.303601

Manichander, T. (Ed.). (2015). *Emerging issues in education*. Laxmi Book Publication.

Maxwell, J. A. (2016). Expanding the history and range of mixed methods research. *Journal of Mixed Methods Research, 10*(1), 12–27. doi:10.1177/1558689815571132

Miles, M. B., Huberman, A. M., & Saldana, J. (2019). *Qualitative Data Analysis, A Methods Sourcebook* (4th ed.). Arizona State University.

Moundy, K., Chafiq, N., & Talbi, M. (2021). Comparative analysis of student engagement in digital textbook use during quarantine. *Education Sciences, 11*(7), 352. Advance online publication. doi:10.3390/educsci11070352

Moundy, K., Chafiq, N., & Talbi, M. (2022a). Digital textbook and flipped classroom: Experimentation of the self-learning method based on the development of soft skills and disciplinary knowledge. *International Journal of Emerging Technologies in Learning, 17*(7), 240–259. doi:10.3991/ijet.v17i07.28933

Moundy, K., Chafiq, N., & Talbi, M. (2022b). A Model for Scripting and Designing a Digital Textbook. *International Journal of Emerging Technologies in Learning, 17*(21), 296–311. doi:10.3991/ijet.v17i21.34603

Mrisse, F. E., Chafiq, N., Talbi, M., & Moundy, K. (2023). The Practices of Online Assessment in a Digital Device in the Context of University Training: The Case of Hassan II University. *International Journal of Advanced Computer Science and Applications*, *14*(1). Advance online publication. doi:10.14569/IJACSA.2023.0140148

Mwenisongole, C. (2021). *Information Communication Technology Through Technical Vocational Education and Training: Experiences from Arusha Tanzania*. The Open University of Tanzania.

National Council for Curriculum and Assessment (NCCA). (2020). *Draft primary curriculum framework*. NCCA, Department of Education, Government of Ireland.

Ngugi, J., & Goosen, L. (2019, October 25). Towards Smart Innovation for Information Systems and Technology Students: Modelling Motivation, Metacognition and Affective Aspects of Learning. Smart Innovation, Systems and Technologies, 111, 90-99. doi:10.1007/978-3-030-03577-8_11

Ornstein, A. C., Levine, D. U., Gutek, G., & Vocke, D. E. (2016). *Foundations of education*. Cengage Learning.

Plano Clark, V. L., & Ivankova, N. V. (2015). *Mixed methods research: A guide to the field* (Vol. 3). Sage publications.

Polikoff, M. S., & Porter, A. C. (2014). Instructional alignment as a measure of teaching quality. *Educational Evaluation and Policy Analysis*, *36*(4), 399–416. doi:10.3102/0162373714531851

Pondiwa, S., El Nabahany, U., & Phiri, M. (2022). Integration of ICT into education: Lessons learnt at the State University of Zanzibar and the Midlands State University in Zimbabwe. In *Computer-Mediated Communication* (Vol. 135). Intechopen. doi:10.5772/intechopen.98441

Poth, C., & Munce, S. E. (2020). Commentary—Preparing today's researchers for a yet unknown tomorrow: Promising practices for a synergistic and sustainable mentoring approach to mixed methods research learning. *International Journal of Multiple Research Approaches*, *12*(1), 56–64. doi:10.29034/ijmra.v12n1commentary

Radwan, O., Razak, A. Z., & Ghavifekr, S. (2019). The mediating effect of organisational culture on academic leadership skills and students' skill-based learning outcomes in saudi higher education. *Malaysian Online Journal of Educational Management*, *8*(1), 39–57. doi:10.22452/mojem/vol8no1.3

Rodríguez-Miranda, F. P., Pozuelos-Estrada, F. J., & León-Jariego, J. C. (2014). The role of ICT coordinator. Priority and time dedicated to professional functions. *Computers & Education*, *72*, 262–270. doi:10.1016/j.compedu.2013.11.009

Sanchez, J. J., & Alemán, E. C. (2011). Teachers' opinion survey on the use of ICT tools to support attendance-based teaching. *Computers & Education*, *56*(3), 911–915. doi:10.1016/j.compedu.2010.11.005

Sefala, M. C. (2021). *Determination of perceptions of social workers about the employee health and wellness programme at the Polokwane Municipality of Limpopo Province*. University of Limpopo.

Shah, S. S. (2022). Teaching and learning with technology: Effectiveness of ICT integration in schools. *Indonesian Journal of Educational Research and Technology*, *2*(2), 133–140. doi:10.17509/ijert.v2i2.43554

Shatri, Z. G. (2020). Advantages and disadvantages of using information technology in learning process of students. *Journal of Turkish Science Education*, *17*(3), 420–428.

Stecuła, K. (2022). Virtual Reality Applications Market Analysis—On the Example of Steam Digital Platform. *Informatics (MDPI)*, *9*(4), 100. Advance online publication. doi:10.3390/informatics9040100

Tairab, A., & Ronghuai, H. (2017). Analyzing ICT Policy in K-12 Education in Sudan (1990-2016). *World Journal of Education*, *7*(1), 71–82. doi:10.5430/wje.v7n1p71

Talukder, M. S., Alam, M. J., & Apu, M. A. (2015). The Impact of ICT on Students' Performance: A Case Study on Undergraduate University Students. *Manarat International University Studies*, *4*(1), 137–147.

Tay, L. Y., Lim, C. P., & Lim, S. K. (2015). Differences in ICT usage across subject areas: A case of an elementary school in Singapore. *Journal of Educational Computing Research*, *53*(1), 75–94. doi:10.1177/0735633115585930

Tondeur, J., Cooper, M., & Newhouse, C. P. (2010). From ICT coordination to ICT integration: A longitudinal case study. *Journal of Computer Assisted Learning*, *26*(4), 296–306. doi:10.1111/j.1365-2729.2010.00351.x

Tũrel, Y. K., & Johnson, E. T. (2012). Teachers' belief and use of interactive whiteboards for teaching and learning. *Journal of Educational Technology & Society*, *15*(1), 381–394.

Uunona, G. N., & Goosen, L. (2023). Leveraging Ethical Standards in Artificial Intelligence Technologies: A Guideline for Responsible Teaching and Learning Applications. In M. Garcia, M. Lopez Cabrera, & R. de Almeida (Eds.), *Handbook of Research on Instructional Technologies in Health Education and Allied Disciplines* (pp. 310–330). IGI Global. doi:10.4018/978-1-6684-7164-7.ch014

Voccia, A. (2011). Knowledge Management for sustainable development in the web 2.0 era: The Triangle of Dichotomies. *Knowledge Management for Development Journal*, *6*(3), 179–193. doi:10.1080/19474199.2011.554323

Wallet, P., & Melgar, B. V. (2015). Information and Communication Technology (ICT) in Education in Sub-Saharan Africa: A comparative analysis of basic e-readiness in schools. United Nations Educational Scientific and Cultural Organization (UNESCO) Institute for Statistics.

KEY TERMS AND DEFINITIONS

Curriculum: The term 'curriculum' refers to a collection of well-thought-out educational opportunities and experiences that are intended to support students' growth and accomplishment of certain learning goals. It includes both the instructional techniques and materials used to support students' learning, as well as the information, abilities, and competences that are required of them. The curriculum describes the subject matter to be covered, the order of teaching, and evaluation procedures. It helps instructors create educational activities and evaluation that are in line with the targeted learning results.

E-Capacity Model Approach: The e-capacity model approach is a framework for evaluating and assessing how well instructors and institutions can incorporate technologies into their educational programs. It focuses on analyzing many aspects of technology integration, including the infrastructure, resources, abilities and skills of teachers, the support of leadership, and the general organizational preparedness. The e-capacity model approach considers both the educational techniques required for successful technology integration, as well as the technical components of technology deployment. In order to increase the effective integration of technology in education, it offers a systematic framework for recognizing teachers' and schools' strengths, shortcomings, and opportunities for growth.

ICT Coordination: ICT coordination entails supervising and coordinating the implementation of ICT projects within a company, institution, or society. To make sure that technology is utilized efficiently and effectively to fulfil organizational goals, it requires coordinating and integrating various ICT resources, systems, and activities. ICT coordination aims to maximize the use of technologies, encourage smooth ICT tool and system integration, and match technological activities with the overarching goals and objectives of the organization.

ICT Infrastructure: ICT infrastructure includes all of the structural and technological components required to support the use and integration of information and communication technologies inside a company, institution, or society. It includes a variety of elements, including networks, software, computer components, and other technological assets, all of which are essential for the effective functioning of ICT systems in educational settings.

ICT Support: ICT support is the term used to describe the help and services offered to people or organizations in connection to their usage of ICTs. It includes providing technical assistance, troubleshooting, direction towards ensuring that ICT systems and tools are operating, setting up and configuring both software and hardware, resolving technical problems, providing instruction regarding ICT tools and applications, and making recommendations on best practices for utilizing ICTs.

ICT Teachers Professional Development: and capacity for integrating information and communication technologies into their pedagogical practices: The main goal is to provide instructors with the fundamental technical know-how and pedagogical strategies necessary to fully use the educational advantages of ICT tools and resources. Teachers are provided with the information, direction, and support they need to successfully integrate ICTs into their teaching practices via a range of organized activities and professional development opportunities. The ultimate objective is to provide instructors with the tools they need to design interactive, student-centered educational settings that foster critical thinking and proficiency with technologies.

Information and Communication Technologies (ICTs): Include a broad variety of resources and technical tools used for communication. Information and communication infrastructure (ICI) and Information Technology (IT) are the two basic divisions into which ICTs may be divided. ICI refers to the real telecommunication systems and networks, including postal services, satellite transmission, cable networks, and mobile communication. In addition, it covers the goods and services that depend on these systems, including the internet, phone and email communication, radio, and television. The software and hardware tools used for activities like data collection, organization, analysis, and presentation, on the other hand, are referred to as IT. The goal of integrating technologies into educational environments is to raise academic success levels and increase institutional effectiveness in general.

Teachers' ICT Competencies: The expertise, abilities, and knowledge that teachers possess in order to utilize ICTs effectively and efficiently in their teaching practices are referred to as teachers' ICT competencies. These skills include a variety of topics, such as the ability to use ICT tools and software proficiently, the ability to integrate ICTs into instructional design and the delivery process, and the capability to make use of electronic assets for purposes of education.

Chapter 7
The Power of AI for the Sake of the Metaverse in Education

Maati Souiet
https://orcid.org/0009-0006-0421-485X
Faculty of Sciences Ben M'Sick, Hassan II University, Casablanca, Morocco

Gaadi Amina
Faculty of Sciences Ben M'Sick, Hassan II University, Casablanca, Morocco

Chafiq Nadia
Faculty of Sciences Ben M'Sick, Hassan II University, Casablanca, Morocco

El Imadi Imane
https://orcid.org/0000-0001-9076-5039
Faculty of Sciences Ben M'Sick, Hassan II University, Casablanca, Morocco

ABSTRACT

The potential for immersive, individualized, and interactive learning experiences for students has made the use of metaverse technology in education an extremely popular subject. This virtual reality environment, "the metaverse," allows users to communicate with other users in a virtual environment by utilizing tools like augmented reality, artificial intelligence, blockchain, and machine learning. Metaverse technology offers higher levels of creativity and customization than conventional e-learning techniques. It enables improved user-environment interaction and can replicate emotional and cognitive processes that are more similar to those encountered in face-to-face learning environments. By providing opportunities that would ordinarily not be available, this innovation creates new chances for enhancing established learning activities. The use of metaverse technology in education has the potential to completely transform the educational process by providing students with an immersive, personalized, and interactive environment.

DOI: 10.4018/979-8-3693-1034-2.ch007

INTRODUCTION

The development of new technologies has brought about tools that are revolutionizing many industries, including education. Metaverse technology is perhaps the most significant example of this. It promises to innovately supplement conventional learning techniques by providing immersive and interactive learning elements as well as a collaborative learning environment. It is clear that metaverse technology holds enormous potential for the young generation alpha cohort, who engage highly with communication technologies such as Instagram, Tik Tok, and other social platforms, as educators investigate this tool's potential for assisting personalized student learning experiences. Technology is extremely important to them. Their entire existence is centered around technology, from entertainment to gaming (PubG, Free Fire, Fortnite, and others), connecting with peers, and even education in the wake of the COVID-19 pandemic.

According to a study by (Turk, 2017), Gen Alpha children can use touchscreens and navigate through different smartphone apps by the age of two, whereas it took their forebears many years to learn how to do so. However, Generation Alpha cautions that we should be aware of the drawbacks of technology use in this situation (Pitchford et al., 2019). For Gen Alpha, the future is promising, but with unsettling and persistent cautions. coming soon. because of the growing population crisis and mental health crisis.

In comparison to traditional media formats, the virtual environment provides more real-life simulations, allowing for better student interactions and access to interdisciplinary connections among diverse subjects in the sciences. According to Getchell et al. (2015), metaverse technology has been identified as a valuable pedagogical asset in game-based education. This study shows that educators can design new learning environments using this innovative platform in a flexible manner, allowing the complement of traditional teaching approaches. The educators' pursuit of exploring educational possibilities in metaverse technology confirms one thing: this innovative tool has the potential to transform student learning experiences (Zhou et al., 2022).

In our study, we aim to provide global quality education in the context of a university by incorporating metaverse in the process of education as an innovative method of education, where the generation alpha is the major category of students considered as the survey's target. Is a tool for getting an idea about students' preconceptions about metaverse as a first step in our research.

Review of Literature

The COVID-19 pandemic has changed the way we connect and meet each other all over the world, to the point where our conception of meeting and collaborating in order to teach or learn has changed (Bokyung et al., 2021). Virtual reality metaverses such as Roblox and Zepeto have created a new social space for people who are unable to leave their homes due to COVID-19, allowing them to congregate in large groups for festivals or concerts. So students can benefit from the advantages of metavers in the context of COVID-19, as well as having the opportunity to communicate with their peers and gain knowledge in a collaborative manner (Bokyung et al., 2021) about this idea said "When schools were closed due to COVID-19 and students could not attend school, the "Classroom Map" among various 3D maps in Zepeto was the most popular." The students went to the Zepeto classroom instead of the regular classroom." So, the metaverse is not only a place to have fun and play, but also to learn. According to (Madiega et al., 2022) in a briefing to the European Parliament, the metaverse is an evolution of the internet towards Web3 that will include a variety of technologies such as blockchain, digital currencies, NFT's, and 5G, but the application of AI in the metaverse to improve the quality of education is still in its early stages due to technological limitations. As (polyviou et al., 2022) clarify, "Educational implementations in the metaverse are still at an early stage, when considering that AI-enabled adaptive learning systems have not yet been widely implemented and the use of IoT for seamless virtual real space interactions remains scarce." From this framework, our research finds a logical purpose: to find a path to implement the metaverse in the field of education, so that we can benefit from the advantages and power of AI to improve educational quality by proposing adaptive educational pathways to students.

What is Metaverse?

Our primary objective is to attain a comprehensive understanding of metavers concept and the difference existed between metaverse and the concept virtual reality, however our researche will also cover the educational part so we try to enhance the quality of education by introducing the metaverse in the area of teaching, considering as a powerful technological tool make the conception of educational scenario more innovative and immersive that encourage the interactivity and collaboration between the students so the teaching will be more creative. In other side and by combining augmented reality and virtual reality, the metaverse creates a digital extension of the physical world, enabling educators to create interactive and collaborative learning environments (López-Belmonte et al., 2022), in this case the same authors said that the application of the metaverse in education offers innovative opportunities for flexible, dynamic, and motivating learning experiences.

The first question that blow our mind is that one referring to the meaning of metavers. to answer that question and bring a clear vision of the the meaning of metavers we propose this figure relate to (Gartner, 2022) that give us clear idea about the meaning of metavers, and then we will move on, to defining this notion, by giving a multiple definitions from experts so we can understand the nature of the concept that we will use it in our research.

Figure 1. The elements of the metaverse

The first step now is to trying to define this concept clearly, so we can understand what it is about, in this case, we propose the fallowing definitions:

A world where humans as avatars interact with each other and with software agents in a three-dimensional space that reflects the real world (Stephenson, 1994).

An immersive environment using a universal and shared digital media network that removes the barriers of time and space by deceiving user's visual sense (Jaynes et al. 2003).

A places where users log in all the time to interact with others in play, commerce, creativity, and exploration (Hazan, 2010).

A next-generation virtual world built on blockchain (Dowling et al., 2021).

An immersive and constant virtual 3D world where people interact through an avatar to enjoy entertainment, make purchases and carry out transaction with crypto-assets, or work without leaving their seat (Council of the European Union, 2022).

Figure 2. Metaverse taxonomy (Park & Kim, 2022)

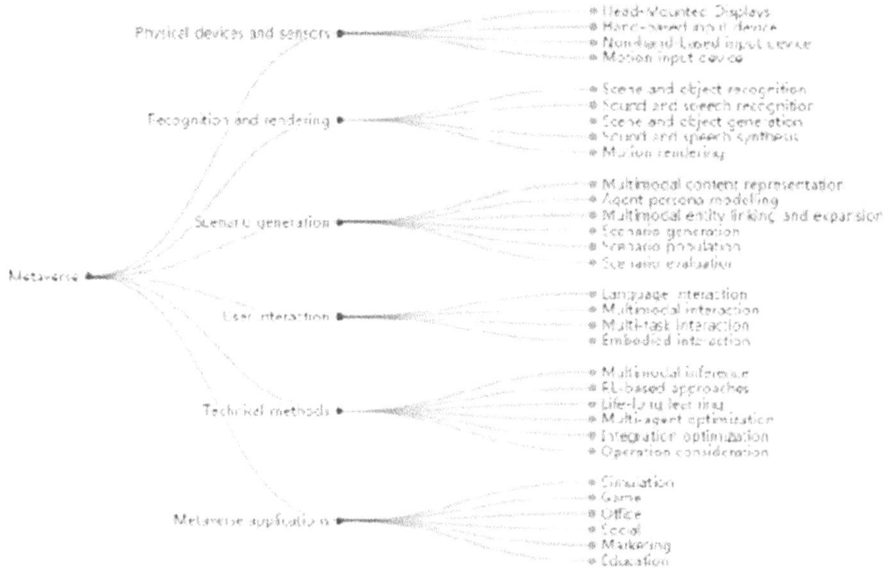

From all this definitions we will try to propose our humble definition the way he's down here:

metaverse it is a immersive virtual world make the interaction between the users possible by using a digital model of avatar make them capable of navigate or shopping, buying, playing, learning or simply communicating around specifics subjects. The interchange of values between the users in the metaverse are guaranteed by the potency of blockchain technology making the transactions possible by using cryptocurrencies is kind of mixing the web3 in a 3D world.

As the European Parliamentary Research Service explain that "the metaverse is commonly considered to be an evolution of the internet towards 'Web3' (Web1 bein the worldwide web and Web2 meaning the rise of social media) in which individuals are empowered and actively involved in the creation of virtual worlds." In addition, the figure below will clarification what we are currently trying to explain.

Figure 3. Evolution of the internet

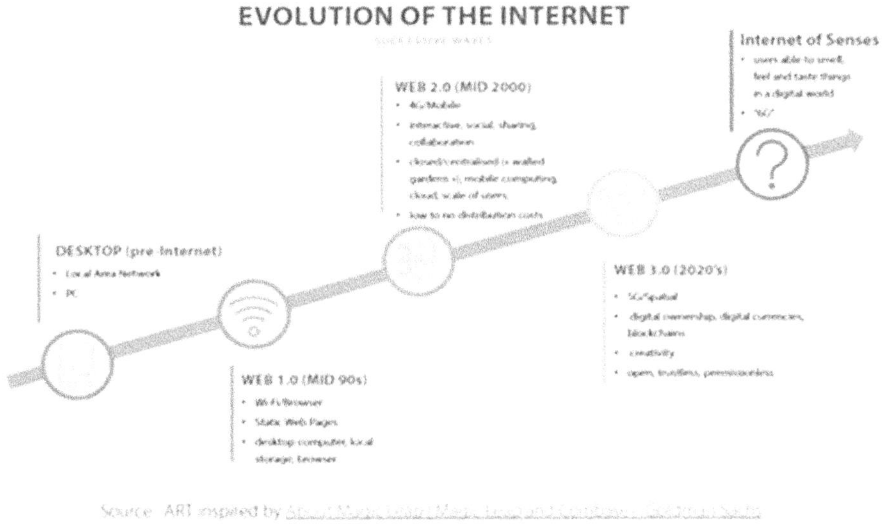

Moreover the European Parliamentary Research Service add also that "we are currently witnessing a transition from a centralised web, where social media channels connect people (web 2.0), to a decentralised internet, where people interact directly (known as "web 3.0). This is driven by blockchain applications, decentralised finance (DeFi) based on cryptoassets (cryptocurrencies, token or NFTs), and more local/niche/targeted service. Some companies claim they have started work on the next generation of an immersive internet called the internet of senses"

In other hand (Cook et al. 2020) said "Though many consider the metaverse as the next web, that is Web 3.0 or the Spatial Web"

While now after we arrive this far the fundamental question may be requested strongly now are:

What Is the Difference Between Metaverse and Virtual Reality?

In this case, we return to what the authors said as Park & Kim (2022), "The Metaverse differs from augmented reality (AR) and virtual reality (VR) in three ways. First, while VR-related studies focus on a physical approach and rendering, Metaverse has a strong aspect as a service with more sustainable content and social meaning. Second, the Metaverse does not necessarily use AR and VR technologies. Even if the platform does not support VR and AR, it can be a Metaverse application. Lastly, the Metaverse has a scalable environment that can accommodate many people is essential to reinforce social meaning."

Also according to a new research Rauschnabel et al. (2022) notes that "Our view of metaverse also implies that XR environments such as AR and VR can exist without a metaverse, but any metaverse cannot exist without AR and/or VR. For example, users can attend personalized trainings through a VR application or try out clothing and fashion accessories through an AR application without being immersed in any type of metaverse. On the other hand, we posit that any meaningful engagement in the metaverse needs to draw on some type of XR environment, such as AR or VR. It is important to note that this view of metaverse aligns well with our proposition of a strict separation between AR and VR, as outlined below. That is, users can either be immersed in AR (leading to local presence) or VR (tied to telepresence), but not both simultaneously"

Furthermore Jadhav & Patil (2022) added too that "Although virtual reality is a part of the metaverse, the metaverse as a whole is far larger."

Now we will propose some clarifications about the useful and essentials terms are combined and involve with the concept of metaverse using in our research for the simple reason, improving teaching and learning processes in the context of education. To make students finally enables to interact more experientially with the immersive environment, allowing them to act out hypothetical situations and actively engage in their own learning.

Adaptive Learning

For teachers, Adaptive learning technology saves teachers time and provides them valuable data about each student's level of progress and their capability to learn. Adaptive learning serves as an assistive platform that enables them to plan an effective personalized teaching experience for every student, build customized resources and activities that address each student's unique learning needs. Also known as assistive scaffolding, it requires teachers to adopt differentiated instruction principles and deliver content that suits each student's learning process. For students, adaptive learning technology allows each student to get the instruction and practice faster and suiting to their capability. Due to scaffolding technique involved, students receive individualized instruction which help them develop their personal potential in and out of the classroom. Besides, adaptive learning helps students to learn through personalized methods based on each student's current skills and performance and receive immediate feedback based on each student's strengths and weaknesses (Castro, 2019).

Avatar

Referring to Park & Kim (2022) An avatar means an alter ego that has descended to the earth, and it started from the concept that a fundamental being (e.g., God) changed its form to human. Previously, the avatar was used as a pre-defined exaggerated form in the virtual world rather than reflecting the real world. However, it gradually changes into an ideal form that projects the outward appearance and reflects the ego. An avatar performs a social role suitable for a job and persona in Metaverse.

Digital Twins

According to Tao et al. (2022) As a digital representation of real-world entities, a DT can synchronize operational assets, processes, and systems with the real world along with some other regular actions, such as monitoring, visualizing, analyzing, and predicting.

Extended Reality

Referring to Thien et al. (2022) XR is defined as an umbrella term that encapsulates VR, AR, mixed reality (MR), and everything in their gaps as shown in Fig. 4. Although some revolutionary experiences are offered for VR and AR, the same original technologies are fueling the innovation and development of MR. While AR provides the experiences of graphics, video streams, and holograms in the physical world and VR offers viewing

Experiences in a fully immersive digital world, MR can deliver a transition experience between AR and VR. Along with these reality technologies, human users can experience the metaverse and enjoy diversified services in both the physical and digital worlds.

Figure 4. The difference between AR, MR, and VR under the umbrella of XR (Thien et al., 2022)

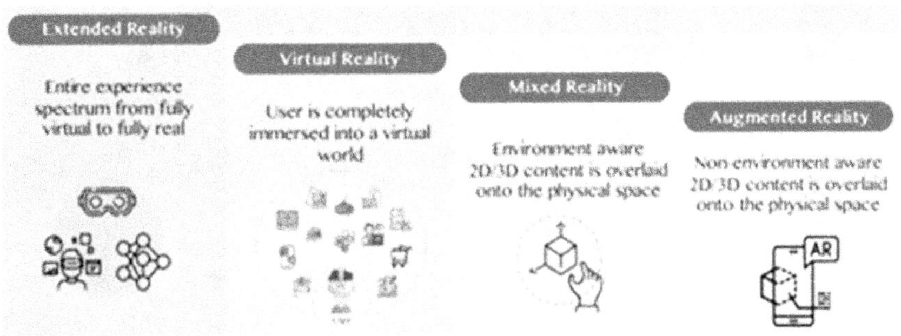

Figure 5. Reality-virtuality (RV) by Milgrame (1994)

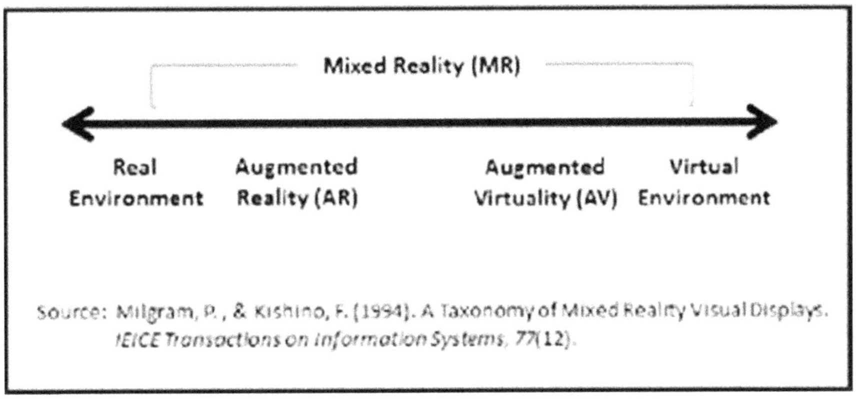

Blockchain

According to Gadekallu et al. (2022) In general, blockchain is defined as a digital ledger that contains a list of recorded transactions and tracked assets interconnected in a business network by using cryptography techniques. Blockchain can provide immediate, shared, and transparent information stored in an immutable and impenetrable ledger which can be accessed by only the network members with permission

Also Cannavo and Lamberti (2021) add to A typical blockchain network can track orders, payments, accounts, and other transactions. In the metaverse, a large amount of data (e.g., videos and other digital contents) is acquired by VR devices, transmitted over networks, and stored in data center without any security and privacy protection mechanisms, which can become the sensitive target of cyberattacks.

In this context, blockchain with several unique features reveals a promising solution for security and privacy issues in the metaverse

As well, Lee et al. (2021) add too Blockchain adopts the proof of work as the consensus mechanism, which requires participants to spend effort on puzzles to guarantee data security.

Figure 6. Blockchain for key enabling technologies of the metaverse (Gadekallu et al., 2022)

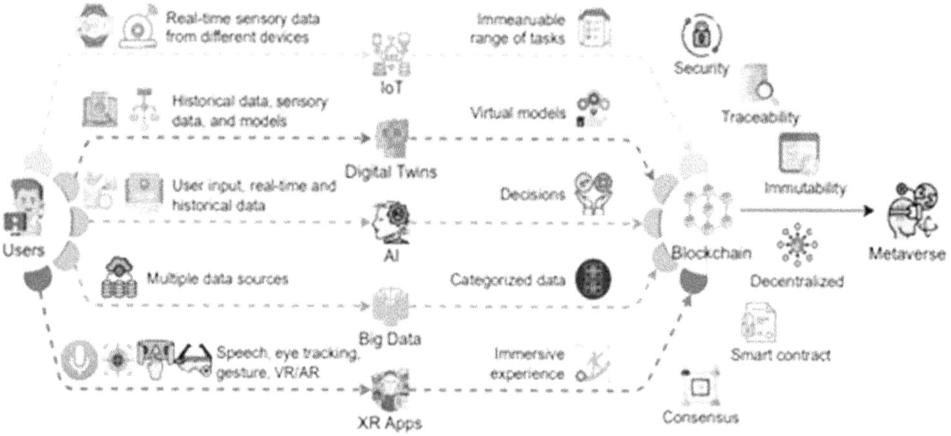

The Artificial Intelligence

Referring to Lee et al. (2021) the application of artificial intelligence, especially deep learning, makes great progress in automation for operators and designers in the metaverse, and achieves higher performance than conventional approaches. However, applying artificial intelligence to facilitate users' operation and improve the immerse experience is lacking. Existing artificial intelligence models are usually very deep and require massive computation capabilities, which is unfriendly for resource-constrained mobile devices. Hence, designing light but efficient artificial intelligence models is necessary.

This is one reason among others why our research was conducted, and the next part of this research it will cover on detail the different elements and ingredients used to establish an educational model based on the integration of metaverse powred by the artificial intelligence in education. The purpose is simple enhancing the educational quality in Moroccan context.

In this case, we propose our humble vision about the model elaborate to be integrate in Moroccan educational context by the use of the combination of AI and the metaverse to create an adaptive pathway make each learner benefit from personalised courses with innovative manner and therefore having the correct and pertinent knowledge. In our model globally based on what we called blended learning the learner will learn properly with their style of learning so the interaction will be more effective and the result the acquisition of knowledge will be more efficient and long lasting.

The pedagogical aspect is very important in our model so we decide to employ the pedagogy of problem solving because it encourages learners to put out more effort (solving educational problems) and successfully gain and acquire knowledge.

In addition, the conception of the courses will be based on the serious games it mean that the pathway will be gamified so it will give a playful aspect in consequently the knowledge acquisition process will be realized in entertainment manner so the educational process will be more efficient.

The metaverse will add a virtual aspect to the education process, allowing the learners to get an immersive experience, and they can be able to gain from learning by the employment of what we called the concept of learn to earn in this system. The achievement of the learning goals and the validation of the transaction are managed by the process of proof of work adopted by the blockchain.

Our model highlights the important role of identifying each learner's preferred method of learning by employing a variety of techniques, such as surveys, observations, and evaluation matrices whether in class or online.

Figure 7. Model of the integration of metaverse combining with the serious game in a blended learning.

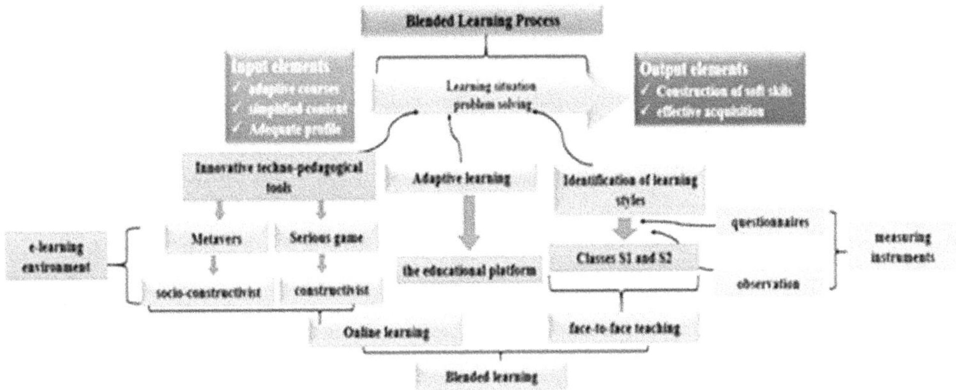

The Big Question Now Is What Is the Role of Artificial Intelligence in This Model?

To begin answering the question above, we will provide an approximate example of what we hope to construct, firstly we give an example about metaverse give the opportunity to players to gain from what we called paly to earn so referring to Bouri et al. (2021) Axie Infinity: As one of the revolutionary Play-to-Earn metaverse projects, Axie Infinity builds a crypto-meet-Pokemon ´ game universe with fantasy creatures, called Axies, that players can collect, raise, breed, and battle for building their Axies kingdoms. Like Decentraland and Sandbox, Axie Infinity has a user-centric economy system that allows players to truly own, sell, buy, and trade in-game resources over gaming activities and contributions to the ecosystem. A key difference between Axie and other traditional games is that the blockchain-based economic mechanism of the Axie metaverse allows players to increase their digital assets by improving in-game skills to reach certain levels.

The only modification we will make to our proposal for an educational metaverse is switching the play to earn concept to learn to earn while preserving the blockchain structure.

In other hand there is another metaverse called star atlas based on AI technology improve the intelligence of non-playable character in tactical planning of actions and fighting strategy in player-NPC combats every time the user play.

In our approach, we work to enhance the immersive adaptive pathway experience that is offered to students by way of artificial intelligence involvement. Every time a student succeeds in passing through an adaptive metaverse pathway. The artificial intelligence intervention will help generate and refine the pathway, and in the next section, we'll explain every step in more depth that is needed.

According to The et al. (2022) By merging AI with other technologies, such as AR/VR, blockchain, and networking, the metaverse can create secure, scalable, and realistic virtual worlds on a reliable and always on platform. he add also "…While XR and AI are distinct sectors, they can be combined to reach a fully immersive in the metaverse."

In very attractive research Gote & Jadhav (2022) said The Study is an example of learning made gamified in practice. Users are rewarded with each class of attended, each video watched, every task is complete. All tasks must be completed. Some rewarded are given NFT crypto collections. Augmented Reality(AR) allows AI (Artificial Intelligence) instructors to show students how to stand, sing, and appear more confident. By using these techniques, people can learn in a completely playful environment and well-known trainers will demonstrate certain skills. This could be a famous surgeon, "the surgeon is rewarded for his teaching, and for the students who receive awards for their education.

Combining all of the authors' previous ideas, we will present a second model that explains how artificial intelligence offers students an exceptional opportunity to receive an outstanding learning experience while AI also making the entire education process based on the metaverse autonomous and evolutionary. This is exactly the purpose of our research.

Figure 8. Model of learning approach based on AI, metaverse, and serious game to enhance education quality in Morocco

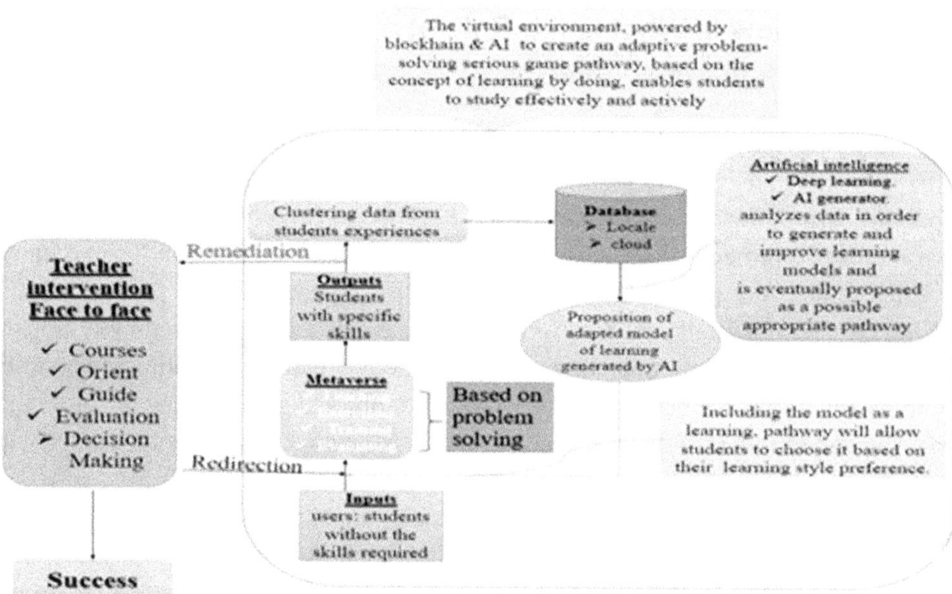

The model give a global idea about the process we will integrate into Moroccan education system to enhance the quality of teaching and education in general, it will be difficult but not impossible.

The model is innovative due to the fact it will raise the bar for education in Morocco; specifically, artificial intelligence will provide the right and appropriate pathway based on the analysis of data from previous educational experiences to generate a new, developed one; additionally, as more students engage in and contribute to their education, the system will assess their participation and suggest a more developed pathway that is better personalized for their learning preferences.

Every student will benefit from a distinct pathway that is more individualized and appropriate to their attention, as the development and evolution of the pathway will be ensured by deep learning and machine learning that give the autonomous aspect to the process so the learner will get the best possible education based on their needs.

The idea is to have an artificial intelligence capable of generating a world in metavers and proposing it to learners. The data and the structure of the world will be provided by deep learning and machine learning. The immersive environment will be generated by the power of the AI so the learners will get a specific immersive situation in the metavers created by the AI. For example, there are multiple AI image and video generators as midjourney and leonardo AI. Every educational situation will be created as a serious game situation based on problem solving.

If learners are rewarded, as they are present in a metaverse the blockchain will fully regulate the process in a secure mode since its purpose is to make transactions easier. And this is capital role of blockchain in our model.

The next step related to this research we will introduce concretely the process in Moroccan educational environment and we will see the impact on the students and the teachers.

CONCLUSION

Finally, the integration of artificial intelligence, blockchain, and metaverse technologies has the potential to revolutionize education in Morocco. Personalized pathways can be generated for each student based on their specific requirements and preferences by employing artificial intelligence technologies to assess data from previous educational experiences. This autonomous procedure ensures that students receive the highest quality education possible, according to their attention and learning styles. AI-created metaverses enable immersive learning experiences through serious game situations designed for problem-solving. Learners can participate in these virtual environments and be rewarded for their efforts to learn. By regulating transactions within the metaverse and maintaining the integrity of the educational experience, blockchain technology improves security and transparency in this process.

REFERENCES

Cheng, R., Wu, N., Chen, S., & Han, B. (2022). Will metaverse be NextG Internet? vision, hype, and reality. *IEEE Network*, *36*(5), 197–204. doi:10.1109/MNET.117.2200055

Crombet, H. (2016). Julien Péquignot, François-Gabriel Roussel, dirs, Les Métavers. Dispositifs, usages et représentations. *Questions De Communication*, *29*(29), 459–461. doi:10.4000/questionsdecommunication.10622

Di Pietro, R., & Cresci, S. (2021). *Metaverse: Security and privacy issues.* doi:10.1109/TPSISA52974.2021.00032

FernandezC. B. (2022, March 25). *Life, the Metaverse and Everything: An overview of privacy, ethics, and governance in metaverse.* doi:10.1109/ICDCSW56584.2022.00058

Gote, R., & Jadhav, S. (2022). MetaHealth – How Metavers will transform healthcare? *International Journal for Research in Applied Science and Engineering Technology*, *10*(12), 988–990. doi:10.22214/ijraset.2022.48077

Guitton, P. (2022, February 25). *Le métavers, quels métavers?* https://inria.hal.science/hal-03599140

Hatzilygeroudis, I. (2022). Article. *Metaverse. Encyclopedia*, *2*(1), 486–497. doi:10.3390/encyclopedia2010031

Huynh-The, T., Gadekallu, T. R., Wang, W., Yenduri, G., Ranaweera, P., Pham, Q., Da Costa, D. B., & Liyanage, M. (2023). Blockchain for the metaverse: A Review. *Future Generation Computer Systems*, *143*, 401–419. doi:10.1016/j.future.2023.02.008

Huynh-The, T., Pham, Q., Pham, X., Nguyen, T., Han, Z., & Kim, D. (2023). Artificial intelligence for the metaverse: A survey. *Engineering Applications of Artificial Intelligence*, *117*, 105581. doi:10.1016/j.engappai.2022.105581

International Journal of Information Management. (2022). *Metaverse beyond the hype: Multidisciplinary perspectives on emerging challenges, opportunities, and agenda for research, practice and policy*. Author.

Jadhav, O. (2022). Blockchain, AI & Web3.0 in Metaverse of Madness. *International Journal for Research in Applied Science and Engineering Technology*, *10*(6), 2378–2385. doi:10.22214/ijraset.2022.44345

JhaA. K. (2020). *Understanding Generation Alpha.* Researchgate. https://doi.org/ doi:10.31219/osf.io/d2e8g

Kaddoura, S., & Husseiny, F. A. (2023). The rising trend of Metaverse in education: Challenges, opportunities, and ethical considerations. *PeerJ*, *9*, e1252. doi:10.7717/peerj-cs.1252 PMID:37346578

Kasiyanto, S., & Kilinc, M. R. (2022). Legal Conundrums of the Metaverse. *Journal of Central Banking Law and Institutions*, *1*(2), 299–322. doi:10.21098/jcli.v1i2.25

Kye, B., Han, N., Kim, E., Park, Y., & Jo, S. (2021). Educational applications of metaverse: Possibilities and limitations. *Journal of Educational Evaluation for Health Professions*, *18*, 32. doi:10.3352/jeehp.2021.18.32 PMID:34897242

Lee, L. C., Braud, T., Zhou, P., Wang, L., Xu, D., Lin, Z., Kumar, A., Bermejo, C., & Hui, P. (2021). *All One Needs to Know about Metaverse: A Complete Survey on Technological Singularity, Virtual Ecosystem, and Research Agenda*. arXiv (Cornell University). https://doi.org//arxiv.2110.05352 doi:10.48550

Logan, S. W., Webster, E. K., Getchell, N., Pfeiffer, K. A., & Robinson, L. E. (2013). Relationship between fundamental motor skill competence and physical activity during childhood and adolescence: A systematic review. *Kinesiology Review (Champaign, Ill.)*, *2*(4), 317–337. doi:10.1123/kr.2013-0012

Madiega, T., Car, P., Niestadt, M., & Van de Pol, L. (2022). *Metaverse Opportunities, risks and policy implications. Members' Research Service PE 733.557.* European Parliamentary Research Service.

Merchant, Z., Goetz, E. T., Cifuentes, L., Keeney-Kennicutt, W., & Davis, T. J. (2014). *Effectiveness of virtual reality-based instruction on students' learning outcomes in K-12 and higher education: A meta-analysis*. Elsevier. doi:10.1016/j.compedu.2013.07.033

Michaud, T. (2017). Julien PÉQUIGNOT et François-Gabriel ROUSSEL (dir.) (2015), Les métavers. Dispositifs, usages et représentations. *Communication*, *34*(2). Advance online publication. doi:10.4000/communication.7166

Outhwaite, L. A., Faulder, M., Gulliford, A., & Pitchford, N. J. (2019). Raising early achievement in math with interactive apps: A randomized control trial. *Journal of Educational Psychology*, *111*(2), 284–298. doi:10.1037/edu0000286 PMID:30774149

Park, S. M., & Kim, Y. (2022). A metaverse: Taxonomy, components, applications, and open challenges. *IEEE Access : Practical Innovations, Open Solutions*, *10*, 4209–4251. doi:10.1109/ACCESS.2021.3140175

Roussel, F. (2015). Culture des métavers et culture académique. *Communication*, *33*(1). Advance online publication. doi:10.4000/communication.5227

Sawiros, M., Lou, R., & Rawash, M. (2022). Next-gen e-commerce in the metaverse. *2022 IEEE International Symposium.*

Chapter 8
University Pedagogy Evaluated by Massification and the Metaverse:
The Case of LANSAD Students at the Mohammedia Faculty of Science and Technology

Loubna Farsi
Faculty of Sciences Ben M'Sick, Hassan II University, Casablanca, Morocco

Hicham Jirari
https://orcid.org/0000-0003-0539-681X
Faculty of Sciences Ben M'Sick, Hassan II University, Casablanca, Morocco

Anouar Hasbaoui
Faculty of Sciences Ben M'Sick, Hassan II University, Casablanca, Morocco

Hasna Fallaki
Faculty of Sciences Ben M'Sick, Hassan II University, Casablanca, Morocco

Mohammed Kahkahy
Faculty of Sciences Ben M'Sick, Hassan II University, Casablanca, Morocco

Abdelilah Satea
Faculty of Sciences Ben M'Sick, Hassan II University, Casablanca, Morocco

Ghizlane Machraoui
Faculty of Sciences Ben M'Sick, Hassan II University, Casablanca, Morocco

ABSTRACT

Learner's access to an immersive, platform-like digital universe would be seen as an invitation to exist in a different way through a process of routine communication with a mentor (tutor) who enables him or her to break out of anonymity and express himself or herself using tools built into the hosting platform. The characteristics and purposes for using a MOODLE-like platform are obviously different from those of 3D virtual worlds. By fostering relational dynamics that encourage students to revalue their personal and academic identities by reviving their digital identities, the authors show how far the hybrid course

DOI: 10.4018/979-8-3693-1034-2.ch008

can counteract the negative effects of massification. Defining the conceptual and theoretical frameworks, as well as a postulate and a problematic, will be done first in order to provide an account of this recent experience. Before presenting and discussing the findings, they first go over the methodology used to gather and analyze the information from students, both in-person (via the placement test) and virtually (via activity reports and satisfaction surveys).

INTRODUCTION

Information and Communication Technologies for Education (ICTE) have an important impact on the learning process. Since the beginning of the 21st[e] century, the teaching/learning process has been benefited from the technological revolution, the relevance of which was massively recognized during the COVID19 crisis. As new *mindset focused* on improving training provision, E-learning" has emerged in the education world, taking advantage of the development of digital tools and pedagogical engineering.

At the level of cross-disciplinary learning modules, particularly in French and communication, there were alarming signals about the low level of language skills among Moroccan students (Chami, 1987; Lamrany-Alaoui, 1998; Amargui, 2006; Chafiq, 2011). These findings are certain about the origins of the language deficiencies that handicap many students who will study most of the academic programs in French. In fact, between the political (the Arabization of education), the societal (the dominant collectivist culture), the conjuncture (the knowledge based economy) and the pedagogical (teacher support) background, teachers have always had different conceptual positions, but they were aware of the need to "embody a technical-pedagogical profile that is constantly being updated" (H. Jirari, 2018) to accommodate, on the one hand, a XXI[e] century full of innovations and, on the other, episodes of complex reform abounding in nomenclatures. Today, the rise of digital platforms and social networks favors the diversification of resources, services, multimedia devices and modalities presiding over teaching-learning paradigms. Under this perspective, was created The Faculté des Sciences et Techniques de Mohammedia (FSTM) in 1994, open to only students with high GPA. Aiming to certify accomplished young citizens both academically and professionally, it has seven disciplinary departments and one interdisciplinary department known as the "Département des Techniques d'Expression et de Communication". The department faculty members was aligned very early on with the practice-research-practice triptych, capitalizing on almost thirty years of professional practice whose key words are: introspection, reflexivity and innovation. We will therefore attempt to analyze the transformation of the restrictive teaching conditions (spatial, referential, human) following an engineering approach through which it was possible to plan a hybrid device (face-to-face, distance learning) within the FSTM and on the MOODLE platform for the spring 2023 session. It was necessary to initiate a change and make it an adjuvant factor to the effectiveness of language and communication teaching for a massive number of students, to meet several needs: organizational (managing amphitheaters), didactic (questioning practices), cognitive (systematization of the vehicular language in specialty courses), pedagogical (knowledge construction), psycho-sociological (inferences from digital identity), etc. This chapter will therefore attempt to show how university pedagogy, as practiced at FSTM, monitor the test implementing the metaverse. Massification is the root of the discomfort that skews the learning process; the metaverse, according to its author Neal Stephenson, represents "a 3D virtual world inhabited by avatars" in a fictional work, *Snow Crash,* published in 1992. Technically speaking today, the metaverse refers to "immersive digital universes that integrate numerous processes and elements such as communications, decentralized finance, video games (P2E), personal profiles, NFTs, etc." (K. Jobin and P. Nadeau, 2022). We assume that the teaching-learning process would result in psycho-cognitive discomfort which would condition the learner's engagement in their own training, especially if it is not compatible with the training space (amphitheater). Consequently, access to an immersive digital platform would be an alternative to exist in a different way, through a process of regular interaction with a guide (tutor) who enables the learner to emerge from anonymity and express him/herself through resources integrated into the hosting platform. Of course, a MOODLE-type platform doesn't have the same properties as 3D virtual worlds, nor the same motivations for using them. However, we will try to test two postulates:

Assumption 1: Hybrid training would be a highly suitable teaching method for LANSAD students in a context of massification.

Assumption 2: ICTE-supported hybrid teaching is a means of actively engaging learners in the construction of the knowledge, in collaborative and contextualized learning activities, to satisfy them in comparison with in class lecture (100% face-to-face) or a distance learning (100%) approach, whose relevance today is increasingly unsupported.

For this purpose, we'll need to demonstrate the extent to which the hybrid course can reverse the disadvantages of massification by creating relational dynamics that help learners to revalue their personal and academic skills by energizing their digital identity. In the section 1, we will present the Moroccan national context, followed with by the theoretical and conceptual background (the section 2), section 3 will discuss the methodology used to collect and process the data collected from students, both face-to-face (placement test) and remotely (activity reports and satisfaction questionnaires), section 4 will present the discussion of the findings and then final conclusion.

Contexts: National and Local

Following the reform of higher education, Morocco created seven Faculties of Science and Technology in the early 90s, four of them in collaboration with the European Union as part of the project entitled "Contribution au renforcement des structures d'enseignement technologique et scientifique" (Project SEM 03/204/006 A Maroc - CEE). Their main missions are:

- Training in scientific and technical fields;
- Continuing education for industrial managers ;
- Promoting applied research;
- Studies on strategic disciplines for regional and national economic development.

The seven FSTs (Settat, Mohammedia, Béni Mellal, Marrakech, Tanger, Errachidia, Fès) operate as a network, each institution develops an expertise in a field to enhance the development of their respective regions. Although Morocco launched a policy of Arabization of education in the 1980s, university courses were still taught in French, which constitues a challenge for science and technology students. To ease students' transition and support them in their academic careers, the Ministry introduced a cross-disciplinary module entitled "Techniques d'Expression et de Communication". This led to the creation of the Techniques d'Expression et de Communication (TEC) departments, designed to fill out the students' linguistic gaps and facilitate their academic learning.

Created in 1994, FSTM has eight departments, one of which is specially dedicated to teaching the LC (Language and Communication) module. It also provides training programs to technicians, engineers and managers in order to respond to companies' requests. It aims to establish partnerships with local and regional established businesses with the objective of initiating mutually beneficial research programs (financed by the companies and carried out by the FSTM scientific laboratories). Because of its geographic location, the FSTM has developed two poles of excellence: Chemical Engineering and Environmental Protection.

When the TEC department was created, the teachers' main concern was to remedy student deficits in the French language. They were also keen to strengthen students' interdisciplinary methodological skills, such as note-taking, academic writing and documentary research.

As the Moroccan university aims not only to train its future graduates, but also to prepare them to face professional challenges and to act in extremely decisive situations (knowing how to promote oneself, knowing how to negotiate, knowing how to undertake...), the TEC department also aimed to help students master professional communication techniques. This will enable them to easily integrate into corporate environment.

At the extra academic level, the Mohammedia FST managed a video workshop in 1995. At the request the students, the cultural activities team decided to direct the workshop's activities on new information and communication technologies, and to offer an ICT teaching module. And since 1997, the TEC department has been cooperating with foreign organizations to enhance the quality of cross-disciplinary teaching.

In that period, as student numbers were small, communication classes were held in the classroom, and student-teacher interaction had its own mutually positive impact. The small class size rightly favored a conducive learning environment where students could enjoy personalized attention, actively participate and receive tailored instruction to their individual needs, stimulating academic success and personal fulfillment.

A few years later, the Mohammedia FST was exposed to the phenomenon of massification. The situation became difficult to manage, with lectures replacing tutorials, with repercussions on the performance of both teachers and students.

In addition, crisis situations, such as the COVID-19 pandemic, have accelerated the adoption of distance learning, causing an abrupt transition to unregulated mode of teaching. While online teaching and the use of platforms have certainly facilitated the transmission of knowledge, it also contributed to the loss of the class interaction.

Today, there are many digital platforms that offer services in all sectors: transport, commerce, tourism, health, social services, etc. These digital advances, which have fundamentally altered our relationship with the world, space, time and the family, are so profound that they have given rise to an anthropological mutation - that of humanity 2.0, to borrow a phrase from American futurologist R.C. Kurzweil. *Homo sapiens* has given way to *homo connectus,* constantly connected online.

At this level, the digitization of education seems amply justified, favorable to Z generation, permanently present and active on social and professional networks such as Facebook, WhatsApp, LinkedIn, Viadeo, etc.

Likened to an "augmented humanity", accustomed to manipulating tablets and smartphones throughout the day, students would in turn be satisfied if faculties effectively integrated digital tools into their teaching practices. Their technological expectation boils down to educational institutions, in harmony with the times, switching to digital use (Stéphane Benoist, 2016).

We also feel it's necessary to clarify a few lexical points. We must be careful not to confuse two terms that we use as interchangeable synonyms: digitization and digitalization. Digitization refers to the conversion of originally analog files into digital files. Digitalization, on the other hand, refers to the use of digital technologies to transform existing processes and business models, automating manual tasks through the use of software or robots. It has to be said that the digitalization of education is becoming an evidence in an environment marked by strong "uberization".

It is worthwhile to mention that Morocco has invested in digitalization as a levy for educational reform to improve the quality of teaching. In 2005, to promote education, the government has set up TV channels such as "l'éducative" and "la quatrième". The aim of these channels is to lessen the illiteracy rate and pass on didactic knowledge. In 2006, the government set up the "projet Génie", aimed at training teaching staff in the use of IT and providing schools with appropriate infrastructure and environment.

An addition, educational authorities, since 2013, have strongly encouraged the use of information and communication technologies (ICT) in higher education institutions. In this regard, the Digital Morocco 2013 program, INJAZ aims to offer benefits to students in the second cycle of higher education, as well as those in certain fields, by enabling them to acquire laptops and offering them a free one year subscription to wifi network.

Moreover, many institutions have equipped the classrooms with modern IT materials and offered wifi access for students. Many university websites have been designed, providing students with digital workspaces (Ent), learning platforms (Loghate) and educational content management platforms (Moodle).

Expanding digital logistics means updating teaching practices, which played crucial role in the wake of the state of emergency following the COVID-19 pandemic. While students of Y generation accustomed to the classical learning mode, expressed some reluctance, the pandemic was a persuasive argument for converting them into users of digital education. Therefore, digital technology remains the only way to learn for students and pupils forced to stay at home for long periods of time. Higher education institutions had no choice but to align themselves with a strategy that would make e-learning an essential component of learning.

Theoretical and Conceptual Framework

The didactic approach adopted for this experiment combines targeted scriptural activities with didactic tasks, using authentic web-based resources to promote learning and action. It is based on a hybrid learning device that combines face-to-face, distance and digital technologies, and the network "[an] integration of a face-to-face component into distance learning" (Nissen, 2006). In a way, it is at the crossroad of three major fields, from which it can draw on the respective contributions of distance learning, face-to-face training and digital and network technologies.

The aim was to place the learner in a genuine situation of collaboration and prolonged production, by transposing physical learning into tutorial action, giving the learner a potentially perfectible digital identity. The face-to-face coaching and distance tutoring were structured around pedagogical scenarios containing realistic macro-tasks with social validity, according to the socio-constructivist paradigm, and training or clarification micro-tasks, according to the cognitivist paradigm.

In addition to the contributions of these two key methods in learning theories, we proceeded with the instrumentation of a set of paradigms, using in particular the conceptual models of Brigitte Denis, Dieudonné Leclercq, John Dewey and Ruben Puentedura. We used the six-paradigm model: sometimes controlled by the teacher ("Imprégnation / Modélisation (Imitation)", "Réception / Transmission (Enseignement)", "Pratique / Guidage (Exercisation)"); sometimes focused on the learner ("Exploration / Approvisionnement (Consultation)", "Expérimentation / Réactivité (Cas- problème)", "Création / Confrontation (Projet)" (Leclercq and Denis, 1998). In many respects, this model is still relevant today. In one hand, it goes beyond traditional teaching frameworks and encourages more flexible and adaptive pedagogical approaches, responding to the changing needs of learners for more interactive and personalized learning methods. On the other hand, this model is associated with dynamic teacher postures, especially when it comes to tutoring. In fact, the tutor profile, essential to our experimentation, covers a range of competencies (technical, disciplinary, methodological, affective, reflective support, etc.) that "must be considered in relation to the training program (constraints, epistemological options, target audience, etc.)" (Denis, 1998).

From another point of view, since the implementation of our hybrid device is accompanied by the intention to empower students in their learning, it becomes necessary to integrate the *learning by doing* method, which makes education a pragmatic process "starting from students' interests, their daily lives and developing their autonomy" (Dewey, 2013).

Finally, the SAMR model initiated by Ruben Puentedura (2010), a theoretical model for integrating digital technology into teaching, will enable us to help students improve their learning practices by partially substituting the digital learning environment for the physical animation in the classroom, and by transforming the learning situation traditionally associated with the classroom to make it remotely achievable, observable and evaluated.

METHODOLOGY

Following the example of all the institutions of the Hassan II University of Casablanca, the FSTM has assist its faculty members to upload their courses on the Moodle platform. In the case of cross-disciplinary teaching, the Département des Techniques d'Expression et de Communication has been able to use the Moodle digital environment to explore different ways of investing digital technology in the teaching-learning process. Indeed, between 1997 and 2021, our representation of the [teacher/student] relationship was to progressively lead to the establishment of a mediation zone in which distance learning was to play a crucial role.

To achieve our academic objective, we are positioned between language didactics - specifically French for LANSAD students - and pedagogical engineering.

In this section, we present the set-up, the research participants, the data collection instruments, the adopted approach and procedure.

Blended Learning Experiment

Unlike the open-access universities, FSTM adopts the "Troncs Communs" system for both the fall and spring semesters. This means that semesters 1 and 2 are offered twice a year. The administration has to simultaneously manage both semesters during each session, and assisting 973 students, spread over two programs, in amphitheaters. This was the case until the spring 2023 semester, when the TEC Department took the initiative to consider a solution that would guarantee modern, efficient learning. Hence the introduction of a hybrid system that would maintain the duplication of semesters 1 and 2, while transforming the spatial and temporal conditions of the teaching-learning process.

In order to implement this approach, we decide to provide four weeks of in class mode (Semester 1), followed by a four weeks of in class (Semester 2), with two hours session per week. For the first four weeks, the in class session of semester 1 coincided with the distance learning session of semester 2, while the in class session of semester 2 coincided with the distance learning session of semester 1. This formula made it possible to divide students into small groups - comprising 40 to 50 - in classrooms that were conducive to individual follow-up.

It is worthwhile to emphasize is that the face-to-face phase was enriched and reinforced by activities and resources available online via the Moodle platform. Consequently, it is more appropriate to describe this period as a four-week "hybrid phase", followed by a distance learning phase. It is crucial to note that the supervision and monitoring of both phases was under the constant supervision of the tutors.

Course Duration

The course lasts eight weeks, the majority of students is divided between individuals or group distance work on the Moodle platform and the equivalent in face-to-face class sessions for orientation, explanation and evaluation. The final stage of our experiment was to gather feedbacks from participants through the satisfaction questionnaire.

Participants and Data Collection Instruments

The sample population is made up of scientific background students enrolled in the first year of the Licence cycle and oriented towards the Biology-Chemistry-Geology (BCG) and Mathematics-Computing-Physics (MIP) courses. A total of 973 students are enrolled, 500 of whom are in semester 1 and 473 in semester 2. Data collection on student performance and success rates is based, respectively, on confrontations and comparisons we have established between participants' individual performance on the pre-test (written final exam of the fall 2022 semester) and post-test (written final exam of the spring 2023 semester) and the results of the two semesters, fall and spring, of the 2022-2023 academic year. Data for the satisfaction survey was collected using two online questionnaires.

Surveys

To conclude the final phase of the hybrid system evaluation, which consisted of a satisfaction survey, we asked students to rate various aspects of the hybrid system. They were invited to express their level of satisfaction using a rating scale ranging from 1 (completely not satisfied) to 5 (very satisfied), via an initial anonymous questionnaire comprising 12 questions. The questionnaire was generated using *Google Forms* and posted online on the FSTM Moodle platform, in the area dedicated to the course and to the distance learning component of the experimental training program. The second questionnaire, comprising 11 questions, was generated and monitored online via *Google Forms*. It should be pointed out that both questionnaires were administered at the end of the course, to ensure maximum authenticity in the students' responses. They display certain similarities in the items assessed, in order to authenticate the students' experience. The aim was both to validate the overall effectiveness of the experiment and to ascertain participants' opinions on the adopted teaching practices, the course content, the chosen subjects, the adopted tools, the followed approach, the pedagogical support and guidance, the workload and the desire to participate in other training courses of the same kind. This reflective attitude is very valuable in raising awareness and motivation among all participants (Narcy-Combes, 2005).

RESULTS

The results of our experiment are based on an examination of the quantitative and qualitative data we collected, enabling us to assess the effectiveness of our hybrid system along three main axes: student performance, success rate and the participant satisfaction.

The results of our experiment are as follows:

Survey 1

Student performance

It should be remembered that the data shown in the graphs in Figure 1 and Figure 2 are drawn from the comparisons we made between the individual performances of the participants in the pre-test and post-test, respectively. They represent the comparison between students' performances in the fall and spring semesters, which corresponds to the period of our experiment.

The data collected, illustrated in Figures 1 and 2, revealed a significant improvement in students' language skills after the hybrid approach, with an average increase of around 15% for written production and 11% for grammatical fluency. Overall, the students have well performed.

Figure 1. Written production as a %

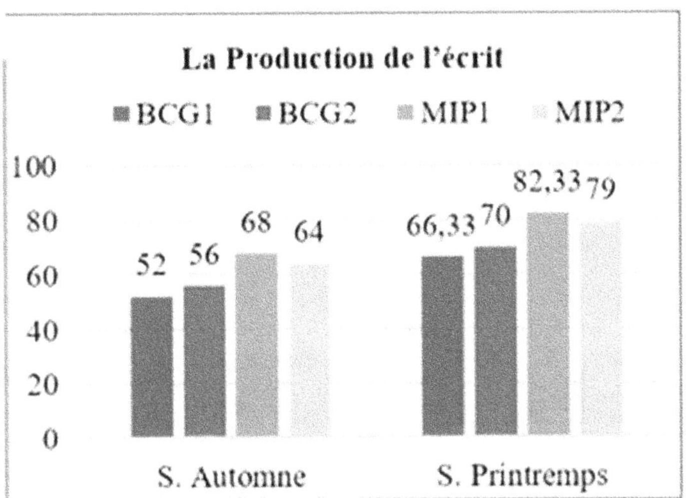

Figure 2. Grammatical fluency as a %

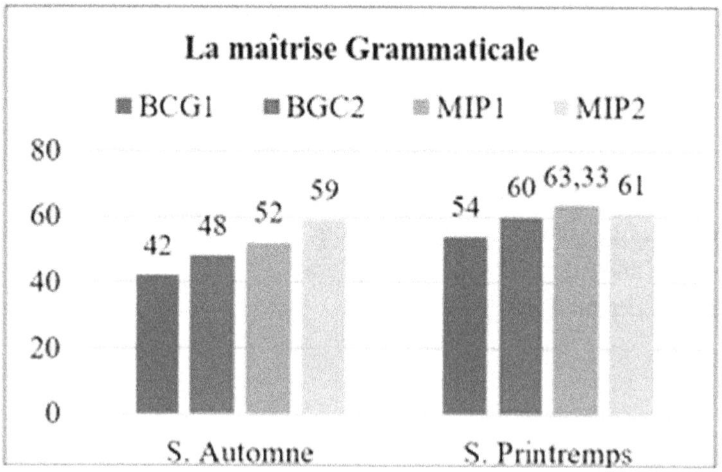

Success rates

With regard to success rates (Figures 3 and 4), we compared students' results after hybrid training in the spring semester with their results in the fall semester, when they took the course in amphitheaters. The data revealed significant increases: of around +11% for BCG1s, +14% for BCG2s, +18% for MIP1s and +33% for MIP2s. These results illustrate the positive effects of the hybrid teaching system and reinforce the effectiveness of the adopted approach.

Figure 3. Average success rate in fall 2022

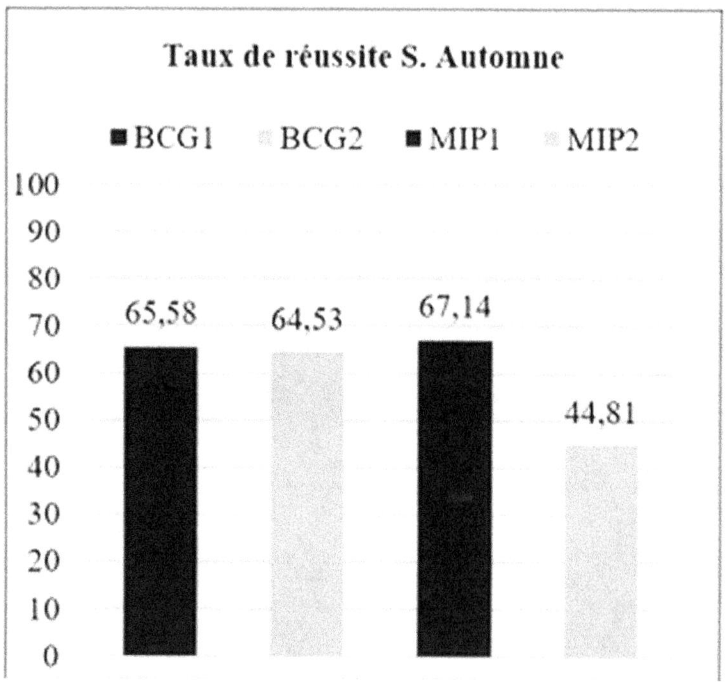

Figure 4. Average success rate in spring 2023

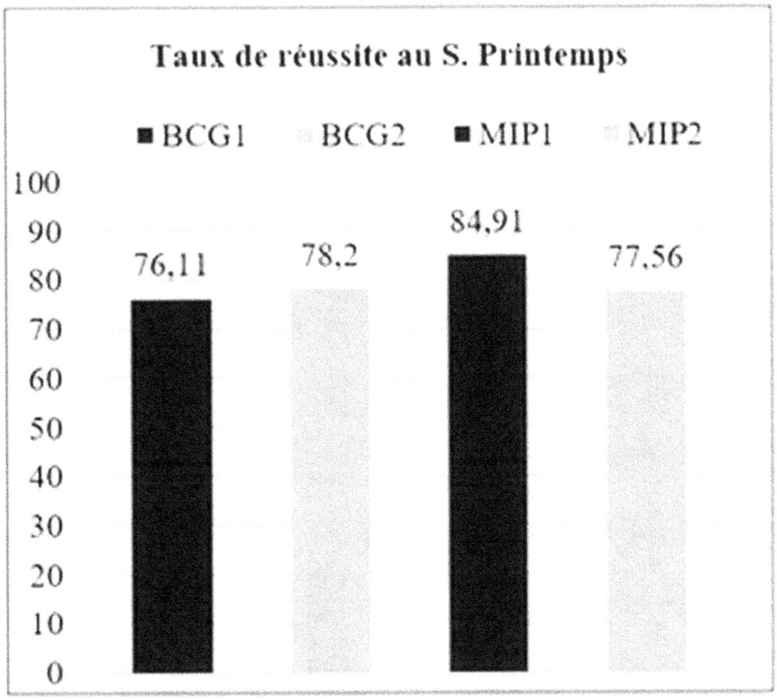

Participant Satisfaction

Students' judgments and impressions are important for measuring the degree of effectiveness of the newly adopted system. On the one hand, this measurement enables us to know whether the hybrid system satisfies the learners' needs and expectations, and on the other, to help us to improve its various aspects. What follows is an illustration and interpretation of the results of the measured items.

Accessing and Using Moodle

All participants, as shown in figure 5, were satisfied with their use of the Moodle platform. 64% were *very satisfied* and 36% were *satisfied* with the platform's performance, ease of access and handling of its various tools. From these responses, we can deduct that the engineering approach we have mobilized for the hybrid system is motivating for students.

Content

In under the heading *Content,* we have included the chosen topics, the course content, the practices and the offered support and assistance (documents, videos, hyperlinks, etc.). According to the data shown in Figure 6, all learners were either *satisfied* or *very satisfied* to varying degrees with the content provided during the course. These positive assessments indicate that, in terms of form and content, the course was neither too complex nor too easy, it met their expectations. The topics, support materials, aids and practices were all appropriate.

Figure 5. Level of satisfaction with Moodle access and use

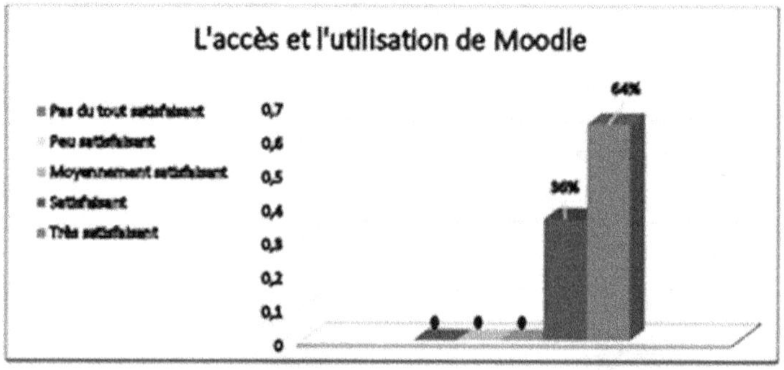

Figure 6. Learner satisfaction with blended learning content

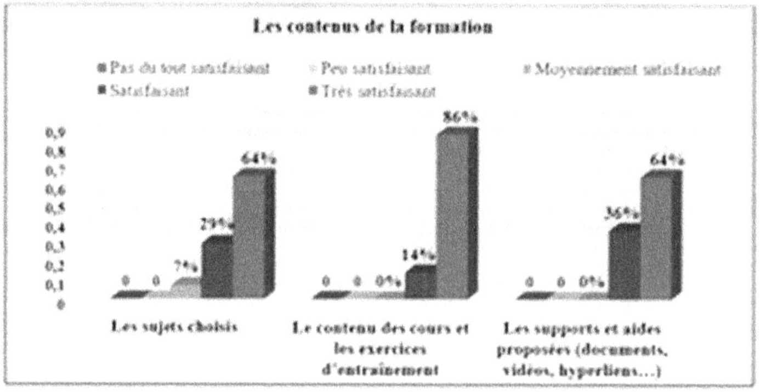

Organizational and pedagogical aspects

By *organizational and pedagogical aspects*, we mean the organization of the course, the sessions and the allocation of tasks to the students. According to the data shown in Figure 7, 64% of participants were *satisfied* with the organizational and pedagogical aspects of the course, 29% were *very satisfied* and 7% were *moderately* satisfied.

Figure 7. Level of satisfaction with organizational and pedagogical aspects

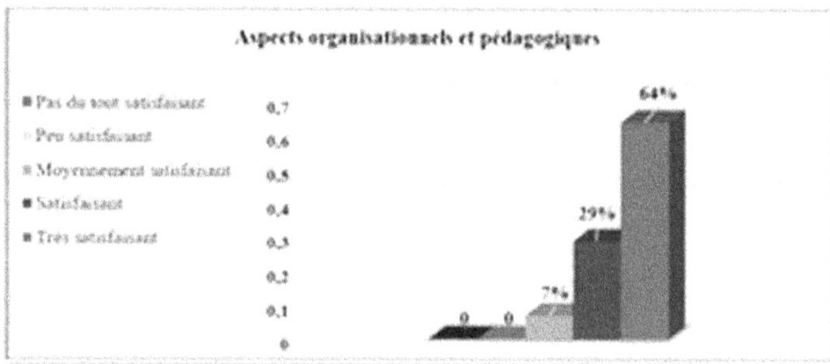

To have a clear idea of this item, we also measured learners' satisfaction in regard to the work methods (individual, in pairs and in groups), face-to-face sessions, the remote workload and the tools recommended to help them complete their tasks (forum, chat, cyberquest, etc.):

Figure 8. Level of satisfaction with the organizational and pedagogical aspects of the course

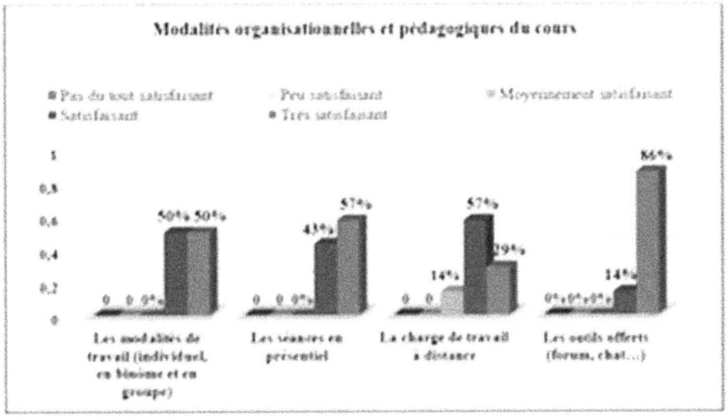

These figures, illustrated in figure 8, confirm the initial findings, all students were satisfied to varying degrees with the organizational and pedagogical aspects of the course. Even if we note a slight difference in favor of face-to-face sessions, distance learning engages students in the same way, showing a growing interest in Moodle work tools. Participants were also accustomed to the teacher's constant physical presence and individualized support online, making "presence in distance" systematic (Poellhubert, Racette and Chirchi, 2012).

Pedagogical Support and Teacher Coaching

As shown in figure 9, all participants were satisfied with the pedagogical support and coaching provided by the teacher. Indeed, 64% were *very satisfied*, and 36% were *satisfied* with the role of the teacher, who in this hybrid course assumes at the same time different roles: coach, tutor, facilitator - in short, a guide for the learner rather than the holder of knowledge. These results are promising, and reflect the learners' ability to be autonomous and familiar with this new way of learning.

Meeting Expectations

According to the data shown in figure 10, 57% of participants stated that their expectations were *Very Satisfied*, and 43% that they were *Satisfied*. We can therefore conclude that the teaching method has achieved its objectives, since the feedback was positive.

Figure 9. Level of satisfaction with teacher support and coaching

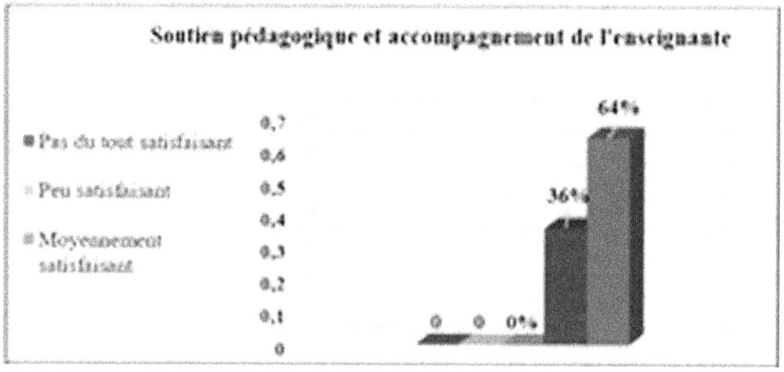

Figure 10. Level of satisfaction

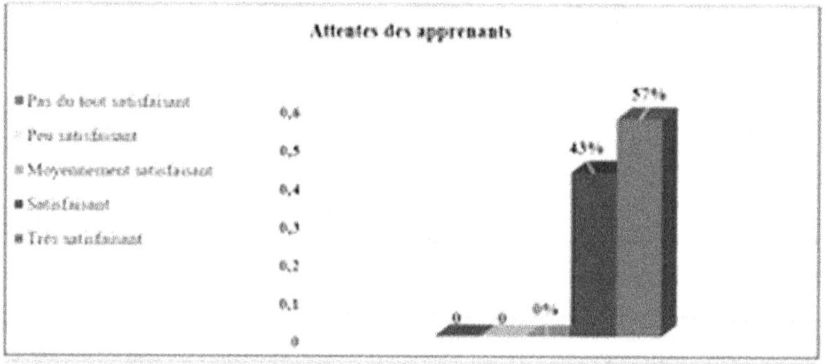

Overall Satisfaction, Desire to Participate in Further Training of This Kind

All participants were satisfied with the training (figure 11). In fact, 72% were very satisfied and 21% were satisfied. This confirms the operation success in terms of optimization and complementarity between face-to-face and distance learning.

Figure 11. Overall satisfaction with training

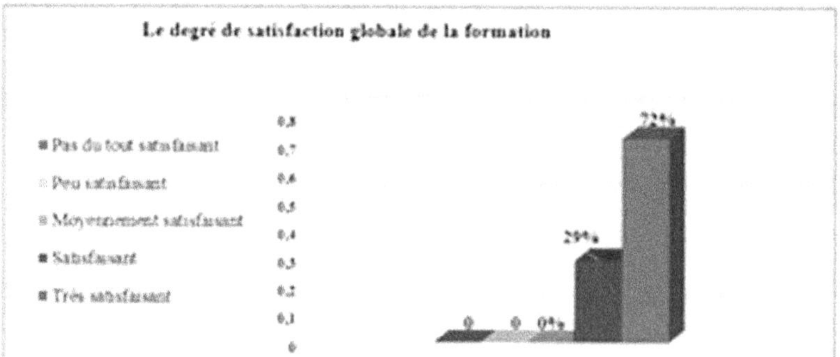

Figure 12. Desire to take part in other hybrid training courses

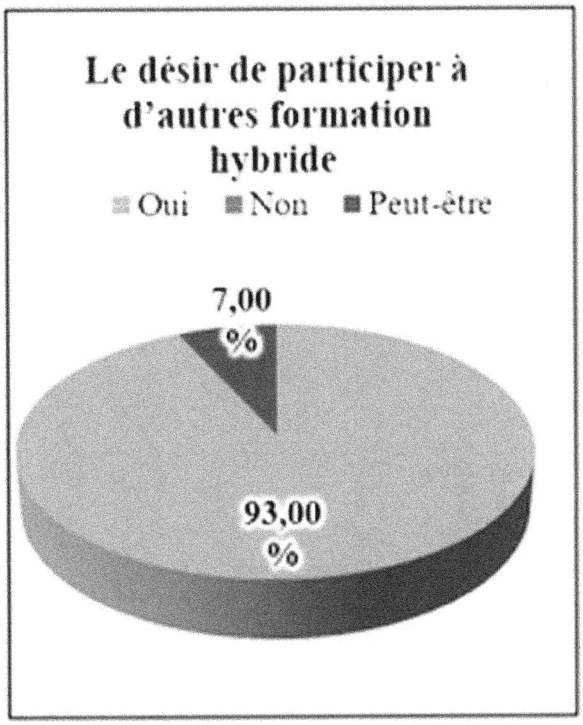

The learners' desire to benefit from another course like the one we've arranged, demonstrates and proves their satisfaction and awareness of their needs and of the benefits of ICTE. The data in Figure 12 show that the majority of students (93%) are keen to repeat the experience. A minority (7%) are hesitant.

Survey 2

Student representation in BCG and MIP courses

Figure 13. Student representation in BCG2 and MIP2 courses

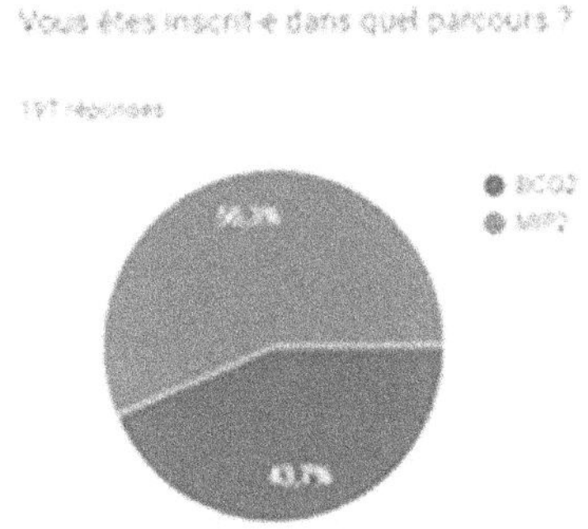

Student representation in TD groups

Figure 14. Student representation in TD groups

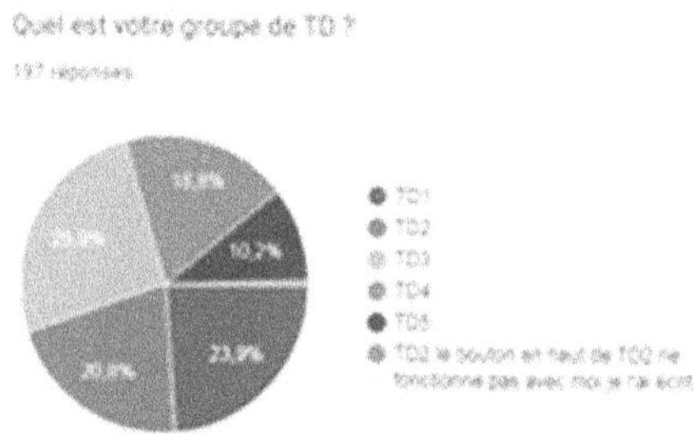

Satisfaction with module programming schedule

Figure 15. Student satisfaction with module programming schedule

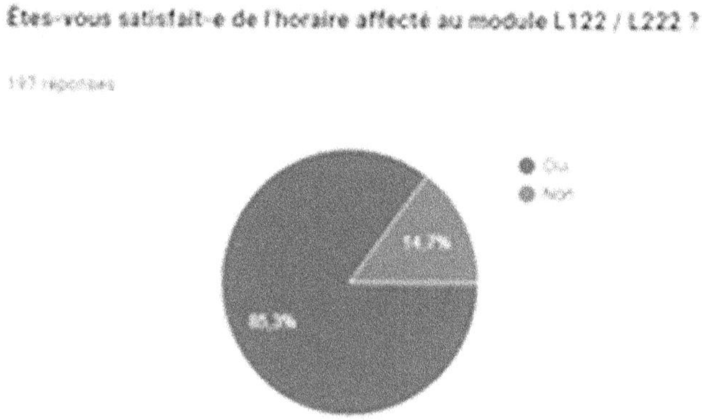

Satisfaction with training space/quality ratio

Figure 16. Student satisfaction with the space/quality ratio of the course

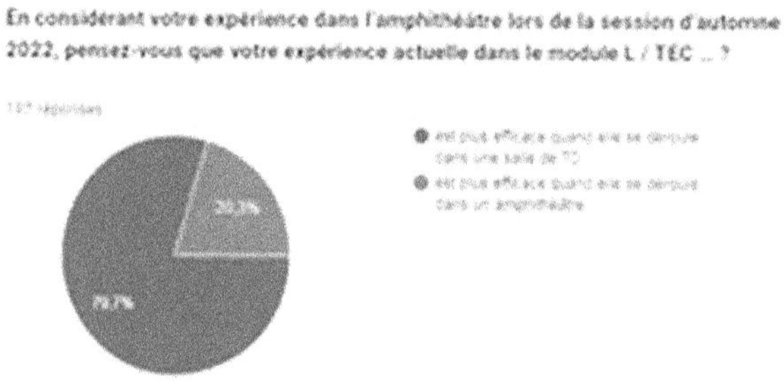

Satisfaction with the content/linguistic comfort ratio

Figure 17. Student satisfaction with the content/linguistic comfort ratio

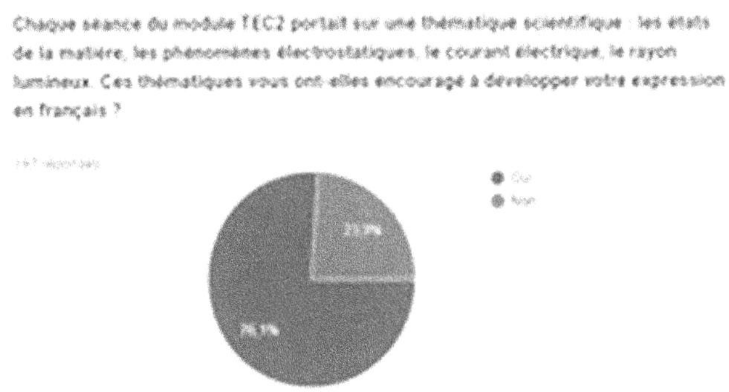

Satisfaction with teacher supervision

Figure 18. Student satisfaction with teacher supervision

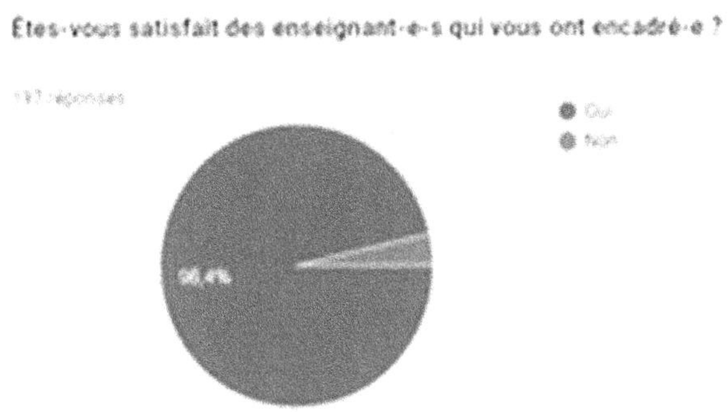

Satisfaction with activities on offer

Figure 19. Student satisfaction with the activities on offer

Satisfaction with teacher guidance

Figure 20. Student satisfaction with teacher guidance

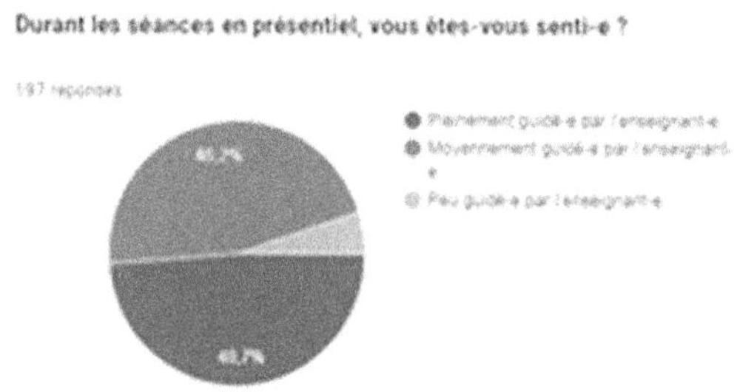

Satisfaction with ease of communication with teacher

Figure 21. Student satisfaction with ease of communication with the teacher

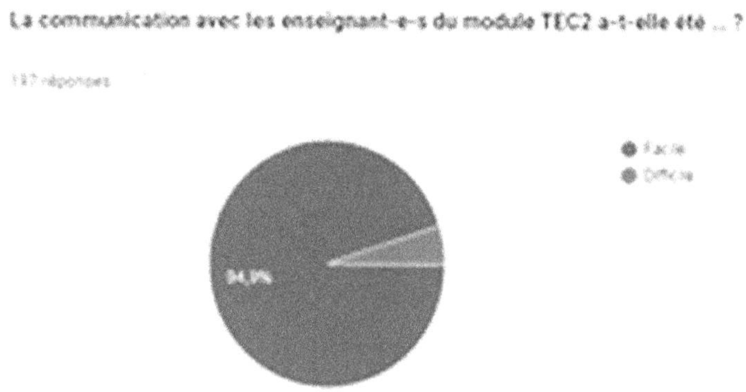

Satisfaction with the impact of the module on interaction with the teacher

Figure 22. Student satisfaction with the impact of the module on their interaction with the teacher

Satisfaction with the hybrid formula

Figure 23. Student satisfaction with the hybrid formula

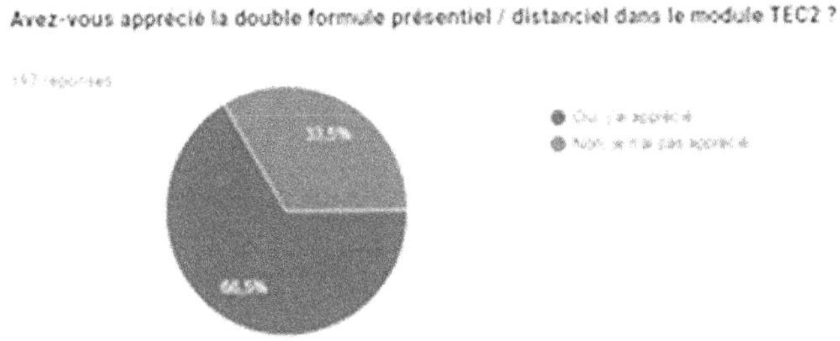

SUMMARY AND DISCUSSION

The experimentation was deemed positive and conclusive, thanks in part to the strengthened guidance provided both face-to-face and remotely, which also resulted in a convincing rate of attendance and commitment to the activities carried out in class and on Moodle:

Table 1. Students' attendances and commitments

BCG Attendance and Commitment Rates1	MIP1 Attendance and Commitment Rates	BCG2 Attendance and Commitment Rates	MIP2 Attendance and Commitment Rates
74%	79%	62%	77%

Table 2. Activity reports of BCG1 on Moodle

BCG1 (Participation Rate: Peak Reached)		
Tool: Quiz	**Tool: Homework**	**Tool: Forum**
75%	72%	63%

Table 3. Activity reports of MIP1 on Moodle

MIP1 (Participation Rate: Peak Reached)		
Tool: Quiz	**Tool: Homework**	**Tool: Forum**
80%	77%	69%

Table 4. Activity reports of BCG2 on Moodle

BCG2 (Participation Rate: Peak Reached)		
Tool: Quiz	Tool: Homework	Tool: Forum
77%	74%	71%

Table 5. Activity reports of MIP2 on Moodle

MIP2 (Participation Rate: Peak Reached)		
Tool: Quiz	Tool: Homework	Tool: Forum
71%	64%	57%

We have just seen that, overall, the hybrid system was satisfactory and beneficial to learners, even if some adjustments still need to be made to the system. The table below summarizes the results obtained from processing the data from the first satisfaction questionnaire, with a view to establishing a satisfaction threshold of 2 out of 4.

Table 6. Surveys results and averages

Variables	0	1	2	3	4	Average Over 4
Accessing/using Moodle	0%	0%	0%	36%	64%	3,64%
Selected topics	0%	0%	7%	29%	64%	3,57%
Course content and training exercises	0%	0%	0%	14%	86%	3,85%
Support and assistance (documents, videos, hyperlinks, etc.)	0%	0%	0%	14%	86%	3,85%
Organizational and pedagogical aspects	0%	0%	7%	29%	64%	3,57%
Work methods (individual, pair and group)	0%	0%	0%	50%	50%	3,50%
Face-to-face sessions	0%	0%	0%	14%	86%	3,85%
Remote workload	0%	0%	14%	57%	29%	3,14%
Tools available (forum, chat, cyberquest, etc.)	0%	0%	0%	14%	86%	3,85%
Pedagogical support and teacher coaching	0%	0%	0%	36%	64%	3,64%
Meeting expectations	0%	0%	0%	14%	86%	3,85%
Overall satisfaction	0%	0%	0%	29%	72%	3,72%

Summary of Surveys Results

***Score**: 0 = minimum / 4 = maximum.

****0** = Not at all satisfactory; 1 = Not very satisfactory; 2 = Moderately satisfactory; 3 = Satisfactory; 4 = Very satisfactory.

***Satisfaction score: 2 out of 4

The data collected show above satisfaction threshold for all the questioner items. They range from 3.85% to 3.14%, with a satisfaction threshold of 2%. It should be noted that 3.14%, which represents the lowest average, corresponds to the item relating to the *workload of distance learning*, which can be explained by the fact that students are not used to this new way of learning, since they were accustomed to attending classroom lectures only. A way that requires autonomy, cooperation and collaboration in the construction of knowledge. Based on these encouraging results, we can say (Narcy-Combes, 2005) that participants' satisfaction is a good indicator of their investment, which is considered as latent variable.

The comparison of student performance and success rates, together with the responses to satisfaction questionnaire, enable us to assess the success of our experiment and to confirm our initial postulate that hybrid teaching is a suitable method to LANSAD students in a context of massification. It could be an improving factor to the teaching and the learning of the French language, and can contribute to the remediation of deficiencies in this language.

Students' satisfaction (3.85%) with the offered tools (forum, chat, cyberquest...) and the provided support and assistance (documents, videos, hyperlinks...) prove that ICTE, in its many and varied forms, has offered several possibilities for communicating, exchanging and collaborating synchronously and asynchronously in group and individual activities. They have made it possible to individualize training and thus facilitate efficient follow-up of learners by giving them the means to be more active in their learning (Lebrun, 2011). Although immersion in virtual reality is an essential feature of the metaverse, students have been able to use a range of multimedia accessories (speakers, headsets) to experience their learning in a digital space that enables them to interact via synchronous tools (BBB for the virtual classroom) and asynchronous tools (forums, wikis) with each other and with their tutors.

In this way, the hybrid training we have provided for FSTM students has been able to play a key role in their collaborative and cooperative learning, developing their autonomy through activities that encourage exchanges of ideas and sharing of proposals. Thanks to digital tools, face-to-face and especially distance learning modes (synchronous/asynchronous), which give learners freedom and choice in terms of the place and pace of work (Pothier, 2003), participants were satisfied with the content, mode, pace and workload of the course.

This type of training fosters autonomy through asynchronous content tailored to the real, individual needs of learners, and through diversified training supports based on the exchange of practices, reflective analysis and the co-construction of knowledge. These practices will eventually make the learner a self-learner, capable of seeking out, selecting and processing information in order to reduce the learning deficiencies and to acquire the needed skills.

We can see from the satisfactory results that the training system we have set up is highly satisfactory for the students. This allows us to validate our second postulate, that's the hybrid teaching supported by ICTE would favor the active engagement of learners in a process of co-construction of knowledge, and how to satisfy them compared to the unique face-to-face (100% face-to-face) or unique distance learning (100%).

Limits

The limitations of our study are related to the following factors:

- Duration of experimentation: the experimentation was carried out in the above configuration, for the first time. The scope of the results will need to be tested upon dynamic approach. Indeed, a longer duration would enable us to evaluate the effects of the hybrid approach in the medium to long term.

- Difficulty accessing classrooms (15-30 minutes delays) due to the prioritization of subject-based teaching.
- Room equipment (video projectors and wifi connection) is not always operational. Hence the challenge of making the rooms practical.
- Generalizability of results: results obtained in the specific context of a regulated-access institution, with LANSAD students enrolled in the FSTM, may not be generalizable to other contexts or student populations in other types of academic institutions.
- Relying on the current digital learning environment, Moodle, now and in the future, teaching by and in the metaverse is still in its infancy.
- The availability of qualified resource persons to provide face-to-face support and remote tutoring is far from systematic. In fact, our experimentation would not have been possible if the five (5) full professors affiliated to the TEC Department had not been reinforced by eleven (11) medium to highly qualified PhD students.

CONCLUSION

Ultimately, the positive results of this experiment confirm our postulates that:

1: Hybrid training would be a highly suitable teaching method for LANSAD students in a context of massification.
2: ICTE-supported hybrid teaching is a means of actively engaging learners in the co-construction of knowledge, collaborative learning and situated, contextualized learning activities.

Indeed, the results converge to underline the advantages of the hybrid approach, notably face-to-face interaction, spatio-temporal flexibility, accompanied self-learning and access to multiple and diversified online teaching resources.

The limitations, as well as some of our results, lead us to formulate some perspectives and avenues of improvement for the future including:

- The development of tools for collecting and storing traces to track the detailed evolution of learners' performance, their interactions and their use of the platform's various tools.
- The development of the digital learning environment (Moodle) so that it can become a sophisticated metaverse, or the adoption of a new platform with immersive metaverse characteristics.

We remain convinced that this type of hybrid device, built around pedagogical engineering centered on the needs of LANSAD learners, is an effective solution to the constraints of massification; and it remains the most appropriate for the Moroccan university context, in several respects. Firstly, the high level of involvement of learners in hybrid training reflects their investment and active commitment to the co-construction of knowledge and to collaborative and cooperative learning. Secondly, the high level of satisfaction expressed by students with the system, and the satisfactory results of this experiment, prove that this type of training can be envisaged for the entire Moroccan university.

REFERENCES

Amargui, L. (2006). L'enseignement de la langue française à l'université marocaine. *Le français aujourd'hui*, *154*, 77-81. https://doi.org/10.3917/lfa.154.0077

Chafiq, N., Benabid, A., Talbi, M., Bergadi, M., & Lima, L. (2011). L'utilisation d'environnements personnels d'apprentissage, une nouvelle façon de remédier aux difficultés langagières chez les étudiants scientifiques. *frantice.net*, *3*, 19-25. http://frantice.net/docannexe/fichier/406/5_Chafiq.pdf

Chami, M. (1987). *L'enseignement du français au Maroc, Diagnostic des difficultés et implications didactiques*. Editions Najah El Jadida.

Denis, B. (2003). Quels rôles et quelle formation pour les tuteurs intervenant dans des dispositifs de formation à distance? *Distances et savoirs*, *1*, 19-46. https://doi.org/10.3166/ds.1.19-46

Dewey, J., & In Reverdy, C. (2013). L'apprentissage par projet : De la recherche. *Revue Technologie*, *186*, 46–54.

Glardon, A. (2021). *Clés pour aider à apprendre*. Wallenried : Editions D'Amont. https://www.meirieu.com/OUTILSDEFORMATION/CpA-14.pdf

Henri, F., & Plante, P. (2018). Qu'est-ce que le e-learning? Un collage de définitions. *TED 1272 : Les TIC et l'apprentissage en milieu de travail*. Université TÉLUQ. https://r-libre.teluq.ca/1746/1/TED1272_texte3.2.pdf

Jirari, H. (2018). Mise en place d'un cours hybride en classe de langue à l'université marocaine : dispositif, approches et action apprenante. Oualili, Cahiers de l'École Normale Supérieure de Meknès, 23, 83-104.

Jobin, K., & Nadeau, P. (2022). *Investir et se développer dans le métavers*. Dunod.

Kurzweil, R. (2007). *Humanité 2.0. La bible du changement* [The Singularity is Near: When Humans Transcend Biology]. Academic Press.

Lamrany-Alaoui, R. (1998). Le scientifique, l'expression, et la communication. Recherches pédagogiques. *Revue de l'AMEF*, *7*, 15–22.

Lebrun, M. (2011). Impacts des TIC sur la qualité des apprentissages des étudiants et le développement professionnel des enseignants : vers une approche systémique. STICEF (Sciences et Technologies de l'Information et de la Communication pour l'Éducation et la Formation), 18, 20.

Leclercq, D., & Denis, B. (1998). Objectifs et paradigmes d'enseignement/apprentissage. In Pour une pédagogie universitaire de qualité. Mardaga.

Ministère de l'Education Nationale, Département de la Technologie. (2002). *Compétice*. https://urlz.fr/mLjO

Narcy-Combes, J.-P. (2005). *Didactique des langues et TIC : vers une recherche-action responsable*. Ophrys.

Nejjari, A., & Bakkali, I. (2017). L'usage des TIC à l'école marocaine : état des lieux et perspectives. *Hermès, La Revue*, *78*, 55-61. https://doi.org/10.3917/herm.078.0055

Nissen, E. (2006). Scénarios de communication en ligne dans des formations hybrides. *Les échanges en ligne dans l'apprentissage et la formation - Le français dans le monde - Recherches et applications*, 44-58. http://edutice.archives-ouvertes.fr/edutice-00124819

Poellhuber, B., Racette, N., & Chirchi, M. (2012). De la présence dans la distance par la visioconférence Web. *Revue internationale des technologies en pédagogie universitaire*, *9*, 63-77. https://doi.org/10.7202/1012903ar

Pothier, M. (2003). *Multimédias, dispositifs d'apprentissage et acquisition des langues*. Ophrys.

Chapter 9
Exploring the Evolution and Impact of Learning Analytics in a Moroccan Context:
A Case Study

Mohamed Housni
https://orcid.org/0000-0001-6199-5249
Faculty of Sciences Ben M'Sick, Hassan II University, Casablanca, Morocco

Mohammed Ait Daoud
https://orcid.org/0000-0002-8627-4429
Faculty of Sciences Ben M'Sick, Hassan II University, Casablanca, Morocco

Khalil Namir
Faculty of Sciences Ben M'Sick, Hassan II University, Casablanca, Morocco

Othmane Aitlmoudden
Faculty of Sciences Ben M'Sick, Hassan II University, Casablanca, Morocco

Mohammed Talbi
Faculty of Sciences Ben M'Sick, Hassan II University, Casablanca, Morocco

ABSTRACT

The chapter evaluates the integration of learning analytics (LA) into Morocco's education system, a task marked by its inherent complexities. A detailed exploration of a case study involving the Provincial Directorate of Education in the Hay Hassani region aids this endeavor. LA's implementation and implications were critically examined, drawing upon the collected data, survey results, and interviews with key stakeholders. A key finding, the Mehnaty project, emerged as a remarkable LA application in the Moroccan context. The analysis indicates that this model, despite logistical and financial constraints, successfully captured age-and-location-based learning requirements, thus informing the design of a more contextually compatible curriculum. This endeavor confirms that implementing LA in the Moroccan educational landscape is viable, albeit with some challenges. The outcome underscores the importance of context in the utilization of LA, advocating for a tailored approach that takes local realities into account to ensure effective learning outcomes.

DOI: 10.4018/979-8-3693-1034-2.ch009

1. INTRODUCTION

The investment in Learning Analytics rest within three issues persisted over the lifespan of the technological development inside the Moroccan educational system (Housni, Namir, Talbi, & Chafiq, 2017):

- Learning is rarely measured at the levels desired by the decision-makers in the organization (Furtado, Souza, Lima, & Oliveira, 2021).
- Most learning activities lacks alignment to the realities of the execution (Xie, Chen, Liu, Kong, & Cao, 2021).
- Learning is considered wasted because learners are not professionally prepared to tackle issues appropriately (Housni, Talbi, & Namir, 2021).

In this prospective this paper finds its roots, aiming at applying Learning Analytics inside the Moroccan environment.

Learners are growing impatient to the traditional learning frameworks because they are networked and empowered by technology that the organization in hole do not take full advantage (Duggal, Gupta, & Singh, 2021).

Technology is the discipline to apply scientific knowledge and skills in an experimental setup to solve real-world problems. However, Applying it does not mean solving (Roll & Winne, 2015).

Therefore, the new application should guide the organization to relocate their resources and converge into creating an effortless learning experience. Those decisions should be based on data that relates to the realities of applications (Chafiq, Housni, & Moussetad, 2019).

The organization aims should be generating an ecosystem for Learning Analytics that apply on: Methods of learning and teaching, created standards, organizational culture, educational content and technological tools . Moreover, new roles should be established such as Learning Engineers and Learning Data Scientists (Chafiq & Housni, 2018).

The complexity of the digitization inside an educational system that have been growing more furiously than ever because of the COVID-19 pandemic dwells in challenging interconnections issues between multitude of systems (Mohammed et al., 2019).

The concerns converge on the Learning Analytics of the instructor/learner relationship environment and the numerical curriculum that adhere to the administrative orientations .

In this paper, the covered subject is Learning Analytics and its applications inside the Moroccan hybrid educational system. In this focus the study converges toward:

1. The importance of the subject matter as an advantageous research opportunity to quantify qualitative measures of learning by the use and integration of Big Data and Learning Management Systems.
2. The technological advancements of Data Mining and its important role in building decision process to describe, prescribe, diagnose and predict environmental outcomes and their influence on learning.
3. Consideration of the punctual needs and requests for analytic on the basis of contextual truths and taking into action the legal and ethical practices for the benefit of all but few.

Furthermore, the digitization process of education goes beyond teachers and students to support resource management systems and nurturing activities. The exigencies of online identity presence and the development of technological skills push forward the agenda of Learning Analytics inside the local educational systems (Mohssine, Bouzekri, & Mohammed, 2019).

The COVID-19 pandemic has accelerated this agenda and pushed forward the implementation of numerical tools to help overcome the trials raised by the virus. Nevertheless, the rise of Learning Analytics caused by the technological advancements and pushed forward by the virus did not change an old strive to understand the learning paradigm, which does not explain the conceptual operations where an individual gains crafts, attitudes, and reasoning attributes (Bentaib et al., s. d.).

This paper questions the meaning of Learning Analytics application in a local context and tries to understand the impact of technology on improving learning activitie. With methodological, analytical research and results, this manuscript will suggest applications answer with suggestions for future endeavors in using technology to solve the learning paradigm (Bentaib et al., s. d.).

Currently, Knowledge is growing exponentially and data is available more than ever, technology of communication and information make the world of knowledge accessible which in return made globalization an established system (Merceron, Blikstein, & Siemens, 2016).

Humans learn informally and formally, this advantage make the human mind more powerful than any current machine that relies on structures and forms (Selwyn, 2019). Moreover, the machines can do more because of its ability to process information at faster rates. Machines can read, model and check data at faster rate but they do not understand its meaning and contextual reality until example data has been provided by developers, engineers or researchers (Selwyn, 2019) .

This complementary between humans and machines is more illustrated in learning and analysis capabilities (Blikstein & Worsley, 2016). Humans acquire knowledge by informal structures that until the present day we can not fully explain and its uniqueness comes from three causes:

- Reading: understanding meaning and impacted experiences of others.
- Doing: Trying in the real-world to solve issues.
- Peering: Transforming circumstantial and relative skills in a closed environment.

2. LITERATURE REVIEW

In literature, results show a growing need for research in Learning Analytics not just because of efficiency and effectiveness in attaining organizational goals with lowest resources allocation possible, but because of the importance of human ingenuity and development by employing the technological advances to its favor (Reich, Tingley, Leder-Luis, Roberts, & Stewart, 2014).

This project focus on providing insights into employing LA technological advances in order to gain intelligence and knowledge. Moreover, developing systems to use data and integrated inside the organizational fabric (Knight, Shum, & Littleton, 2014).

The most commonalities between Learning Analytics applications are:

- Determining learning effectiveness in developing skills and solving problems (Kelly, Thompson, & Yeoman, 2015).
- Identifying gaps or areas of improvements.
- Allocating assets efficiently to answer requests and needs (Gasevic, Dawson, & Jovanovic, 2016).

These similarities constructs general aims for Learning Analytics systems and applications. That should provide key data about seven measurements of efficiency:

1. Learning activities
2. Cost management
3. Learning results
4. Production of information and knowledge
5. Impact of the environment
6. Return on Investments (ROI)
7. Skills development

In the new age of data economy, Learning Analytics become more important than ever to drive value and performance. The greatest asset organization have can be improved at a sustainable growth rate.

Learning Analytics grows in a parallel to the data technology that uses. With the increasing trends in technologies:

- **S**: Security standards
- **S**: Social networks
- **M**: Mobile systems
- **A**: Analysis tools
- **C**: Cloud Computing

In this project, and for the purposes of application inside the local system, the Learning definition describes a cognitive process that aims to acquire skills and knowledge. This characterization needs a decomposition because it refers to multiple vectors that clarify the meaning more. The vectors are cognition, processes, acquisition, skills, and knowledge (Gasevic, Jovanovic, Pardo, & Dawson, 2017).

In this sense, the ontological and epistemological thinking of this project refers to the perceptual capabilities of the Moroccan educational system to integrate Learning Analytics systems that enhances the abilities of learning to the sense of the self and the world (Herodotou, Rienties, Verdin, & Boroowa, 2019).

The project converges into a transformation of the unconscious biases in understanding the realities of mind practices into a data-based conscious, one that can comprehend the mechanisms of identifying the learning ego and the environment in which it resides (Nguyen, Rienties, & Whitelock, 2020).

3. METHODS

Research methods are plans and procedures for research, that starts from a broad assumptions to detailed methods for knowledge collection analysis and interpretations (Shum, Ferguson, & Martinez-Maldonado, 2019).

In this paper, the research plan involves around several decisions, taken in order based on the realities of the context where research occurs, in order to assimilate and present a holistic understanding of the topic.

To examine this research inquiry, six methodological foundations were layout on the basis of creating a hybrid research method that is inspired from quantitative and qualitative methods (Ochoa & Worsley, 2016). The foundations are as follows:

- Collection of data using reliable digital instruments.
- Establishing practices from technological advancements in the local context.
- Applying scientific rigour when processing data using descriptive, predictive, prescriptive and statistical approaches to unlock patterns.
- Interpretation based on practical reality significance.
- Variation in data and visualisation practices to be applied constantly to extract insights.
- Critically thinking about the established hypotheses and theoretical framework and set aside biases to analyse insights and communicate results, in order to provide practical recommendations and lead actions.

In order to deepen the understanding of Learning Analytics applications, it is primordial to ground our work in its contextual reality (Macfadyen, Lockyer, & Rienties, 2020). Analysing Teaching and Learning are a highly complex activities. That requires a high level of skills and knowledge, furthermore resources that arenot available for this (Charleer, Klerkx, & Duval, 2014).

Before digging, there are some assumptions that this project is based on, it will guide our understanding and use the results.

First of all, teachers are considered as facilitator of knowledge and instructional engineers whom reacquired by law to help learners to amass knowledge, values, and skills (Tsai et al., 2018).

Second, Models of instruction employed are systematic development of knowledge specifications using learning abilities and instructional theories to ensure quality. It is represented as an all-inclusive procedure of examination of learning requirements and aspirations beside the expansion of a delivery system to meet those demands (Hernández-Blanco, Herrera-Flores, Tomás, & Navarro-Colorado, 2019). It includes a development of instructional materials and activities; and tryout and evaluation of all instruction and learner activities.

Furthermore, the assumptions insists on starting the process by analyzing the needs of the audience and customize the instruction to the environment where the action of "teaching/learning" occurs (Verschaffel, Depaepe, & Mevarech, 2019).

As a result, decision-making process design, is in a way a framework building to surroundings of the environment of learning/teaching actions to avoid improvising and chaos . In specific terms, the decision-making process is made for:

- Establishing a plan of actions;
- Producing a blueprint for activities;
- Guiding and orienting the deciders;

It shall be noted, that the deciders in an educational setup are the same in most cases, as each one is responsible to make a decision on a level of the organization.

In summery, is up to the deciders to choose which data-driven model is mostly compatible with their context of action, that may or may not be applicable in other particular context .

In this sense, the goal is to provide deciders with the model framework necessary to achieve the best decision based on data and modeling approach that uses generated data during the activities and actions made in their specific circumstances.

As result, revealings of comprehension and decisions is a crucial feature of the analytical process. It translates reality of deciders actions into the context and a factual gap truths related to them. In order to grow this understanding, Our method must pass by three phases:

- **Phase I**: Mining data about learners as key deciders of learning.
- **Phase II**: Visualise and communicate intelligence to other parties responsible in facilitating learning.
- **Phase III**: Integrate Intelligence acquired into actionable products in the Information system.

These phases decomposition are represented in more detailed manner in the next sections of this paper because in their nature they represent the empirical results.

4. RESULTS AND DISCUSSION

While trying to mine data about learners from the provincial direction of education in Hay Hassani region. The official request were denied on the basis of the access limitation by law. However, after interviewing the director Tawfiq AMRANI, there were indications about the structure of the learning data collected from the official MASSAR services (Qazdar, Er-Raha, Cherkaoui, & Mammass, 2019).

The data collected from the learners are not indicating to learning capabilities and only indicate the passing degrees of the learners.

Therefore, a request has been issued to collect data about the working trends in the environments of the learners.

To answer the request and on the basis of the previous methodology described, the Mehnaty project was born as an application of Learning Analytics in the Moroccan system.

4.1. Step 1: Defining Requests

The first step was defining the learning request and identifying the need. Although definitions remain vague and not specific, this research adopted a holistic approach to compromise onn bias of the understanding of the need. And to achieve this a iterative table has been filled to concise the request.

4.2. Step 2: Collecting Data, Measure, Compare, Select

Parallel to the previous request a survey has been conducted to identify the technology profile of the Moroccan population inside the province. There results are illustrated in the table below.

On the basis of the survey results, a software architecture has been proposed to collect, structure and store data from the participants.

The software is an android application that collect location data (GPS) and age with timestamps and device IDs. The software feature is a survey service that adopt The Holland Codes as the measuring instrument for occupational themes and trends in the organization.

Table 1. Analysis table of learning needs according to learners working aspirations.

Organization	**Provincial Direction of Education Hay Hassani - Casablanca-Settat Regional Education and Training Academy Ministry of Education Morocco**
Demand	Identify professional trends in learners orientations and suggest models to decide the type of training to deliver on the basis of location
Current status	Learners describe their educational setup as distant and not compatible with the working aspirations of their environment. Their teachers and administrators describe the same issue. Therefore, the Provincial Direction of education In Hay Hassani wants to analyze the working trends in their environment with a comparison to other environments to decide the training resources allocation of training based on the requested.
Aim	Decide on the engineering model of training compatible with contextual truths and realities of learners.
Project term	One semester (3 months)
Target audience	Learners, Parents and Teachers.
Communication method	Based on past experiences, the provincial director suggests an interactive method of communication and interaction to collect data from the audience. The suggestion also includes a request for digitalization to maximize the reach of communication.
Project resources allocation	No monetary resources were offered. However, full access to information was granted.
Data sources	Due to the nature of the informational system that relies on paperwork, the data available can only be accessed via physical means and require extensive resources for digitalization. Therefore, the dataset should be reconstructed from scratch.
Control /audit body	Research Supervisors / Provincial director

Table 2. Survey results about technology use for learning

Participants Count	**734**				
Period	14/10/2019 — 30/30/2019				
Sexe	Female: 51%		Male: 49%		
Age repartition	12-24	25-34	35-44	45-54	55<
	5%	8%	22%	30%	34%
Used OS	Android	Windows	iOS		Linux
	85%	8%	6%		1%

The Holland Codes serve as an interest assessment tool that survey the trends of the learners in professional horizon. The RIASEC model has been widely used to identify types of personalities and their compatible job profile (Matsui & Tsukamoto, 1991).

The list of trends represented in the Holland model are as fallows:

- **R**: Realistic, assertive and actionable profiles.
- **I**: Investigative, Observer and critical profiles.
- **A**: Artistic, creative and inventive profiles.
- **S**: Social, supportive and helper profiles.

- **E**: Enterprising, adventurous and innovative profiles.
- **C**: Conventional, traditional and organizer profiles.

4.3. Step 3: Audit, Verify

Before consuming further resources a mock-up for the software and the data points measures has been created to be evaluated, verified and audited by research supervisors and provisional director.

Following an Agile management procedure many iterations were applied on the mock-up until the final version has been reached.

The key feedback statements were categorised into groups:

- Design: Adapt the software to the profile of the audience by changing the language to Arabic.
- Functionality: Make the app attractive by offering features to the en-user by reviewing his personal results.
- Value: Propose benefits to the end-user to aid them in choosing career paths.
- Accessibility: make the app accessible via the android official store.
- Extensions: Limiting the scope of the development to answer the request in short time period.
- Limitations: Conformity to legal and ethical conduct and protection of user data.

Figure 1. Software mock-up plan

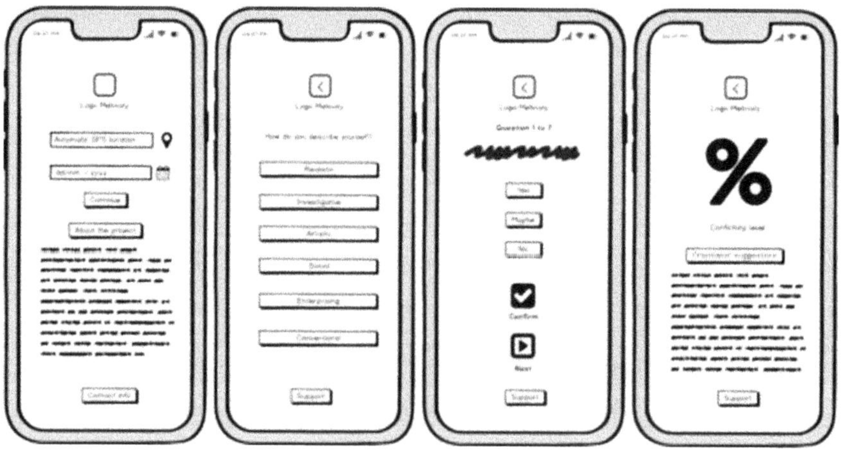

4.4. Step 4: Modeling, Analyse, Decide

After deciding on the architecture of the software and the design. an application was produced using Android Studio software with Firebase as a database for the data. After, the application was published via the Google Play store to gain credibility to be used by the audience.

It was remarkable that the application raised a larger audience from other provinces as it was shared as a solution to identify job compatibility.

For modeling purposes, the research opted for Python. It allows import, cleaning, manipulating and visualizing of data.

Python is an all-purpose development language, conceived by Guido Van Rossum, it is open-source and free for use, plus it is straightforward to build packages, which is a shareable code that solves specific problems. Through time, more and more of these packages specifically built for data science have been developed. Python is a required skill for any aspiring learning data analysts, researchers or professionals (Rossum & Drake, 2001).

Python scripts usually presented in a text file with the extension .py, it is a list of Python commands executed like typing inside a Python Shell line by line. Python is a versatile language used to develop data-driven software to aid and support organizational change and adaptation in new situations and environments. Writing Python scripts does not demand many resources, but a full understanding of the coding language and most importantly. Comments are essential to make sure others can understand the code (Rossum & Drake, 2001).

The source code built is available on GitHub .

4.5. Step 5: Predict Outcomes

The algorithmic model proposed has been iterated multiple times to communicate results in the most efficient way possible. The program takes an input about a specific audience population:

- Age: to reduce the population size, age segmentation.
- Location: physical segmentation of the population.
- Model: Using a specific model enhances the results as the machines where the program is applied is hardware inefficient.
    - Bagging Classifier
    - Ada Boost Classifier
    - XGB Classifier

Figure 2. Example of model inputs: Age, location, and selected modelling process

```
Please enter the age:  65
Please enter the lattitude:  33.6
Please enter the longitude:  7.84
Please enter the model to be used:
model 1: BaggingClassifier
model 2: AdaBoostClassifier
model 3: XGBClassifier
 2
```

After compiling results based on the recent database, the administrator get an probable prediction of the probable answers that the segmented population will deliver.

This prediction help decider to understand the segmented population and communicate effectively with them. Moreover, understanding their trending answers will help the deciders to manage resources effectively especially in training programs that should adhere to the learning profiles and contextual realities of the learners.

Cat1 to 6 refers to the Holland Codes. Therefore: Cat1= Social, Cat2= Conventional, Cat3= Artistic, Cat4= Investigative, Cat5= Enterprising, Cat6= Realistic.

The visualisation above show the models performance in predicting possible trends on the basis of local segmentation. However, the results are insufficient to be conclusive to the deciders, as more structured data is required to build more robust models. Nevertheless, the return on experience is constructive to drive decisions and actions for future endeavour.

Figure 3. Example pf predictions of probable answers

```
Model Chosen:2- AdaBoostClassifier

Best compatible category:        Cat2

Q1- Probability of 0:            32.45%
Q1- Probability of 1:            33.32%
Q1- Probability of 2:            34.23%

Q2- Probability of 0:            32.46%
Q2- Probability of 1:            33.11%
Q2- Probability of 2:            34.43%

Q3- Probability of 0:            39.42%
Q3- Probability of 1:            40.03%
Q3- Probability of 2:            20.55%

Q4- Probability of 0:            20.61%
Q4- Probability of 1:            34.06%
Q4- Probability of 2:            45.33%

Q5- Probability of 0:            35.87%
Q5- Probability of 1:            21.02%
Q5- Probability of 2:            43.11%

Q6- Probability of 0:            32.45%
Q6- Probability of 1:            33.32%
Q6- Probability of 2:            34.23%
```

Table 3. Q references to a profile dimension represented in algorithm results

Q	Realistic	Investigative	Artistic
1	Working on tangible devices	Solving puzzles	Working alone
2	Building and constructing	Trying new tools	Consulting arts and music
3	Caring for animals	Consulting sciences	Writing and sharing ideas
4	Fixing broken furniture	Checking processes	Creating
5	Cooking	Working with numbers and maps	Singing
6	Checking concrete examples	Solving problems	Acting roles
7	Working outdoors	Consulting Mathematics	Drawing
1	Working in groups	Fixing goals and aims	Having a system of organization
2	Orienting and teaching	Persuading and convencing	Setting plans
3	Helping others	Selling and buying	Working according to strategy
4	Aiding the weak and sick	Taking on responsibilities	Attention to details
5	Consulting other cultures	Being a leader	Coordinating paperwork
6	Discussing general issues	Staying in the front	Establishing an action record
7	Answering others needs	Conversing in multi-topics	Acting according to a convention

Figure 4. Comparison graph between the model results to identify trends

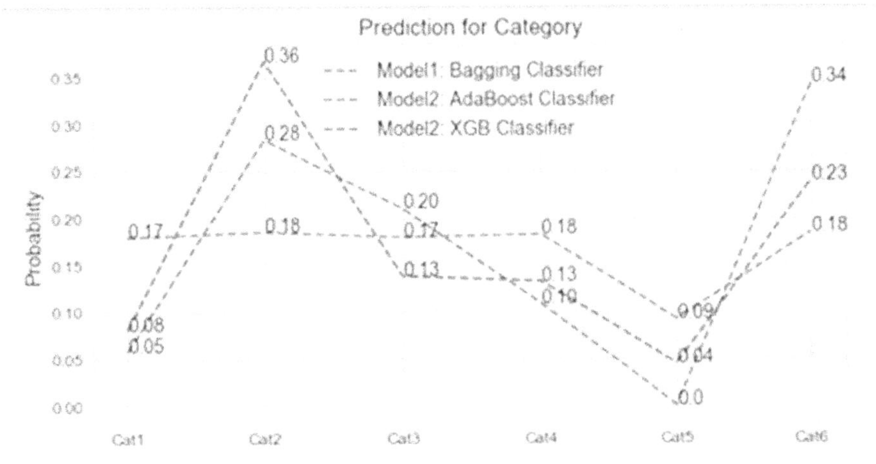

4.6. Notes for Practice

- Learning Analytics application in a hybridized environment such as in Morocco should take into consideration contextual truths of the participants and build upon needs or requests to reduce gaps between desired outcomes and actual situations.
- Singular Learning Analytics applications build upon the needs and requests of the organization are not necessary and they should not be standardized as a one-size-fits-all platform

- Moroccan environment suggests developing Learning Analytics models that can be standardized to take into consideration the environmental contexts of applications and can work upon existing digital and non-digital learning, communication, and information systems.
- The application should be in the organization's convenience and be built upon feedback data provided from participants.
- The Learning Analytics applications help transform the decision process of the Moroccan educational organization and help improve its skills and grow organizational intelligence.

5. CONCLUSION

COVID-19 pandemic has limited previous attempts in Integrating Learning Analytics inside the Moroccan Educational system. As the focus shifted towards keeping the wheel of learning running. Nonetheless, it has accelerated the digitization and the implementation of technological tools to distribute knowledge and content to certify the instructional process's steadiness despite the restrictions posed in many nations worldwide. This opportunity to collect more data about learners and learning that will help construct analytical systems and dashboard to answer deciders needs.

In retrospect, the modeling operations resulted in findings of some critical gaps related to the readiness of the Moroccan system to integrate Learning Analytics.

Moreover, the creation of Data Mining tools and the use of resources that require a reduced amount of monetary assets and logistical efforts only dwell on the ingenuity of the researchers and their technical skills that confirm that the adoption of Learning Analytics in the Moroccan educational system is possible to some extent.

The output of the LA project Mehnaty has been beneficial in getting an inside view of the requirements of learning based on age and location, which in return, help design a learning curriculum that adheres to the perceptual realities of the learners.

Conflicts of Interest

The author(s) declared no potential conflicts of interest with respect to the research, authorship, and/or publication of this article.

Data Availability

The datasets generated during and/or analyzed during the current study are available in the Mehnaty project repository, https://github.com/mohamedhousni/Mehnaty. Furthermore, The articles used to support the findings of this study are included and are cited at relevant places within the text as references.

Funding

This study was not financially supported by the ministry of education nor the university in which it occurs.

ACKNOWLEDGMENT

The inclusion of commercial products and project names in this paper is not an endorsement of these products or projects in any way. The data has been shared in consent of the beholders and was employed for research purposes only. We would like to thank the editor and anonymous reviewers for their constructive comments and suggestions, which have improved the quality of the manuscript.

REFERENCES

Bentaib, M., Daouad, M. A., Touri, B., Namir, A., Labriji, L., Hammed, M., … Talbi, M. (n.d.). *Implementation of a Computing Device to Quality Service in Learning in Higher Education to Enhance Student's Quality of Life*. Academic Press.

Blikstein, P., & Worsley, M. (2016). Multimodal Learning Analytics and Education Data Mining : Using computational technologies to measure complex learning tasks. *Journal of Learning Analytics*, *3*(2), 220–238. doi:10.18608/jla.2016.32.11

Chafiq, N., & Housni, M. (2018). Towards the Design of an Innovative and Social Hybrid Learning Based on the SMAC Technologies. *Smart Innovation, Systems and Technologies*, *111*, 126–133. doi:10.1007/978-3-030-03577-8_15

Chafiq, N., Housni, M., & Moussetad, M. (2019). Towards a dynamics of techno-pedagogical innovation within the university : Case study Hassan II University of Casablanca. *Information Systems and Technologies to Support Learning: Proceedings of EMENA-ISTL 2018, 2*, 118-125.

Charleer, S., Klerkx, J., & Duval, E. (2014). Learning Dashboards. *Journal of Learning Analytics*, *1*(3), 199–202. doi:10.18608/jla.2014.13.22

Duggal, K., Gupta, L. R., & Singh, P. (2021). Gamification and Machine Learning Inspired Approach for Classroom Engagement and Learning. *Mathematical Problems in Engineering*, 1–18. Advance online publication. doi:10.1155/2021/9922775

Furtado, L. S., Souza, R. F. D., Lima, J. L. D. R., & Oliveira, S. R. B. (2021). Teaching Method for Software Measurement Process Based on Gamification or Serious Games : A Systematic Review of the Literature. *International Journal of Computer Games Technology*, 1–35. Advance online publication. doi:10.1155/2021/8873997

Gasevic, D., Dawson, S., & Jovanovic, J. (2016). Ethics and Privacy as Enablers of Learning Analytics. *Journal of Learning Analytics*, *3*(1), 1–4. doi:10.18608/jla.2016.31.1

Gasevic, D., Jovanovic, J., Pardo, A., & Dawson, S. (2017). Detecting Learning Strategies with Analytics : Links with Self-reported Measures and Academic Performance. *Journal of Learning Analytics*, *4*(2), 113–128. doi:10.18608/jla.2017.42.10

Hernández-Blanco, A., Herrera-Flores, B., Tomás, D., & Navarro-Colorado, B. (2019). A Systematic Review of Deep Learning Approaches to Educational Data Mining. *Complexity*, *2019*, 1–22. Advance online publication. doi:10.1155/2019/1306039

Herodotou, C., Rienties, B., Verdin, B., & Boroowa, A. (2019). Predictive learning analytics "at scale" : Towards guidelines to successful implementation in higher education based on the case of the open university UK. *Journal of Learning Analytics*, *6*(1), 85–95. doi:10.18608/jla.2019.61.5

Housni, M., Namir, A., Talbi, M., & Chafiq, N. (2017). Applying Data Analytics and Cumulative Accuracy Profile (CAP) Approach in Real-Time Maintenance of Instructional Design Models. *Advances in Intelligent Systems and Computing*, *756*, 17–25. doi:10.1007/978-3-319-91337-7_2

Housni, M., Talbi, M., & Namir, A. (2021). Simple Technology is an Improved Solution for a Post-Pandemic Informative System : A Reference Model. *International Journal of Emerging Technologies in Learning*, *16*(16), 35–51. doi:10.3991/ijet.v16i16.23211

Kelly, N., Thompson, K., & Yeoman, P. (2015). Theory-led Design of Instruments and Representations in Learning Analytics : Developing a Novel Tool for Orchestration of Online Collaborative Learning. *Journal of Learning Analytics*, *2*(2), 14–43. doi:10.18608/jla.2015.22.3

Knight, S., Shum, S. B., & Littleton, K. (2014). Epistemology, Assessment, Pedagogy : Where Learning Meets Analytics in the Middle Space. *Journal of Learning Analytics*, *1*(2), 23–47. doi:10.18608/jla.2014.12.3

Macfadyen, L. P., Lockyer, L., & Rienties, B. (2020). Learning design and learning analytics : Snapshot 2020. *Journal of Learning Analytics*, *7*(3), 6–12. doi:10.18608/jla.2020.73.2

Matsui, T., & Tsukamoto, S. I. (1991). Relation between career self-efficacy measures based on occupational titles and Holland codes and model environments : A methodological contribution. *Journal of Vocational Behavior*, *38*(1), 78–91. doi:10.1016/0001-8791(91)90019-I

Merceron, A., Blikstein, P., & Siemens, G. (2016). Learning analytics : From big data to meaningful data. *Journal of Learning Analytics*, *2*(3), 4–8. doi:10.18608/jla.2015.23.2

Mohammed, A. D., Khalil, N., Mohssine, B., Rachida, I., Soufiane, B., & Mohammed, T. (2019). Using students' data to improve the quality of the education in Moroccan institution. *International Journal of Open Information Technologies*, *7*(11), 59–65.

Mohssine, B., Bouzekri, T., & Mohammed, T. (2019). Integration of a Computer Device for Learning and Training Situations : The Case of Faculty of Sciences Ben M'sik (FSBM). *International Journal of Emerging Technologies in Learning*, *14*(03), 243–249. doi:10.3991/ijet.v14i03.9355

Nguyen, Q., Rienties, B., & Whitelock, D. (2020). A Mixed-Method Study of How Instructors Design for Learning in Online and Distance Education. *Journal of Learning Analytics*, *7*(3), 64–78. doi:10.18608/jla.2020.73.6

Ochoa, X., & Worsley, M. (2016). Editorial : Augmenting Learning Analytics with Multimodal Sensory Data. *Journal of Learning Analytics*, *3*(2), 213–219. doi:10.18608/jla.2016.32.10

Qazdar, A., Er-Raha, B., Cherkaoui, C., & Mammass, D. (2019). A machine learning algorithm framework for predicting students performance : A case study of baccalaureate students in Morocco. *Education and Information Technologies, 24*(6), 3577-3589. doi:10.1007/s10639-019-09946-8

Reich, J., Tingley, D., Leder-Luis, J., Roberts, M. E., & Stewart, B. (2014). Computer-Assisted Reading and Discovery for Student Generated Text in Massive Open Online Courses. *Journal of Learning Analytics*, *2*(1), 156–184. doi:10.18608/jla.2015.21.8

Roll, I., & Winne, P. H. (2015). Understanding, evaluating, and supporting self-regulated learning using learning analytics. *Journal of Learning Analytics*, *2*(1), 7–12. doi:10.18608/jla.2015.21.2

Rossum, G. V., & Drake, F. L. (2001). *Python Reference Manual Release 2.1.1.* Academic Press.

Selwyn, N. (2019). What's the Problem with Learning Analytics? *Journal of Learning Analytics*, *6*(3), 11–19. doi:10.18608/jla.2019.63.3

Shum, S. B., Ferguson, R., & Martinez-Maldonado, R. (2019). Human-Centred Learning Analytics. *Journal of Learning Analytics*, *6*(2), 1–9. doi:10.18608/jla.2019.62.1

Tsai, Y.-S., Moreno-Marcos, P. M., Jivet, I., Scheffel, M., Tammets, K., Kollom, K., & Gašević, D. (2018). The SHEILA Framework : Informing Institutional Strategies and Policy Processes of Learning Analytics. *Journal of Learning Analytics*, *5*(3), 5–20. doi:10.18608/jla.2018.53.2

Verschaffel, L., Depaepe, F., & Mevarech, Z. (2019). Learning Mathematics in Metacognitively Oriented ICT-Based Learning Environments : A Systematic Review of the Literature. *Education Research International*, *2019*, 1–19. Advance online publication. doi:10.1155/2019/3402035

Xie, S. T., Chen, Q., Liu, K. H., Kong, Q. Z., & Cao, X. J. (2021). Learning Behavior Analysis Using Clustering and Evolutionary Error Correcting Output Code Algorithms in Small Private Online Courses. *Scientific Programming*, *2021*, 1–11. Advance online publication. doi:10.1155/2021/9977977

Chapter 10
Hybridization of Approaches and Gradual Investment in ICTs Toward Innovative University Pedagogy

Chaimae Tailassane
https://orcid.org/0009-0001-0467-4593
Université Moulay Ismail, Morocco

Imane Elimadi
https://orcid.org/0000-0001-9076-5039
Hassan II University, Casablanca, Morocco

ABSTRACT

This research aims to reflect on the integration of digital technologies in teaching French within non-linguistic disciplines. The goal is to think about the academic integration of French in light of various contexts and practices, such as hybrid teaching (both in-person and online via learning platforms dedicated to Edmodo, Moodle, or even MOOCs), combining theory and practice while considering constraints like motivation, organization, and materials. The authors start from the idea that students' poor performance at the university is due to the extensive use of the French language in courses spread over three months, with three hours of class per week. Therefore, various approaches were tested, with a gradual implementation of a hybrid approach known as light in-person classes. Since the fall of 2014, the team of professors has tested three approaches, ranging from enriched in-person classes to 100% online MOOCs. The latter was conducted in the spring of 2016 through a partnership between the Faculty of Sciences at the University Mohammed V in Rabat and the French Institute of Rabat.

DOI: 10.4018/979-8-3693-1034-2.ch010

INTRODUCTION

Our paper is meant to be a reflection on the use of digital technology in the teaching of French in non-language areas. The goal is to pull back from educational practice and reassess certain methods in a creative manner. Our goal is to reflect on the academic integration of French in light of a variety of contexts and practices, such as hybrid teaching (delivered both face-to-face and remotely via dedicated learning platforms such as Edmodo, Moodle, and even Moocs), reconciling theory and practice while keeping a variety of constraints (motivational, organizational, material, and so on) in mind. Nous partons de l'idée selon laquelle la faible performance des étudiants à l'université est due au choix d'une pratique extensive de la langue française à savoir les cours s'étalant sur trois mois à raison d'une séance de trois heures par semaine. Il a été donc question de tester plusieurs dispositif en mettant progressivement en place un dispositif hybride.

Since the autumn of 2014, a group of teachers has been testing all three systems, from enhanced face-to-face courses to the 100% distant MOOC. The latter was the focus of the spring 2016 session as part of a partnership between Mohammed V University's Faculty of Science and the French Institute in Rabat. The Claroline Consortium established it with the goal of providing graduate students with a sufficient amount of digital materials on the FLESUP platform.

THEORETICAL BACKGROUND

Our goal is to present a multi-layered perspective in which we will examine the relationships between French teaching/learning and the incorporation of new technologies by reviewing the scientific literature in the many disciplines affected. We shall also make an effort to present our didactic positioning and goals.

ICT for Learning French: Hybridizing Practices

The incorporation of ICTE into its systems has not evaded the realm of foreign language acquisition, particularly French. New information and communication technologies include those utilized in information processing and transmission. Furthermore, Jean-Pierre Robert (2008: 198) explains:

For teaching and learning purposes, ICTE encompasses a range of knowledge, methods and tools designed and used to produce, store, classify, retrieve and read written, audio and visual documents, as well as to exchange these documents between interlocutors, in real or deferred time.

ICTs are viewed as instruments at the service of instructional initiatives by researchers, didacticians, and pedagogues. They engage in a dynamic relationship with the teacher (Charlier, Daele, & Deschyver, 2002).

Before delving into the qualities of a hybrid device, it is important reviewing the Compétice typology, which is included in the description of ICTE integration at university. In reality, the Compétice typology suggests five different types of hybrid devices based on the degree of ICTE integration. Based on Vetter's (2014) video capsule, we may present the five devices as follows:

Face-to-face multimedia-enhanced teaching: This comprises the use of presentation tools or materials in class, either by the learners or by the teacher.

Pre- and post-course "augmented" or "enhanced" teaching: the teacher makes materials, such as a syllabus or a sitography, available to students before and after the course.

Face-to-face learning is considered lean when it accounts for more than 50% of total learning time.

Reduced face-to-face teaching: most training is done remotely, however specific groups can be planned by the tutor. In a nutshell, these two kinds of training are hybrid.

Face-to-face training is virtually non-existent: this is open, remote learning via a platform that provides access to materials. This sort of Compétice tutoring is both synchronous and asynchronous.

Indeed, because it stresses the alternation of face-to-face and distant training hours, it may be a useful adjuvant. Previously, it was thought to be a way to alleviate students' socio-cognitive and socio-affective isolation. Which led to discouragement and abandonment, as Soubrie (2008: 106) points out. For (Charlier et al., 2006), hybrid systems play an important role in innovation.

It is worth mentioning that the distance-learning component of a hybrid system encourages learners to participate in solo and/or group tasks (see section 1.2.). Face-to-face learning enhances class-group cohesiveness and ensures content coherence, the distance to "slow down the time" of learning (Bruillard, 2003), to lengthen reflection, by taking a step back, or even distance itself. Mangenot (2002) adds that because learners have simple access to the learning environment and hence to mediated resources, this approach encourages learner empowerment. As a consequence, self-learning is assured, with extracurricular activities appraised or utilized within the class group.

As previously said, digital technology has provided fresh impetus to traditional education, which was formerly carried out primarily in the classroom using a teaching technique or textbook. Indeed, adopting this technique has revolutionized the course flow, since the tutor now invites learners to read the course ahead of time at home and intends to go through the tasks with them in class. It also allows for the digitization of the lecture by transferring it to an exchange platform, often in the form of a video capsule. While it is true that ICT provides a means of mediation and improves access to knowledge due to its immediate nature, it is also a tool that must not be used to obscure the educational implications of the flipped classroomtechnique, which are essential.

Similarly, the power of videos was reinforced by (Bergmann and Aaron 2012), who argued that videos had the ability to encourage learners to prepare lessons to be delivered in class, in the presence of the instructor, in order to make the latter more interactive. "Lectures at Home and Homework in Class" was their tagline.

To conclude, Marcel Lebrun (2015, 44) suggests the following points, which are classified as follows:

The flipped classroom is:

- An environment in which students take responsibility for their own learning under the guidance of the teacher. An environment in which students take responsibility for their own learning under the guidance of the trainer;
- a classroom in which the teacher is not the "Sage on the stage", but the "Guide on the side", allowing for different forms of differentiation;
- a fertile blend of direct transmission (I teach) with a constructivist or socio-constructivist approach to learning (it's up to the learners to learn, but we don't learn alone);
- a class in which students who are absent due to illness or extracurricular activities (for sports, field trips) are not left "behind";
- a class where the content worked on (the "subject matter") is accessible all the time for revision, exams and remediation;

- a class where students are more engaged in their learning
  -a place where students can receive personalized support

We can't describe the "inverted classroom" approach without referencing the three stages identified by Marcel Lebrun and Julie Lecoq in Classes inversées, enseigner et apprendre à l'endroit, from novice to expert.

Table 1. The two levels of the flipped classroom

	Level 1	Level 2
		motivation, contexts, tasks, problems
Distance	videos, texts	Documentary research Field work activity preparation
presence	debates, questions, answers, etc.	presentations, animations, discussions, modeling activities

The first level appears to be overly stiff, and it may even constitute a retreat to the deductive process if it becomes electronically transmissive. Its upside, though, is that it allows for more action in the classroom and redefines the roles of instructor and student.

Level 2 of the Lebrun-Lecoq typology is a more dynamic approach in which the student is more engaged and involved in the course's creation. Level 2 students are required to do remote activities such as documentary research, fieldwork, and activity preparation in order to complete in-person activities such as presentations, presentations, debates, and modeling activities.

Marcel Lebrun and Julie Lecoq define level 3 based on the Kolb cycle as follows (Lebrun, Lecoq, 2015: 17):

A third level of the inverted classroom could combine the previous two, by considering the events described above in the form of a cycle. This would go beyond the deterministic linearity of "before class/ during class" to become a spiral made up of successive contextualization (the meaning of knowledge, practices, contexts), decontextualization (invariants, principles, models, theories) and recontextualization (applications, situations, transfer), alternating face-to-face and distance activities, or individual and group work.

In this level, the course is built in 4 steps:

- At home: Research, teach the notion
- In class: Present, share
- At home: Learning
- In class: Contextualization, practice formerly done at home.

At this point, we're discussing a hybrid method, because this degree of inversion implies a hybridization of distant learning and traditional, face-to-face learning. The student is significantly more independent and accountable for his or her own learning in level 3, and far less reliant. It is no more a matter of flipping the roles of theory and practice, but of reimagining work spaces and time division in a cyclical manner.

The Task-Based Approach to Learning

As previously stated, ICTE provides significant functionality and practical solutions, notably for jobs within devices. Learners may be able to demonstrate their inventiveness and assess their language demands on the one hand, while comparing their activities with others on the other.

In didactics, the task has become increasingly prevalent. It is important in the context of teaching/learning FLE (Ellis, R., 2003; Nunan, D., 2004, Narcy-Combes, J.-P., 2005; Mangenot, F., & Louveau, E., 2006) as well as in the socio-cultural setting in which the learner inscribes himself and creates his knowledge.

Tasks are classified into two types: macro-tasks and micro-tasks (see R. Ellis 2003, Narcy-Combes 2005). Realistic macro-tasks are defined. They rely on observing "authentic" communication scenarios, or "staging" jobs as they are referred to (Demaiziere & J. P. Narcy-Combes, 2005: 45-46). These macro-tasks lead to open-ended language production because they are carried out in a social interaction context that encourages meaning negotiation, aiding the acquisition of FLE and permitting the establishment of PAS (Potentially Acquirable Situations).

In terms of micro-activities, these are regarded analytical tasks that rely mostly on language. They are less realistic and concentrate on controlling meaning and drawing attention to significant phenomena. These assignments are chosen based on the requirements of the L2 program; they are training tasks. In actuality, they are mostly centered on multimedia activities, owing to the availability of "general public" software, educational resources, and equipment on the Internet. Demaizière and J. P. Narcy-Combes (2005: 45-64) suggest that micro-tasks will be more operational if they inspire learners to notice, to have "mini-SPAs" experiences. These mini-SPAs will help the student gain his or her bearings during language exchanges in some way. As previously stated, micro-tasks and macro-tasks are corollaries. In other words, micro-tasks come into play after identifying linguistic barriers during macro-tasks. In this situation, the teacher/tutor's intervention or mediation is intended to provide learners with micro-tasks for remediation and language training based on their requirements.

In result, the hybrid approach will be efficient and cost-effective in a situation where students may participate in face-to-face instruction via micro-assignments and practice tasks, as well as weekly and remote sessions with the tutor. The instructor will examine and remark on the platform's work, making recommendations (referrals to valuable sites, focused reading, etc.).

Representative Experiments

This article, as previously stated, reports on three tests conducted with students from the Faculty of Science at Mohammed V University in Rabat. The first consists of three weeks of intense classes followed by a standard session of regular courses. In reality, the two epochs complement one another. Indeed, the goals of this immersion session were to contextualize scientific facts in current events and daily life, to promote learning through an action-based language method, to encourage autonomy, to reinforce the use of language as a tool for communication and social action, to encourage language risk-taking, and, most importantly, to make a gradual transition from general French to French for Specific Purposes (FOS).

1st Experiment: Language Immersion Session

The current experiment involves a hybrid device (enhanced classroom) that is based on an action-based strategy that appears to be suitable for dealing with the aforementioned challenges.

- 80% face-to-face: identify linguistic points in texts and visuals chosen by topic professors.
- 20% distant learning: on the one hand, supporting group and/or individual learning, and on the other, mediation via mediatization. It inspires students by decomposing the learning environment, hence empowering them. The distanciel entailed sending students to see films created specifically for the immersion session, explain their content in an attempt to comprehend the phenomena, and lastly communicate with the supervisor via e-mail or social media.

The French teachers collaborate closely with each other during the course, through meetings, encounters, the blog (http://immersionlinguistique2014.blogspot.com/), and with the subject teachers.

The audiovisual documents on which the subject instructors will work are taken from a variety of websites and television shows, including "Kezako,".

Each two-hour French class is separated into two one-hour sequences, each of which is associated with two subjects. If the papers are basic, the first half-hour of the class can be spent to rectifying an assignment given the day before (a brief survey/research, a presentation), and the second half-hour to drafting the afternoon's document. If the paper is more difficult, you can commit an entire hour to prepare it for the afternoon. The work done in French classes is not just about lexis, but also on syntax, depending on the subject and the unique language issues it causes. To do this, improvisations, role-playing, riddles, mind maps, crossword puzzles, and other activities were on the schedule.

A new environment was established in the classroom as a result of video projection, multimedia, and activity modification. This mood was improved further when students were directed to YouTube videos rather than a complicated out-of-class task. The classic transmission/reception approach was therefore coupled with the flipped classroom idea, allowing students to process and organize what they had previously done at home in the classroom, resulting in "a classroom or laboratory environment that adapts to the students' learning pace and style."

The second follows, lasting three months from October to December 2014. It satisfies a number of criteria, including the obligation to certify scientific university profiles so that students can continue their studies. The stakes are high inasmuch as French transmits all of the content related with these curricula, because learners should have capitalized on the language tool as an essential talent for their transition to higher education by the conclusion of the first year of the licensing cycle. As a result, the FOS framework employs the flipped classroom method and two systems (enriched face-to-face / augmented face-to-face), as well as experiments with a hybrid system (lightened face-to-face).

As the operational mode of the immersion session was extended into the normal session, this session was a continuation and assessment of the immersion session. Indeed, the students were eager and motivated to continue their language and terminology course under the same conditions as the previous session, which had focused on video projection, improvisations, role-playing, riddles, mental maps, crosswords, and so on. This was the mode of operation for the immersion session throughout the autumn of 2014.

These three months were also utilized to integrate the remaining students in A2 and upwards, increasing the total number of pupils each class to 40/60. The supervisors had a significant barrier in individualizing follow-up and consolidating joint effort. As a result, the majority of instructors invested in enhanced face-to-face instruction, whereas decreased face-to-face instruction was maintained on an experimental basis for the SMPC > A04, C03, D01, and F01 groups. To build a space for sharing and conversation, it was required to develop digital communities on Google+ for each of these groups:

Figure 1.

For this reason, this simulation piqued the interest of other students who had only had face-to-face training. Informally, we noted that several students in our group requested us to join the community to have a better understanding of what we do remotely. As a consequence, the community has grown to 38 members.

Figure 2.

The value of alternating face-to-face and distance learning was confirmed on an informational level, when it came to reminding students of important dates and events, and on a communicational level, when it came to bringing students and teachers closer together on a socio-pedagogical level.

Figure 3.

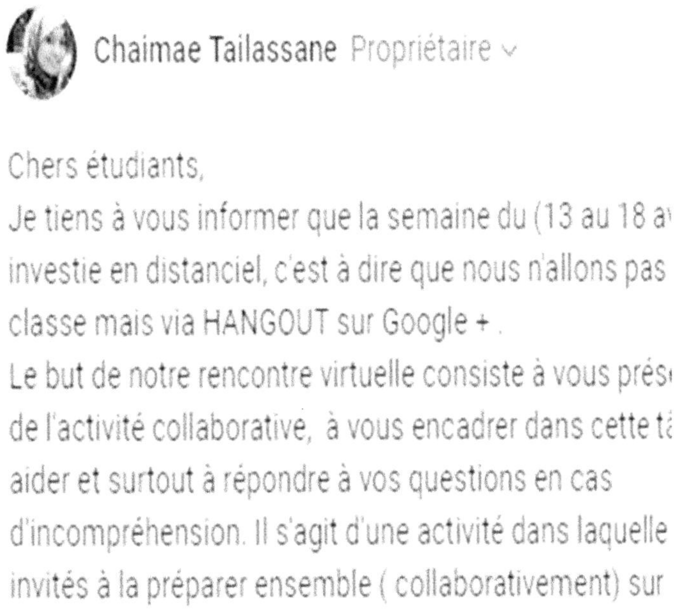

Figure 4.

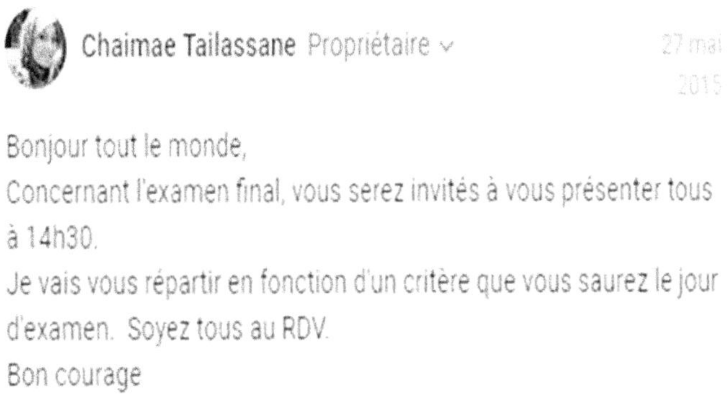

In terms of effectiveness, the most significant barrier we encountered was the target audience's irregular participation, which occurred for a variety of reasons (lack of computerized classrooms at the Faculty, precarious economic conditions for some students, late membership in the communities, difficult investment by the teacher/tutor given his or her hourly workload).

Furthermore, including a hybrid device into French lectures has proven to be a stimulating element not just for students enrolled in the communities, but also for other SMPC students. Exchanges with part-time colleagues were documented in a private digital community, the major assets of which are the dissemination of information, constant monitoring by coordinators, and the reaction of members in the case of a problem. We came to a variety of conclusions, one of which was crucial. A large number of kids were absent from class.

Figure 5.

2nd Experiment: Spring/Autumn 2015 Session

The second experiment was progressively incorporating new technologies into the course in order to make it into a hybrid device. This integration will allow us to assess students' engagement in a FOU course as well as the influence of device hybridization on their motivation. In these two sessions (spring and fall 2015), we attempted to collaborate with various platforms to give assistance during the E/A process of French at university. We initially chose Google+, which had already proven useful in reinforcing collaborative work during the normal autumn 2014 session.

Second, we selected Edmodo as a learning platform. This is a learning network that connects all students to the people and resources they need to reach their greatest potential. The platform is intended to turn the classroom into a community through social networking, while also providing instructors with complete control over their digital classrooms. According to the website, the instructor may rapidly establish groups, assign homework, schedule tests, track progress, and more with straightforward tools and limitless storage.

It is worth mentioning that in the spring of 2015, the SMPC industry was divided into seven parts (A, B, C, D, E, F, G), each of which was further broken into four groups. Through the formation of a digital community on Google+, each of these groups was given a dynamic identity. These communities, it goes without saying, deepen the bonds between the learners themselves, who are frequently disadvantaged by geographical distance, as well as between them and the teacher. The teacher has been overseeing the students' work as part of his or her tutorial obligations (described above). His efforts were centered on visually marking the community as well as giving important information to it.

Figure 6. Google+community

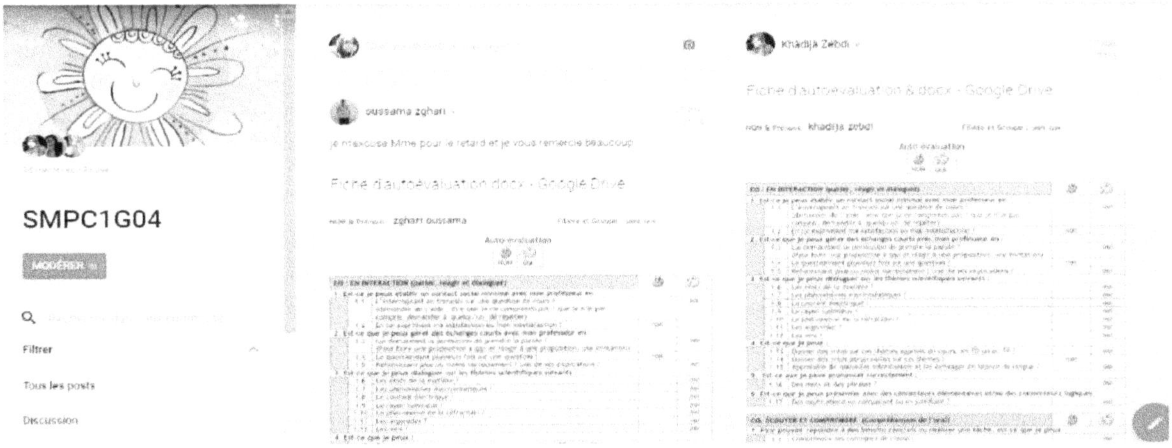

The activities suggested on the community are unquestionably an extension of the course in that they allow students to prepare for the ultimate end-of-year presentation in class, which is a scientific demonstration in small groups.

Six dossiers with glossaries were created on these issues. They were worked on in class, following a sequence that led to knowledge systematization through out-of-class activities, the completion of which was to lead to posts (publications) in the communities. Here's an example from dossier 3 "Electrical current":

Figure 7.

<table>
<tr>
<td>Continuez l'histoire qui suit en imaginant des causes et des conséquences :

Une compagnie d'eau et d'électricité décide de suspendre le compte de l'un de ses clients qui refuse de payer ses factures. Le client en question est une personne connue par son avarice. En effet, en restant indifférent à la décision de la compagnie, il pense qu'il n'a pas besoin de ses services et qu'il peut lui-même s'approvisionner en eau et électricité...</td>
<td>La suite de l'histoire doit être aussi courte que possible et contenir les mots suivants :
>Un jour
>Panneaux photovoltaïque
>Biomasse
>Puits</td>
</tr>
</table>

The alternating of in-class and distant learning approaches allowed the student to exhibit his or her effort to practice, because the student gained from reinforcement to increase his or her sense of self-efficacy with relation to previously unresolved or unfeeling challenges. This alternative exhibits "characteristics of methods more open to technology's effective role." We cite: - an authentic, relevant, and demanding work as the trigger for this open didactic setting; - the complexity of the skills performed and mastered by learners in a wide range of domains (cognitive, social, technical, etc.); - the teacher's role as guide", emphasizes Lebrun (2002:176).

Students were required to develop cross-disciplinary skills, whether intellectual, inherent in the coherence of contextually-adapted statements (via definition, explanation, and justification), communicative, consubstantial in the use of gestures, or methodological, primarily related to the deployment of technology for successful final demonstrations. The technical competence associated with the regular use of TIC double l'utilisation personnel free environment digital a didactic codified use. Learners are fully aware of this, and demonstrate their need for new manipulations by progressively engaging them in action and conversation, even if deadlines are missed.

They occasionally reverse positions on the community, assisting the instructor in resolving or responding to a student's query. For example, valuable time was saved due to the attentiveness of one of our pupils. A student had asked for the link to a film on the community wall, and while we were taking our time to respond, another student took care of it to save time. Here's an example:

Figure 8.

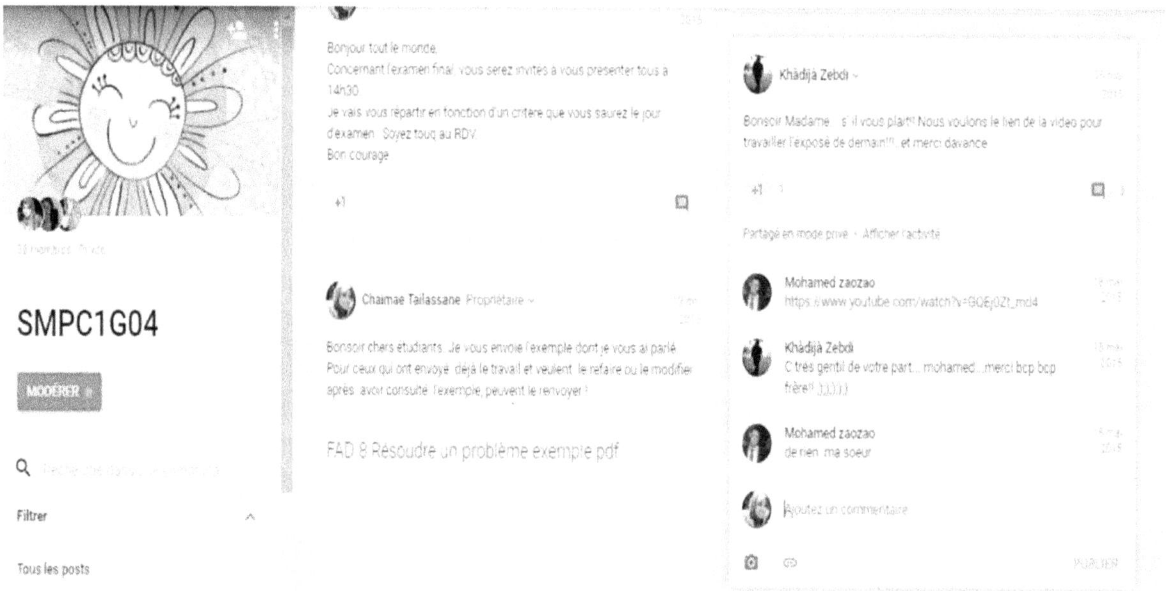

Furthermore, we had to measure the target audience's effort in connection to the academic rhythm experienced to the fullest by the stream most resistive to French courses within the Faculty of Science. The learners were not disappointed by the programming of a collaborative activity (including a group performance). A collaborative activity, as the name implies, describes the interactions of a group around a piece of work. This exercise inspired them to tell others about it. Furthermore, the majority of class groups were enthusiastic about the exercise. The community had 38 members, and all pupils liked to work in groups.

Take the following example:

We ask the students to complete the macro-task. The assignment is to create a PowerPoint deck that presents the answer to a problem that involves two separate physical quantities. The presentation must adhere to the teacher's strategy, which will serve as an outline to assist students in designing their slideshow. The strategy is as follows:

- The first micro-task (one slide) is to formulate the aim using the infinitive.
- Second microtask (one slide): Create a question stating the problem. The learner is expected to grasp the interrogative phrase.
- Third microtask (one slide): The student must specify the experiment's accessories using enumeration and coordination.
- 4th micro-task (six slides): This micro-task requires you to describe the experiment. The learner will employ logical linkages and derivation at this stage.
- 5th micro-task: Explanation of the experiment (one to two slides).
- 6th micro-task: Post the slide presentation on your community's website. The student must demonstrate proficiency with digital technologies.

Figure 9.

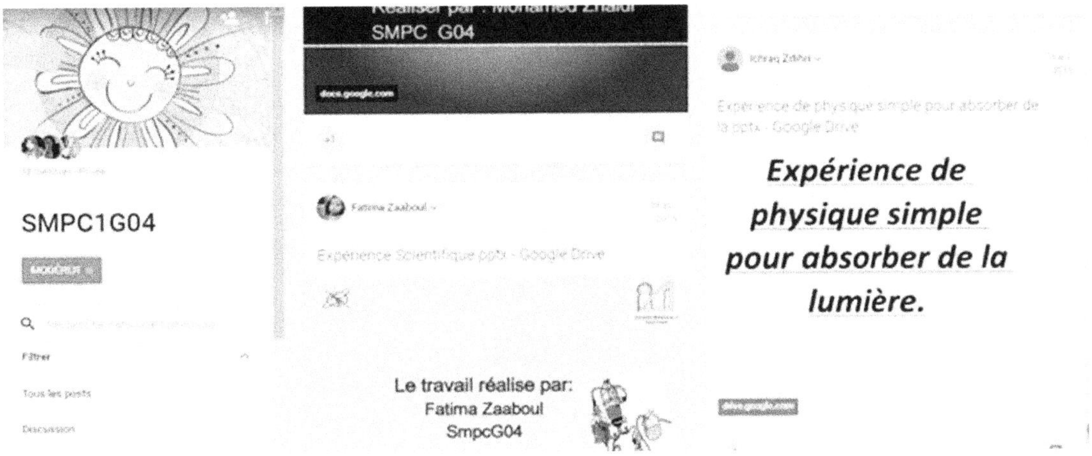

To verify the experiment, it was important to go over the previously developed learning goals. In reality, validation was evaluated both subjectively (through questionnaires and assessment grids) and statistically (by the session success rate, which indicated the success of the final test). In this way, evaluation was both formative and summative. Formative, in that it included regular feedback during the teaching period via face-to-face and distance learning sessions via Google+, and summative, in that it was the subject of the mark awarded for work done in and out of class (increased to 25%) and the mark for the final written test (increased to 75%).

Figure 10.

Some drawbacks have been overcome by adapting this working methodology, such as overcrowding in classes, the sociolinguistic insecurity of weaker students vis-à-vis students with a good command of the language (feeling of intimidation), and a lack of follow-up due to the large number of students in a class....

Figure 11. The number of students assessed and validated in the fall 2014 and spring 2015 sessions

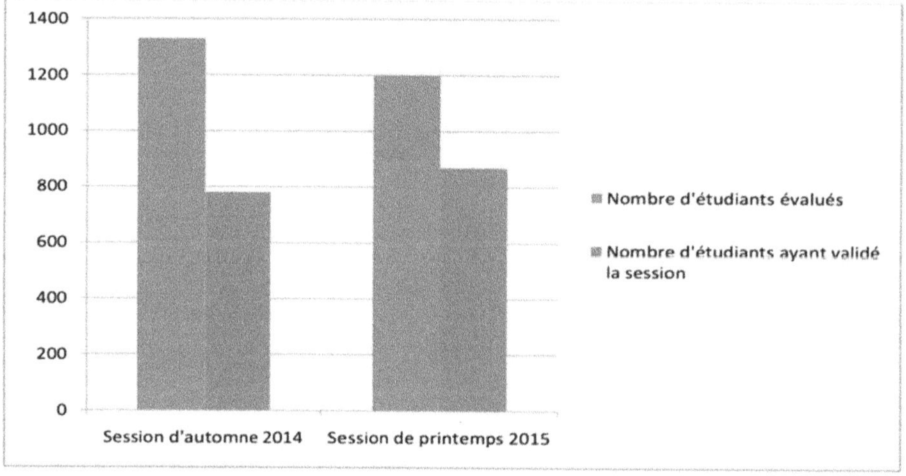

The teaching team selected Edmodo as a platform to make the language and terminology training more practical. This platform enabled the provision of supporting papers to supplement those shown in class, resulting in greater in-depth work on the language. The exercises built on this platform using questionnaires included lexical aspects not addressed in class owing to time constraints, and frequently ensured previous comprehension of the issues to be examined in the face-to-face courses.

These activities also allowed students to rectify and reinforce grammatical points learned in class. The development of distance learning activities addressed a deficiency identified during the classroom course, in which time was insufficient to study in depth on each skill or language topic. As a result, face-to-face and remote learning became interdependent, with the activities offered at a distance having to be performed in order to continue with the face-to-face course.

The effects of the hybrid system's implementation are difficult to assess over such a short period of time, considering that the pupils only had three months of lectures. We mostly relied on learners' replies to an opinion questionnaire provided on the platform at the end of the session to establish its impact. The findings offered evidence of the system's favorable characteristics. We were able to determine that the pupils' comments attested to the platform's usefulness. Furthermore, various tools (Padlet) were set up to assist and guide them in their task. They were never left to their own devices, whether in the classroom or remotely. Students might utilize the in-person course structure to ask questions or seek clarification on certain activities. Remote tutorial assistance was also available via the group wall and message system. This analysis considered not only the completed questionnaires, but also the final assessment marks.

Figure 12. Theplatform used to support students at adistance Edmodo

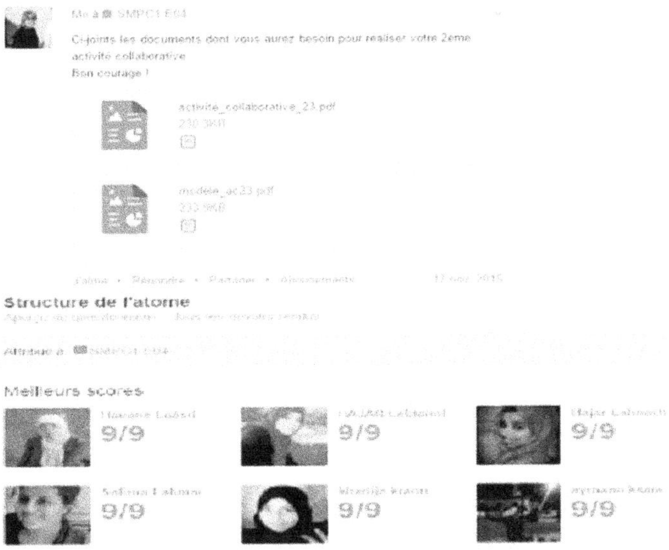

The utility of alternating face-to-face and distance learning has thus been confirmed, not only at the learning level, by providing an interesting and even strategic potential for encouraging the acquisition and development of discourse skills in students and increasing the number of interactions between peers, but also at the informational or communicational level, as evidenced by the data collected. Overall, the hybridization of methodologies and ICTE's ongoing investment in French learning have ensured an innovative university pedagogy that fosters student enthusiasm and empowerment. However, it should be noted that ICTE integration alone is insufficient to overcome the problems connected with learning French, as well as to encourage and engage learners. Didactic selections and tutoring are also important in getting the desired results.

3rd Experiment

The new reform has made the higher education system more flexible, which did not exist previously. This reform is still evolving, and it is always attempting to balance the disciplinary and the interdisciplinary, even though this appears to be a tough undertaking to sustain. Indeed, this reform has focused attention on the integration of ICT into the higher education system, and this has coincided with the introduction of a MOOC for student benefit, the goal of which was to assist students enrolled in the first year of the bachelor's degree cycle in achieving academic success.

Before presenting this experimentation, which is part of a process of improvement, it is important to note that two training courses were set up prior to the experimentation, with the goal of familiarizing tutors with the MOOC context, specifically the FLESUP platform, and making them more aware of the importance of collaborative work. Because the MOOC was created by Tunisian universities, the training content has to be tailored to the Moroccan setting. The goal of these preparatory training courses was to help teachers become more independent in managing training material by developing the suggested content (courses) using video

Figure 13. The platform's various functions

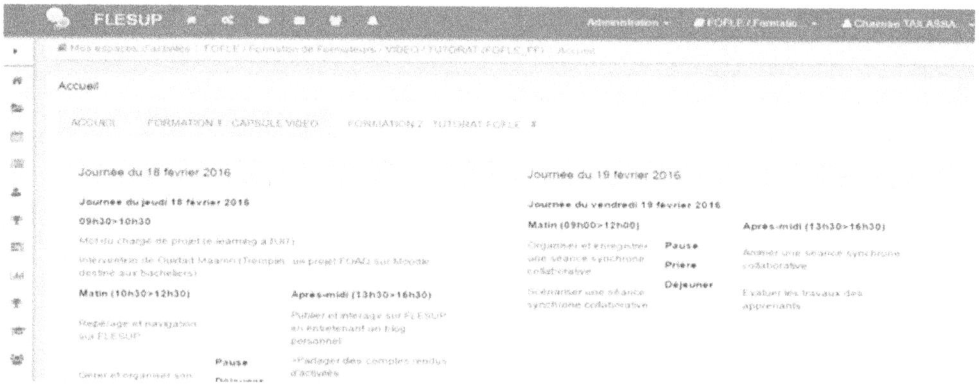

Figure 14. A video explaining the different routes on offer

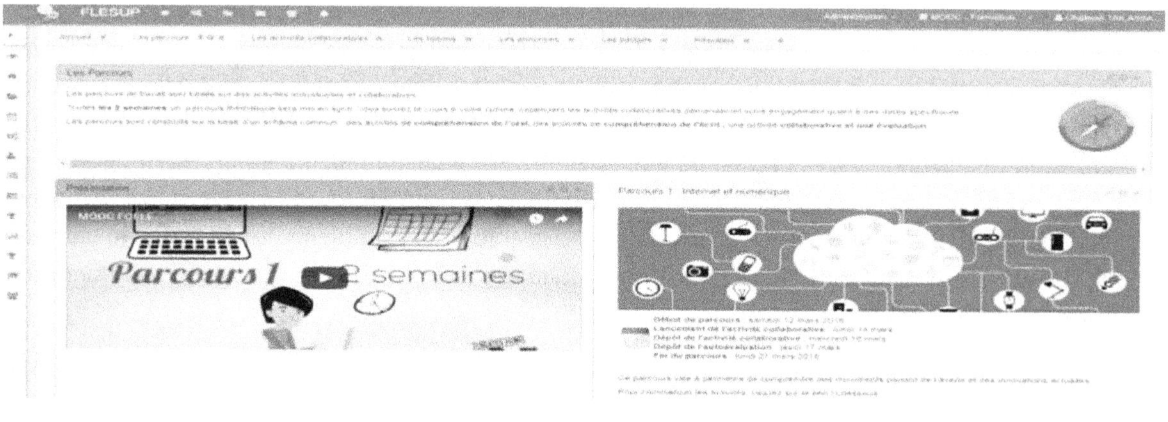

As this was the students' first experience with a 100% distance learning course, we found that their tenacity resulted in a late response during the first and second weeks. It takes time to become acquainted with the digital environment. Due to the tardy response of the target population, the training course was launched on Saturday, March 12, 2016 rather than Monday, March 7, 2016. Only a dozen students turned up for the first course's start. And, because the number of connected students was significantly fewer than the number of registered students, a movie for the FOFLE MOOC (https://www.youtube.com/watch?v=ffe6vH8QnmA) was immediately created to persuade the registered public and dispel their skepticism.

The themes of the proposed sequences are the product of Claroline:

Option 1: Internet and digital technology
Option 2: Discovery and the future
Option 3: Environment and progress
Option 4: Science and research
Option 5: Arts and Society
Option 6: Media and International Exchanges

Figure 15. Our support for the FLESUP platform

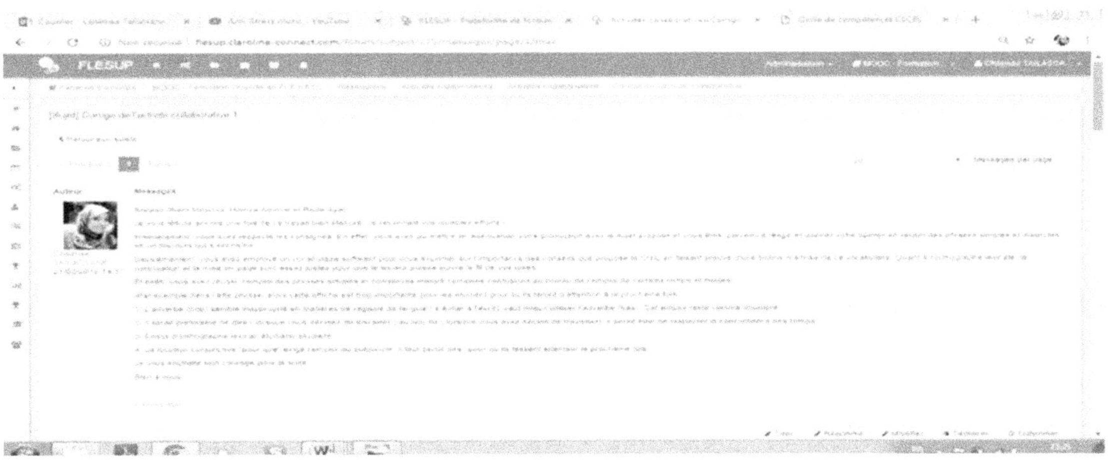

With this initial step of our project, we created a digital area at the SMPC unit (Google+). Registration for this new environment was required, and there was a deadline for joining the community formed for this purpose.

The technology side contributed to the design and organization of the activities, since experimenting with Web 2.0 technologies ensured online engagement, such as the spaces created in the Google+ communities, the "Padlet" walls, and linkages to YouTube, for example.

The Google+ community with its various spaces, the Edmodo platform and wall, and Padlet proved to be appropriate for our research's goals insofar as they allowed us to give students access to their own environments that contained (individual and collaborative) activities to do, notices and announcements, discussion space, etc. The Padlet wall provided a variety of sharing possibilities, making it possible to set up collaborative work.

Figure 16. The Padlet wall

Our goal is to evaluate the educational impact of our intervention. We concentrated on how students felt about taking part in the MOOC, especially the many group projects. In fact, starting in the final week of the MOOC, a satisfaction survey was made available on the course's home page in order to assess the course's pros and cons, as well as to more thoroughly examine participant feedback on the tutors' direction and support. In actuality, the questionnaire's suggested questions centered on the expectations of students, the challenges they faced, and the elements that contributed to their success.

Overall, the evaluation was favorable from the perspective of the MOOC participants. We were interested in learning whether students have used new tools to study French when we asked the first question. The results revealed that 53.6% had already utilized them and 46.3% had never done so, indicating that the latter group had insufficient access to the Internet and were still learning about this. Therefore, it is necessary to mentor them in this new technique and to set them up to effectively use the platform.

Taking note of the fact that several students expressed dissatisfaction with the number of exercises provided, citing the possibility that their lack of access to the internet at home would prohibit them from completing the tasks and staying current.

Additionally, we made an effort to learn what they thought of the courses they had taken. In fact, given their favorable ratings of 63% and 44.4%, classes 3 and 4—entitled "Environment and Progress" and "Science and Research," respectively—appear to have been favorites of the students. The scientific content of these two courses and their connection to the course advised in the first semester can be used to support their success.

We were able to determine the following strengths and areas for development based on the instructors' feedback

However, the majority of students reaffirmed their preference for independent study. The converse is demonstrated by the fact that collaborative projects are completed. Despite the fact that they were conducted utilizing internet tools (dictionaries, reference materials, translators, etc.), their effectiveness had a favorable effect on the written product.

Figure 17. Students' use of new technologies

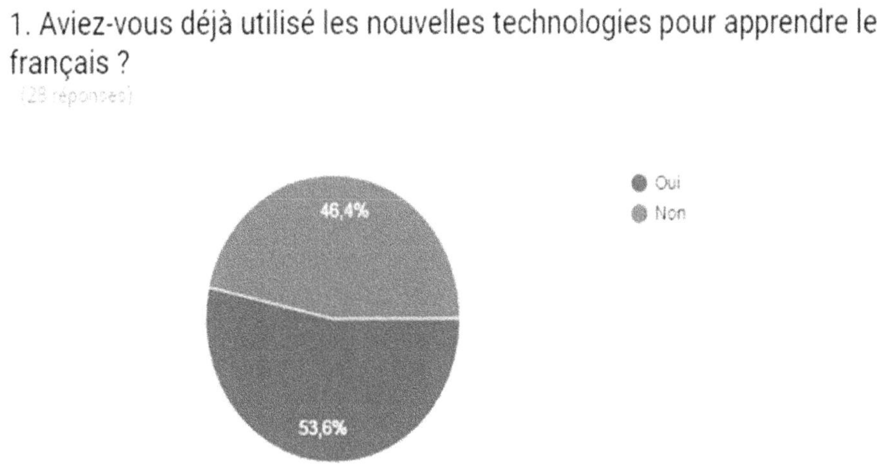

Figure 18. Responses

D'abord merci pour cette expérience et pour les efforts de tous les tuteurs, j'ai bien apprécie le travail dans le MOOC FOFLE; ma remarque ce qu'il y'a beaucoup d'activités et je ne trouve pas le temps pour compléter toutes les activités car je n'ai pas un accès 'WIFI' j'ai seulement la 3G , danc je ne peux pas être a jour.Merci

J'ai trouvé que ces parcours sont en ligne avec notre ère et nos études.

j'ai aimé les parcours par rapport au programme du 1er semestre

j'aime bien les sciences et donc j'ai bien apprécié le parcours 4

parce que ce parcours donne la chance pour comprend les phenomenes scientifiques et essaye de connaitre les étapes des expériences .

j'aime les 4 parcours car adresses des sujet scientifique et culturels .

Table 2. Feedback

Strong Points	Points à Revoir
The course modification to the participants' level is the first noteworthy positive. They were able to comprehend any scientific paper from the written and audio supports, as well as learn about the world of research and be able to communicate a scientific fact, thus courses 3 and 4 precisely matched their requirements and expectations. We should also mention the interaction between the coordinator and the tutors, which could be considered a strong point insofar as the tutors felt supervised and guided in their mission. 100% of tutors wanted to repeat this remote tutoring experience. The following screenshot illustrates this point:	When it came to submitting activities, the forums did not meet the tutors' expectations. Collaborative activities had to be reorganized because the unavailability of some participants was disrupting their progress. Several open-ended questions were proposed to allow for more subjectivity in participants' answers, which could increase supervision time and become a burden for some tutors. It would have been appropriate to include a week 0, which could have been considered as an introduction to the use of the platform, in particular to the method of posting documents on the forum, and thus guarantee a good follow-up to the first course.

This result demonstrates that the participants valued this kind of equipment. The success of hybrid or non-hybrid systems, however, depends on a number of individuals, including educators, technologists, administrators, and partners from civic society, as we shall see in the general discussion at the conclusion of our research.

General Overview of the System

The work that the students turned in and the surveys they answered (cf. appendix) allowed us to gauge not only how satisfied they were with the MOOC but also how far along they were in the course. Students gave their participation in the various courses positive ratings, as we have previously seen. More than half of respondents thought the exercises were level-appropriate. Additionally, we saw that students were motivated by the reference materials to better organize their works, which supports the development of their correction as a result of their involvement in practically all of the courses.

The effect of the device on the participants was measured through the development of language elements in their written productions:

Table 3. Effect of the device on participants

Advanced Language Elements	Observed Gain
polite request expression	use of the conditional to express a polite request
the connectors	introduction of more and more connectors, leading to an increase in written output (recycling of input)
colloquial/ fluent language	less colloquial expression and use of common formulas
Glossary / morphosyntax	vocabulary enrichment and correction

These gains may be viewed as dynamic inasmuch as they embody an emergentist and socioconstructivist perspective of the textual production activity, incorporating the traces of interactions and feedback in a particular production environment. These findings can only be trusted if we consider additional factors, such as the circumstances that encouraged appropriation, as a consequence of the interactions between students and tutors and the reference books (input). Thus, the latter have promoted the development of SPAs.

Despite being open to it, the students favored solo work over collaborative work when it came to teamwork. Since the goal of collaborative activity is to promote group work, exchange, mutual aid, and dialogue, their resistance to this modality was evident in the fact that some projects were completed by a single student under the pretext that he was unable to connect with other students. We recommend actions like those suggested by Storch (2013) to prevent any opposition to collaborative work:

- Find out about learners' attitudes to collaborative writing by filling in short questionnaires.
- Let students choose,
- Highlight the strengths of collaborative work if this is a new way of working for them.

Some students gave the excuse that they lacked a computer or access to the Internet as justification for their resistance to working on the platform. This excuse, however, was not very convincing since after looking at their responses, it became clear that they had another reason for not publishing: they were still learning French and were concerned that posting their work on the forum would make them look weak.

In forums where misconceptions are more likely to occur, tutor support is crucial in assisting students in identifying problems.

Overall, just 58% of students passed the module satisfactorily. On the forum side, modifications must be done, though. Given that certain students frequently drop out of their courses, it is also clear that it is crucial to instill greater responsibility in them.

We need to reflect on certain aspects that remain transmissive and sometimes contradict the given positioning. We feel that greater support for the informal or non-formal is needed, letting students create their own tasks, even in scientific courses.

CONCLUSION

We have been able to advance in an institutional structure that is incorporating innovative educational techniques more and more thanks to our engagement in the teaching field. The favorable outcomes with our target audience have strengthened our will to enhance our practices and services in the future, based on a corrective strategy that will answer the challenges and requirements of a student population that is inextricably linked to a digital technology environment.

In fact, Web 2.0 technologies are essential for the deployment of an efficient hybrid system since they foster online communication, teamwork, and task management. As students grow more aware of their linguistic demands and limitations, they become more attentive but most importantly reflexive. We employed Google+ for one semester of task organization and Edmodo for the following semester. During these two semesters, we saw increased student engagement. Based on the underlying ideas, these tools and resources were employed to strengthen the impact of the activities that were suggested (Catroux, 2006; Narcy-Combes, 2005).

ICT's original contribution also makes it feasible to replicate abilities that are often used in higher education, such as note-taking, oral and written communication, and reformulation. However, they also provide linguistic empowerment, which appears to us to be a given in hybrid university instruction. We are discussing "disciplinary content" in this instance. The exercises we suggest are different from those taught in language classes and are geared on developing the five CEFR-recommended abilities of interaction, articulation, lexis, and grammar, as well as oral and written production, comprehension, and production.

However, it is preferable to work on some of these aspects face-to-face, because it's more practical without having to use the digital environment to mediate them; and others remotely, because in the digital space, the Internet represents a valuable source for finding information, provided that the research steps are well mastered. It should be noted that written production is a skill favored by the distance mode.

There were certain drawbacks, including the participant's isolation and the lack of genuine touch with the teacher, even if the students enjoyed the implementation of a 100% distance learning method. Thus, social contacts and exchanges between students and tutors are abolished, despite the fact that in some learning scenarios, particularly when it comes to training activities, students require face-to-face pedagogical support.

In summary, ICTs provide the entire educational system a virtually limitless supply of new practices and a significant potential for pedagogical innovation (Bentaib, M., 2012). Insofar as they have the capacity to stimulate the development of intellectual skills in the learner, such as the capacity to reason, learn to learn, interact, explore, experiment, etc., they are in fact seen as mental amplifiers, cognitive triggers that reinforce the means of executing and controlling effective actions, favoring constant interaction (Mangenot, 2001), and ensuring the practically unlimited transmission of data (Linard, 2001).

REFERENCES

Bentaib, M. (2012). *Higher Education Facing New Technologies: A Contractual Digital Space*. EPI Association.

Bergmann, J., & Sams, A. (2012). *Flip Your Classroom: Reach Every Student in Every Class Every Day*. International Society for Technology in Education.

Catroux, M. (2006). *Co-actional Perspective and ICT: Convergences for Specialized Language Teaching*. Presented at the Study Days of EA 2025, IUT Bordeaux. http://www.aplvlanguesmodernes.org/spip.php?article933

Charlier, Daele, & Deschryver. (2002). Towards an Integrated Approach to Information and Communication Technologies in Teaching Practices. *Pedagogical Integration of ICT: Research and Training, 28*(2).

Charlier, Deschryver, & Peraya. (2006). Learning in Presence and at a Distance: A Definition of Hybrid Devices. In *Distances et savoirs* (Vol. 4). Academic Press.

Ellis, R. (2003). *Task-based Language Learning and Teaching. Oxford Applied Linguistics*. Oxford University Press.

Lebrun, M. (2002). *Theories and Pedagogical Methods for Teaching and Learning. What is the Role of ICT in Education? col. Perspectives in Education and Training*. De Boeck University.

Lebrun, M., & Lecoq, J. (2015). *Flipped Classes, Teaching and Learning the Right Way!* Canope Editions.

Linard, M. (2001). *ICT: Tools for Teaching and Learning Differently*. http://www.scolanet.org

Mangenot, F. (2002). *Pedagogical and Institutional Integration of ICT. Psychology of Learning and Multimedia*. Armand Colin.

Mangenot, F., & Louveau, É. (2006). *Internet and the Language Classroom*. CLE-International.

Narcy-Combes, J.-P. (2005). *Language Teaching and ICT: Towards Responsible Action Research*. Ophrys.

Nunan, D. (2004). *Task-based Language Teaching*. Cambridge University Press. doi:10.1017/CBO9780511667336

Robert, J-P. (2008). Practical Dictionary of FFL Didactics. In Essential French (2nd ed.). Ophrys.

Soubrié, T. (2008). A New Framework for Designing ICT Activities: The Communicative Perspective of the CEFR. In *Bizarro, Teaching and Learning Foreign Languages and Cultures Today: What Perspectives?* (pp. 68–81). Areal Editores.

Storch, N. (2013). *Collaborative Writing in L2 Classrooms*. Multilingual Matters. doi:10.21832/9781847699954

Chapter 11
Rapid Learning in the Teaching of Physical Education and Sport

Gaadi Amina
Hassan II University, Casablanca, Morocco

Souiet Maati
Hassan II University, Casablanca, Morocco

Chakli Abdelhak
Hassan II University, Casablanca, Morocco

Sefri Youssef
Hassan II University, Casablanca, Morocco

Chafiq Nadia
Hassan II University, Casablanca, Morocco

ABSTRACT

Integration of information and communication technologies in education has become a significant phenomenon that provides educators with the resources they need to improve teaching and learning processes. When used on a regular basis, ICTE promotes program objectives and increases student engagement in learning. This can lead to learning experiences that are rapid, interactive, and impactful. Furthermore, the usage of ICTE increases student motivation and simplifies the teaching process. In recent years, there has been considerable growth in the use of tools designed to promote quick learning in many different kinds of countries. These innovative methods aim to simplify the teaching and learning process by speeding up acquisition and decreasing time spent on traditional explanations. Teachers are invited to use these tools to improve the effectiveness of their instruction.

DOI: 10.4018/979-8-3693-1034-2.ch011

INTRODUCTION

Today's generation of teenagers and young adults is very attached to social networks, video games, and digital technologies, and these have grown steadily to become essential tools in classrooms in many parts of the world. The case of European countries, which have declared that the integration of information and communication technologies is becoming a primary objective in their education systems. Morocco in turn, like all developing countries, has understood the importance of integrating and using ICT in its education system and has long been committed to projects promoting the integration and widespread use of ICTE in its education system. To this end, numerous reforms have been carried out over the last two decades, thanks to the implementation of multiple digital strategies designed to energize and revolutionize the world of teaching and learning. However, ICTE requires frequent and regular use by teachers and students to maximize the benefits of these technologies and ensure rapid, interactive, and meaningful learning. (Dias, 1999) asserts that technologies are integrated when used on an ongoing basis to support and further program objectives and stimulate student engagement in learning. Furthermore, the use of ICTE in the pedagogical context enhances learner motivation and facilitates the teaching and learning process (Klein, 2013). Today, the exploitation of tools that promote rapid learning for teaching and learning has seen a flagrant boom in several countries, as an innovative method with the aim of accelerating, catalyzing, and facilitating acquisition and learning without wasting time in conventional explanations, which consume a lot of session time. It is therefore very interesting for teachers to exploit these tools to simplify the teaching and learning process, promote educational success and enhance professional practice.

During training at the regional center for education and training professions (CRMEF) Casablanca. We noticed that future physical education and sports teachers need tools that will help them manage the time devoted to the session, given that the nature of the subject is virtually practical and is based on the performance of physical and sports activities (PSAs) whose learners know nothing about either their rules or their phases of execution, which requires a great effort on the part of the teachers to explain the principles of action and the rules of play of PSAs, Hence the need to use efficient tools to catalyze and accelerate the teaching and learning process.

Definition of Rapid Learning

Rapid Learning is a method that has become fashionable in recent years in the educational world. It is essentially aimed at transmitting and acquiring knowledge in a short, rapid way. It is characterized by the very short duration of the modules, from 1 to 6 minutes. Its content is structured into short units of meaning, designed to anchor it firmly in the memory. Rapid Learning can be used to transform Powerpoint-formatted training materials into training courses enriched with sound, video, web links, or quizzes. And with learners looking for faster, simpler access to learning resources, this is the perfect opportunity to make use of this technological tool. Rapid Learning support is developing rapidly, as the name suggests. It enables training managers to react quickly to requests from operational staff. Using the material used in face-to-face training or virtual classrooms is also a way of getting trainers accustomed to digitizing their content. A major advantage of Rapid Learning is the simplicity of the tools used. This gives training managers and their teams the autonomy to adapt and update digitized content. Several configurations are possible. The training department can autonomously use one of the dedicated software solutions already present in the company. It can also integrate a software solution and train teaching teams in its use. The simplicity of the tools does not mean that the approach does not require in-house design and graphics resources. That's why it's also possible to entrust the creation and updating of your materials to a service provider. (Alicia.K, 2017)

The concept of Rapid Learning in PES Teaching

Rapid Learning is today becoming a pedagogy massively chosen by schools in the developed world and sees itself as a pedagogically relevant way of enabling teachers to work with digital devices that facilitate and accelerate the teaching-learning process. For PES teaching, Rapid Learning will play a very important role in the smooth running and time management of PE sessions, since the time set aside for a PE session is two hours a week, divided into two sessions lasting one hour each, which doesn't give learners the opportunity to get the most out of the new activity they're about to embark on, since it takes time to understand it before it's performed, which must be done correctly to avoid the risk of trauma, Generally speaking, the PE teacher asks a volunteer to give a demonstration so that his or her peers can understand the principle and flow of the movement, but despite this, the teacher falls into the trap of explaining and re-explaining so that the learners can carry out their tasks correctly. This wastes a lot of time and energy, hence the need to use Rapid Learning to make it easier for students to understand the content of the session, using sophisticated technological tools and resources that are easy to use and quickly assimilated. Rapid Learning can be used on the spot in PE sessions as it can be used as a means in flipped classrooms for the purpose of engendering psychic arousal in learners and preparing them ahead to the scenario of the next session. (Elourdani.k, 2015).

Rapid Learning has become a successful technique for improving time management and the teaching-learning process in physical education. Digital tools are used in this pedagogical approach to facilitate and speed up the learning process, enabling teachers to make the most of the brief time allocated for physical education classes.

Rapid Learning has become a successful technique for improving time management and the teaching-learning process in physical education. This method is especially useful in PES situations where a lack of instructional time makes it difficult to guarantee that students thoroughly understand new activities before participating in them. In the past, physical education instructors relied on frequent explanations and volunteer demonstrations to help students comprehend and accurately carry out activities. But doing this takes a lot of time and effort.

Rapid Learning promotes using innovative technical tools and resources that are easily accessible to learners. It can be used in PE lessons or as part of flipped classrooms, allowing students to become familiar with the material in advance and improve their readiness for subsequent lessons.

Without relying entirely on profound clarifications from the teacher, Rapid Learning enables pupils to quickly digest knowledge and comprehend the flow of movement.

Materials and Methods

The practical study of this research was made within the Regional Center of Education and Training of Casablanca, by the participation of 80 teacher trainees of the subject of EPS, for studying the perceptions of future teachers around the use of rapid technological tools in PSE sessions. By analyzing the results obtained from the questionnaire, we could draw up circular diagrams for each item, interpret them and then discuss them in light of the research results related to this context.

Rapid Learning in Reverse Classes

Rapid Learning is an educational tool that occupies the role of the key lies in the possibility of taking the PSE lesson out of its usual framework to a framework of the inverted approach that considers itself a means of preparing the student quickly for the lesson he will be going live, It is essential to talk about the teaching content that we approach through a reverse PSE class to leave a trace to learnings and give learners the opportunity to learn the content of the upcoming session.

Reverse classes allow PSE teachers to get rid of the waste of time in explaining and re-exploiting content to learners, however, techniques related to learning situations will be disseminated presenting in a reverse classroom as an interactive presentation, a descriptive sheet with illustrations or with the help of an educational video to take advantage of the time of the session in the practice of physical and sports activities. Rapid Learning in the reverse classroom allows for optimizing the time of practice in face-to-face class and develop the various motor skills in the learners in the same session, promoting access to knowledge at any time to further develop the learner's skills during PSE, allowing the student to observe, analyze and provide regulated feedback on their activities.

However, seeking to mobilize knowledge outside of the PSE course thus lengthens the learning time, promotes continuity between courses, develops a spirit of cooperation and mutual aid, gives more meaning to learning, and improves autonomy, motivation, and the feeling of responsibility of the students in their learning.

Students learning with the reverse class method will of course develop technical knowledge and know-how that will be necessary for them to pursue higher education or to integrate into the digital society of today and tomorrow (Julien, T,2017).

Figure 1. Familiarizing future PE teachers with the term rapid learning

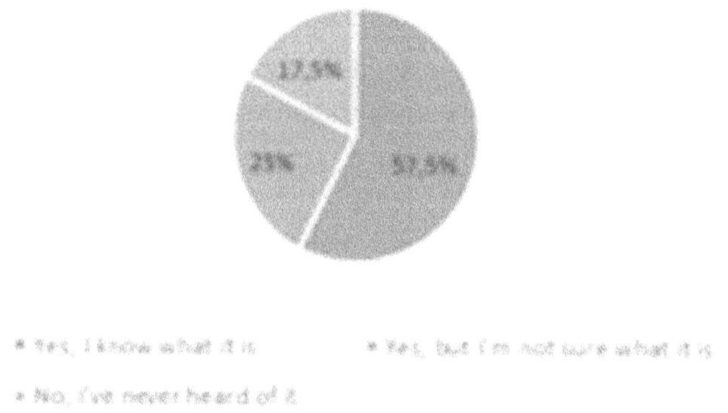

RESULTS

According to the above statistics, 57.50% of participants claim to know about Rapid Learning, while 17.50% are aware of this new method but do not know what it is, and 25.00% have never heard of the term.

These results show that a large proportion of future teachers are aware of the latest world of digital technologies dedicated to teaching and learning, that they have learned, and that they are curious to seek out and discover the technological means, methods, and didactics to improve and achieve honorable results in terms of academic results in academic success.

Figure 2. Measuring the need for rapid tools in the PES teaching and learning process

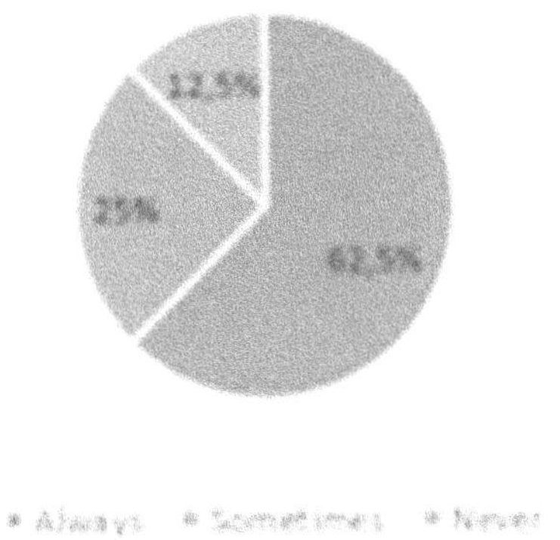

Based on the above results, we can see that 62.50% of future PES teachers say they always need to use quick tools during sessions, while 25% say they sometimes need them, and 12.5% say they do not need them at all. Say they do not need them at all.

These results lead us to believe that the majority of teachers need Rapid learning tools, which will help them to ensure that their professional practice is not linear. a kind of attraction and dynamism to avoid the boredom of cognitive overload and cognitive overload and create the right conditions for learning.

Deployment of the statistical data reveals that 48.75% of participants said they preferred to use short instructional videos, 25.00% were in favor of the use of data sheets, 17.50% preferred to explain using dynamic presentations, and 8.75% preferred to work with educational applications.

These results show that teachers will exploit various types of tools to energize teaching and accelerate learning. These tools are designed and used to produce, exchange, retrieve and read digital documents for teaching and learning purposes. The modernity and diversity of these tools motivate learners and encourage them to participate more fully in learning situations.

According to the results obtained from the graph in Figure 4, we note that the following statistics show that 56.25% of participants want to use Rapid Learning tools to facilitate student understanding and learning, while 23.7% state that they want to apply Rapid Learning tools to optimize session time. Apply Rapid Learning tools to optimize session time, while 20% said they would announce that they are going to use Rapid Learning devices to improve the flow of the physical and sports education sessions.

However, it can be said from these results that Rapid Learning tools can be used for many educational objectives and in developing multiple competencies in future PES teachers and their learners.

Figure 3. Tools preferred by future PES teachers

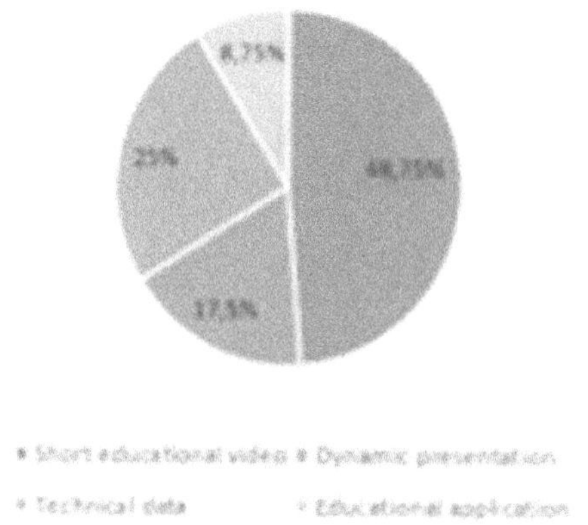

Figure 4. The interest of future teachers in using rapid learning tools

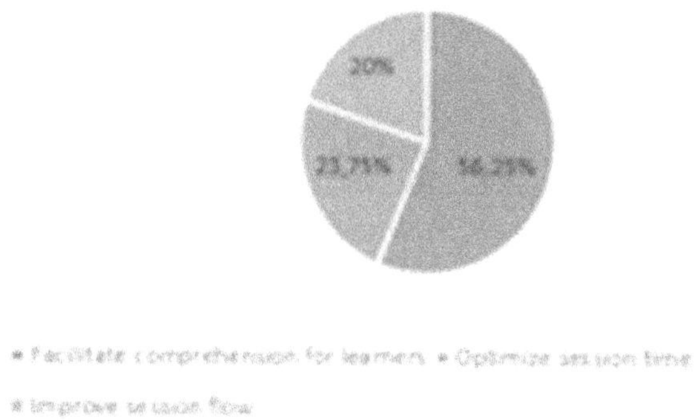

Figure 5. Percentage of teachers motivated to apply rapid learning tools

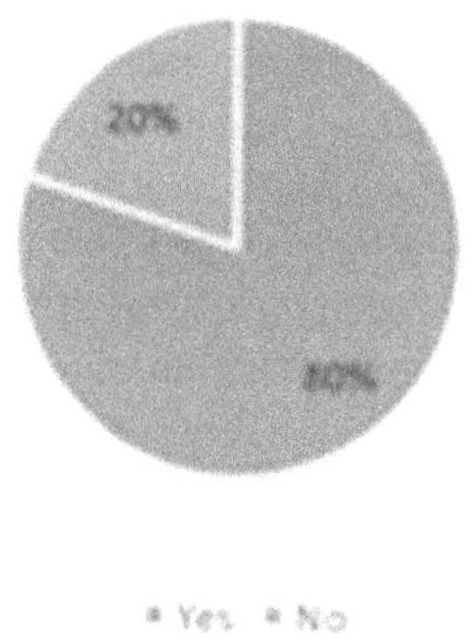

From the results of the pie chart, we find that 80.% of the participants declare that they are motivated to apply the tools that offer rapid learning, while 20% of them announce that they are not motivated to use these tools during PE sessions.

However, we can say that most future teachers are motivated to accelerate the improvement of the quality of the teaching system thanks to the flexibility, complementarity, and multitude of Rapid Learning tools, which encourage teaching cops to apply them to facilitate teaching and learning to apply them in order to facilitate the teaching and learning of the PES subject.

DISCUSSION

The results of our study show that future PES teachers are aware of the importance of teaching the subject of physical education and sport with the help of technological tools, which offer a different kind of teaching, one that is innovative in its method and in which they will work with a multitude of tools that enable them to improve their technological skills.

Future PES teachers need to exploit quick, easy-to-develop tools that catalyze the teaching and learning process during PES sessions and this is what the Rapid Learning model offers, which sees itself as a method of rapid learning using efficient ICT tools at the service of active pedagogies. These gentle, uncomplicated tools enable rapid understanding of learning situations and optimize session time.

Although there are studies showing that there is no significant difference between the use of ICT tools or not at the level of learning (Clarke et al, 1999), other studies have come up with a series of findings confirming the positive role that ICT tools can play in this new conception of learning and teaching, and in particular in their higher, authentic, autonomous and high-level dimensions. (Jorge.M, 2011).

One of the major challenges to be met to fully integrate educational technologies in the delivery of PES sessions is acquiring and supplying schools with suitable equipment.

All the above shows the interest that staff have in fast ICTE tools. All that remains is the willingness of teachers to apply Rapid Learning in the field to physical and sports physical and sports education sessions as a preferred animation tool in the modern management of learning situations, and even if many are going to try, their attempts are only personal initiatives, since they are not aware of the official texts that require to introduce technology into schools. What's more, appropriate training courses from time to time for those who have difficulty making professional use of them. If this is done, we will enable Moroccan schools to rise to the challenge of inclusive and equitable quality education in physical education and sport.

In addition to the advantages indicated in the excerpted document, there are a number of other thoughts that emphasize the significance of utilizing technology in physical education and sport. First of all, utilizing technology gives a fresh method of instruction that might increase students' interest in the material. This is crucial in physical education, since practical applications are essential to learning. Teachers may make the most of class time and foster an engaging learning environment by utilizing effective ICT tools, such those provided by the Rapid Learning model.

In addition, research indicates that using ICT tools in physical education can improve students' academic results. Even though certain studies might not be interesting.

CONCLUSION

The new Information and Communication Technologies in Education (NICTE) are seen as a means to an end, rather than an end in themselves, in the service of teaching and learning. They are supports, and adjuncts, on which teachers rely, to enrich teaching methods, make them more attractive, increase pupils' interest, and facilitate their learning (Bastian & Riplinger, 2016). These digital artifacts (Norman, 1993) provide data to complement and enrich traditional teaching-learning learning environments. They strongly instrument PSE practices, increasingly leading learners to become motivators and actors in their own learning (Andrieu & Burel, 2014; Morieux & Andrieu, 2014).

Even if the pedagogical use of digital tools is sometimes restrictive, PE teachers PES teachers recognize that their integration is beneficial, under certain conditions of use. of use, i.e. in optimizing the timing of the session, hence the interest of Rapid Learning which plays a facilitating and catalyzing role in the act of teaching-learning by offering rapid learning for learners, and presents itself as an efficient model for integrating of integrating these technologies into teaching and learning practices. (Lemeur & Tomaszower, 2015; Morieu, 2016).

In this research, we wanted to demonstrate that Rapid Learning could provide real benefits in learning, knowledge appropriation, and the appropriation of knowledge and development of skills during physical and sports physical and sports education.

The resources mobilized using Rapid Learning in PES can also be transposed to other disciplines since there is interdisciplinary interaction between school subjects. We hope to use this work to raise awareness of new possibilities for making learners more motivated, committed, and involved in their own learning.

The integration of Rapid Learning at the heart of our learning sessions is prompting us to rethink our pedagogical and didactic and didactic processes, our concern being to demonstrate that these are possibilities our concern is to show that today's possibilities are within everyone's reach and that we are convinced of their effects.

REFERENCES

Bruchon, F., & Tomaszoer, Y. (2017). *Les TICE au service des apprentissages en EPS*. Academic Press.

Camille, D., & Galyen, K. (2011). E-Learning, online learning, and distance learning environments: Are they the same? Academic Press.

Castelli, D., & Gromacki, E. (2015). *Active Education: Growing Evidence on Physical Activity and Academic Performance*. Academic Press.

Curry & Sarazin. (2001). *Les théories de la motivation et pratiques sportives: l'état des recherches*. Academic Press.

El Haddadi, A. (2009). *Les orientations pédagogiques et programmes d'enseignement d'EPS dans le cycle collégial*. Academic Press.

El Ouardani, K. (2015). *Qu'est-ce qu'une intégration efficace des TIC à l'école?* Academic Press.

Gaëlle, L. (2014). *Analyser la pratique d'enseignement sous l'angle des orientations de valeur études de cas en éducation physique et sportive*. Academic Press.

Gikas, J., & Grant, M. (2013). *Internet and Higher Education Mobile computing devices in higher education: Student perspectives on learning with cellphones, smartphones & social media*. Academic Press.

Hamann, D. (2015). *The Construction and Validation of an M-Learning Framework for Online and Blended Learning Environments*. Nova Southeastern University.

Jorge & Molina. (2009). *Tice-education*. Academic Press.

King, A. (2019). *Qu'est-ce que le Rapid Learning*. https://myskillcamp.com

Klein, C. (2013). *Les usages du numérique pour l'enseignement.* Academic Press.

Kroote, L., & Bucher, A. (2007). *Management of Physical Education and Sport.* Academic Press.

Marc, M. (2017). *Dispositifs technologiques en EPS et convergence numérique*. Academic Press.

Martin, F., & Snider, J. (2012). Developing Mobile Based Instruction. *TechTrends*, *56*(5), 46–51. doi:10.1007/s11528-012-0598-9

Mazouak, A. (2007). *Les orientations pédagogiques 2007.* Academic Press.

Messaoudi, F. (2013). *Dispositifs de e-Learning*. Academic Press.

Morieux, M. (2014). *De l'innovation à l'intégration*. Academic Press.

Nejjari, A., & Bakkali, I. (2017). *L'usage des TIC à l'école marocaine: état des lieux et perspectives.* Academic Press.

Chapter 12
Student and Teacher Assessment of Digital Education During the COVID-19 Pandemic and After:
The Case of Cadi Ayad and Sultan Moulay Slimane Universities

Rachid Agliz
Faculte de Lettre Marrakech, Morocco

ABSTRACT

COVID-19 spread through the entire world and has automatically changed student and teacher perceptions of the entire educational system. This serious pandemic has totally affected students and teachers in their diverse pedagogical tasks. It was therefore important to cope with the far-reaching implications of the virus at the educational level. Obviously, those tremendous implications and changes have given us a glimpse at how the whole system of education could actually change for the better or worse. Most governments around the world have taken swift decisions in order to mitigate the impact of this dangerous and full blown pandemic. Like the rest of the world, the Moroccan government opted for the online education as an alternative to secure a good education for thousands and thousands of students in urban and rural areas. Distance education has completely revolutionized the Moroccan society. Surely, after the pandemic, the students are free to opt for the kind of learning that suits their own interests.

DISTANCE LEARNING AS AN ALTERNATIVE IN THE MOROCCAN EDUCATIONAL SYSTEM

Suddenly within a matter of weeks, (COVID 19) spread through the entire world and has completely changed how students are educated. Obviously, those tremendous changes give us a glimpse at how the

DOI: 10.4018/979-8-3693-1034-2.ch012

whole system of education could change for the better or the worse in the long run. With the coronavirus spreading quickly across Asia, Europe, the Middle East, North Africa as well as the United States, governments have taken swift and some decisive actions in order to ward off the danger and to mitigate the impact of a dangerous and full blown pandemic. In the whole world, there have been diverse announcements suspending attendance at schools and universities. In March, 2020, most schools and universities in Morocco were closed and the government opted for distance learning as an alternative to secure a good education for the majority of students in both rural and urban areas and to save lives. Yet, digital education proved to be effective for those who have access to the internet and turned out to be useless for those who live in rural areas as they do not have access to the internet at all. Morocco like other countries has tried to come up with some measures to help students and professors to instill an inviting learning environment by providing certain virtual learning platforms like moodle, miscrosoft teams to initially enhance the contact between the two and to exchange lessons and assignments on line. Surely, Morocco is a huge geographical landscape and the quality of learning depends heavily on both the level and the quality of digital access. Nowadays, more than 60 percent of the globe's population use the diverse sophisticated technological means to communicate, to learn foreign languages and to do business. In Morocco, there is a huge discrepancy between social classes. Hence, only wealthy families can benefit from the sophisticated digital platforms to secure a good education for their children. In some private universities and schools in Morocco, a whole range of material is delivered on line. Virtual classes on personal tablets may be the norm in some urban areas in the country. Yet, many students in poor rural areas are denied such a privilege. At this stage, one may wonder what does distance education mean in the first place? What are its advantages and drawbacks? To what extent has Morocco been able to implement the digital system in its diverse schools and universities? Are professors and students really satisfied with digital education? These are some of the questions that must be addressed and dealt with in this study. After all, one of the main objectives of this conceptual and empirical study is to come up with some pertinent results concerning the impact of distance learning on the whole educational system in Morocco and to show whether the country is ready to opt for the digital education at the detriment of the traditional face to face learning. The data presented in this study reflects the university professors and students remarks concerning the flexibility and importance of distance learning.

Before presenting the data gathered in this empirical study, it is crucial to define the concept and see how it is different from other types of learning. Distance education is completely different from the traditional face to face learning. The term "Distance learning" or "Distance education" has been the target of different critical studies. The concept seems to be open to different interpretations and cannot therefore be pinned down to one particular approach or perspective. In their illuminating article, "Distance Education: Definition and Overview", the authors strongly argue that the term "Distance Education" has never been clearly defined. The concept was rather used interchangeably with phrases like "education by correspondence" Historically speaking, there have been several attempts to define the term in simple and straightforward words. A good definition is surely provided by Zigerell (1984:10) who states that distance learning or education is a type of instruction that is essentially marked by "the physical separation of teacher from student, except for the occasional face to face meeting allowed for by some projects". (p.10). To further back up his approach, Zigerell (1984) points out that there is "a difference between presupposes opportunities for student interaction whether live or mediated, as well as for student independence." (p.14). Still, Wedemeyer (1983) defines distance education taking into account the role of the learning. According to him, distance learning essentially entails the "learning undertaken in a transactional relationship with educational programs and institutions, but entered into the choice of the learner on the basis of his or her own needs, concerns and aspirations". (p.9). So much focus here is on the learner who is the one concerned with the choice of such a system taking into account his or her dire needs. It seems that such a choice is governed and dictated by certain institutions which provide some digital platforms that suit the learner's urgent need. Furthermore, in some European countries like France, distance education is clearly defined by law as "an educational situation that does not presuppose the presence of a teacher or where a teacher is physically present only occasionally." (p.9). Above all, distance learning as a system aims at providing some learning chances to people who could not actually afford time or the necessary financial means for traditional classes or who lived in some remote areas from schools.

In the same vein, digital education, online learning, E-learning and distance learning are terms which overlap and which are used interchangeably to refer to the whole process of learning which is essentially mediated through the use of the pedagogical platforms. For Kramer (2002), E-learning is basically "a system and a process that connects learners with learning resources in the same electronic space, with the constrictions of time". (pp.23-24). Still, UNESCO defines E-learning as "an educational process and system in which all or a significant proportion of the teaching is carried out by someone or something removed in space and time from the learner". (Burns, 2011:9). The importance of this mode of learning resides in the flexibility of the technological devices to instill an inviting and very stimulating environment for the learners to overcome the constraints of time and space and therefore learn efficiently and easily.

There are different forms of distance learning. The most common ones are the fully online learning, the hybrid mode of learning and the web assisted mode of learning. According to Mamatta (2006) and Gillespie, et.al, (2007), the fully online learning is essentially a type of learning in which there is no physical contact whatsoever between the instructor and the learners. The fully online education is meant to be asynchronous in nature so much so that learners are ready to use asynchronous technological tools to interact with each other. Unlike the fully online learning, the hybrid mode of learning refers to the use of both face to face education and online learning. This mixed type of learning is beneficial both for the instructor and the learners. All the lecturing, students assessment are done face to face while all the assignments, oral presentations and learning materials are presented online. This type of learning is used to ensure the flexibility and efficiency of the teaching and learning process and to reduce the hours of face to face education. The other important form of E-learning is the web assisted mode. Through this mode, all the teaching and learning process are conducted through the use of web sites and virtual classrooms. The web assisted mode is quite similar to the fully online mode in the sense that it is done exclusively on line. Yet, unlike the fully online mode, it uses the synchronous forms and the diverse tools of education in such a way as to guarantee an efficient and strong interaction between the instructor and the learners.

Significantly, there are different methods or ways to implement distance learning. According to Smart and Cappel (2006), the implementation of the E-learning can be done through the use of the synchronous or the asynchronous forms. When it comes to the synchronous type of learning, we can say that it is used basically in real time circumstances and interactions through the use of the internet. Obviously, one of the main objectives and concerns of this form of learning is to pave the way for the engagement of different learners in diverse locations at the same time through the internet. Hence, learners and instructors interact with each other in the same time using diverse technological devices like web conferencing, audio conferencing and messages. Apart from this, the asychronous form of learning entails the learners self-directed engagement in which they are supposed to learn without the constrictions of time. According to Kocur and Kosc (2009), the asynchronous type of learning is very flexible in the sense that learners are not fully required to indulge in live interactions. The learners can learn individually using streaming audios, databases, e-books and website links. (Mamattha, 2006, p.8).

Another important issue that is worth to be investigated at length is the social nature of distance learning. In fact, there are certain stereotypes and drawbacks associated with this sophisticated means of communication. According to Eastmond (1995:46), what is actually wrong with distance education is "the loneliness of the long distance learner". Digital education can be both isolating and highly interactive. Electronic or digital connectedness is essentially a different sort of interaction that is meant to suit the urgent needs of consumers in the new globalized world and this can be achieved at the detriment of traditional schools. Still, in some less developed economies, there are some learners who are uncomfortable with this highly sophisticated means of communication. In Morocco, for instance, students who use the moodle and the Microsoft team platforms find it sometimes difficult to interact with their teachers on line and this may be due to the lack of nonverbal cues or to the weakness of the digital system in some remote rural areas and this can create some misunderstanding between the professor and the students. It is obvious that traditional classrooms are gradually losing their status and position in the age of globalization. Cook (1995) contends that there are communities within the digital system. As a matter of fact, the existence of a sense of community within the traditional classrooms is out of question and is totally false. Hence, the digital class environment is different from the traditional face to face education. If in the classroom, the students interact with their teachers and share certain interests, there is still room for those who use the virtual and digital platforms to interact with each other and to create communities on line. Electronic communities are possible and exist everywhere. According to Dede (1996), most of the courses presented on line feature a remarkable group of projects through which a community of learners can develop their skills through collaboration.

DATA ANALYSIS

The data presented in this empirical study reveals the informants views concerning the future of distance learning in Morocco. In Sultan Moulay Slimane University in Beni Mellal for instance, the university professors were asked to fill in a questionnaire which encompasses ten questions. The following tables shed light on the professors' feedback concerning the adequacy of the technological devices available in Morocco and which can to some extent ensure a very inviting learning environment for both the students and the professors.

Table 1. Distance learning in Morocco

Distance Learning in Morocco	Frequency	Percentage
Poor	3	37,5%
Average	3	37,5%
Good	2	25%
Excellent	0	0%
Total	8	100%

Table 2. Time spent on distance learning

Time Spent on Distance Learning	Frequency	Percentage
1-3 Hours	7	87,5%
3-6 Hours	1	12,5%
6-10 Hours	0	0%
10 Hours and More	0	0%
Total	8	100%

Table 3. Efficiency of distance learning for professors and students

Efficiency of Distance Learning for Professors and Students	Frequency	Percentage
Extremely important	0	0%
Very Effective	4	50%
Not Effective at all	4	50%
Total	8	100

Table 4. Moulay Slimane University and the adequacy of the technological resources

Moulay Slimane University and the Adequacy of the Technological Resources	Frequency	Percentage
Yes	3	37,5%
To some extent	5	62.5%
Not at all	0	0%
Total	8	100%

Table 5. Enjoying distance learning

Enjoying Distance Learning	Frequency	Percentage
Yes surely	4	50%
Not at all, there have been a few problems and challenges	3	37,5%
Morocco is still a developing country that has to ensure an effective and strong technological system	1	12,5%
Total	8	100%

The above frequency tables provide us with some pertinent results concerning the future of digital education in Morocco. Obviously, the government and the ministry of higher education are doing their best to implement the necessary technological platforms in different parts of the country to help both the professors and the students to interact with each other virtually. Yet, despite all these efforts, there are still some technological lacunas which hinder both parties from attaining an equal and thrilling learning environment. For instance, in Table 1, 37 percent of the informants argue that distance learning in Morocco is very poor. One of the informants in this study stated that he had two different experiences with remote learning. In March 2020, as a high school teacher and under the effect of the pandemic, the unexpected lockdown came as a bolt from the blue and the teacher suddenly found himself compelled to fall back on the means at his disposal to keep in touch with the students and engage them into distance learning. Unfortunately, this kind of learning had limited success for a variety of reasons, the most salient of which were the teachers' lack of experience in using some sophisticated online platforms such as Microsoft Teams and the utter improvisation that marked the regional academy's response to the repercussions of the lockdown. Though the teachers could finally manage the crisis by dint of resorting to creating what is up groups, only very few students reacted positively to this sort of online learning. It was noticed that those who were active in the actual presence of the teacher in class were also active in his virtual presence through what is up. Still, for his other experience, as a university professor in the year 2021, his high expectations of online learning as a possible alternative to in class interactions with actual human beings were likewise thwarted. In the fall semester, he was eager to try distance learning with almost two thousand freshmen and sophomores, but his enthusiasm suddenly came to a halt for different reasons. Not all students unfortunately could have access to Microsoft Teams. Some complained about the absence of connectivity, others could not afford the internet due to poor social conditions, while others simply could not have a smart phone or a laptop. This created a digital divide. Most teachers themselves are dissatisfied with the overall circumstances surrounding remote learning mostly due to technical problems that kept cropping up in the course of online lecturing and accordingly the smooth flow of the lecture that occurs in face to face teaching was repeatedly blocked for one reason or another. Last but not least, this professor concurs with sheer reticence that learning through the internet could supplement rather than supplant face to face teaching and learning exchange. In the same vein, when professors were asked whether distance learning has actually enhanced the social interaction between professors and students, some professors point out that distance learning has meaning only as a discursive reality. In other words, what imparts meaning and significance to it is discourse. The existence of this kind of learning as an object in itself, outside discourse is meaningless. If we speak about the social interaction between students and teachers, I believe that the only possible way to enhance it is through face to face teaching as online or virtual teaching does not allow direct social contact.

Apart from this, in Table 2, the statistics show that 87,5% of the professors spend more than 2 hours on line interacting with their students. This proves that digital education is a good option during this pandemic. At least, the students can consolidate that social contact to grab the sort of information they need virtually. Still, in this study, 50 percent of the professors contend that it is high time to question the validity and the adequacy of the technological platforms and resources used to ensure a good and strong interaction between the students and their professors on line. To back up this, we need to consider again the professors attitudes and views concerning the value of such devices in the Moroccan universities. If we take Sultan Moulay slimane University as an example, we will find out that 62,5 percent of the professors believe that the university has been able to provide the students with the necessary technological tools as well as the diverse digital platforms to ensure an effective and instilling learning environment.

In relation to the above facts, the study has also touched upon digital education as a source of enjoyment for both students and professors. Table 5, for instance shows that 50 percent of the informants have enjoyed themselves while using Microsoft teams and Moodle whereas 37,5 percent state that they have not really enjoyed themselves while using the different digital platforms. It seems that they have their own reasons for not choosing virtual classes. Most of them assert that their everyday virtual sessions were coupled with a lot of problems and challenges. One of these serious problems is connectivity which is not equally shared by all the students in Morocco.

Apart from this, the data gathered at Cadi Ayad University in Marrakech reveals some pertinent results concerning the future of digital education in Morocco. Both the students and professors at the faculty of Letters have expressed diverse opinions and views concerning the implementation of online courses in the curriculum during the Covid 19 pandemic and even after. The results of the students and teachers assessment of distance learning at the faculty of Letters in Marrakech are presented in the following frequency tables:

Table 6. Distance learning in Morocco: The student case

Distance Learning in Morocco	Frequency	Percentage
Poor	26	33,76%
Average	37	48,05%
Good	14	18,18%
Excellent	0	0%
Total	77	99,99

Table 7. Time spent on distance learning: The student case

Time Spent on Distance Learning	Frequency	Percentage
1-3 Hours	60	77,92%
3-6 Hours	16	20,77%
6-10 Hours	1	1,29%
10 Hours and More	0	0%
Total	77	99,98%

Table 8. Efficiency of distance learning for students

Efficiency of Distance Learning for Students	Frequency	Percentage
Extremely Important	26	33.76%
Very Effective	28	36,36%
Not Effective at all	23	29,87%
Total	77	99,99%

Table 9. Cadi Ayad University and the adequacy of the technological resources: The student case

Cadi Ayad University and the Adequacy of the Technological Resources	Frequency	Percentage
Yes	17	22,07%
To some extent	56	72,72%
Not at all	4	5,19%
Total	77	99,98%

Table 10. Enjoying distance learning: The student case

Enjoying Distance Learning	Frequency	Percentage
Yes surely	13	16,88%
Not at all, there have been a few problems and challenges	40	51,94%
Morocco is still a developing country that has to ensure an effective and strong technological system	24	31,16%
Total	77	99,98%

Table 11. Distance learning in Morocco: The professor case

Distance Learning in Morocco	Frequency	Percentage
Poor	2	50%
Average	1	25%
Good	1	25%
Excellent	0	0%
Total	4	100%

Table 12. Time spent on distance learning: The professor case

Time Spent on Distance Learning	Frequency	Percentage
1-3 Hours	3	75%
3-6 Hours	1	25%
6-10 Hours	0	0%
10 Hours and More	0	0%
Total	4	100%

Table 13. Efficiency of distance learning for professors

Efficiency of Distance Learning for Professors	Frequency	Percentage
Extremely Important	0	0%
Very Effective	3	75%
Not effective at all	1	25%
Total	4	100%

Table 14. Cadi Ayad University and the adequacy of the technological resources: The professor case

Cadi Ayad University and the Adequacy of the Technological Resources	Frequency	Percentage
Yes	1	25%
To some extent	2	50%
Not at all	1	25%
Total	4	100%

Table 15. Enjoying distance learning: The professor case

Enjoying Distance Learning	Frequency	Percentage
Yes surely	2	50%
Not at all, there have been a few problems and challenges	2	50%
Morocco is still a developing country that has to ensure an effective and strong technological system	0	0%
Total	4	100%

The present survey conducted in Marrakech, at the faculty of letters, Caddi Ayyad University is mainly intended to investigate the students and teachers assessment of digital education in the Moroccan context which has abruptly adopted distance education at all levels. During the pandemic, there was an abrupt shift from the classical face to face education to the online learning with the help of different online media in all higher education institutions. The following data deals specifically with the university students and teachers experience by both assessing and exploring their perceptions and attitudes concerning the online learning mode. The questionnaire was given to four professors and seventy seven students. When asked about whether distance learning has actually enhanced the social interaction between professors and students, most of the teachers argue that digital education has actually enhanced communication and interaction between professors and students. Accordingly, through distance learning professors can help their students solve some problems in their learning and students in turn, can communicate with their professors by sending their questions or remarks and interacting with instructors either synchronously or asynchronously. The professors in this survey tend to diverge in their perception and attitude toward distance learning. One of the professors in this study has pointed out that distance education or online learning was a new mode of teaching. As a matter of fact, it was very stressful for different reasons. First, it is the first time that both professors and students switch to this new mode of learning. Second, students and professors have no training whatsoever in how to use distance learning. Third, lack of equipment plays a very crucial role in the success of distance learning such as laptops, access to internet connection and the quality of internet network, especially in rural and remote areas. Concerning the importance of digital education in Morocco, the statistics reveal that 50% of the respondents maintain that this mode of learning is new in Morooco and can in no way replace the traditional classroom. Virtual classrooms are highly required in such difficult circumstances. Yet, the country is lagging behind when it comes to the implementation of the adequate technological tools and devices to ensure a very strong and effective learning environment. The statistics also depict the number of hours spent on distance learning. 75 percent of the professors tend to spend at least three hours on line and state that the online learning is a very effective method that has essentially broken the barriers between the learner and the instructor. It seems that this mode of learning has somewhat consolidated a strong bond between the instructors and learners in terms of sharing the information and in engaging both parties in very long sequences of interaction.Through the platforms, all the assignments and presentations were provided to probe the learners and instructors abilities to instill a very intimate and effective teaching and learning environment. Yet, though Cadi Ayyad University has somewhat ensured the use of very pertinent technological tools in its different institutions. Still, further steps are needed to be taken to secure the implementation of adequate technological devices to help both the instructors and learners to achieve their teaching and learning objectives. The statistics show that 50 percent of the professors strongly believe that digital education is a dire necessity both during the pandemic and after. However, like the other universities in Morocco, the use of platforms is coupled with difficulties and challenges. When asked about whether they have enjoyed the use of the platforms and other online facilities, 50 percent of the respondents maintain that they surely have enjoyed online learning. However, such enjoyment is sometimes short lived or experienced as there have been a few problems and challenges that have hindered both the professors and the students from maintaining the social interactions needed to learn efficiently.

By the same stroke, the survey has revealed some pertinent results concerning the students' attitude and perception about the future of distance learning in Morocco. At the faculty of letters, 48,05 percent of the respondents highlight that distance learning in Morocco is a new phenomenon. 33,76 percent of the students think that this mode of learning in Morocco is not highly appreciated. The informants in this study tend to value much the traditional classroom or the face to face learning. Only 18,18 percent of them consider digital education as a good means of interaction between the instructors and learners. The face to face education is of paramount importance for the students at Caddi Ayyad university. Yet, the different platforms can be qualified as good enunciative spaces to share all the sorts of visual material to help the students to receive the knowledge missed in the actual traditional classroom. Obviously, digital education is to some extent a good alternative of learning. Again, the data gathered show that 77,92 percent of the respondents spend 3 hours interacting with their professors. In addition to this, 20, 77 percent of my informants in this study have demonstrated their keen interest in the websites and other pedagogical platforms such as moodle and zoom to retrieve the information they need. The students spend sometimes four or six hours on line with professors asking questions about the lectures delivered. Regardless this abrupt switch from the traditional education to the virtual learning, the study has divulged the students innate tendency to learn online better than to be caught within the traditional classroom and to wait for the instructors to deliver diverse lectures and get the knowledge and the information they need on the spot. The data unveil that 36,36 percent of the respondents think that the digital learning is very crucial in such difficult circumstances. 33.76 percent of them contend that the traditional classroom is still the most appreciated option for those who are much attached to their professors physically. Yet, virtual classrooms are extremely important as they compensate to some extent for the absence of the instructors and learners physically. Still, those sophisticated pedagogical platforms implemented in Caddi Ayyad University have reinforced the social and emotional bond between the instructors and learners. Last but not least, the statistics further consolidate the students positive attitude toward the use of the technological tools in Caddi Ayyad University. When asked about the future of online learning in Morocco, 72.72 percent of the respondents have demonstrated their readiness to devote so much of their precious time on line to learn different subjects. This relatively high percentage of the informants are happy with the technological resources available in Caddi Ayad institutions. It seems that the adequacy of the sophisticated pedagogical platforms is unquestionable. Yet, despite all the efforts done by the government and the high officials in the Ministry of Higher education, digital education still remains at an early stage of development in Morocco. Hence, 51.94 percent of my informants in this study assert that digital learning is of a paramount importance to the future generations. Yet, enjoying the online virtual classes is never completely achieved easily as the use of those pedagogical platforms is hampered by certain technological problems namely the burning issue of connectivity which is not very high to suit the desires and the ambitions of both instructors and learners. Still, 31.16 percent of the respondents in this empirical study concur that Morocco is still a developing country that has to ensure an effective and strong technological system.

CONCLUSION

Distance learning can be resorted to as a follow up and not as an alternative. In the entire world, academics and researchers tend to instrumentalize the fateful crisis of Covid and give more importance to remote learning than it deserves. I am very confident that digital education or remote learning provides a cosmetic and short lived solution to the crisis. Yet, it will never replace face to face encounters with real people (in this case our students). It is true that a very considerable number of students are dissatisfied with the software and technological tools they are using to interact virtually with their professors. Such dissatisfaction emanates from the weakness of connectivity which is not equally shared by all the students in urban and remote rural areas. Due to this pandemic, most students were unable to use the digital platforms effectively. Students still seem to be attached to in classroom learning experiences and are therefore incapable of being autonomous learners. They still rely on the teacher as the only pedagogical source. I am afraid that in Morocco in the near future, the traditional education or face to face communication will lose its position to give a sort of hegemony to the digital education. Obviously, despite the technical problems and challenges professors and students are exposed to in virtual classes, there is a sheer amount of discourse that tends to normalize and legitimate distance learning at the detriment of its counterpart. According to Foucault, we are living in a society where normalizing power is given more weight and significance than repressive power. These concepts also evoke Louis Althusser's notions of repressive state apparatus (this one is no longer tenable) versus ideological state apparatus (this one is applicable and hence efficient in this rapid contemporary digital era). Globalization has surely spanned the entire world and has changed the way we assess and evaluate things. Following Althusser's vision, we are born into ideology and we collude with it in the construction of its subjects.

The Questionnaire

1- How do you feel about distance learning in Morocco?
   - a)- Poor.
   - b)- Average.
   - c)- Good.
   - d)- Excellent.

2- Do you use a special device for learning online? Explain.

3- Do you think that distance learning has actually enhanced the social interaction between professors and students? Explain.

4- How much time do you spend each day on distance learning?
   - a)- 1-3 Hours.
   - b)- 3-6 Hours.
   - c)- 6-10 Hours.
   - d)- 10 hours and more.

5- How effective has distance learning been for both students and professors?
   - a)- Extremely important.
   - b)- Very effective.
   - c)- Not effective at all.

6- Have Sultan Moulay Slimane and Caddi Ayyad Universities been able to provide its learners and professors with the adequate resources to ensure an effective and instilling learning environment?
   a)- Yes.
   b)- To some extent.
   c)- Not at all.
7- In your opinion is distance education stressful during the Covid 19 pandemic?
8- Have you enjoyed distance learning?
   a)- Yes, surely.
   b)- Not at all, there have been a few problems and challenges.
   c)- Morocco is still a developing country that has to ensure an effective and strong technological system.
9- Are teachers and students satisfied with the technology and software they are using for online education?
10- Do you think that distance learning is less important than the traditional face to face communication.?

REFERENCES

Burns, M. (2011). *Distance Education for Teacher Training: Modes, Models and Methods*. Education Development Center.

Cook, D. L. (1995). Community and Computer Generated Learning Environments. *New Directions for Adult and Continuing Education*, *1995*(67), 33–39. doi:10.1002/ace.36719956706

Dede, C. (1996). Emerging Technologies in Distance Education for Business. *Journal of Education for Business*, *71*(4), 197–204. doi:10.1080/08832323.1996.10116784

Eastmond, D. V. (1995). *Alone But Together: Adult Distance Study Through Computer Conferencing*. Hampton Press.

Gillespie, H., Boulton, H., Hrmiak, A., & Williamson, R. (2007). *Learning and Teaching with Virtual Learning Environments*. Troubridge, Wiltshire Learning Matters Ltd.

Kocur, D., & Kosc, P. (2009). E-Learing Implementation in Higher Education. *Acta Electrotechnica et Informatica*, *9*(1), 20–26.

Kramer, C. (2002). *Success in On Line Learning*. DELMAR Thomson Learning.

Mamathah, R. S. (2016). Students Perceptions of E-Learning. Department of Behavioural Sciences and Learning, Linkoping University.

Sewart, D., Keegan, D., & Holmberg, B. (1983). *Distance Education: International Perspectives*. St. Martin's.

Smart, K. L., & Cappel, J. J. (2006). Students Perceptions of Online Learning: A Comparative Study. *Journal of Information Technology Education*, *5*, 201–219. doi:10.28945/243

Sylvia & Willis. (1987). Distance Education: Definition and Overview. *Journal of Education for Library and Information Science, 27*(4), 223-232.

Zigerell, J. (1984). *Distance Education: An information Age Approach to Adult Education.* National Center Publications, National Center for Research in Vocational Education.

Compilation of References

Aamro, E. H., Chafiq, N., Radid, M., & Talbi, M. (2023). The Effect of Parental Social Status in Academia: Comparative Case of the Public/Private University in Morocco. *International Journal of Engineering Pedagogy*, *13*(3), 80–99. doi:10.3991/ijep.v13i3.33973

Abensour, C., & Gomariz, F. (2018). L'édition d'éducation face aux défis du numérique (1re éd.). Éditions du Cercle de la Librairie.

Abouhanifa, S., Benmadani, M., Khalfaoui, M., Hanini, M., & Kabbaj, M. (2008). *L'outil informatique : Analyse des obstacles qui entravent son utilisation efficace en classe du secondaire*. Association EPI.

Adade, R. (2022, December). Status of ICT Infrastructure towards the inclusion of ICT in the new curriculum in the Hohoe Municipality, Ghana. *International Journal of Research in Engineering and Science*, *10*(12), 568–572.

Adas, H. A., Shetty, S., & Hargrove, S. K. (2013, October). *Virtual and augmented reality based assembly design system for personalized learning. In 2013 Science and Information Conference*. IEEE.

Agarwal, R., & Karahanna, E. (2000). Time flies when you're having fun : Cognitive absorption and beliefs about information technology usage. *Management Information Systems Quarterly*, *24*(4), 665–694. doi:10.2307/3250951

Agbatogun, A. O. (2012). Investigating Nigerian primary school teachers' preparedness to adopt personal response system in ESL classroom. *International Electronic Journal of Elementary Education*, *4*(2), 377–394.

Agrawal, S. R., & Bech, S. (2023). Immersion in audiovisual experiences. In *Sonic Interactions in Virtual Environments* (pp. 319–351). Springer. doi:10.1007/978-3-031-04021-4_11

Ahenkora, S., Adubofour, E. B., Osei, E. G., & Ibrahim, A. (2023). Technology Use Among Ghanaian Junior High School Mathematics Teachers in the Ahafo-Ano South District. *Journal of Education and Training Studies*, *11*(3), 78–87. doi:10.11114/jets.v11i3.6066

Ahmed, N., Lataifeh, M., Alhamarna, A. F., Alnahdi, M. M., & Almansori, S. T. (2021, September). LeARn: A collaborative learning environment using augmented reality. In *2021 IEEE 2nd International Conference on Human-Machine Systems (ICHMS)* (pp. 1-4). IEEE. 10.1109/ICHMS53169.2021.9582643

Ahn, S. J. G., Nowak, K. L., & Bailenson, J. N. (2022). Unintended consequences of spatial presence on learning in virtual reality. *Computers & Education*, *186*, 104532. doi:10.1016/j.compedu.2022.104532

Aidoo, B., Macdonald, M. A., Vesterinen, V. M., Pétursdóttir, S., & Gísladóttir, B. (2022). Transforming Teaching with ICT Using the Flipped Classroom Approach: Dealing with COVID-19 Pandemic. *Education Sciences*, *12*(6), 421. doi:10.3390/educsci12060421

Alalwan, N., Cheng, L., Al-Samarraie, H., Yousef, R., Alzahrani, A. I., & Sarsam, S. M. (2020). Challenges and prospects of virtual reality and augmented reality utilization among primary school teachers: A developing country perspective. *Studies in Educational Evaluation, 66*, 100876. doi:10.1016/j.stueduc.2020.100876

Al-Azawi, R. (2018, April). Embedding augmented and virtual reality in educational learning method: present and future. In *2018 9th International Conference on Information and Communication Systems (ICICS)* (pp. 218-222). IEEE. 10.1109/IACS.2018.8355470

Alha, K., Leorke, D., Koskinen, E., & Paavilainen, J. (2023). Augmented play: An analysis of augmented reality features in location-based games. *Convergence (London), 29*(2), 342–361. doi:10.1177/13548565231156495

Aljowaysir, N., Ozdemir, T. O., & Kim, T. (2019, June). Differentiated learning patterns with mixed reality. In *2019 IEEE Games, Entertainment, Media Conference (GEM)* (pp. 1-4). IEEE.

Allal-Chérif, O. (2022). Intelligent cathedrals: Using augmented reality, virtual reality, and artificial intelligence to provide an intense cultural, historical, and religious visitor experience. *Technological Forecasting and Social Change, 178*, 121604. doi:10.1016/j.techfore.2022.121604

Altman, P. (2000). I-M@NUEL Une nouvelle génération de Manuels scolaires. *La Revue De l'Epi*, 99.

Amargui, L. (2006). L'enseignement de la langue française à l'université marocaine. *Le français aujourd'hui, 154*, 77-81. https://doi.org/10.3917/lfa.154.0077

Amirrudin, M., Nasution, K., & Supahar, S. (2021). Effect of variability on Cronbach alpha reliability in research practice. *Jurnal Matematika, Statistika dan Komputasi, 17*(2), 223-230.

Ancient, C., & Teeuw, R. (2020, July). Augmented reality interface design to support visualisation of 'risk landscapes'. In *International Conference on Human-Computer Interaction* (pp. 391-408). Springer. 10.1007/978-3-030-49760-6_28

Angra, S., Sharma, B., & Sharma, K. D. (2022, April). Amalgamation of virtual reality, augmented reality and machine learning: A review. In *2022 2nd International Conference on Advance Computing and Innovative Technologies in Engineering (ICACITE)* (pp. 2601-2604). IEEE. 10.1109/ICACITE53722.2022.9823716

Annetta, L. A., Minogue, J., Holmes, S. Y., & Cheng, M. T. (2009). Investigating the impact of video games on high school students' engagement and learning about genetics. *Computers & Education, 53*(1), 74–85. doi:10.1016/j.compedu.2008.12.020

Ansu-Kyeremeh, E. K., & Goosen, L. (2022). Exploring the Socioeconomic Facet of Online Inclusive Education in Ghana: The Effects of Technological Advancement in Academia. In M. Garcia (Ed.), *Socioeconomic Inclusion During an Era of Online Education* (pp. 47–66). IGI Global. doi:10.4018/978-1-6684-4364-4.ch003

Apostolakis, K. C., Margetis, G., & Stephanidis, C. (2020, November). Pleistocene Crete: A narrative, interactive mixed reality exhibition that brings prehistoric wildlife back to life. In *2020 IEEE International Symposium on Mixed and Augmented Reality Adjunct (ISMAR-Adjunct)* (pp. 237-240). IEEE. 10.1109/ISMAR-Adjunct51615.2020.00069

Arce-Lopera, C., Gomez, A., & Montoya, C. (2019, November). User engagement for collaborative learning on a mobile and desktop augmented reality application. In *2019 International Conference on Virtual Reality and Visualization (ICVRV)* (pp. 193-195). IEEE. 10.1109/ICVRV47840.2019.00045

Asai, K., Kobayashi, H., & Kondo, T. (2005, July). Augmented instructions-a fusion of augmented reality and printed learning materials. In *Fifth IEEE International Conference on Advanced Learning Technologies (ICALT'05)* (pp. 213-215). IEEE. 10.1109/ICALT.2005.71

Aslam, A. M., Chaudhary, R., Bhardwaj, A., Budhiraja, I., Kumar, N., & Zeadally, S. (2023). Metaverse for 6G and Beyond: The next revolution and deployMent ChallenGes. *IEEE Internet of Things Magazine*, *6*(1), 32–39. doi:10.1109/IOTM.001.2200248

Ayo, C. K., Mbarika, V., & Oni, A. A. (2015). The influence of trust and risk on intention to use e-democracy in Nigeria. *Mediterranean Journal of Social Sciences*, *6*(6), 477–486. doi:10.5901/mjss.2015.v6n6s1p477

Azuma, R. T. (1997). A survey of augmented reality. *Presence (Cambridge, Mass.)*, *6*(4), 355–385. doi:10.1162/pres.1997.6.4.355

Azuma, R., Baillot, Y., Behringer, R., Feiner, S., Julier, S., & MacIntyre, B. (2001). Recent advances in augmented reality. *IEEE Computer Graphics and Applications*, *21*(6), 34–47. doi:10.1109/38.963459

Baabdullah, A. M., Alsulaimani, A. A., Allamnakhrah, A., Alalwan, A. A., Dwivedi, Y. K., & Rana, N. P. (2022). Usage of augmented reality (AR) and development of e-learning outcomes: An empirical evaluation of students' e-learning experience. *Computers & Education*, *177*, 104383. doi:10.1016/j.compedu.2021.104383

Bagozzi, R. P. (2007). The legacy of the technology acceptance model and a proposal for a paradigm shift. *Journal of the Association for Information Systems*, *8*(4), 3. doi:10.17705/1jais.00122

Bahuguna, Y., Verma, A., & Raj, K. (2018, February). Smart learning based on augmented reality with android platform and its applicability. In *2018 3rd International Conference on Internet of Things: Smart Innovation and Usages (IoT-SIU)* (pp. 1-5). IEEE. 10.1109/IoT-SIU.2018.8519853

Bandura, A. (1997). *The anatomy of stages of change*. Academic Press.

Bandura, A. (2003). Social cognitive theory for personal and social change by enabling media. In *Entertainment-education and social change* (pp. 97–118). Routledge.

Banerjee, I. (2019). Integration of ICT in pedagogy of teacher education: Influence of constructive thinking in global society. *International Journal of Scientific Research and Review*, *7*(6), 130–136.

Bank, A. D. (2017). Innovative Strategies for Accelerated Human Resource Development in South Asia: Information and Communication Technology for Education: Special Focus on Bangladesh, Nepal, and Sri Lanka. Asian Development Bank.

Barham, B. L., Chavas, J. P., Fitz, D., Salas, V. R., & Schechter, L. (2014). The roles of risk and ambiguity in technology adoption. *Journal of Economic Behavior & Organization*, *97*, 204–218. doi:10.1016/j.jebo.2013.06.014

Barreto, M., & Ellemers, N. (2015). Detecting and experiencing prejudice : New answers to old questions. *Advances in Experimental Social Psychology*, *52*, 139–219. doi:10.1016/bs.aesp.2015.02.001

Belarbi, N., Chafiq, N., Talbi, M., Namir, A., & Benlahmar, E. (2019a, January 17). User profiling in a SPOC: A method based on user video clickstream analysis. *International Journal of Emerging Technologies in Learning*, *14*(1), 110–124. doi:10.3991/ijet.v14i01.9091

Belarbi, N., Chafiq, N., Talbi, M., Namir, A., & Benlahmar, H. (2019b, February 22). A recommender system for videos suggestion in a SPOC: A proposed personalized learning method. In *Big Data and Smart Digital Environment* (pp. 92–101). Springer International Publishing. doi:10.1007/978-3-030-12048-1_12

Belarbi, N., Namir, A., Talbi, M., & Chafiq, N. (2020). A Multi-Objectives Optimization to Develop the Mobile Dimension in a Small Private Online Course (SPOC). *International Journal of Advanced Computer Science and Applications*, *11*(1), 473–480. doi:10.14569/IJACSA.2020.0110158

Ben Youssef, A., Dahmani, M., & Ragni, L. (2022). ICT Use, Digital Skills and Students' Academic Performance: Exploring the Digital Divide. *Information (Basel), 13*(3), 129. doi:10.3390/info13030129

Bentaib, M. (2012). *Higher Education Facing New Technologies: A Contractual Digital Space.* EPI Association.

Bentaib, M., Daouad, M. A., Touri, B., Namir, A., Labriji, L., Hammed, M., … Talbi, M. (n.d.). *Implementation of a Computing Device to Quality Service in Learning in Higher Education to Enhance Student's Quality of Life*. Academic Press.

Bergmann, J., & Sams, A. (2012). *Flip Your Classroom: Reach Every Student in Every Class Every Day.* International Society for Technology in Education.

Bhat, S., Raju, R., Bhat, S., & D'Souza, R. (2020). Redefining Quality in Engineering Educa-tion through the Flipped Classroom Model. *Procedia Computer Science, 172*, 906–914. doi:10.1016/j.procs.2020.05.131

Bichlmeier, C., Wimmer, F., Heining, S. M., & Navab, N. (2007). Contextual anatomic mimesis: Hybrid in-situ visualization method for improving multi-sensory depth perception in medical augmented reality. IEEE. 1 – 10.

Billinghurst, M., & Duenser, A. (2012). Augmented reality in the classroom. *Computer, 45*(7), 56–63. doi:10.1109/MC.2012.111

Birgili, B., Seggie, F. N., & Oğuz, E. (2021). The trends and outcomes of flipped learning re-search between 2012 and 2018: A descriptive content analysis. *Journal of Computers in Education, 8*(3), 365–394. doi:10.1007/s40692-021-00183-y

Blikstein, P., & Worsley, M. (2016). Multimodal Learning Analytics and Education Data Mining : Using computational technologies to measure complex learning tasks. *Journal of Learning Analytics, 3*(2), 220–238. doi:10.18608/jla.2016.32.11

Blum, L., Broll, W., & Müller, S. (2009). Augmented reality under water. In *SIGGRAPH'09* (pp. 1–1). Posters.

Bojic, L. (2022). Metaverse through the prism of power and addiction: What will happen when the virtual world becomes more attractive than reality? *European Journal of Futures Research, 10*(1), 1–24. doi:10.1186/s40309-022-00208-4

Bolaji, H. O., & Adeoye, M. A. (2022). Accessibility, Usability, and Readiness Towards ICT Tools for Monitoring Educational Practice in Secondary Schools in Ilorin Metropolis. *Indonesian Journal of Multidiciplinary Research, 2*(2), 257–264.

Bonn, M. A., Kim, W. G., Kang, S., & Cho, M. (2015). Purchasing Wine Online : The Effects of Social Influence, Perceived Usefulness, Perceived Ease of Use, and Wine Involvement. *Journal of Hospitality Marketing &amp\math-semicolon. Journal of Hospitality Marketing & Management, 25*(7), 841–869. doi:10.1080/19368623.2016.1115382

Börsting, I., Shulikina, E., & Gruhn, V. (2021, September). Interdisciplinary Collaboration in augmented reality development—A process model. In *International Conference on Augmented Reality, Virtual Reality and Computer Graphics* (pp. 178-194). Springer, Cham. 10.1007/978-3-030-87595-4_14

Bouaziz, R., Alhejaili, M., Al-Saedi, R., Mihdhar, A., & Alsarrani, J. (2020, December). Using marker based augmented reality to teach autistic eating skills. In *2020 IEEE International Conference on Artificial Intelligence and Virtual Reality (AIVR)* (pp. 239-242). IEEE. 10.1109/AIVR50618.2020.00050

Boulahcen, A. (2005). Le processus d'orientation scolaire au Maroc. *Revue internationale d'éducation de Sèvres*, (38), 25-34. doi:10.4000/ries.1427

Bourguet, M. L., & Romero-Gonzalez, M. (2021, May). Work-In-Progress-Teaching invisible phenomena and virtual experiments: Immersion or augmentation? In *2021 7th International Conference of the Immersive Learning Research Network (iLRN)* (pp. 1-3). IEEE.

Bourguet, M. L., Ye, W., & Romero-Gonzalez, M. (2022, May). Work-In-Progress—Developing materials science experiments using augmented reality: How much reality is needed? In *2022 8th International Conference of the Immersive Learning Research Network (iLRN)* (pp. 1-3). IEEE.

Brangier, É., & Barcenilla, J. (2003). *Concevoir un produit facile à utiliser*. Paris: Editions d'organisation.

Brinkmann, F., & Weinzierl, S. (2023). Audio quality assessment for virtual reality. In *Sonic Interactions in Virtual Environments* (pp. 145–178). Springer. doi:10.1007/978-3-031-04021-4_5

Broll, W. (2022). Augmented reality. In *Virtual and Augmented Reality (VR/AR)* (pp. 291–329). Springer. doi:10.1007/978-3-030-79062-2_8

Broll, W., Weidner, F., Schwandt, T., Weber, K., & Doerner, R. (2022). Authoring of VR/AR applications. In *Virtual and Augmented Reality (VR/AR)* (pp. 371–400). Springer. doi:10.1007/978-3-030-79062-2_10

Bruchon, F., & Tomaszoer, Y. (2017). *Les TICE au service des apprentissages en EPS*. Academic Press.

Bruillard, É. (2015). Digital textbooks Current trends in secondary education in France. In Digital Textbooks: What's new? Universidade de Santiago de Compostela.

Bruillard, É. (2020, mars). *Les modes d'appropriation des ressources numériques: Caractériser l'offre des ressources numériques éducatives*. Groupes thématiques de la Direction du numérique pour l'Éducation. https://eduscol.education.fr/2115/groupe-thematique-numerique-6-mode-d-appropriation-des-ressources

Bruni, L. E., Dini, H., & Simonetti, A. (2021, July). Narrative cognition in mixed reality systems: Towards an empirical framework. In *International Conference on Human-Computer Interaction* (pp. 3-17). Springer. 10.1007/978-3-030-77599-5_1

Buabeng-Andoh, C. (2012). Factors influencing teachers' adoption and integration of information and communication technology into teaching: A review of the literature. *International Journal of Education and Development using ICT, 8*(1), 136-155.

Buiu, C., Buga, A., & Coman, A. M. (2013, November). Teaching robotics and virtual reality in a synergistic approach. In *2013 7th IEEE International Conference on e-Learning in Industrial Electronics (ICELIE)* (pp. 71-75). IEEE. 10.1109/ICELIE.2013.6701275

Burns, M. (2011). *Distance Education for Teacher Training: Modes, Models and Methods*. Education Development Center.

Cahyadi, E., Santoso, H. A., Bandung, Y., & Langi, A. Z. (2012, April). Augmented reality Virtual Class Box for digital learning services. In *2012 International Conference on Cloud Computing and Social Networking (ICCCSN)* (pp. 1-4). IEEE. 10.1109/ICCCSN.2012.6215754

Calle-Bustos, A. M., Juan, M. C., Abad, F., & Mollá, R. (2019, July). An augmented reality app for therapeutic education and suitable for mobile devices with different features. In *2019 IEEE 19th International Conference on Advanced Learning Technologies (ICALT)* (Vol. 2161, pp. 337-339). IEEE. 10.1109/ICALT.2019.00106

Calvo, P. (2020). The ethics of Smart City (EoSC): Moral implications of hyperconnectivity, algorithmization and the datafication of urban digital society. *Ethics and Information Technology, 22*(2), 141–149. doi:10.1007/s10676-019-09523-0

Camille, D., & Galyen, K. (2011). E-Learning, online learning, and distance learning environments: Are they the same? Academic Press.

Carreras, A., & Sora, C. (2009, October). Coupling digital and physical worlds in an AR magic show performance: Lessons learned. In *2009 IEEE International Symposium on Mixed and Augmented Reality-Arts, Media and Humanities* (pp. 25-28). IEEE. 10.1109/ISMAR-AMH.2009.5336729

Castelli, D., & Gromacki, E. (2015). *Active Education: Growing Evidence on Physical Activity and Academic Performance.* Academic Press.

Catroux, M. (2006). *Co-actional Perspective and ICT: Convergences for Specialized Language Teaching.* Presented at the Study Days of EA 2025, IUT Bordeaux. http://www.aplvlanguesmodernes.org/spip.php?article933

Chafiq, N., Benabid, A., Talbi, M., Bergadi, M., & Lima, L. (2011). L'utilisation d'environnements personnels d'apprentissage, une nouvelle façon de remédier aux difficultés langagières chez les étudiants scientifiques. *frantice. net, 3*, 19-25. http://frantice.net/docannexe/fichier/406/5_Chafiq.pdf

Chafiq, N., Elimadi, I., Ghazouani, M., & Talbi, M. (2023). Commercial Metaverse and the Customer: What Are the Realities, Challenges, and Perspectives for Brands? In Influencer Marketing Applications Within the Metaverse (pp. 87-101). IGI Global.

Chafiq, N., Housni, M., & Moussetad, M. (2019). Towards a dynamics of techno-pedagogical innovation within the university : Case study Hassan II University of Casablanca. *Information Systems and Technologies to Support Learning: Proceedings of EMENA-ISTL 2018, 2*, 118-125.

Chafiq, N., Elimadi, I., Talbi, M., & Ghazouani, M. (2023). Comodal Education in a COVID-19 Pandemic Context: Perceptions and Outcomes. In *The Role of Educators as Agents and Conveyors for Positive Change in Global Education* (pp. 295–314). IGI Global. doi:10.4018/978-1-6684-7869-1.ch013

Chafiq, N., & Housni, M. (2018). Towards the Design of an Innovative and Social Hybrid Learning Based on the SMAC Technologies. *Smart Innovation, Systems and Technologies, 111*, 126–133. doi:10.1007/978-3-030-03577-8_15

Chafiq, N., & Housni, M. (2019). Towards the Design of an Innovative and Social Hybrid Learning Based on the SMAC Technologies. In *Information Systems and Technologies to Support Learning: Proceedings of EMENA-ISTL 2018* (pp. 126-133). Springer.

Chafiq, N., Housni, M., & Moussetad, M. (2019). Towards a dynamics of techno-pedagogical innovation within the university: Case study Hassan II University of Casablanca. In *Information Systems and Technologies to Support Learning: Proceedings of EMENA-ISTL 2018* (pp. 118-125). Springer International Publishing.

Chami, M. (1987). *L'enseignement du français au Maroc, Diagnostic des difficultés et implications didactiques.* Editions Najah El Jadida.

Chang, H. Y., Yu, Y. T., Wu, H. K., & Hsu, Y. S. (2016, July). The impact of a mobile augmented reality game: Changing students' perceptions of the complexity of socioscientific reasoning. In *2016 IEEE 16th International Conference on Advanced Learning Technologies (ICALT)* (pp. 312-313). IEEE.

Chang, W., & Tan, Q. (2010, December). Augmented reality system design and scenario study for location-based adaptive mobile learning. In *2010 13th IEEE International Conference on Computational Science and Engineering* (pp. 20-27). IEEE. 10.1109/CSE.2010.66

Chang, R. C., & Yu, Z. S. (2017, May). Application of augmented reality technology to promote interactive learning. In *2017 International Conference on applied system Innovation (ICASI)* (pp. 1673-1674). IEEE. 10.1109/ICASI.2017.7988257

Chang, S.-C., & Tung, F.-C. (2008). An empirical investigation of students' behavioural intentions to use the online learning course websites. *British Journal of Educational Technology, 39*(1), 71–83. doi:10.1111/j.1467-8535.2007.00742.x

Chapelle, O., & Li, L. (2011). An empirical evaluation of Thompson sampling. *Advances in Neural Information Processing Systems*, *24*, 2249–2257.

Charleer, S., Klerkx, J., & Duval, E. (2014). Learning Dashboards. *Journal of Learning Analytics*, *1*(3), 199–202. doi:10.18608/jla.2014.13.22

Charlier, Daele, & Deschryver. (2002). Towards an Integrated Approach to Information and Communication Technologies in Teaching Practices. *Pedagogical Integration of ICT: Research and Training, 28*(2).

Charlier, Deschryver, & Peraya. (2006). Learning in Presence and at a Distance: A Definition of Hybrid Devices. In *Distances et savoirs* (Vol. 4). Academic Press.

Chen, Z., Wu, J., Gan, W., & Qi, Z. (2022). Metaverse security and privacy: An overview. In *2022 IEEE International Conference on Big Data (Big Data)* (pp. 2950-2959). IEEE.

Cheng, R., Wu, N., Chen, S., & Han, B. (2022). Will metaverse be NextG Internet? vision, hype, and reality. *IEEE Network*, *36*(5), 197–204. doi:10.1109/MNET.117.2200055

Chen, J. Y., Liu, C. H., Hsieh, C. H., Huang, S. Y., Wang, W. K., & Nien, B. H. (2017, May). Kinect augmented reality gear game design. In *2017 International Conference on Applied System Innovation (ICASI)* (pp. 373-375). IEEE. 10.1109/ICASI.2017.7988429

Chen, M., Mao, S., & Liu, Y. (2014). Big data : A survey. *Mobile Networks and Applications*, *19*(2), 171–209. doi:10.1007/s11036-013-0489-0

Chen, Y. C. (2013, June). Learners' motivation in an augmented reality E-learning system. In *2013 International Conference on Engineering, Technology and Innovation (ICE) & IEEE International Technology Management Conference* (pp. 1-6). IEEE. 10.1109/ITMC.2013.7352609

Chen, Z. Y., Li, Y. J., Wang, M., Steinicke, F., & Zhao, Q. (2021, October). A reinforcement learning approach to redirected walking with passive haptic feedback. In *2021 IEEE International Symposium on Mixed and Augmented Reality (ISMAR)* (pp. 184-192). IEEE. 10.1109/ISMAR52148.2021.00033

Cherif, S., & Gekiere, G. (2017). *Enseigner Autrement Avec Le Numérique: La Boîte à Outils Du Professeur*. Dunod.

Chin, K. Y., Hou, C. X., Wang, C. S., & Lee, K. F. (2017, July). Using augmented reality technology for the development of historic building teaching application: A Mackay Culture Course. In *2017 IEEE 17th International Conference on Advanced Learning Technologies (ICALT)* (pp. 87-88). IEEE. 10.1109/ICALT.2017.7

Chiou, Y. M., & Barrnaki, R. (2019, March). [DC] learning tornado formation via collaborative mixed reality. In *2019 IEEE Conference on Virtual Reality and 3D User Interfaces (VR)* (pp. 1369-1370). IEEE. 10.1109/VR.2019.8798339

Choppin, A. (1992). *Les Manuels scolaires: histoire et actualité*. Hachette Éducation Paris.

Chukwu, O. L. (2021). *Neoliberalism and the University: An Analysis of Patterns of Transformation within Nigerian Private and Public Institutions*. University of York.

Collins, J., Regenbrecht, H., & Lanalotz, T. (2018, October). Back to the future: Constructivist learning in virtual reality. In *2018 IEEE International Symposium on Mixed and Augmented Reality Adjunct (ISMAR-Adjunct)* (pp. 45-46). IEEE. 10.1109/ISMAR-Adjunct.2018.00030

Conroy, M., Houchins, D., Hitchcock, J., & Anderson, J. (2023). Use of Mixed Methods in Emotional/Behavioral Disorders Intervention Research. *Behavioral Disorders*, *48*(3), 163–173. doi:10.1177/01987429231160283

Cook, D. L. (1995). Community and Computer Generated Learning Environments. *New Directions for Adult and Continuing Education, 1995*(67), 33–39. doi:10.1002/ace.36719956706

Costa, I. V., Queiroz, V. F., Miranda, B. P., de Freitas, A. A., dos Santos, C. G. R., & Meiguins, B. S. (2019, July). A card-based interaction to design visualizations in augmented reality environments. In *2019 23rd International Conference in Information Visualization??? Part II* (pp. 52-55). IEEE.

Courant, J., de Falco, M., Gonnord, S., Filliâtre, J.-C., Conchon, S., Dowek, G., & Wack, B. (2013). *Informatique pour tous en classes préparatoires aux grandes écoles : Manuel d'algorithmique et programmation structurée avec Python.* Eyrolles.

Cox, D. F., & Rich, S. U. (1964). Perceived Risk and Consumer Decision-Making—The Case of Telephone Shopping. *JMR, Journal of Marketing Research, 1*(4), 32–39. doi:10.1177/002224376400100405

Craig, P., Willemsen, P., Downs, E., Lover, A., & Barber, W. (2022, March). Learning environments in AR: Comparing tablet and head-mounted augmented reality devices at room and table scale. In *2022 IEEE Conference on Virtual Reality and 3D User Interfaces Abstracts and Workshops (VRW)* (pp. 892-893). IEEE. 10.1109/VRW55335.2022.00297

Creane, S., Crotty, Y., & Farren, M. (2015). A proposed use of virtual and augmented reality for supporting inquiry based learning. *Proceedings of the 2015 International Conference on Interactive Mobile Communication Technologies and Learning,* 393 – 395.

Creswell, J. W., & Creswell, J. D. (2018). *Research design: qualitative, quantitative, and mixed methods approaches* (5th ed.). SAGE.

Creswell, J. W., & Plano Clark, V. L. (2017). *Designing and conducting mixed methods research.* Sage publications.

Crombet, H. (2016). Julien Péquignot, François-Gabriel Roussel, dirs, Les Métavers. Dispositifs, usages et représentations. *Questions De Communication, 29*(29), 459–461. doi:10.4000/questionsdecommunication.10622

Cubillo, J., Martín, S., Castro, M., Diaz, G., Colmenar, A., & Boticki, I. (2014, October). A learning environment for augmented reality mobile learning. In 2014 IEEE Frontiers in Education Conference (FIE) Proceedings (pp. 1-8). IEEE. doi:10.1109/FIE.2014.7044039

Curry & Sarazin. (2001). *Les théories de la motivation et pratiques sportives: l'état des recherches.* Academic Press.

Daher, S. (2017, March). *Optical see-through vs. spatial augmented reality simulators for medical applications. In 2017 IEEE Virtual Reality (VR).* IEEE.

Daniel, D. B., & Woody, W. D. (2013). E-textbooks at what cost? Performance and use of electronic v. print texts. *Computers & Education, 62,* 18–23. doi:10.1016/j.compedu.2012.10.016

Davcev, D., Trajkovic, V., Kalajdziski, S., & Celakoski, S. (2003, August). Augmented reality environment for dance learning. *International Conference on Information Technology: Research and Education, 2003 Proceedings. ITRE2003,* 189–193.

Davis, F. D. (1985). *A technology acceptance model for empirically testing new end-user information systems : Theory and results* [PhD Thesis]. Massachusetts Institute of Technology.

Davis, F. D. (1989a). Perceived Usefulness, Perceived Ease of Use, and User Acceptance of Information Technology. *Management Information Systems Quarterly, 13*(3), 319. doi:10.2307/249008

De Backer, P., Simoens, J., Creemers, H., Vermijs, S., Matthys, R., Bravi, C. A., Sarchi, L., Piazza, P., Paciotti, M., Farinha, R., Debbaut, C., Desender, L., Van Praet, C., Mottrie, A., & Decaestecker, K. (2022). Augmented reality instrument detection: Enabling 3D model-instrument interaction through deep learning. *European Urology Open Science*, *44*, S406. doi:10.1016/S2666-1683(22)02254-6

De Grove, F., Bourgonjon, J., & Van Looy, J. (2012). Digital games in the classroom? A contextual approach to teachers' adoption intention of digital games in formal education. *Computers & Education*, *59*(4), 1155–1166.

De Michelis, G., De Paoli, F., Pluchinotta, C., & Susani, M. (2000, April). Weakly augmented reality: Observing and designing the work-place of creative designers. In *Proceedings of DARE 2000 on Designing Augmented Reality Environments* (pp. 81-91). 10.1145/354666.354675

Dede, C. (1996). Emerging Technologies in Distance Education for Business. *Journal of Education for Business*, *71*(4), 197–204. doi:10.1080/08832323.1996.10116784

Degeratu, A. M., Rangaswamy, A., & Wu, J. (2000). Consumer choice behavior in online and traditional supermarkets : The effects of brand name, price, and other search attributes. *International Journal of Research in Marketing*, *17*(1), 55–78. doi:10.1016/S0167-8116(00)00005-7

Del Gallego, N. P. (2020, November). A proposed learning content for teaching handheld augmented reality in a classroom setting. In *2020 22nd Symposium on Virtual and Augmented Reality (SVR)* (pp. 111-118). IEEE. 10.1109/SVR51698.2020.00030

Demba, M., Kapasa, R. L., Camara, T., Halabi, N., Abdelaziz, H., Oumnia, B., ... Coppieters't Wallant, Y. (2023). Knowledge, attitudes, and practices toward COVID-19 among the general population: A cross-sectional study in Kankan, Guinea. *Journal of Public Health in Africa*, *14*(3). Advance online publication. doi:10.4081/jphia.2023.2231 PMID:37197262

Demski, J. (2012). Rebuilding the LMS for the 21st Century. *Campus Technology*, *25*(8), 34–37.

Denis, B. (2003). Quels rôles et quelle formation pour les tuteurs intervenant dans des dispositifs de formation à distance? *Distances et savoirs*, *1*, 19-46. https://doi.org/10.3166/ds.1.19-46

Dennis, A. (2011). *E-Textbooks at Indiana University: A Summary of Two Years of Research. Indiana University Kelly School of Busness Research Report*. Indiana University.

Derby, J. L., & Chaparro, B. S. (2022). The development and validation of an augmented and mixed reality usability heuristic checklist. In *International Conference on Human-Computer Interaction* (pp. 165-182). Springer. 10.1007/978-3-031-05939-1_11

Deutsch, M. (1958). Trust and suspicion. *The Journal of Conflict Resolution*, *2*(4), 265–279. doi:10.1177/002200275800200401

Dewey, J., & In Reverdy, C. (2013). L'apprentissage par projet : De la recherche. *Revue Technologie*, *186*, 46–54.

Di Pietro, R., & Cresci, S. (2021). *Metaverse: Security and privacy issues*. doi:10.1109/TPSISA52974.2021.00032

Di Pietro, R., & Cresci, S. (2021). Metaverse: security and privacy issues. In *2021 Third IEEE International Conference on Trust, Privacy and Security in Intelligent Systems and Applications (TPS-ISA)* (pp. 281-288). IEEE.

Doerner, R. (2022). Mathematical Foundations of VR/AR. In *Virtual and Augmented Reality (VR/AR)* (pp. 401–412). Springer. doi:10.1007/978-3-030-79062-2_11

Doerner, R., Broll, W., Jung, B., Grimm, P., Göbel, M., & Kruse, R. (2022). Introduction to virtual and augmented reality. In *Virtual and Augmented Reality (VR/AR)* (pp. 1–37). Springer. doi:10.1007/978-3-030-79062-2_1

Doerner, R., & Horst, R. (2022). Overcoming challenges when teaching hands-on courses about Virtual Reality and Augmented Reality: Methods, techniques and best practice. *Graphics and Visual Computing*, *6*, 200037. doi:10.1016/j.gvc.2021.200037

Doerner, R., & Steinicke, F. (2022). Perceptual aspects of VR. In *Virtual and Augmented Reality (VR/AR)* (pp. 39–70). Springer. doi:10.1007/978-3-030-79062-2_2

Domingo, J. R., & Bradley, E. G. (2018). Education student perceptions of virtual reality as a learning tool. *Journal of Educational Technology Systems*, *46*(3), 329–342. doi:10.1177/0047239517736873

Dong, Y., Yin, H., Du, S., & Wang, A. (2021). The effects of flipped classroom characterized by situational and collaborative learning in a community nursing course: A quasi-experimental design. *Nurse Education Today*, *105*, 105037. doi:10.1016/j.nedt.2021.105037 PMID:34247009

Doswell, J. T. (2008). Pedagogy play: Virtual instructors for wearable augmented reality during hands-on learning and play. *Second IEEE International Conference on Digital Game and Intelligent Toy Enhanced Learning,* 215 – 216.

Doswell, J. T., & Mosley, P. H. (2006, July). Robotics in mixed-reality training simulations: augmenting STEM learning. In *Sixth IEEE International Conference on Advanced Learning Technologies (ICALT'06)* (pp. 864-868). IEEE. 10.1109/ICALT.2006.1652579

Downey, G. L., Lucena, J. C., Moskal, B. M., Parkhurst, R., Bigley, T., Hays, C., Jesiek, B. K., Kelly, L., Miller, J., Ruff, S., Lehr, J. L., & Nichols-Belo, A. (2006). The globally competent engineer : Working effectively with people who define problems differently. *Journal of Engineering Education*, *95*(2), 107–122. doi:10.1002/j.2168-9830.2006.tb00883.x

Drljević, N., Wong, L. H., & Botički, I. (2017). Where does my Augmented Reality Learning Experience (ARLE) belong? A student and teacher perspective to positioning ARLEs. *IEEE Transactions on Learning Technologies*, *10*(4), 419–435. doi:10.1109/TLT.2017.2690426

Duan, H., Li, J., Fan, S., Lin, Z., Wu, X., & Cai, W. (2021). Metaverse for social good : A university campus prototype. *Proceedings of the 29th ACM international conference on multimedia*, 153-161. 10.1145/3474085.3479238

Dubois, E., & Nigay, L. (2000, April). Augmented reality: which augmentation for which reality? In *Proceedings of DARE 2000 on Designing Augmented Reality Environments* (pp. 165-166). 10.1145/354666.354695

Dudeney, G. (2010). *The Internet and the language classroom* (Vol. X). Cambridge University Press.

Duggal, K., Gupta, L. R., & Singh, P. (2021). Gamification and Machine Learning Inspired Approach for Classroom Engagement and Learning. *Mathematical Problems in Engineering*, 1–18. Advance online publication. doi:10.1155/2021/9922775

Durairaj, M., & Aurelia, P. S. (2017, July). A modernistic and contemporary mobile augmented reality erudition system. In *2017 International Conference on Computing Methodologies and Communication (ICCMC)* (pp. 1109-1112). IEEE. 10.1109/ICCMC.2017.8282645

Dutrieux, L. (2016). *De quelles manières la mise en page et la présentation graphique des manuels scolaires peuvent-elles aider le jeune en apprentissage?* (Olivier Ruol, interview réalisé le 28 avril 2016). https://medium.com/liove/de-quelles-mani%C3%A8res-la-mise-en-page-et-la-pr%C3%A9sentation-graphique-des-manuels-scolaires-peuvent-1afdca651ea2

Eastmond, D. V. (1995). *Alone But Together: Adult Distance Study Through Computer Conferencing*. Hampton Press.

El Haddadi, A. (2009). *Les orientations pédagogiques et programmes d'enseignement d'EPS dans le cycle collégial.* Academic Press.

El Kabtane, H., Mourdi, Y., El Adnani, M., & Sadgal, M. (2015, March). The integration of augmented reality in the virtual learning environment for practical activities. In *2015 International Conference on Electrical and Information Technologies (ICEIT)* (pp. 363-368). IEEE. 10.1109/EITech.2015.7162960

El Ouardani, K. (2015). *Qu'est-ce qu'une intégration efficace des TIC à l'école?* Academic Press.

Elkoubaiti, H., & Mrabet, R. (2018, May). A generic architecture of augmented and virtual reality in classrooms. In *2018 6th International Conference on Multimedia Computing and Systems (ICMCS)* (pp. 1-4). IEEE. 10.1109/ICMCS.2018.8525976

Ellis, R. (2003). *Task-based Language Learning and Teaching. Oxford Applied Linguistics*. Oxford University Press.

El-Shinnawy, A. H., Badawi, A. H., & Nassar, A. M. (2010). Two-step scheduling algorithm for IEEE802.16 wireless networks. In *2010 IEEE 12th International Conference on Communication Technology*. IEEE. 10.1109/ICCT.2010.5688935

Eriksson, K., Kerem, K., & Nilsson, D. (2005). Customer acceptance of internet banking in Estonia. *International Journal of Bank Marketing*, *23*(2), 200–216. doi:10.1108/02652320510584412

Erofeeva, M., & Klowait, N. O. (2021, May). The impact of virtual reality, Augmented reality, and interactive whiteboards on the attention management in secondary school STEM teaching. In *2021 7th International Conference of the Immersive Learning Research Network (iLRN)* (pp. 1-5). IEEE.

Fatima-zahra, G., & Khadija, D. (2016). Modernization of a domain E-orientation metamodel. In *2016 11th International Conference on Intelligent Systems: Theories and Applications (SITA)*. IEEE. 10.1109/SITA.2016.7772308

FernandezC. B. (2022, March 25). *Life, the Metaverse and Everything: An overview of privacy, ethics, and governance in metaverse*. doi:10.1109/ICDCSW56584.2022.00058

Fitri, E. Y., Siahaya, J., Nugraha, A., & Arief, I. (2022). Analysis of the role of parents in online learning in the covid-19 pandemic. *International Journal of Demos*, *4*(1), 352–363. doi:10.37950/ijd.v4i1.210

Fominykh, M., Wild, F., Klamma, R., Billinghurst, M., Costiner, L. S., Karsakov, A., ... Smolic, A. (2020). Model augmented reality curriculum. In *Proceedings of the Working Group Reports on Innovation and Technology in Computer Science Education* (pp. 131-149). 10.1145/3437800.3439205

Frutos-Pascual, M., Gale, C., Harrison, J. M., Creed, C., & Williams, I. (2021, August). Character input in augmented reality: An evaluation of keyboard position and interaction visualisation for head-mounted displays. In *IFIP Conference on Human-Computer Interaction* (pp. 480-501). Springer. 10.1007/978-3-030-85623-6_29

Furtado, L. S., Souza, R. F. D., Lima, J. L. D. R., & Oliveira, S. R. B. (2021). Teaching Method for Software Measurement Process Based on Gamification or Serious Games : A Systematic Review of the Literature. *International Journal of Computer Games Technology*, 1–35. Advance online publication. doi:10.1155/2021/8873997

Gaëlle, L. (2014). *Analyser la pratique d'enseignement sous l'angle des orientations de valeur études de cas en éducation physique et sportive*. Academic Press.

Gao, Y. F., Wang, H. Y., & Bian, X. N. (2016, July). Marker tracking for video-based augmented reality. In *2016 International Conference on Machine Learning and Cybernetics (ICMLC)* (Vol. 2, pp. 928-932). IEEE. 10.1109/ICMLC.2016.7873011

Garača, Ž., & ... (2011). Factors related to the intended use of ERP systems. *Management*, *16*(2), 23–42.

García-Pazo, P., Lopez, F. P., Coll, A. B., Moreno, C., & Brogi, L. (2023). Low cost 360 degree virtual reality video creation for nursing intensive care unit practices: A descriptive study. *EDULEARN23 Proceedings*, 6957-6957.

Gargrish, S., Mantri, A., & Kaur, D. P. (2020). Augmented reality-based learning environment to enhance teaching-learning experience in geometry education. *Procedia Computer Science*, *172*, 1039–1046. doi:10.1016/j.procs.2020.05.152

Garzotto, F., Torelli, E., Vona, F., & Aruanno, B. (2018, December). HoloLearn: Learning through mixed reality for people with cognitive disability. In *2018 IEEE International Conference on Artificial Intelligence and Virtual Reality (AIVR)* (pp. 189-190). IEEE. 10.1109/AIVR.2018.00042

Gasevic, D., Dawson, S., & Jovanovic, J. (2016). Ethics and Privacy as Enablers of Learning Analytics. *Journal of Learning Analytics*, *3*(1), 1–4. doi:10.18608/jla.2016.31.1

Gasevic, D., Jovanovic, J., Pardo, A., & Dawson, S. (2017). Detecting Learning Strategies with Analytics : Links with Self-reported Measures and Academic Performance. *Journal of Learning Analytics*, *4*(2), 113–128. doi:10.18608/jla.2017.42.10

Gasteiger, N., van der Veer, S. N., Wilson, P., & Dowding, D. (2022, March). Exploring how, for whom and in which contexts extended reality training 'works' in upskilling healthcare workers: A realist review. In *2022 IEEE Conference on Virtual Reality and 3D User Interfaces Abstracts and Workshops (VRW)* (pp. 734-735). IEEE. 10.1109/VRW55335.2022.00218

Gee, J. P. (2003). What Video Games Have to Teach Us About Learning and Literacy. *Computers in Entertainment*, *1*(1), 20–20. doi:10.1145/950566.950595

Gefen, D., Karahanna, E., & Straub, D. W. (2003). Trust and TAM in online shopping : An integrated model. *Management Information Systems Quarterly*, *27*(1), 51–90. doi:10.2307/30036519

Gérard, F. M., & Roegiers, X. (2009). *Des manuels scolaires pour apprendre. Concevoir, évaluer, utiliser*. De Boeck Supérieur. doi:10.3917/dbu.gerar.2009.01

Geroimenko, V. (2022). *Augmented reality art* (3rd ed.). Springer. doi:10.1007/978-3-030-96863-2

Ghamya, K., Yadav, C. C., Pranav, D. V. S., Reddy Madhavi, K., & Patel, A. (2023). Metaverse: The Potential Threats in the Virtual World. In *Proceedings of Fourth International Conference on Computer and Communication Technologies: IC3T 2022* (pp. 59-67). Singapore: Springer Nature Singapore.

Ghana National Association of Teachers. (2021). *One Laptop, One Teacher, Kick Start*. Retrieved from https://www.ghanateachers.com/news-media/gnat-news/one-laptop-one-teacher

GhanaWeb. (2019). *New Schools' Curriculum Starts in September 2019*. Retrieved from https://www.ghanaweb.com/GhanaHomePage/NewsArchive/New-schools-curriculum-starts-in-September-2019-766446

Ghasemi, Y., Jeong, H., Choi, S. H., Park, K. B., & Lee, J. Y. (2022). Deep learning-based object detection in augmented reality: A systematic review. *Computers in Industry*, *139*(103661), 1–15. doi:10.1016/j.compind.2022.103661

Ghazouani, M., Chafiq, N., Zaher, N., Azouazi, M., & Chakir, A. (2023). Merging Big Data With the Metaverse: A Proposed Architecture With Multiple Layers. In Influencer Marketing Applications Within the Metaverse (pp. 263-287). IGI Global. doi:10.4018/978-1-6684-8898-0.ch017

Ghazwani, Y., & Smith, S. (2020, February). Interaction in augmented reality: Challenges to enhance user experience. In *Proceedings of the 2020 4th International Conference on Virtual and Augmented Reality Simulations* (pp. 39-44). 10.1145/3385378.3385384

Ghouaiel, N., Cieutat, J. M., & Jessel, J. P. (2014, April). Adaptive augmented reality: plasticity of augmentations. In *Proceedings of the 2014 Virtual Reality International Conference* (pp. 1-4). Academic Press.

Ghulamani, S., & Zareen, S. (2018, March). Educating students in remote areas using augmented reality. In *2018 International Conference on Computing, Mathematics and Engineering Technologies (iCoMET)* (pp. 1-6). IEEE. 10.1109/ICOMET.2018.8346350

Gikas, J., & Grant, M. (2013). *Internet and Higher Education Mobile computing devices in higher education: Student perspectives on learning with cellphones, smartphones & social media*. Academic Press.

Gillespie, H., Boulton, H., Hrmiak, A., & Williamson, R. (2007). *Learning and Teaching with Virtual Learning Environments*. Troubridge, Wiltshire Learning Matters Ltd.

Glardon, A. (2021). *Clés pour aider à apprendre*. Wallenried : Editions D'Amont. https://www.meirieu.com/OUTILS-DEFORMATION/CpA-14.pdf

Glass, I., & Evans, T. L. (1981). A period–luminosity relation for Mira variables in the Large Magellanic Cloud. *Nature*, *291*(5813), 303–304. doi:10.1038/291303a0

Gómez-Galán, J. (2020). Media Education in the ICT Era: Theoretical Structure for Innovative Teaching Styles. *Information (Basel)*, *11*(5), 276. doi:10.3390/info11050276

Gonzalez, A. V., Koh, S., Kapalo, K., Sottilare, R., Garrity, P., Billinghurst, M., & LaViola, J. (2019, October). A comparison of desktop and augmented reality scenario based training authoring tools. In *2019 IEEE International Symposium on Mixed and Augmented Reality (ISMAR)* (pp. 1199 - 1200). IEEE. 10.1109/VR.2019.8797973

Goosen, L. (2018a). Sustainable and Inclusive Quality Education Through Research Informed Practice on Information and Communication Technologies in Education. In L. Webb (Ed.), *Proceedings of the 26th Conference of the Southern African Association for Research in Mathematics, Science and Technology Education (SAARMSTE)* (pp. 215 - 228). Gabarone: University of Botswana.

Goosen, L. (2019). Information Systems and Technologies Opening New Worlds for Learning to Children with Autism Spectrum Disorders (Á. Rocha, & M. Serrhini, Eds.). Smart Innovation, Systems and Technologies, 111, 134-143. doi:10.1007/978-3-030-03577-8_16

Goosen, L., & Van Heerden, D. (2017). Beyond the Horizon of Learning Programming with Educational Technologies. In U. I. Ogbonnaya, & S. Simelane-Mnisi (Ed.), *Proceedings of the South Africa International Conference on Educational Technologies* (pp. 78 - 90). Pretoria: African Academic Research Forum.

Goosen, L. (2018b). Ethical Information and Communication Technologies for Development Solutions: Research Integrity for Massive Open Online Courses. In C. Sibinga (Ed.), *Ensuring Research Integrity and the Ethical Management of Data* (pp. 155–173). IGI Global. doi:10.4018/978-1-5225-2730-5.ch009

Goosen, L., & Naidoo, L. (2014). Computer Lecturers Using Their Institutional LMS for ICT Education in the Cyber World. In C. Burger, & K. Naudé (Ed.), *Proceedings of the 43rd Conference of the Southern African Computer Lecturers' Association (SACLA)* (pp. 99-108). Port Elizabeth: Nelson Mandela Metropolitan University.

Gote, R., & Jadhav, S. (2022). MetaHealth – How Metavers will transform healthcare? *International Journal for Research in Applied Science and Engineering Technology*, *10*(12), 988–990. doi:10.22214/ijraset.2022.48077

Gouws, P., & Goosen, L. (2019). Technologies to Inspire Education in Science, Engineering and Technology Through Community Engagement in South Africa. *Smart Innovation, Systems and Technologies*, *111*, 144–153.

Grabe, M., & Grabe, C. (2007). *Integrating technology for meaningful learning* (5th ed.). Houghton Mifflin.

Grubert, J. (2023). Mixed Reality Interaction Techniques. In *Springer Handbook of Augmented Reality* (pp. 109–129). Springer International Publishing. doi:10.1007/978-3-030-67822-7_5

Guerss, F., Aitdaoud, M., Douzi, K., Guemmat, K., Namir, A., & Talbi, M. (2015). *Towards a new ontology of the Moroccan Post-baccalaureate learner profile for the E-orientation system "MMSyOrientation"*. Academic Press.

Guitton, P. (2022, February 25). *Le métavers, quels métavers?* https://inria.hal.science/hal-03599140

Gundala, D. S. A., Alamuri, S. S., Firdaus, A., & Kumar, G. K. (2022, February). Implementing augmented reality using OpenCV. In 2022 IEEE Delhi Section Conference (DELCON) (pp. 1-4). IEEE.

Guo, R., Cui, J., Zhao, W., Li, S., & Hao, A. (2021, March). Hand-by-hand mentor: An AR based training system for piano performance. In *2021 IEEE Conference on Virtual Reality and 3D User Interfaces Abstracts and Workshops (VRW)* (pp. 436-437). IEEE. 10.1109/VRW52623.2021.00100

Hamann, D. (2015). *The Construction and Validation of an M-Learning Framework for Online and Blended Learning Environments*. Nova Southeastern University.

Hamari, J., Koivisto, J., & Sarsa, H. (2014). Does gamification work? — A literature review of empirical studies on gamification. *2014 47th Hawaii international conference on system sciences,* 3025-3034.

Han, J., Liu, G., & Gao, Y. (2023). Learners in the Metaverse: A systematic review on using Roblox in learning. *Education Sciences*, *13*(3), 296. doi:10.3390/educsci13030296

Hannoun, A., Chafiq, N., Raji, M., Elkouali, M. H., & Razine, R. (2023). Physicians' perception of health topics covered by traditional media in Morocco: Opinion of physicians as consumers of the media. *Journal of Public Health in Africa*, *14*(5). Advance online publication. doi:10.4081/jphia.2023.2275 PMID:37441121

Harrington, M. C. (2020, June). Connecting user experience to learning in an evaluation of an immersive, interactive, multimodal augmented reality virtual diorama in a natural history museum & the importance of story. In *2020 6th International Conference of the Immersive Learning Research Network (iLRN)* (pp. 70-78). IEEE. 10.23919/iLRN47897.2020.9155202

Henri, F., & Plante, P. (2018). Qu'est-ce que le e-learning? Un collage de définitions. *TED 1272 : Les TIC et l'apprentissage en milieu de travail*. Université TÉLUQ. https://r-libre.teluq.ca/1746/1/TED1272_texte3.2.pdf

Hensen, B., & Klamma, R. (2020, July). Comparing authoring workflows and learning paths in Web & mixed reality environments. In *2020 IEEE 20th International Conference on Advanced Learning Technologies (ICALT)* (pp. 319-321). IEEE. 10.1109/ICALT49669.2020.00102

Hernández-Blanco, A., Herrera-Flores, B., Tomás, D., & Navarro-Colorado, B. (2019). A Systematic Review of Deep Learning Approaches to Educational Data Mining. *Complexity*, *2019*, 1–22. Advance online publication. doi:10.1155/2019/1306039

Hernandez-Ortega, B. (2011). The role of post-use trust in the acceptance of a technology : Drivers and consequences. *Technovation*, *31*(10-11), 523–538. doi:10.1016/j.technovation.2011.07.001

Herodotou, C., Rienties, B., Verdin, B., & Boroowa, A. (2019). Predictive learning analytics "at scale" : Towards guidelines to successful implementation in higher education based on the case of the open university UK. *Journal of Learning Analytics*, *6*(1), 85–95. doi:10.18608/jla.2019.61.5

Hill, A., Barba, E., MacIntyre, B., Gandy, M., & Davidson, B. (2011, July). Mirror worlds: experimenting with heterogeneous AR. In *2011 International Symposium on Ubiquitous Virtual Reality* (pp. 9-12). IEEE. 10.1109/ISUVR.2011.28

Hill, R. J., Fishbein, M., & Ajzen, I. (1977). Belief, Attitude, Intention and Behavior : An Introduction to Theory and Research. *Contemporary Sociology*, *6*(2), 244. doi:10.2307/2065853

Hiyama, A., Fujino, H., Kashiwagi, G., & Hirose, M. (2011, September). Ubiquitous augmented reality: expanding augmented reality environment with wireless tags and visible light communication projector. In *Proceedings of the 13th International Conference on Ubiquitous Computing* (pp. 597-598). 10.1145/2030112.2030231

Hoang-Oanh, T. T. (2020). The Impact of a Flipped Classroom on Student Learning Achieve-ments in EFL Classrooms. Education. *Language and Sociology Research, 1*(2), 13. doi:10.22158/elsr.v1n2p13

Hossain, M. F., Barman, S., & Haque, A. B. (2019, October). Augmented reality for education; AR children's book. In TENCON 2019-2019 IEEE Region 10 Conference (TENCON) (pp. 2568-2571). IEEE.

Hou, H. T., & Lin, Y. C. (2017, July). The development and evaluation of an educational game integrated with augmented reality and virtual laboratory for chemistry experiment learning. In *2017 6th IIAI International Congress on Advanced Applied Informatics (IIAI-AAI)* (pp. 1005-1006). IEEE. 10.1109/IIAI-AAI.2017.14

Housni, M., Namir, A., Talbi, M., & Chafiq, N. (2019). Applying Data Analytics and Cumulative Accuracy Profile (CAP) Approach in Real-Time Maintenance of Instructional Design Models. In Lecture Notes in Real-Time Intelligent Systems (pp. 17-25). Springer.

Housni, M., Namir, A., Talbi, M., & Chafiq, N. (2017). Applying Data Analytics and Cumulative Accuracy Profile (CAP) Approach in Real-Time Maintenance of Instructional Design Models. *Advances in Intelligent Systems and Computing, 756*, 17–25. doi:10.1007/978-3-319-91337-7_2

Housni, M., Talbi, M., & Namir, A. (2021). Simple Technology is an Improved Solution for a Post-Pandemic Informative System : A Reference Model. *International Journal of Emerging Technologies in Learning, 16*(16), 35–51. doi:10.3991/ijet.v16i16.23211

Hughes, C. E., & Ingraham, K. M. (2016, March). *De-escalation training in an augmented virtuality space. In 2016 IEEE Virtual Reality (VR)*. IEEE.

Hu, P. J.-H., Lin, C., & Chen, H. (2005). User acceptance of Intelligence and Security Informatics technology : A study of COPLINK. *Journal of the American Society for Information Science and Technology, 56*(3), 235–244. doi:10.1002/asi.20124

Hussain, A. J., Morgan, S., & Al-Jumeily, D. (2011, December). How Does ICT Affect Teachings and Learning within School Education. In *Developments in E-systems Engineering (DeSE), 2011* (pp. 250–254). IEEE. doi:10.1109/DeSE.2011.50

Hussain, S. (2023, April). Metaverse for education–Virtual or real? *Frontiers in Education, 8*, 1177429. doi:10.3389/feduc.2023.1177429

Huynh, B., Orlosky, J., & Höllerer, T. (2019, March). In-situ labeling for augmented reality language learning. In *2019 IEEE Conference on Virtual Reality and 3D User Interfaces (VR)* (pp. 1606-1611). IEEE. 10.1109/VR.2019.8798358

Huynh-The, T., Gadekallu, T. R., Wang, W., Yenduri, G., Ranaweera, P., Pham, Q., Da Costa, D. B., & Liyanage, M. (2023). Blockchain for the metaverse: A Review. *Future Generation Computer Systems, 143*, 401–419. doi:10.1016/j.future.2023.02.008

Huynh-The, T., Pham, Q., Pham, X., Nguyen, T., Han, Z., & Kim, D. (2023). Artificial intelligence for the metaverse: A survey. *Engineering Applications of Artificial Intelligence, 117*, 105581. doi:10.1016/j.engappai.2022.105581

Iatraki, G., Delimitros, M., Vrellis, I., & Mikropoulos, T. A. (2021, July). Augmented and virtual environments for students with intellectual disability: design issues in Science Education. In *2021 International Conference on Advanced Learning Technologies (ICALT)* (pp. 381-385). IEEE. 10.1109/ICALT52272.2021.00122

Ienaga, N., Bork, F., Meerits, S., Mori, S., Fallavollita, P., Navab, N., & Saito, H. (2016, September). First deployment of diminished reality for anatomy education. In *2016 IEEE International Symposium on Mixed and Augmented Reality (ISMAR-Adjunct)* (pp. 294-296). IEEE. 10.1109/ISMAR-Adjunct.2016.0099

Ihya, R., Aitdaoud, M., Namir, A., Guerss, F. Z., & Haddani, H. (2020). Using Machine Learning Algorithms to Predict the E-orientation Systems Acceptancy. In *Innovations in Smart Cities Applications* (3rd ed., pp. 117–130). Springer International Publishing. doi:10.1007/978-3-030-37629-1_10

Ihya, R., Namir, A., Elfilali, S., Guerss, F. Z., & Daoud, M. A. (2019). Modeling the Acceptance of the E-Orientation Systems by Using the Predictions Algorithms. In *Learning and Analytics in Intelligent Systems* (pp. 27–31). Springer International Publishing. doi:10.1007/978-3-030-36778-7_3

Ihya, R., Namir, A., Filali, S. E., Daoud, M. A., & Guerss, F. Z. (2019). J48 algorithms of machine learning for predicting user's the acceptance of an E-orientation systems. In *Proceedings of the 4th International Conference on Smart City Applications*. ACM. 10.1145/3368756.3368995

Inceoglu, M. M., & Ciloglugil, B. (2022). Use of Metaverse in education. In *International conference on computational science and its applications* (pp. 171-184). Cham: Springer International Publishing.

Interactive Design Foundation. (2020). *Augmented reality—The past, the present and the future*. Retrieved Dec. 19, 2022, from https://www.interaction-design.org/literature/article/augmented-reality-the-past-the-present-and-the-future

International Journal of Information Management. (2022). *Metaverse beyond the hype: Multidisciplinary perspectives on emerging challenges, opportunities, and agenda for research, practice and policy*. Author.

International Society for Technology in Education (ISTE). (2023). *ISTE Standards: Educators*. Retrieved from https://www.iste.org/standards/iste-standards-for-teachers

Iqbal, M. Z., Mangina, E., & Campbell, A. G. (2019, October). Exploring the use of augmented reality in a kinesthetic learning application integrated with an intelligent virtual embodied agent. In *2019 IEEE International Symposium on Mixed and Augmented Reality Adjunct (ISMAR-Adjunct)* (pp. 12-16). IEEE. 10.1109/ISMAR-Adjunct.2019.00018

Irawati, S., Green, S., Billinghurst, M., Duenser, A., & Ko, H. (2006, October). " Move the couch where?": developing an augmented reality multimodal interface. In *2006 IEEE/ACM International Symposium on Mixed and Augmented Reality* (pp. 183-186). IEEE. 10.1109/ISMAR.2006.297812

Jadhav, O. (2022). Blockchain, AI & Web3.0 in Metaverse of Madness. *International Journal for Research in Applied Science and Engineering Technology*, *10*(6), 2378–2385. doi:10.22214/ijraset.2022.44345

Jagatheesaperumal, S. K., Ahmad, K., Al-Fuqaha, A., & Qadir, J. (2022). Advancing education through extended reality and internet of everything enabled metaverses: applications, challenges, and open issues. *arXiv preprint arXiv:2207.01512*.

Jain, K., & Choi, Y. M. (2020, July). Authoring interactions for tangible augmented reality. In *International Conference on Human-Computer Interaction* (pp. 43-50). Springer.

Jamieson-Proctor, R., Albion, P., Finger, G., Cavanagh, R., Fitzgerald, R., Bond, T., & Grimbeek, P. (2013). Development of the TTF TPACK Survey Instrument. *Australian Educational Computing*, *27*(3), 26–35.

Jang, J., Ko, Y., Shin, W. S., & Han, I. (2021). Augmented reality and virtual reality for learning: An examination using an extended technology acceptance model. *IEEE Access : Practical Innovations, Open Solutions*, *9*, 6798–6809. doi:10.1109/ACCESS.2020.3048708

Jauhiainen, J. S., Krohn, C., & Junnila, J. (2022). Metaverse and Sustainability: Systematic Review of Scientific Publications until 2022 and Beyond. *Sustainability (Basel)*, *15*(1), 346. doi:10.3390/su15010346

Javeed, F., Shahzad, B., Shaikh, A., Reshan, A., Saleh, M., Ahmad, S., ... Rajab, K. (2022). Strengthening Software Make vs. Buy Decision: A Mixed-Method Approach. *Intelligent Automation & Soft Computing, 32*(1), 193–205. Advance online publication. doi:10.32604/iasc.2022.021769

JhaA. K. (2020). *Understanding Generation Alpha.* Researchgate. https://doi.org/ doi:10.31219/osf.io/d2e8g

Jin, Y., & Schmidt-Crawford, D. A. (2017). Parents' perceptions of the first-year implementation of a one-to-one laptop initiative in a Midwestern high school. *Computers in the Schools, 34*(1-2), 73–87. doi:10.1080/07380569.2017.1293470

Jirari, H. (2018). Mise en place d'un cours hybride en classe de langue à l'université marocaine : dispositif, approches et action apprenante. Oualili, Cahiers de l'École Normale Supérieure de Meknès, 23, 83-104.

Jobin, K., & Nadeau, P. (2022). *Investir et se développer dans le métavers.* Dunod.

Johnson, A. S., & Sun, Y. (2013, March). *Exploration of spatial augmented reality on person. In 2013 IEEE Virtual Reality (VR).* IEEE.

Johnson, E. R. (1990). *Psychological adjustment of mainstream adolescents: physically disabled and nondisabled.* Arizona State University.

Jorge & Molina. (2009). *Tice-education.* Academic Press.

Jovanović, A., & Milosavljević, A. (2022). VoRtex Metaverse platform for gamified collaborative learning. *Electronics (Basel), 11*(3), 317. doi:10.3390/electronics11030317

Junco, R., & Clem, C. (2015). Predicting course outcomes with digital textbook usage data. *The Internet and Higher Education, 27*, 54–63. doi:10.1016/j.iheduc.2015.06.001

Kaddoura, S., & Al Husseiny, F. (2023). The rising trend of Metaverse in education: Challenges, opportunities, and ethical considerations. *PeerJ. Computer Science, 9*, e1252. doi:10.7717/peerj-cs.1252 PMID:37346578

Kao, G. Y. M., & Ruan, C. A. (2022). Designing and evaluating a high interactive augmented reality system for programming learning. *Computers in Human Behavior, 132*, 107245. doi:10.1016/j.chb.2022.107245

Karahanna, E., & Straub, D. W. (1999). The psychological origins of perceived usefulness and ease-of-use. *Information & Management, 35*(4), 237–250. doi:10.1016/S0378-7206(98)00096-2

Kasiyanto, S., & Kilinc, M. R. (2022). Legal Conundrums of the Metaverse. *Journal of Central Banking Law and Institutions, 1*(2), 299–322. doi:10.21098/jcli.v1i2.25

Kaur, D. P., Mantri, A., & Horan, B. (2020). Enhancing student motivation with use of augmented reality for interactive learning in engineering education. *Procedia Computer Science, 172*, 881–885. doi:10.1016/j.procs.2020.05.127

Kaviyaraj, R., & Uma, M. (2022, January). Augmented reality application in classroom: An immersive taxonomy. In *2022 4th International Conference on Smart Systems and Inventive Technology (ICSSIT)* (pp. 1221-1226). IEEE.

Kelly, N., Thompson, K., & Yeoman, P. (2015). Theory-led Design of Instruments and Representations in Learning Analytics : Developing a Novel Tool for Orchestration of Online Collaborative Learning. *Journal of Learning Analytics, 2*(2), 14–43. doi:10.18608/jla.2015.22.3

Kiat, L. B., Ali, M. B., Abd Halim, N. D., & Ibrahim, H. B. (2016, October). Augmented reality, virtual learning environment and mobile learning in education: A comparison. In *2016 IEEE Conference on e-Learning, e-Management and e-Services (IC3e)* (pp. 23-28). IEEE. 10.1109/IC3e.2016.8009034

Kim, S., Song, K., Lockee, B., Burton, J., Kim, S., Song, K., & Burton, J. (2018). *What is gamification in learning and education?* Springer International Publishing. doi:10.1007/978-3-319-47283-6

King, A. (2019). *Qu'est-ce que le Rapid Learning.* https://myskillcamp.com

Klein, C. (2013). *Les usages du numérique pour l'enseignement.* Academic Press.

Klippel, A., Wallgrün, J. O., Masrur, A., Zhao, J., & LaFemina, P. (2019, March). Warping space and time-xR reviving educational tools of the 19th Century. In *2019 IEEE Conference on Virtual Reality and 3D User Interfaces (VR)* (pp. 1022-1023). IEEE. 10.1109/VR.2019.8797897

Knight, S., Shum, S. B., & Littleton, K. (2014). Epistemology, Assessment, Pedagogy : Where Learning Meets Analytics in the Middle Space. *Journal of Learning Analytics, 1*(2), 23–47. doi:10.18608/jla.2014.12.3

Knox, J. (2022). The Metaverse, or the Serious Business of Tech Frontiers. *Postdigital Science and Education, 4*(2), 207–215. doi:10.1007/s42438-022-00300-9

Knyazev, A., & Cheremukhina, J. (2022, May). Regulatory and methodological support for the mixed reality technology in education. In *2022 2nd International Conference on Technology Enhanced Learning in Higher Education (TELE)* (pp. 37-39). IEEE. 10.1109/TELE55498.2022.9801029

Kocur, D., & Kosc, P. (2009). E-Learing Implementation in Higher Education. *Acta Electrotechnica et Informatica, 9*(1), 20–26.

Kolstee, Y., & Van Eck, W. (2011, October). The augmented Van Gogh's: Augmented reality experiences for museum visitors. In *2011 IEEE International Symposium on Mixed and Augmented Reality-Arts, Media, and Humanities* (pp. 49-52). IEEE. 10.1109/ISMAR-AMH.2011.6093656

Koufaris, M., & Hampton-Sosa, W. (2004). The development of initial trust in an online company by new customers. *Information &amp\mathsemicolon. Information & Management, 41*(3), 377–397. doi:10.1016/j.im.2003.08.004

Koychev, I., Nikolov, R., & Dicheva, R. (2009). Smartbook -The future e-book and educatonal hypermedia. *10th IFIP Working Conference on Virtual Enterprises*, Thessaloniki, Greece.

Kramer, C. (2002). *Success in On Line Learning.* DELMAR Thomson Learning.

Krogh, P. G. (2000, April). Interactive rooms—augmented reality in an architectural perspective. In *Proceedings of DARE 2000 on Designing Augmented Reality Environments* (pp. 135-137). 10.1145/354666.354681

Kroote, L., & Bucher, A. (2007). *Management of Physical Education and Sport.* Academic Press.

Krüger, J. M., Palzer, K., & Bodemer, D. (2022). Learning with augmented reality: Impact of dimensionality and spatial abilities. *Computers and Education Open, 3*, 100065. doi:10.1016/j.caeo.2021.100065

Kumar, A., & Kumar, S. (2021). A new normal. *In the Proceedings of SIGGRAPh '21 Immersive Pavilion,* 1 – 2.

Kumar, V. V., Carberry, D., Beenfeldt, C., Andersson, M. P., Mansouri, S. S., & Gallucci, F. (2021). Virtual reality in chemical and biochemical engineering education and training. *Education for Chemical Engineers, 36*, 143–153. doi:10.1016/j.ece.2021.05.002

Kundu, S. N., Muhammad, N., & Sattar, F. (2017, December). Using the augmented reality sandbox for advanced learning in geoscience education. In *2017 IEEE 6th International Conference on Teaching, Assessment, and Learning for Engineering (TALE)* (pp. 13-17). IEEE. 10.1109/TALE.2017.8252296

Kurniawan, M. P., Purwanto, A., & Mansur, M. F. (2019, November). Augmented Reality of Android-based learning media of sun and earth structure. In *2019 4th International Conference on Information Technology, Information Systems and Electrical Engineering (ICITISEE)* (pp. 85-90). IEEE. 10.1109/ICITISEE48480.2019.9003985

Kurzweil, R. (2007). *Humanité 2.0. La bible du changement* [The Singularity is Near: When Humans Transcend Biology]. Academic Press.

Kye, B., Han, N., Kim, E., Park, Y., & Jo, S. (2021). Educational applications of metaverse: Possibilities and limitations. *Journal of Educational Evaluation for Health Professions*, *18*, 32. doi:10.3352/jeehp.2021.18.32 PMID:34897242

Lahlali, A., Chafiq, N., Radid, M., Moundy, K., & Srour, C. (2023). The Effect of Integrating Interactive Simulations on the Development of Students' Motivation, Engagement, Interaction and School Results. *International Journal of Emerging Technologies in Learning*, *18*(12), 193–207. doi:10.3991/ijet.v18i12.39755

Lakshmiprabha, N. S., Santos, A., Mladenov, D., & Beltramello, O. (2014, September). [Poster] An augmented and virtual reality system for training autistic children. In *2014 IEEE International Symposium on Mixed and Augmented Reality (ISMAR)* (pp. 277-278). IEEE. 10.1109/ISMAR.2014.6948448

Lampropoulos, G., Keramopoulos, E., & Diamantaras, K. (2020). Enhancing the functionality of augmented reality using deep learning, semantic web and knowledge graphs: A review. *Visual Informatics*, *4*(1), 32–42. doi:10.1016/j.visinf.2020.01.001

Lamrany-Alaoui, R. (1998). Le scientifique, l'expression, et la communication. Recherches pédagogiques. *Revue de l'AMEF*, *7*, 15–22.

Landrum, R. E., Gurung, R. A. R., & Spann, N. (2012). Assesments of textbook usage and the relarionship to student course performance. *College Teaching*, *60*(1), 17–24. doi:10.1080/87567555.2011.609573

Lang, T., MacIntyre, B., & Zugaza, I. J. (2008, March). *Massively multiplayer online worlds as a platform for augmented reality experiences. In 2008 IEEE Virtual Reality Conference*. IEEE.

Lebrun, M. (2011). Impacts des TIC sur la qualité des apprentissages des étudiants et le développement professionnel des enseignants : vers une approche systémique. STICEF (Sciences et Technologies de l'Information et de la Communication pour l'Éducation et la Formation), 18, 20.

Lebrun, M. (2002). *Theories and Pedagogical Methods for Teaching and Learning. What is the Role of ICT in Education? col. Perspectives in Education and Training*. De Boeck University.

Lebrun, M. (2011). Impacts des TIC sur la qualité des apprentissages des étudiants et le développement professionnel des enseignants: Vers une approche systémique. *Sciences et Technologies de l'Information et de la Communication pour l'Éducation et la Formation*, *18*(1), 287–316. doi:10.3406/stice.2011.1028

Lebrun, M., & Lecoq, J. (2015). *Flipped Classes, Teaching and Learning the Right Way!* Canope Editions.

Leclercq, D., & Denis, B. (1998). Objectifs et paradigmes d'enseignement/apprentissage. In Pour une pédagogie universitaire de qualité. Mardaga.

Leduc, S., Valléry, G., Bellhari, S., & Gaston, S. (2013). *Ergonomie des interfaces logicielles : Recommandations pour la conception, le développement et l'évaluation des applications*. Hermès.

Lee, L. C., Braud, T., Zhou, P., Wang, L., Xu, D., Lin, Z., Kumar, A., Bermejo, C., & Hui, P. (2021). *All One Needs to Know about Metaverse: A Complete Survey on Technological Singularity, Virtual Ecosystem, and Research Agenda*. arXiv (Cornell University). https://doi.org//arxiv.2110.05352 doi:10.48550

Lee, L. H., Braud, T., Zhou, P., Wang, L., Xu, D., Lin, Z., . . . Hui, P. (2021). All one needs to know about metaverse: A complete survey on technological singularity, virtual ecosystem, and research agenda. *arXiv preprint arXiv:2110.05352.*

Lee, L.-H., Braud, T., Zhou, P., Wang, L., Xu, D., Lin, Z., … Hui, P. (2021). All One Needs to Know about Metaverse : A Complete Survey on Technological Singularity, Virtual Ecosystem, and Research Agenda. *ArXiv, abs/2110.05352.*

Lee, H.-H., & Kim, J. (2008). The effects of shopping orientations on consumers' satisfaction with product search and purchases in a multi-channel environment. *Journal of Fashion Marketing and Management*, *12*(2), 193–216. doi:10.1108/13612020810874881

Lee, J.-S., Cho, H., Gay, G., Davidson, B., & Ingraffea, A. (2003). Technology acceptance and social networking in distance learning. *Journal of Educational Technology & Society*, *6*(2), 50–61.

Lee, W., Jeong, P., Choi, H., Kim, J., & Moon, B. (2022). Online illumination learning for interactive global illumination in augmented reality. *IEEE Access : Practical Innovations, Open Solutions*, *10*, 109498–109509. doi:10.1109/ACCESS.2022.3214516

Legendre, R. (2005). Dictionnaire actuel de l'éducation (3e éd.). Guérin éditeur Montréal.

Legris, P., Ingham, J., & Collerette, P. (2003). Why do people use information technology? A critical review of the technology acceptance model. *Information & Mathsemicolon. Information & Management*, *40*(3), 191–204. doi:10.1016/S0378-7206(01)00143-4

Leiva, G., Grønbæk, J. E., Klokmose, C. N., Nguyen, C., Kazi, R. H., & Asente, P. (2021, October). Rapido: Prototyping Interactive AR Experiences through Programming by Demonstration. In *The 34th Annual ACM Symposium on User Interface Software and Technology* (pp. 626-637). ACM.

Lengsfeld, J. (2019). *Digital era framework.* Academic Press.

Liao, S. C., & Kuo, M. J. (2020, November). An analysis for motivating sketching practice with augmented reality in Da Vinci Eye. In *2020 International Symposium on Computer, Consumer and Control (IS3C)* (pp. 95-97). IEEE. 10.1109/IS3C50286.2020.00032

Liao, Y. T., Yu, C. H., & Wu, C. C. (2015, April). Learning geometry with augmented reality to enhance spatial ability. In *2015 International Conference on Learning and Teaching in Computing and Engineering* (pp. 221-222). IEEE. 10.1109/LaTiCE.2015.40

Lichty, P. (2020). Making inside the augment: Augmented reality and art/design education. In *Augmented Reality in Education* (pp. 261–278). Springer. doi:10.1007/978-3-030-42156-4_15

Li, G., Liu, Y., & Wang, Y. (2018, December). An empirical evaluation of labelling method in augmented reality. In *Proceedings of the 16th ACM SIGGRAPH International Conference on Virtual-Reality Continuum and its Applications in Industry* (pp. 1-9). 10.1145/3284398.3284422

Li, M. (2023). Chinese mathematics teachers' TPACK and attitudes toward ICT integration in the post-pandemic era. *Eurasia Journal of Mathematics, Science and Technology Education*, *19*(7), em2301. Advance online publication. doi:10.29333/ejmste/13346

Lin, H., Wan, S., Gan, W., Chen, J., & Chao, H. C. (2022). Metaverse in education: Vision, opportunities, and challenges. In *2022 IEEE International Conference on Big Data (Big Data)* (pp. 2857-2866). IEEE.

Linard, M. (2001). *ICT: Tools for Teaching and Learning Differently.* http://www.scolanet.org

Lin, Y. T. (2019). Impacts of a flipped classroom with a smart learning diagnosis system on students' learning performance, perception, and problem-solving ability in a software engineering course. *Computers in Human Behavior, 95*, 187–196. doi:10.1016/j.chb.2018.11.036

Liu, W., Lai, B., Wang, C., Bian, X., Yang, W., Xia, Y., ... Li, J. (2020, March). Learning to match 2d images and 3d lidar point clouds for outdoor augmented reality. In *2020 IEEE Conference on Virtual Reality and 3D User Interfaces Abstracts and Workshops (VRW)* (pp. 654-655). IEEE. 10.1109/VRW50115.2020.00178

Li, X. Z., Chen, C. C., & Kang, X. (2022, July). Research on Intangible cultural heritage education inheritance based on augmented reality technology. In *2022 IEEE International Conference on Consumer Electronics-Taiwan* (pp. 49-50). IEEE. 10.1109/ICCE-Taiwan55306.2022.9869146

Li, Y., Hicks, D., Lages, W. S., Lee, S. W., Sharma, A., & Bowman, D. A. (2021, March). ARCritique: Supporting remote design critique of physical artifacts through collaborative augmented reality. In *2021 IEEE Conference on Virtual Reality and 3D User Interfaces Abstracts and Workshops (VRW)* (pp. 585-586). IEEE. 10.1109/VRW52623.2021.00175

Liying, F., Weng, N. G., Liyao, M., Maozheng, F., & Xiaoping, Q. (2021, December). Research on the application of augmented reality technology in the transformation and development of cultural and creative industries. In *International Conference on Intelligent Technologies for Interactive Entertainment* (pp. 295-308). Springer.

Logan, S. W., Webster, E. K., Getchell, N., Pfeiffer, K. A., & Robinson, L. E. (2013). Relationship between fundamental motor skill competence and physical activity during childhood and adolescence: A systematic review. *Kinesiology Review (Champaign, Ill.), 2*(4), 317–337. doi:10.1123/kr.2013-0012

Lopes, A. P., & Soares, F. (2018). Perception and performance in a flipped Financial Mathe-matics classroom. *International Journal of Management Education, 16*(1), 105–113. doi:10.1016/j.ijme.2018.01.001

Lunding, M. S., Grønbæk, J. E. S., Bilstrup, K. E. K., Sørensen, M. L. S. K., & Petersen, M. G. (2022, April). ExposAR: Bringing augmented reality to the computational thinking agenda through a collaborative authoring tool. In *CHI Conference on Human Factors in Computing Systems* (pp. 1-14). 10.1145/3491102.3517636

M'rhaouarh, I., Chafiq, N., & Namir, A. (2021, November). Toward Using Cloud Computing at Universities in Developing Countries Considering the Covid-19 Crisis. *The Proceedings of the International Conference on Smart City Applications* (pp. 733-743). Cham: Springer International Publishing.

M'Rhaouarh, I., Moutamanni, H., Labzai, A., Namir, A., & Chafiq, N. (2021). Mathematical modeling and optimal control of abstaining attitude of could computing adoption. *Journal of Mathematical and Computational Science, 11*(4), 4411–4427.

M'rhaouarh, I., Namir, A., & Chafiq, N. (2021). The use of the performance measures of queuing model to optimize profit in a Cloud Computing environment. *International Journal of Computer Science and Information Security, 19*(11). Advance online publication. doi:10.5281/zenodo.5831851

Maaloul, I., & Mezghani, L. (2003). L'implantation des ERP et ingénierie du changement : Les déterminants de la satisfaction des utilisateurs d'un ERP dans les entreprises tunisiennes. *XIIème Conférence de l'Association Internationale de Management Stratégique*.

Macfadyen, L. P., Lockyer, L., & Rienties, B. (2020). Learning design and learning analytics : Snapshot 2020. *Journal of Learning Analytics, 7*(3), 6–12. doi:10.18608/jla.2020.73.2

Madiega, T., Car, P., Niestadt, M., & Van de Pol, L. (2022). *Metaverse Opportunities, risks and policy implications. Members' Research Service PE 733.557*. European Parliamentary Research Service.

Maguire, M. (2020, July). An exploration of low-fidelity prototyping methods for augmented and virtual reality. In *International Conference on Human-Computer Interaction* (pp. 470-481). Springer. 10.1007/978-3-030-49760-6_33

Maier, P., & Klinker, G. (2013, September). Augmented chemical reactions: An augmented reality tool to support chemistry teaching. In *2013 2nd Experiment@ International Conference (exp. at'13)* (pp. 164-165). IEEE.

Makoza, F. (2022). A Review of Critical Studies on National ICT Policy in the Context of Africa. *International Journal of Information Systems and Social Change*, *13*(1), 1–22. doi:10.4018/IJISSC.303601

Mamathah, R. S. (2016). Students Perceptions of E-Learning. Department of Behavioural Sciences and Learning, Linkoping University.

Mangenot, F. (2002). *Pedagogical and Institutional Integration of ICT. Psychology of Learning and Multimedia.* Armand Colin.

Mangenot, F., & Louveau, É. (2006). *Internet and the Language Classroom.* CLE-International.

Mangina, E. (2017, October). 3D learning objects for augmented/virtual reality educational ecosystems. In *2017 23rd International Conference on virtual system & Multimedia (VSMM)* (pp. 1-6). IEEE.

Manichander, T. (Ed.). (2015). *Emerging issues in education.* Laxmi Book Publication.

Manzano-León, A., Camacho-Lazarraga, P., Guerrero, M. A., Guerrero-Puerta, L., Aguilar-Parra, J. M., Trigueros, R., & Alias, A. (2021). Between level up and game over: A systematic literature review of gamification in education. *Sustainability (Basel)*, *13*(4), 2247. doi:10.3390/su13042247

Maqableh, W. F., & Sidhu, M. S. (2010, March). From boards to augmented reality learning. In *2010 International Conference on Information Retrieval & Knowledge Management (CAMP)* (pp. 184-187). IEEE. 10.1109/INFRKM.2010.5466920

Marc, M. (2017). *Dispositifs technologiques en EPS et convergence numérique.* Academic Press.

Martin, F., & Snider, J. (2012). Developing Mobile Based Instruction. *TechTrends*, *56*(5), 46–51. doi:10.1007/s11528-012-0598-9

Matsui, T., & Tsukamoto, S. I. (1991). Relation between career self-efficacy measures based on occupational titles and Holland codes and model environments : A methodological contribution. *Journal of Vocational Behavior*, *38*(1), 78–91. doi:10.1016/0001-8791(91)90019-I

Maxwell, J. A. (2016). Expanding the history and range of mixed methods research. *Journal of Mixed Methods Research*, *10*(1), 12–27. doi:10.1177/1558689815571132

Mazouak, A. (2007). *Les orientations pédagogiques 2007.* Academic Press.

McHaney, R., Reiter, L., & Reychav, I. (2018). Immersive simulation in constructivist-based classroom e-learning. *International Journal on E-Learning*, *17*(1), 39–64.

Memaï, A., & Rouag, A. (2017). Le manuel scolaire: Au-delà de l'outil pédagogique, l'objet politico-social. *Éducation et socialisation*, 43. doi:10.4000/edso.2014

Merceron, A., Blikstein, P., & Siemens, G. (2016). Learning analytics : From big data to meaningful data. *Journal of Learning Analytics*, *2*(3), 4–8. doi:10.18608/jla.2015.23.2

Merchant, Z., Goetz, E. T., Cifuentes, L., Keeney-Kennicutt, W., & Davis, T. J. (2014). *Effectiveness of virtual reality-based instruction on students' learning outcomes in K-12 and higher education: A meta-analysis.* Elsevier. doi:10.1016/j.compedu.2013.07.033

Messaoudi, F. (2013). *Dispositifs de e-Learning*. Academic Press.

Michaud, T. (2017). Julien PÉQUIGNOT et François-Gabriel ROUSSEL (dir.) (2015), Les métavers. Dispositifs, usages et représentations. *Communication, 34*(2). Advance online publication. doi:10.4000/communication.7166

Mikropoulos, T. A., Delimitros, M., Gaintatzis, P., Iatraki, G., Stergiouli, A., Tsiara, A., & Kalyvioti, K. (2020, June). Acceptance and user experience of an augmented reality system for the simulation of sensory overload in children with autism. In *2020 6th International Conference of the Immersive Learning Research Network (iLRN)* (pp. 86-92). IEEE. 10.23919/iLRN47897.2020.9155113

Miles, M. B., Huberman, A. M., & Saldana, J. (2019). *Qualitative Data Analysis, A Methods Sourcebook* (4th ed.). Arizona State University.

Milgram, P., & Kishino, F. (1994). A taxonomy of mixed reality visual displays. *IEICE Transactions on Information and Systems, 77*(12), 1321–1329.

Ministère de l'Education Nationale, Département de la Technologie. (2002). *Compétice*. https://urlz.fr/mLjO

Mohamed, B., & Mohamed, B. (2012, July). Proposition of a 3d pattern for e-learning augmented reality applications based on artoolkit library. In *International Conference on Education and e-Learning Innovations* (pp. 1-4). IEEE. 10.1109/ICEELI.2012.6360672

Mohammed, A. D., Khalil, N., Mohssine, B., Rachida, I., Soufiane, B., & Mohammed, T. (2019). Using students' data to improve the quality of the education in Moroccan institution. *International Journal of Open Information Technologies, 7*(11), 59–65.

Mohssine, B., Bouzekri, T., & Mohammed, T. (2019). Integration of a Computer Device for Learning and Training Situations : The Case of Faculty of Sciences Ben M'sik (FSBM). *International Journal of Emerging Technologies in Learning, 14*(03), 243–249. doi:10.3991/ijet.v14i03.9355

Molnár, G., & Sik, D. (2019, October). Smart devices, smart environments, smart students-A review on educational opportunities in virtual and augmented reality learning environments. In *2019 10th IEEE International Conference on Cognitive Infocommunications (CogInfoCom)* (pp. 495-498). IEEE. 10.1109/CogInfoCom47531.2019.9089984

Monaco, S., & Sacchi, G. (2023). Travelling the metaverse: Potential benefits and main challenges for tourism sectors and research applications. *Sustainability (Basel), 15*(4), 3348. doi:10.3390/su15043348

Morieux, M. (2014). *De l'innovation à l'intégration*. Academic Press.

Motejlek, J., & Alpay, E. (2021). Taxonomy of virtual and augmented reality applications in education. *IEEE Transactions on Learning Technologies, 14*(3), 415–429. doi:10.1109/TLT.2021.3092964

Motokawa, Y., & Saito, H. (2006, October). Support system for guitar playing using augmented reality display. In *2006 IEEE/ACM International Symposium on Mixed and Augmented Reality* (pp. 243-244). IEEE. 10.1109/ISMAR.2006.297825

Moundy, K., Chafiq, N., & Talbi, M. (2021). Comparative Analysis of Student Engagement in Digital Textbook Use during Quarantine. *Education Sciences, 11*(7), 352. doi:10.3390/educsci11070352

Moundy, K., Chafiq, N., & Talbi, M. (2022a). Digital textbook and flipped classroom: Experimentation of the self-learning method based on the development of soft skills and disciplinary knowledge. *International Journal of Emerging Technologies in Learning, 17*(7), 240–259. doi:10.3991/ijet.v17i07.28933

Moundy, K., Chafiq, N., & Talbi, M. (2022b). A Model for Scripting and Designing a Digital Textbook. *International Journal of Emerging Technologies in Learning, 17*(21), 296–311. doi:10.3991/ijet.v17i21.34603

Mrisse, F. E., Chafiq, N., Talbi, M., & Moundy, K. (2023). The Practices of Online Assessment in a Digital Device in the Context of University Training: The Case of Hassan II University. *International Journal of Advanced Computer Science and Applications, 14*(1). Advance online publication. doi:10.14569/IJACSA.2023.0140148

Murillo-Zamorano, L. R., López Sánchez, J. N., & Godoy-Caballero, A. L. (2019). How the flipped classroom affects knowledge, skills, and engagement in higher education: Effects on students' satisfaction. *Computers & Education, 141*, 103608. doi:10.1016/j.compedu.2019.103608

Murodillaevich, N. F., Eshpulatovich, G. U., & Kuvondik, K. (2020, November). Improve teaching and learning approach 3D primitives with Virtual and Augmented Reality. In *2020 International Conference on Information Science and Communications Technologies (ICISCT)* (pp. 1-7). IEEE. 10.1109/ICISCT50599.2020.9351418

Mwenisongole, C. (2021). *Information Communication Technology Through Technical Vocational Education and Training: Experiences from Arusha Tanzania*. The Open University of Tanzania.

Mystakidis, S. (2022). Metaverse. *Metaverse. Encyclopedia, 2*(1), 486–497. doi:10.3390/encyclopedia2010031

Nadi-Ravandi, S., & Batooli, Z. (2022). Gamification in education: A scientometric, content and co-occurrence analysis of systematic review and meta-analysis articles. *Education and Information Technologies, 27*(7), 10207–10238. doi:10.1007/s10639-022-11048-x PMID:35431599

Nantel, J.-A., & Tellier, C. (1992). L'achat par services télématisés : Qui en sont les utilisateurs et pourquoi? *Technologies de l'Informatique et Société, 4*(3), 333-350.

Nanthanasit, A., & Wongta, N. (2018, February). Approach augmented reality real-time rendering for understanding light and shade in art education. In *2018 International Conference on Digital Arts, Media and Technology (ICDAMT)* (pp. 71-74). IEEE. 10.1109/ICDAMT.2018.8376498

Narcy-Combes, J.-P. (2005). *Didactique des langues et TIC : vers une recherche-action responsable*. Ophrys.

Narcy-Combes, J.-P. (2005). *Language Teaching and ICT: Towards Responsible Action Research*. Ophrys.

National Council for Curriculum and Assessment (NCCA). (2020). *Draft primary curriculum framework*. NCCA, Department of Education, Government of Ireland.

Nejjari, A., & Bakkali, I. (2017). L'usage des TIC à l'école marocaine : état des lieux et perspectives. *Hermès, La Revue, 78*, 55-61. https://doi.org/10.3917/herm.078.0055

Nejjari, A., & Bakkali, I. (2017). *L'usage des TIC à l'école marocaine: état des lieux et perspectives*. Academic Press.

Ngugi, J., & Goosen, L. (2019, October 25). Towards Smart Innovation for Information Systems and Technology Students: Modelling Motivation, Metacognition and Affective Aspects of Learning. Smart Innovation, Systems and Technologies, 111, 90-99. doi:10.1007/978-3-030-03577-8_11

Nguyen, Q., Rienties, B., & Whitelock, D. (2020). A Mixed-Method Study of How Instructors Design for Learning in Online and Distance Education. *Journal of Learning Analytics, 7*(3), 64–78. doi:10.18608/jla.2020.73.6

Nguyen, V. T., & Dang, T. (2017, October). Setting up virtual reality and augmented reality learning environment in unity. In *2017 IEEE International Symposium on Mixed and Augmented Reality (ISMAR-Adjunct)* (pp. 315-320). IEEE. 10.1109/ISMAR-Adjunct.2017.97

Nie, G. Y., Liu, Y., Wang, C., Liu, Y., & Wang, Y. (2019, March). Exploring stereovision-based 3-D scene reconstruction for augmented reality. In *2019 IEEE Conference on Virtual Reality and 3D User Interfaces (VR)* (pp. 1100-1101). IEEE. 10.1109/VR.2019.8797778

Ning, H., Wang, H., Lin, Y., Wang, W., Dhelim, S., Farha, F., ... Daneshmand, M. (2023). A Survey on the Metaverse : The State-of-the-Art, Technologies, Applications, and Challenges. *IEEE Internet of Things Journal.*

Nissen, E. (2006). Scénarios de communication en ligne dans des formations hybrides. *Les échanges en ligne dans l'apprentissage et la formation - Le français dans le monde - Recherches et applications*, 44-58. http://edutice.archives-ouvertes.fr/edutice-00124819

Noorasura, A. D., & Sazilah, S. (2011, June). A model of mobile learning object design for concept comprehension using reciprocal teaching strategies and augmented reality. In *2011 IEEE International Conference on Computer Science and Automation Engineering* (Vol. 3, pp. 717-720). IEEE. 10.1109/CSAE.2011.5952775

Nooteboom, B. (2000). *Trust as a governance device. In Cultural factors in economic growth.* Springer.

Norouzi, N., Kim, K., Bruder, G., Bailenson, J. N., Wisniewski, P., & Welch, G. F. (2022). The advantages of virtual dogs over virtual people: Using augmented reality to provide social support in stressful situations. *International Journal of Human-Computer Studies, 165*, 102838. doi:10.1016/j.ijhcs.2022.102838

Nunan, D. (2004). *Task-based Language Teaching.* Cambridge University Press. doi:10.1017/CBO9780511667336

Ochoa, X., & Worsley, M. (2016). Editorial : Augmenting Learning Analytics with Multimodal Sensory Data. *Journal of Learning Analytics*, *3*(2), 213–219. doi:10.18608/jla.2016.32.10

Oliveira, T. A., Marranghello, N., Silva, A. C. R., & Pereira, A. S. (2018). Virtual laboratories development using 3D environments. In *Virtual and augmented reality: Concepts, methodologies, tools, and applications* (pp. 733–758). IGI Global. doi:10.4018/978-1-5225-5469-1.ch035

Ornstein, A. C., Levine, D. U., Gutek, G., & Vocke, D. E. (2016). *Foundations of education.* Cengage Learning.

Ortiz, J. S., Guevara, B. S., Espinosa, E. G., Santana, J., Tamayo, L. R., & Andaluz, V. H. (2020, June). 3D virtual content for education applications. In *2020 15th Iberian Conference on Information Systems and Technologies (CISTI)* (pp. 1-5). IEEE.

Osato, Y., & Koizumi, N. (2020). Compact optical system displaying mid-air images movable in depth by rotating light source and mirror. *Computers & Graphics*, *91*, 290–300. doi:10.1016/j.cag.2020.08.006

Oswald, P., Tost, J., & Wettach, R. (2014, November). The real augmented reality: real-time game editor in a spatial augmented environment. In *Proceedings of the 11th Conference on Advances in Computer Entertainment Technology* (pp. 1-4). 10.1145/2663806.2663853

Otto, J. E., & Ritchie, J. B. (1995). Exploring the quality of the service experience: A theoretical and empirical analysis. *Advances in Services Marketing and Management, 4*(1), 37-61.

Outhwaite, L. A., Faulder, M., Gulliford, A., & Pitchford, N. J. (2019). Raising early achievement in math with interactive apps: A randomized control trial. *Journal of Educational Psychology*, *111*(2), 284–298. doi:10.1037/edu0000286 PMID:30774149

Öza, G. Z., & Abaan, S. (2021). Use of a flipped classroom "Leadership in Nursing" course on nursing students' achievement and experiences: A quasi-experimental study. *Journal of Professional Nursing*, *37*(3), 562–571. doi:10.1016/j.profnurs.2021.02.001 PMID:34016315

Palomino, P. T., Toda, A. M., Oliveira, W., Cristea, A. I., & Isotani, S. (2019). Narrative for gamification in education: why should you care? In *2019 IEEE 19th International Conference on Advanced Learning Technologies (ICALT)* (Vol. 2161, pp. 97-99). IEEE. 10.1109/ICALT.2019.00035

Panessai, I. Y., Iksan, N., Zahari, S. A., Abdulbaqi, A. S., Modi Lakulu, M. M. B., Husin, M. R., . . . Wahyudiono, P. H. (2021, March). Learning Internet of Things by using augmented reality. In *2021 the 5th International Conference on Virtual and Augmented Reality Simulations* (pp. 17-20). 10.1145/3463914.3463926

Park, S. M., & Kim, Y. (2022). A metaverse: Taxonomy, components, applications, and open challenges. *IEEE Access : Practical Innovations, Open Solutions, 10*, 4209–4251. doi:10.1109/ACCESS.2021.3140175

Park, S., & Kim, S. (2022). Identifying world types to deliver gameful experiences for sustainable learning in the metaverse. *Sustainability (Basel), 14*(3), 1361. doi:10.3390/su14031361

Patil, S., Prabhu, C., Neogi, O., Joshi, A. R., & Katre, N. (2016, August). E-learning system using Augmented Reality. In *2016 International Conference on Computing Communication Control and automation (ICCUBEA)* (pp. 1-5). IEEE.

Pavlou, P. A. (2003). Consumer acceptance of electronic commerce : Integrating trust and risk with the technology acceptance model. *International Journal of Electronic Commerce, 7*(3), 101–134. doi:10.1080/10864415.2003.11044275

Peng, N., & Dredze, M. (2016). Improving named entity recognition for chinese social media with word segmentation representation learning. *arXiv preprint arXiv:1603.00786.* doi:10.18653/v1/P16-2025

Pereira, L. F., da Silva, M. M., Roberto, R. A., Teichrieb, V., & Cavalcante, P. S. (2020, November). Virtual playground: An augmented reality application to improve English learning. In *2020 22nd Symposium on Virtual and Augmented Reality (SVR)* (pp. 83-91). IEEE.

Pérez-López, D., Contero, M., & Alcaniz, M. (2010, July). Collaborative development of an augmented reality application for digestive and circulatory systems teaching. In *2010 10th IEEE International Conference on Advanced Learning Technologies* (pp. 173-175). IEEE. 10.1109/ICALT.2010.54

Perez-Sanagustin, M., Hernández-Leo, D., Santos, P., Kloos, C. D., & Blat, J. (2014). Augmenting reality and formality of informal and non-formal settings to enhance blended learning. *IEEE Transactions on Learning Technologies, 7*(2), 118–131. doi:10.1109/TLT.2014.2312719

Petrigna, L., & Musumeci, G. (2022). The Metaverse: A New Challenge for the Healthcare System: A Scoping Review. *Journal of Functional Morphology and Kinesiology, 7*(3), 63. doi:10.3390/jfmk7030063 PMID:36135421

Pew Research Center. (2014). *E-Reading Rises as Device Ownership jumps.* WayBackMachine. https://web.archive.org/web/20140327053903/http://www.pewinternet.org/files/old-media/Files/Reports/2014/PIP_E-reading_011614.pdf

Pisano, S. (2018). *Students' experiences with games and their academic potential: An interpretative phenomenological analysis* [Doctoral dissertation]. Northeastern University.

Plano Clark, V. L., & Ivankova, N. V. (2015). *Mixed methods research: A guide to the field* (Vol. 3). Sage publications.

Poellhuber, B., Racette, N., & Chirchi, M. (2012). De la présence dans la distance par la visioconférence Web. *Revue internationale des technologies en pédagogie universitaire, 9*, 63-77. https://doi.org/10.7202/1012903ar

Polikoff, M. S., & Porter, A. C. (2014). Instructional alignment as a measure of teaching quality. *Educational Evaluation and Policy Analysis, 36*(4), 399–416. doi:10.3102/0162373714531851

Pondiwa, S., El Nabahany, U., & Phiri, M. (2022). Integration of ICT into education: Lessons learnt at the State University of Zanzibar and the Midlands State University in Zimbabwe. In *Computer-Mediated Communication* (Vol. 135). Intechopen. doi:10.5772/intechopen.98441

Poth, C., & Munce, S. E. (2020). Commentary—Preparing today's researchers for a yet unknown tomorrow: Promising practices for a synergistic and sustainable mentoring approach to mixed methods research learning. *International Journal of Multiple Research Approaches, 12*(1), 56–64. doi:10.29034/ijmra.v12n1commentary

Pothier, M. (2003). *Multimédias, dispositifs d'apprentissage et acquisition des langues.* Ophrys.

Prabadevi, B., Deepa, N., Victor, N., Gadekallu, T. R., Maddikunta, P. K. R., Yenduri, G., . . . Liyanage, M. (2023). Metaverse for Industry 5.0 in NextG Communications: Potential Applications and Future Challenges. *arXiv preprint arXiv:2308.02677.*

Pranoto, H., & Panggabean, F. M. (2019). Increase the interest in learning by implementing augmented reality: Case studies studying rail transportation. *Procedia Computer Science, 157*, 506–513. doi:10.1016/j.procs.2019.09.007

Qazdar, A., Er-Raha, B., Cherkaoui, C., & Mammass, D. (2019). A machine learning algorithm framework for predicting students performance : A case study of baccalaureate students in Morocco. *Education and Information Technologies, 24*(6), 3577-3589. doi:10.1007/s10639-019-09946-8

Rabah, J., Cassidy, R., & Beauchemin, R. (2018). Gamification in education: Real benefits or edutainment. In *17th European Conference on e-Learning, Athens, Greece* (pp. 489-497). Academic Press.

Radu, I., & Antle, A. (2017, March). Embodied learning mechanics and their relationship to usability of handheld augmented reality. In *2017 IEEE Virtual Reality Workshop on K-12 Embodied Learning through Virtual & Augmented Reality (KELVAR)* (pp. 1-5). IEEE. 10.1109/KELVAR.2017.7961561

Radwan, O., Razak, A. Z., & Ghavifekr, S. (2019). The mediating effect of organisational culture on academic leadership skills and students' skill-based learning outcomes in saudi higher education. *Malaysian Online Journal of Educational Management, 8*(1), 39–57. doi:10.22452/mojem/vol8no1.3

Rambach, J., Pagani, A., & Stricker, D. (2023). Principles of Object Tracking and Mapping. In *Springer Handbook of Augmented Reality* (pp. 53–84). Springer International Publishing. doi:10.1007/978-3-030-67822-7_3

Reich, J., Tingley, D., Leder-Luis, J., Roberts, M. E., & Stewart, B. (2014). Computer-Assisted Reading and Discovery for Student Generated Text in Massive Open Online Courses. *Journal of Learning Analytics, 2*(1), 156–184. doi:10.18608/jla.2015.21.8

Resch, G., Manzone, J., Welsh, T., Nitsche, M., & Mazalek, A. (2021, July). Goal-directed reaching in real, augmented, and virtual environments. In *2021 International Conference on Advanced Learning Technologies (ICALT)* (pp. 398-400). IEEE. 10.1109/ICALT52272.2021.00127

Resnyansky, D., Billinghurst, M., & Lee, G. (2022, March). A tangible augmented reality programming learning environment for textual languages. In *2022 IEEE Conference on Virtual Reality and 3D User Interfaces Abstracts and Workshops (VRW)* (pp. 662-663). IEEE. 10.1109/VRW55335.2022.00182

Richter, S., & Richter, A. (2023). What is novel about the Metaverse? *International Journal of Information Management, 73*, 102684. doi:10.1016/j.ijinfomgt.2023.102684

Ripka, G., Tiede, J., Grafe, S., & Latoschik, M. E. (2020). *Teaching and Learning Processes in Immersive VR – Comparing Expectations of Preservice Teachers and Teacher Educators.* Academic Press.

Robert, J-P. (2008). Practical Dictionary of FFL Didactics. In Essential French (2nd ed.). Ophrys.

Roblox Corporation. (2022, November 1). *The New School's Parsons School of Design and Roblox Partner to Educate on Digital Fashion Design and Trends.* Roblox Corporation. Available at: https://corp.roblox.com/2022/11/01/the-new-schools-parsons-school-of-design-and-roblox-partner-to-educate-on-digital-fashion-design-and-trends/

Roblox Corporation. (2023, August 28). *Curiosity*. Roblox Corporation. Available at: https://www.robloxschool.com/

Rodríguez, F. C., Dal Peraro, M., & Abriata, L. A. (2022). Online tools to easily build virtual molecular models for display in augmented and virtual reality on the web. *Journal of Molecular Graphics & Modelling*, *114*, 108164. doi:10.1016/j.jmgm.2022.108164 PMID:35325844

Rodríguez-Miranda, F. P., Pozuelos-Estrada, F. J., & León-Jariego, J. C. (2014). The role of ICT coordinator. Priority and time dedicated to professional functions. *Computers & Education*, *72*, 262–270. doi:10.1016/j.compedu.2013.11.009

Roll, I., & Winne, P. H. (2015). Understanding, evaluating, and supporting self-regulated learning using learning analytics. *Journal of Learning Analytics*, *2*(1), 7–12. doi:10.18608/jla.2015.21.2

Romero, E., Artal-Sevil, J. S., Casanova, O., & Serrano, R. M. (2017). Flipped learning + ICT: An instructional model in higher education. *INTED Proceedings*. 10.21125/inted.2017.2201

Rossum, G. V., & Drake, F. L. (2001). *Python Reference Manual Release 2.1.1*. Academic Press.

Roussel, F. (2015). Culture des métavers et culture académique. *Communication*, *33*(1). Advance online publication. doi:10.4000/communication.5227

Rozinaj, G., Vančo, M., Vargic, R., Minárik, I., & Polakovič, A. (2018, June). Augmented/virtual reality as a tool of self-directed learning. In *2018 25th International Conference on Systems, Signals and Image Processing (IWSSIP)* (pp. 1-5). IEEE.

Salazar, J. L. H., Pacheco-Quispe, R., Cabeza, J. D., Salazar, M. J. H., & Cruzado, J. P. (2020, October). *Augmented reality for solar system learning. In 2020 IEEE ANDESCON*. IEEE.

Salkin, S. (1999). Fear of buying. *Logistics Management and Distribution Report*, *8*(5), 101–104.

Sá, M. J., & Serpa, S. (2023). Metaverse as a learning environment: Some considerations. *Sustainability (Basel)*, *15*(3), 2186. doi:10.3390/su15032186

Sanchez, J. J., & Alemán, E. C. (2011). Teachers' opinion survey on the use of ICT tools to support attendance-based teaching. *Computers & Education*, *56*(3), 911–915. doi:10.1016/j.compedu.2010.11.005

Santos, M. E. C., Chen, A., Taketomi, T., Yamamoto, G., Miyazaki, J., & Kato, H. (2013). Augmented reality learning experiences: Survey of prototype design and evaluation. *IEEE Transactions on Learning Technologies*, *7*(1), 38–56. doi:10.1109/TLT.2013.37

Saparudin, M., Rahayu, A., Hurriyati, R., & Sultan, M. A. (2020). Exploring the role of trust in mobile-banking use by Indonesian customer using unified theory of acceptance and usage technology. *International Journal of Financial Research*, *11*(2), 51–60. doi:10.5430/ijfr.v11n2p51

Saritha, R. C., Mankad, U., Venkataswamy, G., & Bapu, S. B. (2018, December). An augmented reality ecosystem for learning environment. In *2018 IEEE International Conference on Advanced Networks and Telecommunications Systems (ANTS)* (pp. 1-6). IEEE. 10.1109/ANTS.2018.8710093

Saßmannshausen, S. M., Radtke, J., Bohn, N., Hussein, H., Randall, D., & Pipek, V. (2021, June). Citizen-Centered Design in Urban Planning: How Augmented Reality can be used in Citizen Participation Processes. In *Designing Interactive Systems Conference 2021* (pp. 250-265). 10.1145/3461778.3462130

Sawiros, M., Lou, R., & Rawash, M. (2022). Next-gen e-commerce in the metaverse. *2022 IEEE International Symposium.*

Schlemmer, E., & Backes, L. (2018). The Real Virtuality of Metaverses. In Virtual and Augmented Reality: Concepts, Methodologies, Tools, and Applications (pp. 47-64). IGI Global. doi:10.4018/978-1-5225-5469-1.ch003

Schraffenberger, H., & van der Heide, E. (2016, November). Multimodal augmented reality: The norm rather than the exception. In *Proceedings of the 2016 Workshop on Multimodal Virtual and Augmented Reality* (pp. 1-6). 10.1145/3001959.3001960

Scotto, F. (2022). Sculpting in augmented reality. In *International Conference on Human-Computer Interaction* (pp. 91-107). Springer.

SDTICE. (2009). *Les manuels numériques CG*. CNDP. http://www.cndp.fr/crdp-rouen/images/cddp27/pdf/tuic/les_manuels_numeriques_cg.pdf

Sefala, M. C. (2021). *Determination of perceptions of social workers about the employee health and wellness programme at the Polokwane Municipality of Limpopo Province*. University of Limpopo.

Séguin, R. (1989). *L'élaboration des manuels scolaires: Guide méthodologique. Division des sciences de l'éducation contenus et méthodes*. UNESCO.

Selwyn, N. (2019). What's the Problem with Learning Analytics? *Journal of Learning Analytics*, *6*(3), 11–19. doi:10.18608/jla.2019.63.3

Séré, A., & Bassy, A.-M. (2010, juillet). *Le manuel scolaire à l'heure du numérique: Une « nouvelle donne » de la politique des ressources pour l'enseignement* (No 087). Ministère de l'éducation nationale ministère de l'enseignement supérieur et de la recherche. https://www.vie-publique.fr/sites/default/files/rapport/pdf/114000048.pdf

Sewart, D., Keegan, D., & Holmberg, B. (1983). *Distance Education: International Perspectives*. St. Martin's.

Seymour, L., Makanya, W., & Berrangé, S. (2007). End-users' acceptance of enterprise resource planning systems : An investigation of antecedents. *Proceedings of the 6th annual ISOnEworld conference*, 1-22.

Shah, S. S. (2022). Teaching and learning with technology: Effectiveness of ICT integration in schools. *Indonesian Journal of Educational Research and Technology*, *2*(2), 133–140. doi:10.17509/ijert.v2i2.43554

Shanmugam, M., Sudha, M., Lavitha, K., Venkatesan, V. P., & Keerthana, R. (2019, March). Research opportunities on virtual reality and augmented reality: a survey. In *2019 IEEE International Conference on System, Computation, Automation and Networking (ICSCAN)* (pp. 1-6). IEEE. 10.1109/ICSCAN.2019.8878796

Shashaank, N., & Feiner, S. (2022, March). Synesthesia AR: Creating sound-to-color synesthesia in augmented reality. In *2022 IEEE Conference on Virtual Reality and 3D User Interfaces Abstracts and Workshops (VRW)* (pp. 874-875). IEEE.

Shatri, Z. G. (2020). Advantages and disadvantages of using information technology in learning process of students. *Journal of Turkish Science Education*, *17*(3), 420–428.

Shen, D., Laffey, J., Lin, Y., & Huang, X. (2006). Social influence for perceived usefulness and ease-of-use of course delivery systems. *Journal of Interactive Online Learning*, *5*(3), 270–282.

Shen, S., Xu, K., Sotiriadis, M., & Wang, Y. (2022). Exploring the factors influencing the adoption and usage of augmented reality and virtual reality applications in tourism education within the context of COVID-19 pandemic. *Journal of Hospitality, Leisure, Sport and Tourism Education*, *30*, 100373. doi:10.1016/j.jhlste.2022.100373 PMID:35069015

Sheppard, B. H., & Sherman, D. M. (1998). The grammars of trust : A model and general implications. *Academy of Management Review*, *23*(3), 422–437. doi:10.2307/259287

Shin, D.-H., Biocca, F., & Choo, H. (2013). Exploring the user experience of three-dimensional virtual learning environments. *Behaviour & Mathsemicolon Information Technology, 32*(2), 203-214. doi:10.1080/0144929X.2011.606334

Shum, S. B., Ferguson, R., & Martinez-Maldonado, R. (2019). Human-Centred Learning Analytics. *Journal of Learning Analytics*, *6*(2), 1–9. doi:10.18608/jla.2019.62.1

Simon-Liedtke, J. T., & Baraas, R. C. (2022). The Need for Universal Design of eXtended Reality (XR) Technology in Primary and Secondary Education. In *International Conference on Human-Computer Interaction* (pp. 121-141). Springer. 10.1007/978-3-031-06015-1_9

Smart, K. L., & Cappel, J. J. (2006). Students Perceptions of Online Learning: A Comparative Study. *Journal of Information Technology Education*, *5*, 201–219. doi:10.28945/243

Soubrié, T. (2008). A New Framework for Designing ICT Activities: The Communicative Perspective of the CEFR. In *Bizarro, Teaching and Learning Foreign Languages and Cultures Today: What Perspectives?* (pp. 68–81). Areal Editores.

Southgate, E., & Smith, S. P. (2017, March). Designing and conducting research using immersive technologies in schools: Seven observations. In *2017 IEEE Virtual Reality Workshop on K-12 Embodied Learning through Virtual & Augmented Reality (KELVAR)* (pp. 1-3). IEEE. 10.1109/KELVAR.2017.7961564

Stanoevska-Slabeva, K. (2022). Opportunities and challenges of metaverse for education: a literature review. *EDULEARN22 Proceedings*, 10401-10410. 10.21125/edulearn.2022.2527

Statista. (2022, November 28). *Metaverse - Statistics & Facts*. Statista. Available at: https://www.statista.com/topics/8652/metaverse

Stecuła, K. (2022). Virtual Reality Applications Market Analysis—On the Example of Steam Digital Platform. *Informatics (MDPI)*, *9*(4), 100. Advance online publication. doi:10.3390/informatics9040100

Stefan, P., Wucherer, P., Oyamada, Y., Ma, M., Schoch, A., Kanegae, M., & Navab, N. (2014, March). *An AR edutainment system supporting bone anatomy learning. In 2014 IEEE Virtual Reality (VR)*. IEEE.

Steinkuehler, C., & Duncan, S. (2008). Scientific habits of mind in virtual worlds. *Journal of Science Education and Technology*, *17*(6), 530–543. doi:10.1007/s10956-008-9120-8

Stephenson, N. (2003). *Snow crash: A novel*. Spectra.

Storch, N. (2013). *Collaborative Writing in L2 Classrooms*. Multilingual Matters. doi:10.21832/9781847699954

Strelan, P., Osborn, A., & Palmer, E. (2020). The flipped classroom: A meta-analysis of ef-fects on student performance across disciplines and education levels. *Educational Research Review*, *30*, 100314. doi:10.1016/j.edurev.2020.100314

Strong, S. (2006). *Early childhood education and care*. Organization for Economic Co-operation and Development.

Stylianou, A. C., & Jackson, P. J. (2007). A comparative examination of individual differences and beliefs on technology usage : Gauging the role of IT. *Journal of Computer Information Systems*, *47*(4), 11–18.

Sun, J., Gan, W., Chao, H. C., & Yu, P. S. (2022). Metaverse: Survey, applications, security, and opportunities. *arXiv preprint arXiv:2210.07990.*

Sun, R., Haraldsson, H., Zhao, Y., & Belongie, S. (2019, October). Anon-Emoji: An optical see-Through augmented reality system for children with autism spectrum disorders to promote understanding of facial expressions and emotions. In *2019 IEEE International Symposium on Mixed and Augmented Reality Adjunct (ISMAR-Adjunct)* (pp. 448-450). IEEE. 10.1109/ISMAR-Adjunct.2019.00052

Swacha, J. (2021). State of research on gamification in education: A bibliometric survey. *Education Sciences*, *11*(2), 69. doi:10.3390/educsci11020069

Sylvia & Willis. (1987). Distance Education: Definition and Overview. *Journal of Education for Library and Information Science, 27*(4), 223-232.

Tabach, M., & Trgalová, J. (2020). Teaching mathematics in the digital era: Standards and beyond. *STEM teachers and teaching in the digital era: Professional expectations and advancement in the 21st century schools*, 221-242.

Tairab, A., & Ronghuai, H. (2017). Analyzing ICT Policy in K-12 Education in Sudan (1990-2016). *World Journal of Education, 7*(1), 71–82. doi:10.5430/wje.v7n1p71

Talukder, M. S., Alam, M. J., & Apu, M. A. (2015). The Impact of ICT on Students' Performance: A Case Study on Undergraduate University Students. *Manarat International University Studies, 4*(1), 137–147.

Tayal, S., Rajagopal, K., & Mahajan, V. (2022). Virtual reality based metaverse of gamification. In *2022 6th International Conference on Computing Methodologies and Communication (ICCMC)* (pp. 1597-1604). IEEE. 10.1109/ICCMC53470.2022.9753727

Tay, L. Y., Lim, C. P., & Lim, S. K. (2015). Differences in ICT usage across subject areas: A case of an elementary school in Singapore. *Journal of Educational Computing Research, 53*(1), 75–94. doi:10.1177/0735633115585930

Teixeira, N., Lahm, B., Peres, F. F. F., Mauricio, C. R. M., & Teixeira, J. M. (2021). Augmented reality on museums: The Ecomuseu Virtual Guide. *Proceedings of the SVR '21*, 147 – 156.

Tondeur, J., Cooper, M., & Newhouse, C. P. (2010). From ICT coordination to ICT integration: A longitudinal case study. *Journal of Computer Assisted Learning, 26*(4), 296–306. doi:10.1111/j.1365-2729.2010.00351.x

Tönnis, M., Klein, L., & Klinker, G. (2008, September). Perception thresholds for augmented reality navigation schemes in large distances. In *2008 7th IEEE/ACM International Symposium on Mixed and Augmented Reality* (pp. 189-190). IEEE. 10.1109/ISMAR.2008.4637360

Tripathi, S. (2019, October). Integration of virtual reality and augmented reality for immersive gaming and learning. In *2019 2nd International Conference on Power Energy, Environment and Intelligent Control (PEEIC)* (pp. 63-66). IEEE. 10.1109/PEEIC47157.2019.8976608

Tsai, Y.-S., Moreno-Marcos, P. M., Jivet, I., Scheffel, M., Tammets, K., Kollom, K., & Gašević, D. (2018). The SHEILA Framework : Informing Institutional Strategies and Policy Processes of Learning Analytics. *Journal of Learning Analytics, 5*(3), 5–20. doi:10.18608/jla.2018.53.2

Tűrel, Y. K., & Johnson, E. T. (2012). Teachers' belief and use of interactive whiteboards for teaching and learning. *Journal of Educational Technology & Society, 15*(1), 381–394.

Udemy. (2022, November 1). *Metaverse Masterclass: Learn Everything About the Metaverse*. Udemy. Available at: https://www.udemy.com/course/metaverse-masterclass-learn-everything-about-the-metaverse/

UNESCO. (2005). Stratégie globale d'élaboration des manuels scolaires et des matériels didactiques. Paris: UNESCO: Organisation des Nations unies pour l'éducation, la science et la culture.

UNESCO. (2008). *Comment promouvoir l'égalité entre les sexes par les manuels scolaires? Guide méthodologique à l'attention des acteurs et actrices de la chaîne du manuel scolaire*. UNESCO.

Université du Québec. (2013). *Guide de conception et d'utilisation du manuel numérique universitaire*. https://www.puq.ca/catalogue/livres/guide-conception-utilisation-manuel-numerique-universitaire-2664.html

Uribe, J., Harmon, D., Laguna, B., & Courtier, J. (2022). Augmented-reality Enhanced Anatomy Learning (A-REAL): Assessing the utility of 3D holographic models for anatomy education. *Annals of 3D Printed Medicine*, 100090.

Uunona, G. N., & Goosen, L. (2023). Leveraging Ethical Standards in Artificial Intelligence Technologies: A Guideline for Responsible Teaching and Learning Applications. In M. Garcia, M. Lopez Cabrera, & R. de Almeida (Eds.), *Handbook of Research on Instructional Technologies in Health Education and Allied Disciplines* (pp. 310–330). IGI Global. doi:10.4018/978-1-6684-7164-7.ch014

Venkatesh, V., & Davis, F. D. (1996). A Model of the Antecedents of Perceived Ease of Use : Development and Test. *Decision Sciences*, *27*(3), 451–481. doi:10.1111/j.1540-5915.1996.tb01822.x

Venkatesh, V., & Davis, F. D. (2000). A Theoretical Extension of the Technology Acceptance Model : Four Longitudinal Field Studies. *Management Science*, *46*(2), 186–204. doi:10.1287/mnsc.46.2.186.11926

Verschaffel, L., Depaepe, F., & Mevarech, Z. (2019). Learning Mathematics in Metacognitively Oriented ICT-Based Learning Environments : A Systematic Review of the Literature. *Education Research International*, *2019*, 1–19. Advance online publication. doi:10.1155/2019/3402035

Vertucci, R., D'Onofrio, S., Ricciardi, S., & De Nino, M. (2023). History of Augmented Reality. In *Springer Handbook of Augmented Reality* (pp. 35–50). Springer International Publishing. doi:10.1007/978-3-030-67822-7_2

Vinumol, K. P., Chowdhury, A., Kambam, R., & Muralidharan, V. (2013, May). Augmented reality based interactive text book: An assistive technology for students with learning disability. In *2013 XV Symposium on Virtual and Augmented Reality* (pp. 232-235). IEEE. 10.1109/SVR.2013.26

Voccia, A. (2011). Knowledge Management for sustainable development in the web 2.0 era: The Triangle of Dichotomies. *Knowledge Management for Development Journal*, *6*(3), 179–193. doi:10.1080/19474199.2011.554323

Vrellis, I., Delimitros, M., Chalki, P., Gaintatzis, P., Bellou, I., & Mikropoulos, T. A. (2020, July). Seeing the unseen: User experience and technology acceptance in Augmented Reality science literacy. In *2020 IEEE 20th International Conference on Advanced Learning Technologies (ICALT)* (pp. 333-337). IEEE.

Wallet, P., & Melgar, B. V. (2015). Information and Communication Technology (ICT) in Education in Sub-Saharan Africa: A comparative analysis of basic e-readiness in schools. United Nations Educational Scientific and Cultural Organization (UNESCO) Institute for Statistics.

Wang, J., Liang, H. N., Monteiro, D. V., Xu, W., Chen, H., & Chen, Q. (2020, November). Real-time detection of simulator sickness in virtual reality games based on players' psychophysiological data during gameplay. In *2020 IEEE International Symposium on Mixed and Augmented Reality Adjunct (ISMAR-Adjunct)* (pp. 247-248). IEEE. 10.1109/ISMAR-Adjunct51615.2020.00071

Wang, Y., Su, Z., Zhang, N., Xing, R., Liu, D., Luan, T. H., & Shen, X. (2022). A survey on metaverse: Fundamentals, security, and privacy. *IEEE Communications Surveys and Tutorials.*

Wang, Z., Nguyen, C., Asente, P., & Dorsey, J. (2021, May). DistanciAR: Authoring site-specific augmented reality experiences for remote environments. In *Proceedings of the 2021 CHI Conference on Human Factors in Computing Systems* (pp. 1-12). 10.1145/3411764.3445552

Weisberg, M. (2011). Student Attitudes and Behaviors Towards Digital Textbooks. *Publishing Research Quarterly, 27*(2), 188-196. doi:10.1007/s12109-011-9217-4

Wei, X., Weng, D., Liu, Y., & Wang, Y. (2016, March). *A tour guiding system of historical relics based on augmented reality. In 2016 IEEE Virtual Reality (VR)*. IEEE.

Wiederhold, B. K. (2022). *Ready (or Not) player one : Initial musings on the metaverse*. Mary Ann Liebert, Inc.

Wientapper, F., Wuest, H., & Kuijper, A. (2011, May). Reconstruction and accurate alignment of feature maps for augmented reality. In *2011 International Conference on 3D Imaging, Modeling, Processing, Visualization and Transmission* (pp. 140-147). IEEE. 10.1109/3DIMPVT.2011.25

Wild, F. (2016). The future of learning at the workplace is augmented reality. *Computer*, *49*(10), 96–98. doi:10.1109/MC.2016.301

Willemsen, P., Jaros, W., McGregor, C., Downs, E., Berndt, M., & Passofaro, A. (2018, March). Memory task performance across augmented and virtual reality. In *2018 IEEE Conference on Virtual Reality and 3D User Interfaces (VR)* (pp. 723-724). IEEE. 10.1109/VR.2018.8446457

Wouters, P., van Nimwegen, C., van Oostendorp, H., & van Der Spek, E. D. (2013). A meta-analysis of the cognitive and motivational effects of serious games. *Journal of Educational Psychology*, *105*(2), 249–265. doi:10.1037/a0031311

Xie, S. T., Chen, Q., Liu, K. H., Kong, Q. Z., & Cao, X. J. (2021). Learning Behavior Analysis Using Clustering and Evolutionary Error Correcting Output Code Algorithms in Small Private Online Courses. *Scientific Programming*, *2021*, 1–11. Advance online publication. doi:10.1155/2021/9977977

Xu, M., Murcia-López, M., & Steed, A. (2017, March). *Object location memory error in virtual and real environments. In 2017 IEEE Virtual Reality (VR)*. IEEE.

Yadav, S., & Aalam, Z. (2021, October). Meta-analysis of learning strategies in teaching using: Augmented reality technology. In *2021 4th International Conference on Recent Developments in Control, Automation & Power Engineering (RDCAPE)* (pp. 224-229). IEEE.

Yang, F., Caballero, J. M., & Juanatas, R. A. (2022). Designing of Chinese ancient poetry app based on iOS platform augmented reality and machine learning. *Proceedings of the 2022 7th International Conference on Business and Industrial Research,* 285 – 288.

Yang, M. T., Liao, W. C., & Shih, Y. C. (2013, July). VECAR: Virtual English classroom with markerless augmented reality and intuitive gesture interaction. In *2013 IEEE 13th International Conference on Advanced Learning Technologies* (pp. 439-440). IEEE.

Yi, M. Y., & Hwang, Y. (2003). Predicting the use of web-based information systems : Self-efficacy, enjoyment, learning goal orientation, and the technology acceptance model. *International Journal of Human-Computer Studies*, *59*(4), 431–449. doi:10.1016/S1071-5819(03)00114-9

Young, J. (2013). The object formerly known as the textbook. *The Chronicle of Higher Education.*

Yount, Z. F., Kass, S. J., & Arruda, J. E. (2022). Route learning with augmented reality navigation aids. *Transportation Research Part F: Traffic Psychology and Behaviour*, *88*, 132–140. doi:10.1016/j.trf.2022.05.019

Yousafzai, S. Y., Foxall, G. R., & Pallister, J. G. (2007). Technology acceptance : A meta-analysis of the TAM: Part 1. *Journal of Modelling in Management*, *2*(3), 251–280. doi:10.1108/17465660710834453

Yu, J. (2017). A light-field journey to virtual reality. *IEEE MultiMedia*, *24*(2), 104–112. doi:10.1109/MMUL.2017.24

Zahra, G. F., Mohammed, A., Khadija, D., Mohammed, T., & Abdelouahed, N. (2015). Implementation of a Computerized System for the Orientation of the Moroccan Student in the University. *Procedia - Social and Behavioral Sciences, 182*, 381-387. doi:10.1016/j.sbspro.2015.04.797

Zallio, M., & Clarkson, P. J. (2022). Designing the metaverse: A study on inclusion, diversity, equity, accessibility and safety for digital immersive environments. *Telematics and Informatics*, *75*, 101909. doi:10.1016/j.tele.2022.101909

Zeithaml, V. A. (1988). Consumer Perceptions of Price, Quality, and Value : A Means-End Model and Synthesis of Evidence. *Journal of Marketing*, *52*(3), 2–22. doi:10.1177/002224298805200302

Zhang, H., Cui, Y., Shan, H., Qu, Z., Zhang, W., Tu, L., & Wang, Y. (2020, June). Hotspots and trends of virtual reality, augmented reality and mixed reality in education field. In *2020 6th International Conference of the Immersive Learning Research Network (iLRN)* (pp. 215-219). IEEE. 10.23919/iLRN47897.2020.9155170

Zhang, X., Chen, Y., Hu, L., & Wang, Y. (2022). The metaverse in education: Definition, framework, features, potential applications, challenges, and future research topics. *Frontiers in Psychology*, *13*, 6063. doi:10.3389/fpsyg.2022.1016300 PMID:36304866

Zhang, Z. (2020, November). Understanding physical common sense in symmetrical reality. In *2020 IEEE International Symposium on Mixed and Augmented Reality Adjunct (ISMAR-Adjunct)* (pp. 275-276). IEEE. 10.1109/ISMAR-Adjunct51615.2020.00077

Zhao, Y., Forte, M., & Kopper, R. (2018, March). VR touch museum. In *2018 IEEE Conference on Virtual Reality and 3D User Interfaces (VR)* (pp. 741-742). IEEE. 10.1109/VR.2018.8446581

Zhou, X., Tang, L., Lin, D., & Han, W. (2020). Virtual & augmented reality for biological microscope in experiment education. *Virtual Reality & Intelligent Hardware*, *2*(4), 316–329. doi:10.1016/j.vrih.2020.07.004

Zhou, Y., Chen, J., & Wang, M. (2022). A meta-analytic review on incorporating virtual and augmented reality in museum learning. *Educational Research Review*, *36*, 100454. doi:10.1016/j.edurev.2022.100454

Zigerell, J. (1984). *Distance Education: An information Age Approach to Adult Education*. National Center Publications, National Center for Research in Vocational Education.

Zonaphan, L., Northus, K., Wijaya, J., Achmad, S., & Sutoyo, R. (2022). Metaverse as A Future of Education: A Systematic Review. In *2022 8th International HCI and UX Conference in Indonesia (CHIuXiD)* (Vol. 1, pp. 77-81). IE. 10.1109/CHIuXiD57244.2022.10009854

Zuo, T., Spek, E. D., Hu, J., & Birk, M. V. (2021, December). Investigating the motivational effect of fantasy and similarity through avatar identification in AR game-based learning. In *International Conference on Intelligent Technologies for Interactive Entertainment* (pp. 279-294). Springer, Cham.

About the Contributors

Nadia Chafiq is professor-researcher at the Faculty of Sciences Ben M'Sick, Hassan II University of Casablanca. Director of the laboratory "Sciences and Technologies of Information and Education" (LA.S.T.I.E) and head of the department of Communication Sciences and Humanities. She is a specialist in educational technology and author of several publications in this field. She is currently pursuing her research in the field and is more specifically dedicated to educational engineering and digital learning. She is currently directing doctoral theses on (distance learning, hybrid devices, comodal devices, flipped classes, collaborative platforms, serious games, MOOCS, SPOCS, mobile learning, learning analytics, blockchain, metaverse, etc.

* * *

Mohammed Ait Daoud is a Ph.D. in Educational Data Analysis from the Faculty of Sciences Ben M'Sik, Hassan II University of Casablanca, Morocco. He is currently a professor at the same faculty. Also, he is a member of the Laboratory of Technologies for Information and Modeling (LTIM) and also a member of the Observatory of Research in Didactics and University Pedagogy (ORDIPU). His research interests include educational technologies, distance training engineering, techniques of training, information systems, IoT, Data Mining and Process Mining.

Ruth S. Contreras-Espinosa is a Doctor in Multimedia Engineering. Researcher/Coordinator in International Research projects funded by the European Union. Areas of activity: UX-UI, UX Research, Game studies, Game based learning, Gamification, Technology enhanced learning, Serious Games, Interaction design. Lecturer in Higher Education. Women in Games Ambassador.

Hasna Fallaki is Qualified Professor and Teacher of Communication Techniques at the Faculty of Sciences and Techniques of Mohammedia (FSTM), affiliated with the Hassan II University of Casablanca since October 1995. Her areas of expertise include the design of programs adapted to the target audience, coaching in academic and professional guidance as well as personal development and relational skills. As an active member in the LALITRA laboratory at Hassan II University, she is involved in exploring themes related to the sustainable development of education. In addition, Hasna Fallaki is also responsible for supervising doctoral theses and monitoring doctoral students. As a volunteer within several associations, she is actively involved in social projects and adopt an approach which consists of systematically involving my students, thus introducing them to volunteering while promoting the development of their relational and personal skills.

Loubna Farsi is a teacher-researcher at the Faculty of Sciences and Technology of Mohammedia (FSTM), Hassan II University in Casablanca. She is a member of GARCCO - Research Action Group in Communication, Culture and Organization - (EST-Essaouira) and associated with the "language and society" laboratory (FLSH-Kénitra). PhD in language teaching and a DUESS in Ecotourism, Heritage Management and Sustainable Development, her work focuses on Soft-skills, didactics and educational engineering, in particular on ICT and their investment in flipped pedagogy and in the teaching/learning process of FOS (French on Specific Objectives) and FOU (French on University Objectives). Her latest research falls within the framework of soft skills and personal development.

Jose Luis Gomez is a Doctor in Digital Communication. Researcher and lecturer, Barcelona School of Industrial Engineering (ETSEIB), Polytechnic University of Catalonia. Areas of activity: Serious Games, Game based learning, Gamification, Technology enhanced learning.

Leila Goosen is a full professor in the Department of Science and Technology Education of the University of South Africa. Prof. Goosen was an Associate Professor in the School of Computing, and the module leader and head designer of the fully online signature module for the College for Science, Engineering and Technology, rolled out to over 92,000 registered students since the first semester of 2013. She also supervises ten Masters and Doctoral students, and has successfully completed supervision of 43 students at postgraduate level. Previously, she was a Deputy Director at the South African national Department of Education. In this capacity, she was required to develop ICT strategies for implementation. She also promoted, coordinated, managed, monitored and evaluated ICT policies and strategies, and drove the research agenda in this area. Before that, she had been a lecturer of Information Technology (IT) in the Department for Science, Mathematics and Technology Education in the Faculty of Education of the University of Pretoria. Her research interests have included cooperative work in IT, effective teaching and learning of programming and teacher professional development.

Shalin Hai-Jew works as a grant writer at Hutchinson Community College. Just prior, she worked as an instructional designer at Kansas State University (for 17.5 years). She has taught at the university and college levels for many years (including four years in the People's Republic of China) and was tenured at Shoreline Community College but left tenure to pursue instructional design work. She has Bachelor's degrees in English and psychology, a Master's degree in Creative Writing from the University of Washington (Hugh Paradise Scholar), and an Ed.D in Educational Leadership with a focus on public administration from Seattle University (where she was a Morford Scholar). She tested into the University of Washington at 14. She reviews for several publishers and publications. She has worked on a number of instructional design projects, including public health, biosecurity, one health, mental health, PTSD, grain science, turfgrass management, social justice, and others. She has authored and edited a number of books. Hai-Jew was born in Huntsville, Alabama, in the U.S. Currently, she is working on multiple projects. She has successfully pursued grant funding for various projects over the years, both solo and as part of a team.

Anouar Hasbaoui, PhD in finance, worked for the university of San Antonio as tutor for two years, he also worked for the city of San Antonio as Budget Officer. Anouar Hasbaoui teaches entrepreneurship and portfolio management. He has published many articles of finance mainly the prediction of time series and few articles on risk management. He is actually full teacher for the Hassan II University at the Faculty of Sciences and Technology of Mohammedia (FSTM) since 2017.

Mohamed Housni is a Multidisciplinary Researcher, Data Scientist, Business Analyst and Data Analyst. A Computer Science doctor, and a Mathematics teacher. Specialized in Data Analytics in Communication Technologies and Information in an educational setup. Passionate about leveraging Data in transforming the teaching/learning experience, to deliver the best quality to learners.

Tarek Ihya graduated with a Master degree in computer sciences in 2016 from Abdelmalek Essaadi University in Morocco, His research interests include Metaverse, machine learning, Data Mining and Process Mining.

Hicham Jirari holds a PhD in French, Francophone and comparative literature. He studied in Mohammed V University (Rabat), Ibn Tofail University (Kenitra) and University of Montréal (Canada). He is a teacher-researcher at the Faculty of Sciences and Technology of Mohammedia (FSTM), Hassan II University in Casablanca, a permanent member of the "Sciences de l'ingénieur et biosciences" laboratory (FST-Mohammedia), and an associate member of the "linguistique appliquée, communication et didactique du fle" (FLSH-Oujda) and "Littérature, Arts et Ingénierie pédagogique" (FLSH-Kenitra) laboratories. He is also certified in expression and communication techniques and psychology. His publications cover literary studies, educational engineering and social psychology. In 2020, he created the Interuniversity Network for Research and Science (RIRS >), a network driven by the initiatives of its members from different academic backgrounds, associated in the promotion of universal humanist values.

Mohammed Kahkahy is teacher-researcher at the Faculty of Sciences and Technology of Mohammedia (FSTM), Hassan II University of Casablanca. He teaches french and communication. He is a member of the ICM Lab (Interculturality, Communication and Modernity) and is part of the reading committee of the electronic journal "RIRS", Interuniversity Network for Research and Science. Holder of an aggregation in French language and a PhD in literature French and comparative obtained at Bordeaux Michel de Montaigne III (France), he is preparing a master's degree in Clinical Psychology. He is the author of the novel *Les orties de l'amour* as well as several short stories and items. As a Moroccan teacher, he is interested in various themes linked notably postcolonialism, intersectional feminism, otherness, management of difference, and to the individual in the Arab world.

Ghizlane Machraoui is an eminent Moroccan professional. She enjoys a rewarding career in teaching and communication. She possesses a diverse set of skills and professional qualities. She is also qualified in organizational communication, has strong computer skills and is trained in NLP as a Helper Practitioner. A graduate of the Université Stendhal Grenoble III, Mrs. Machraoui currently holds the position of Qualified Professor and Teacher of Communication Techniques at the Faculty of Sciences and Technology of Mohammedia and is also a permanent member of the " Material Membrane and Environment Laboratory ". She embodies the combination of a dedicated educator and a skilled professional, contributing significantly to a field of expertise while being involved in rewarding activities outside work.

Kamal Moundy is a PhD in Educational Science and Technology at the Laboratoryof Sciences and Technologies of Information and Education, Faculty of Sciences BenM'Sick, Hassan II University, Casablanca, Morocco.

Chaimae Tailassane is a professor-researcher at the National School of Commerce and Management, under the Moulay Ismail University of Meknes. Chaimae Tailassane holds a PhD degree in language teaching, particularly in Fle and Fos. His research-action focused on the progressive investment of ICT in the learning of French. She is involved in several disciplinary fields such as linguistics and communication. She is also an examiner for orals and authorized to correct DELF-DALF tests at the French Institute in Rabat. She participated as a tutor in a MOOC offered by the FSR and the IF of Rabat on the Claroline connect platform. His areas of interest also extend to engineering and educational scripting integrating ICT.

Mohammed Talbi is a Ph.D. in Sciences and Processes of Analysis from the University Pierre et Marie Curie of Paris. He is currently the Dean of the Faculty of Sciences Ben M'Sik at Hassan II University, B.P 7955 Sidi Othmane, Casablanca, Morocco, and the Director of the Observatory of Research in Didactics and University Pedagogy (ORDIPU) since 2014. He is an Expert in the fields of teaching and research on educational technologies, engineering of distance training, techniques of training, and information systems. He is the author of several national and international awards and has accumulated more than 30 years of scientific productions.

Index

R

S

T

U

V

W

Z

www.ingramcontent.com/pod-product-compliance
Lightning Source LLC
LaVergne TN
LVHW062146300926
849161LV00010B/2644